NURSING RESEARCH

NURSING RESEARCH
Principles, process and issues

Kader Parahoo

palgrave

Published by
PALGRAVE MACMILLAN
Houndmills, Basingstoke, Hampshire RG21 6XS and
175 Fifth Avenue, New York, N. Y. 10010
Companies and representatives throughout the world

PALGRAVE MACMILLAN is the global academic imprint of the Palgrave
Macmillan division of St. Martin's Press, LLC and of Palgrave Macmillan Ltd.
Macmillan® is a registered trademark in the United States, United Kingdom
and other countries. Palgrave is a registered trademark in the European
Union and other countries.

ISBN 0–333–69918–1 paperback

This book is printed on paper suitable for recycling and
made from fully managed and sustained forest sources.

A catalogue record for this book is available from the British Library.

13   12   11   10
07   06   05   04   03

Printed and bound in Great Britain by
Creative Print and Design (Wales), Ebbw Vale

To *nani* and *nana*, who had little but gave a lot.
To them, I am eternally grateful.

ACKNOWLEDGEMENTS

This book would not have been possible without the contribution and help from a number of people. I would like to thank Jenny Boore, Vidar Melby, Neal Cook and Kate Sullivan for reading and commenting on the earlier drafts and Averil Callaghan, Helen Houston and Liz Millar for typing the manuscript.

In particular, I thank Ros Bryar, Catherine Henshaw and Marion Wright for their advice, comments and attention to detail, Richenda Milton-Thompson for her professionalism, unswerving support and confidence in the project, Martin Liu for getting it off the ground in the first place and the Faculty of Social and Health Sciences and Education, University of Ulster for granting me time to complete it.

I am particularly grateful to Eilís McCaughan for her support, patience, comments, advice and encouragement. Her belief in me has been the 'wind beneath my wings'.

Finally this book draws on the work of others. I am thankful to all those from whom I borrowed extensively.

Publisher's acknowledgements

The author and publishers wish to thank the following for permission to use copyright material.

Blackwell Science and the *Journal of Advanced Nursing* for permission to use the following extracts:
- Page 55, from Rukholm E *et al.* 1991 **16**:920
- Page 153, from MacKenzie A E 1992 **17**:682
- Page 157, from Brydolf M and Segesten K 1996 **23**:39
- Pages 167–8, from Fielding J and Weaver S H 1994 **19**:1196
- Page 169, from Crotty M 1993 **18**:151
- Page 237, from Dalgas-Pelish P L 1993 **18**:437–8
- Pages 356–7, from Hogston R 1995 **21**:118.

Churchill Livingstone for permission to use the following extracts:
- Pages 145 and 294, from Bluff R and Holloway I 1994 *Midwifery* **10**:158–9
- Pages 355–6, from Hallgren A *et al.* 1995 *Midwifery* **11**:131–2.

John Wiley & Sons for permission to use:
- Page 110, from Wyper M A 1990 *Research in Nursing and Health* **13**:423, Figure 1.

Nursing Times for the three tables on pages 344 and 345, where these first appeared with the article by Sutton J, Standen P and Wallace A 1994 Incidence and documentation of patient accidents in hospital, *Nursing Times* **90**(33):29–35, and the article by Wilmott Y 1994 Career opportunities in the nursing service for prisoners, *Nursing Times* **90**(24):29–30.

Every effort has been made to trace all the copyright holders but if any have been inadvertently overlooked the publishers will be pleased to make the necessary arrangement at the first opportunity.

CONTENTS

Introduction   1

1   RESEARCH AND NURSING PRACTICE   **4**
The Development of Nursing Research   4
The Meaning of Nursing Research   7
Knowledge for Nursing Practice   8
Research and Clinical Effectiveness   13
Research and Professional Development   16
The Role of Nurses in Research   18
Research-mindedness   19
Research Utilisation   22
The Role of Nurses in the Conduct of Research   23
Funding Nursing Research   24

2   KNOWLEDGE, SCIENCE AND RESEARCH   **31**
The Need for Knowledge   31
Belief Systems   32
Science and Knowledge   35
Science and Research   36
Paradigms   39
The Influence of Paradigms   46

3   QUANTITATIVE AND QUALITATIVE RESEARCH   **50**
Differentiating between Quantitative and Qualitative Approaches   50
The Value of the Quantitative Approach to Nursing   54
Limitations of the Quantitative Approach   58
The Value of the Qualitative Approach to Nursing   59
Limitations of the Qualitative Approach   62
Mixing Quantitative and Qualitative Approaches   64

4   THE RESEARCH PROCESS   **71**
The Meaning of 'Research Process'   71
The Research Process and the Nursing Process   72
The Process in Quantitative Research   72
Stages of the Research Process   73
The Process in Qualitative Research   75
Understanding the Research Process   76
Critiquing the Research Process   77
Ethics and the Research Process   78

5   THE LITERATURE REVIEW   81
    The Need to Review the Literature   81
    What is Meant by 'The Literature'?   82
    Primary and Secondary Sources   84
    Assessing the Value of Publications   85
    Literature Search and Literature Review   88
    Systematic Reviews   94
    Critiquing the Literature Review   96

6   RESEARCH AND THEORY   100
    What is a Theory?   100
    Defining a Theory   101
    Types of Theory   102
    Levels of Theory   103
    Practice, Research and Theory   105
    Theory and Research   107
    Theoretical Framework, Conceptual Framework and
    Conceptual Model   109
    Conceptual Frameworks in Quantitative Research   112
    Conceptual Frameworks in Qualitative Research   116
    Nursing Theories versus Other Theories as Frameworks
    for Nursing Research   117
    Evaluating the Use of Conceptual Frameworks in Research   118

7   RESEARCH QUESTIONS AND OPERATIONAL DEFINITIONS   122
    Formulating Research Questions   122
    Operational Definitions   128
    Evaluating Operational Definitions   131
    Research Questions and Operational Definitions in
    Qualitative Research   136
    Critiquing Research Questions and Operational Definitions   139

8   RESEARCH DESIGNS   142
    Research Design or Methodology   142
    Selecting a Design   143
    Levels of Research in Quantitative Studies   143
    Types of Research Design   148
    Designs in Qualitative Research   150
    Ethnographic Studies   150
    Phenomenological Studies   152
    Grounded Theory   154
    Variations of Research Design   156

9   EXPERIMENTS   179
    The Meaning and Purpose of Experiments   179
    Research Experiments   180
    Intervention   181
    Control   183

Placebos and Blind Techniques   188
Randomisation   189
Single-subject Experiment   190
Quasi-experiments   192
Internal and External Validity of Experiments   196
Ethics of Experiments   203
Problems in Conducting Experiments   207
Randomised Controlled Trials in Nursing   208
Putting Experiments into Context   211
Evaluating Experiments   212

10   SAMPLES AND SAMPLING   218
Samples and Populations   218
Sampling in Quantitative and Qualitative Research   236
Critiquing Samples and Sampling   240

11   QUESTIONNAIRES   246
Use of Questionnaires in Nursing   246
What is a Questionnaire?   247
Questionnaires in Nursing Research   248
Question Formats   250
Rating Scales   257
Advantages and Disadvantages of Questionnaires   262
Validity and Reliability of Questionnaires   264
Enhancing Validity   270
Enhancing Reliability   273
Critiquing Questionnaires   275
Ethical Aspects of Questionnaires   276

12   INTERVIEWS   281
Interviews in Clinical Practice   281
Research Interviews   282
Structured Interviews   283
Qualitative Interviews   286
Semistructured Interviews   293
Focus Group Interviews   296
Ethical Implications of Interviewing   301
Critiquing Interviews   306

13   OBSERVATIONS   310
Observation and Nursing Practice   310
Observation in Nursing Research   311
Structured Observation   314
Unstructured Observation   322
Participation in Observation   327
Participant Observation and Ethnography   330
Ethical Implications of Observation   332
Critiquing Observations   334

14   **MAKING SENSE OF DATA**   **338**
What Does Making Sense of Data Mean?   338
Quantitative Data Analysis   339
Statistical Levels   341
Descriptive Statistics   342
Inferential Statistics   350
Selecting a Test   351
Qualitative Data Analysis   353

15   **EVALUATING RESEARCH STUDIES**   **360**
Critiquing Skills   360
A Structure for Evaluation   361
Sources of Bias   366
Omission and Exaggeration   366
The Role of Researchers in Facilitating Evaluation   367

16   **THE UTILISATION OF RESEARCH**   **369**
Using Research in Practice   369
Barriers to the Implementation of Research Findings   372
Strategies to Facilitate the Use of Research   378
Using Research: Whose Responsibility is it Anyway?   384

Glossary   391

Index   398

INTRODUCTION

There is worldwide consensus that qualified practitioners must be able to read, comprehend and make use of research in decision-making and in their practice. The European Health Committee (1996) published a report on nursing research and made a number of recommendations, one of which is that all qualified nurses should:

- (be) able to read and critically assess research literature relating to their field of work;
- have a basic knowledge and understanding of the strengths and limitations of different data-collection instruments and methods of analysis;
- recognise the importance of research and application of research-based knowledge for the improvement of nursing practice and patient care.

One can add that nurses need to understand the ethical implications of different methodologies in order to be in a better position to protect patients from potential harm when participating in research and to safeguard their rights.

To do this, they must first acquire the necessary skills and knowledge. There is sometimes a naïve view that they can start critiquing research articles without a prior knowledge of the basics of research. One student, when asked to critique a research article after a 2-hour introduction to research, remarked that 'the cart was being put in front of the horse'. No-one would dare attempt a sociological analysis without first learning concepts such as class, socialisation and social structure.

This book is written mainly for preregistration students and for nurses, health visitors and midwives who have little or no prior knowledge of research. It is intended to equip them with a comprehensive understanding of the concepts and principles of nursing research so that they can begin to read research critically. Undergraduate and postgraduate students will also find sections of the book useful.

What constitutes nursing research and research evidence is itself problematic. There are different perspectives on research, on how it should be carried out and on its actual and potential benefits. The debate about the value of quantitative and qualitative approaches to nursing has been going on for at least the last 30 years. This book deals with many of the issues raised in this debate. The potential contribution of both approaches is compared and contrasted, and the benefits and drawbacks of mixing them are explored. The strengths and weaknesses of a range of methodologies, in particular research methods, are also discussed.

Research can help as well as harm people. The ethical implications of various types of methodology are explored at length. An understanding of these issues is as vital for evaluating studies as is a knowledge of research techniques.

All practising nurses are expected to base their practice on research evidence. Yet there are many problems with research utilisation. This book explores the relationship between research and practice, examines research evidence relating to factors which facilitate and those which impede research utilisation, and discusses the role of nurses, managers, educators and others in enhancing research-based practice.

CONTENT AND LAYOUT

Chapter 1 examines closely the role of practitioners in research and discusses research in the context of other ways of knowing, such as intuition, tradition and experience, as well as the potential contribution of research to clinical effectiveness and to the development of nursing as a profession. The next two chapters discuss the relationship between knowledge, science and research, and explore the value and limitations of qualitative and quantitative approaches to the study of nursing phenomena. Unavoidably, a large number of concepts and issues are introduced at this stage. They are, however, dealt with further throughout the book. For example, concepts such as induction and deduction, or approaches such as ethnography and grounded theory, are pursued again at relevant points. Discussions on the validity, reliability and ethical aspects of research are fully integrated in the text.

The rest of the chapters follow closely the stages of the research process. Chapter 4 outlines the process in quantitative and qualitative research. Chapters 5 and 6 deal respectively with the literature review and the relationship between theory and research in quantitative and qualitative studies, while Chapter 7 deals with the formulation of questions and operational definitions.

Although a range of research designs is discussed in Chapter 8, experimental and quasi-experimental designs are given a separate and lengthy treatment in Chapter 9. The current emphasis on the evaluation of, and comparisons between, treatment programmes have focused attention on a lesser-used design in nursing research – that of the randomised controlled trial (RCT). The strengths and weaknesses of the RCT, as well as its appropriateness for the study of nursing phenomena, are considered.

Data collection methods, samples and sampling techniques are described and discussed in Chapters 10, 11, 12 and 13, while Chapters 14 and 15 are designed to help readers make sense of research findings. The utilisation of research in practice warrants a chapter on its own (Chapter 16), not least because of the current realisation that the research–practice gap is still very wide.

One of the main features of the book is the use of examples to explain abstract concepts. In these Research Examples (REs, boxed), the relevant parts of the articles are described or quoted, followed by comments designed to illustrate concepts or issues raised in the text. Therefore they should be treated as part of the text. These excerpts stand on their own, but readers who may wish to read the original articles will not find them difficult to access. The rationale for using real examples is that one useful way to learn about research is to find out how research studies are carried out.

Finally, in an attempt to avoid the clumsy and inelegant form 'she/he', the female gender is used in this book to refer to researchers. The flipping of a coin was the 'scientific' strategy used to select the pronoun. It is, of course, acknowledged that researchers are both men and women.

To conclude, this book is not designed to teach how to do research but to help readers to acquire a thorough and comprehensive understanding of research principles, concepts, processes and issues in order to be able to read research critically. The view taken here is that both qualitative and quantitative approaches have a contribution to make towards advancing knowledge. Research is put in context of other ways of knowing. Throughout this book, both the potential benefits of research and the danger of blind faith in research findings are emphasised.

REFERENCE

European Health Committee (1996) *Nursing Research: Report and Recommendations*. Strasbourg: CDSP.

1   RESEARCH AND NURSING PRACTICE

> Research without practice is like building castles in the air.
> Practice without research is building castles on slippery
> grounds.

INTRODUCTION

This introductory chapter will provide an overview of the development
of nursing research world wide. It will discuss the relationship between
research and practice, in particular the role of research-based and other
sources of knowledge in decision-making, and the justifications for
nursing research. The meaning of nursing research and the roles of
nurses in promoting efficient and effective care through research-based
practice will also be explored.

THE DEVELOPMENT OF NURSING RESEARCH

In most industrialised countries, the development of nursing research
occurred in the post-Second World War period; in the US, however,
according to LoBiondo-Wood and Haber (1994), it started in the early
part of the 20th century. Referring to the UK, Simpson, in a preface to
MacLeod Clark and Hockey (1979), wrote:

> In the 1950s nurses were beginning to join in research and in the 1960s
> the earliest studies of nursing began to appear alongside the studies of
> nurses, their education, organisation and management. The 1970s have
> seen a steady build up of nursing research resources and reports.

The past two decades have seen a rapid increase in the number of
nurses trained in research, in nursing research books, in journals, and
in research conferences and workshops. Not only has the number of
researchers and research publications increased, but there has also been
a groundswell of interest in research among nurses in the UK, according
to Lelean and Clarke (1990), who offer as evidence the following:

- the increasing number of local research interest groups;
- the development of nursing practices and policies based on research
  findings;

- funding by health authorities of nurses to undergo degree courses and other forms of research training;
- involvement of groups of nurses in district wide and multi-centre research projects.

Writing about the rest of Europe, Farrell and Christensen (1990), commented:

> Nursing research in Europe has undergone change in the past ten years. The number and variety of publications, projects, studies, and courses have grown at a considerable rate. Community and hospital services have developed research elements as part of overall evaluation, and schools and university programmes include research as part of the curriculum.

Not much is written about nursing research in developing countries. The lack of funds and the low status of nursing in many of these countries have been factors contributing to the slow development of nursing research. According to Mangay-Maglacas (1992), nursing research in the developing and least developed countries is 'in its infancy', although 'much development has taken place in improved educational patterns and increased recognition of nursing as an important element of health care systems'. Examining data from the International Council of Nurses (ICN) 1990 *Directory of Nursing Research Units*, Mangay-Maglacas noted:

> Of the 20 countries that responded to the ICN worldwide survey, only four (Brazil, Egypt, Jamaica and Panama) could be considered to fall into the category of developing countries having only 14 out of a total of 115 surveyed nursing research units. And 46% of all research units are in only one country, the United States of America.

Marshall-Burnett (1990), writing about Jamaica and the Caribbean, echoes the same observations made by Mangay-Maglacas above when she states that 'nursing research remains in its infancy even in 1989, lagging behind the successes recorded by many other countries'.

Although the pace of development world wide has not been the same, there are a number of similarities that can be noted. These are that:

- early nursing research was carried out mostly by researchers from other disciplines;
- most early research was conducted mainly on nurses;
- the amount of clinical research has been growing steadily;
- the link of nursing education with higher education has been a catalyst in the growth of interest and training in research;

- the lack of funding for nursing research relative to medicine;
- the dominance of the quantitative approach in the formative years of nursing research.

MacLeod Clark and Hockey (1986) remarked that, in the UK, 'up to the last 20 years or so nurses have been dependent on members of other disciplines, especially the social scientists, for the study of their own profession'. According to Flaherty (1990), 'although Canadian nurses have been involved in research for more than half a century, in the beginning the research activity consisted largely of co-operation with and/or assistance to members of other disciplines'. In New Zealand, 'prior to 1973 the history of nursing research is scant and very much a history of research on nurses, conducted mostly by non-nurses and always from the perspective of another discipline' (Chick, 1987). In a guest editorial featured in the journal *Nursing Research* in 1956 (cited in LoBiondo-Wood and Haber, 1994), Virginia Henderson commented that, in the US, 'studies about nurses outnumber clinical studies 10 to 1'. In 1974 the American Nursing Association 'resolved that for the next decade, nursing research would focus on the practice of nursing' (Jennings, 1995). The success of this resolution in the last 20 years has been such that Jennings (1995) calls for a redirection of nursing research from clinical practice to the environmental domain of nursing, more specifically to nursing administration.

Midwifery research in the US shows the same trends as nursing research. Lydon-Rochelle and Albers (1993) found that 83 per cent of research topics in the *Journal of Nurse-Midwifery* between 1987 and 1992 were clinical. In the UK, although there are currently more nursing research journals than there were 5 years ago, and despite the fact that more clinical research is reported, there are indications that the focus still remains on the profession. Smith (1994) carried out an analysis in 1992 of all articles in all the issues of three UK-based journals: the *Journal of Advanced Nursing*, the *International Journal of Nursing Studies* and the *Journal of Clinical Nursing*. She reported that 'research on nurses was a prominent theme across all three nursing journals' and that 'the clinical category came second to the theoretical papers even in the *Journal of Clinical Nursing*'.

The introduction of research into nursing curricula and the integration of nurse education into higher education have greatly contributed to the increase in interest and training in research. There is evidence that graduates are able to carry out small-scale projects, many of which are eventually published, as part of their role as practitioners (Kemp, 1988).

The role of nursing organisations has been crucial in supporting nursing research in a number of countries in Europe and in the USA. The Royal College of Nursing (RCN) has been at the forefront of the development and promotion of nursing research in the UK. Among other contributions, it has set up the Daphne Heald Research Unit (with funds from an endowment) and created a chair in nursing research in Wales (with funds raised by its membership in Wales). The Centre for Policy in Nursing Research was opened in 1995, as a joint venture between the RCN and the London School of Hygiene and Tropical Medicine; funding has been provided by the Nuffield Provincial Hospitals Trust for an initial period of 5 years. The RCN is also in the process of setting up its own Research and Development Co-ordinating Centre, aimed at giving coherence and structure to its research strategy. The RCN Research Society provides a forum for the discussion of nursing research issues and organises annual research conferences.

The development of nursing research, in particular issues related to funding, is discussed in more detail later on in this chapter.

The Meaning of Nursing Research

'Nursing research' is an umbrella term for all research into nursing practice and issues related to it. It can be defined as the systematic and rigorous collection and analysis of data on the organisation, delivery, uses and outcomes of nursing care for the purpose of enhancing clients' health. It is not only about what nurses do, but also about clients' behaviour, knowledge, beliefs, attitudes, perceptions and other factors influencing how they make use of, and experience, care and treatment.

Crow in 1982 listed four approaches that research could take in order to contribute to better nursing practice. These are:

1. research that will provide *insights* into our practice;
2. research that will *deepen our understanding* of the concepts central to our care;
3. research that is concerned with the *development of new and improved* methods of caring; and
4. research which is designed to *test the effectiveness* of the care we give.

More than a decade later, we can see – judging by papers in nursing journals and at conferences in the UK – that, although some progress has been made, much remains to be achieved.

KNOWLEDGE FOR NURSING PRACTICE

The main sources of knowledge which nurses use in their practice are tradition, intuition, experience and research.

Traditional knowledge

The bulk of our knowledge has been accumulated over centuries and passed down to us through literature, art, music, oral history and other such media. Traditional nursing knowledge is learnt mainly from books and journals, by word of mouth and by observing the practice of others. Much traditional practice takes the form of rituals. For example, it may be a tradition in some hospitals that, after patients are washed, talcum powder is dusted over their body. This ritual is performed consistently with little thought to the rationale behind it. Walsh and Ford (1990) explain:

> Ritual action implies carrying out a task without thinking it through in a problem-solving, logical way. The nurse does something because this is the way it has always been done. Perhaps actions have become enshrined in the holy tablets of stone known as the procedure book, or just: 'This is the way Sister likes it done'. Either way, the nurse does not have to think about the problem and work out an individual solution; the action is ritual.

O'Brien and Davison (1994), referring to the routine taking of blood pressure 'at fixed and pre-determined times unrelated to the clinical status of the individual patients', suggest what such practices mean to practitioners:

> Once established, such rituals readily became part of the nursing culture and provided comfort and certainty to nurses in their daily work. It is not surprising that nurses are reluctant to challenge cherished and established approaches to practice, especially when the alternatives demand individualised considerations, notions of appropriate clinical decision making and professional accountability.

Traditions are important not only in passing down knowledge, but also in giving groups in society a sense of identity, belonging and pride. Through socialisation, we learn the culture of those who have gone before us. Similarly, traditional nursing knowledge and practice are learnt by novice nurses through the process of socialisation in colleges of nursing, universities and clinical areas. Much of this traditional knowledge and many ritual practices are the outcomes of sound reasoning. Today's new knowledge and practices will likewise eventually become traditional. The term 'traditional' is sometimes used in a negative sense, meaning backward, outdated or unprogressive. For example, pre-Project 2000 courses are referred to as 'traditional training', giving the impression the course might be inferior. Knowledge in itself is harmless; it is the use people make of it which can be harmful or beneficial. It should neither be rejected too quickly nor clung to rigidly if we are to benefit from the experiences of our predecessors and continue to make progress.

Intuition

There has been an increasing interest in the role of intuition in nursing and midwifery practice (Rew, 1986). Intuition is a form of knowing and behaving not apparently based on rational reasoning. The use of intuition in nursing is only beginning to attract nurse researchers, so not much is known about 'how' nurses come to know there is something 'wrong' or whether they have a 'sixth' sense to know what to do. According to Kenny (1994), nurses use empathetic intuition in their daily practice:

> This type of intuitive thinking often occurs within the context of a nursing situation, and feeling, rather than conscious thinking, seems to predominate. Nurses know that there is something wrong but cannot explain what it is.

Despite the recognition that intuition is an important 'tool' in the human repertoire of knowing, concern has been raised regarding the 'process of apprehension and action without apparent reason' (Aggleton and Chalmers, 1986). Even the strongest intuitions are sometimes proved false when put to an empirical test (Polgar and Thomas, 1991).

Experience

Nurses and midwives base their practice in great part on their own experience and to a lesser extent on the experience of others. A study by Luker and Kenrick (1992) of 47 community nurses from four district health authorities in Britain shows that:

> The effects of past experience and situational variables were identified by all the nurses as having an important impact on the decision-making process, and both these influences were deemed to be practice-based knowledge, with experience having 82% (n = 39) agreement and the situational context having 76% (n = 36) agreement. Another factor which all nurses identified as being an important source of influence was discus-

sions with nurse colleagues, described as experiential knowledge by 82% (n = 39) of respondents.

Mander (1992) interviewed 40 midwives and found that 'knowledge derived from their occupational experience was of overwhelming significance' to them.

Experience is a useful way of learning. There is a wealth of untapped knowledge embedded in the practice and 'know-how' of expert nurse clinicians (Benner, 1984). It is also reckoned that what we learn by experience is more enduring than what we are taught. However, our experience is in itself rather narrow. For example, in treating depression, a nurse may use one or two approaches. While the experience obtained is invaluable, she will be unfamiliar with other treatments and may either be reluctant to try them or may reject them out of hand. Nurses are not alone in relying on their experience. Rosenberg and Donald (1995), writing about doctors, commented that they continue to base their clinical decisions 'on increasingly out of date primary training or the over interpretation of experiences with individual patients'.

There is also a degree of trial and error when learning by experience. While this may be inevitable in a few cases, there is, by and large, a risk of reinventing the wheel and a greater risk of unsafe practice. Experience is therefore an important source of nursing knowledge, but relying solely on it and overstating its importance can be detrimental to nursing practice.

Research

Research, on the other hand, is a systematic way of knowing and lays bare its methods for all to see. Cang (1979) explains:

> Anyone who tries to observe and remember and learn from experience, whether that experience has to do with forecasting the weather or caring for a patient under some given circumstances, is broadly speaking engaged in research. No questionnaires, no computers, no overalls are necessarily required: just the attempt to find out something about something.

The main difference between this type of activity and research is that the latter collects and analyses data systematically and rigorously, and this process is described to others by means of oral and/or written presentation. Research findings by themselves are not solutions to problems. They provide new insight into phenomena or add to, confirm or reject what is already known. Decisions still have to be taken about whether they should be used or not, and how.

The value of research as a source of information must, however, be put into context. Research can produce inconclusive results. In fact, it only attempts to answer questions the researcher wants answered. It rarely looks at a phenomenon (anything which occurs about which curiosity is aroused) from a holistic perspective but investigates only part of a problem. For example, in an experiment to find out whether a model of nursing has any impact on patient care, other factors, such as the skills, knowledge and nursing care abilities of nurses, will be controlled for rather than studied (see Chapter 9).

Not all research findings can be believed. Hunt (1987) points out that 'derided "old wives' tales" and traditional beliefs sometimes have been found to have sound rationales while research can be erroneous and even fraudulent'. While it is likely very few researchers are dishonest, it is possible many more carry out research to justify their practice or support their perceptions of particular issues, thereby inadvertently more than consciously, introducing bias to their studies. For example, a nurses' organisation carried out research showing that the morale of health visitors in one health authority was low. The health authority then employed a research consultancy firm that produced 'evidence' to the contrary. The cynical manipulation of research does discredit to an otherwise potentially enlightening enterprise.

Rundell (1992) cautions against the blind acceptance of research findings 'in the same way we used to base our work on "Sister says..."'. It is not uncommon to hear nurses say research has 'proved' or 'shown' something or other. All that research does is answer the questions which the researcher asks. Good research can only provide insights into the problem being investigated and nothing more. Research findings, like traditional knowledge, are not definitive; they eventually have to be built upon. Research reports must be read critically, and if the findings are found to be valid and reliable (see Chapter 2), only then can they be taken into account in decision-making. Reflections in practice can only partly achieve the same effect. Assessing one's actions and motives can shed some light on one's practices, but this remains a subjective exercise. Research, on the other hand, is a public exercise that can benefit more than just the people who undertake it.

One may argue that, by using common sense, nurses can take the right decisions. However, they still need relevant and valid information in order to do so. What may seem simple and straightforward is not necessarily so. For example, in many developing countries babies suffering from diarrhoea are not given fluids because it is believed that this will aggravate the situation. To the parents, it makes sense that in order to stop the baby from passing 'watery' faeces, they must stop the administration of fluids. In doing this, the baby is put at risk of dying from dehydration. Jackson (1994) recalls that in midwifery practice 'it used to be commonsense to give an enema to prevent soiling during delivery until Romney and Gordon (1981) published their research which showed that this procedure was not necessary'.

An impression sometimes created by those who advocate the use of research is that traditions should be rejected. This makes nurses feel that what they did in the past was wrong, putting them on the defensive with the result that they continue to cling to harmful practices even in the face of evidence to the contrary. Reed and Procter (1995) point out that one of the problems inherent in the 'research knowledge is best' position is 'the assumption that practitioners can choose between science and experience' and that they 'can adopt a scientific stance which excludes and forgets any understanding they have developed during their practice'.

The limitations of research, tradition, intuition and experience, far from diminishing their value, should point to the need to treat all kinds of information with scepticism, to question what we do and to search for ways to practise that are effective, efficient and above all humane. Tradition, intuition, experience and research together provide the knowledge on which nursing practice is based. Even when a nurse carries out a nursing ritual such as piping oxygen in a wound without stopping to ask why this is necessary (Walsh and Ford, 1990), she has taken a decision not to update her knowledge or to ignore research in favour of what traditionally is practised. Studies of decision-making 'illustrate that, although nurses may display a high level of skill, much of their practice is unsupported by an underlying rationale' (Luker and Kenrick, 1992).

One of the important factors in decision-making is the availability of relevant and up-to-date information. Benton and Avery (1993) pointed out that 'in the past, many district health authorities made major policy decisions with only partial information'. Traditional knowledge, although an important source of information, needs to be updated. What was relevant a decade ago may not be so now, as illustrated by Jackson (1994):

> Many of the observations that we make on pregnant women today were probably implemented when the health of the pregnant population was much less robust than it is today. In many instances, the pregnant woman would have been less than well and this probably influenced the way she was cared for.

Research has the potential to provide up-to-date information that may facilitate decision-making. Whether research data are superior to other forms of knowledge depends on the quality of the research and the beliefs of the people using them. Traditional knowledge may have suited a world in which 'authority' was not questioned, people did what they were told and things were right because someone 'important' said so. We now live in an age when most clients are no longer passive recipients of services and those who hold the purse strings require business plans for the allocation and use of funds. The need to justify one's practice is greater now than it has ever been.

RESEARCH AND CLINICAL EFFECTIVENESS

The primary goal of nursing research is to improve the quality of care given to clients. Research has the potential to do so because it provides the opportunity for nurses to ask questions about their practice and seek answers, producing data that can thereafter facilitate decision-making. For example, a study on catheter blockages by Getcliffe (1993) sought to determine 'whether patients could be classified in one or two groups: "blockers" who suffer frequent and recurrent catheter blockage due to encrustations, and "non-blockers" who do not form encrustations even when the catheter is left in place for several weeks or months'. It was hoped that 'early recognition of patients as blockers would allow the development of a planned individualised programme of care instead of relying on "crisis care" in response to leakage or retention' (Getcliffe, 1993).

It is not always necessary to carry out new research in order to address nursing problems. There is a large amount of existing research which is waiting to be used. The potential contribution of research will not be realised if practice is not based on research findings.

Research plays a key role in providing evidence on the value and limitations of clinical interventions and on their cost-effectiveness. In the UK, the Department of Health (DOH) launched the NHS Research and Development Strategy (DOH, 1992), the focus of which is evidence-based health care (EBHC). EBHC simply means basing practice on evidence. Sackett et al. (1996) explain what this means in relation to evidence-based medicine:

> [It] is the conscientious, explicit, and judicious use of current best evidence in making decisions about the care of individual patients. The practice of evidence based medicine means integrating individual clinical expertise with the best available external clinical evidence from systematic research. By individual clinical expertise we mean the proficiency and judgement that individual clinicians acquire through clinical experience and clinical practice. Increased expertise is reflected in many ways, but especially in more effective and efficient diagnosis and in the more thoughtful identifica-

tion and compassionate use of individual patients' predicaments, rights, and preferences in making clinical decisions about their care.

The RCN (1996a) gives a similar description when it describes EBHC as:

rooted in best available scientific evidence and takes into account patient's views of effectiveness and clinical expertise in order to promote clinically effective services. This is essential in ensuring that health care practitioners do the things that work and are acceptable to patients and do not do the things which do not work.

There is, however, no consensus about the nature of 'research' or 'scientific' evidence. There are those who believe that the gold standard is the randomised controlled trial (RCT) (see Chapter 9) and that nothing else will do. Others favour an approach that values evidence from other research designs, provided they show evidence of rigour (see Chapter 5 for further discussion on this topic).

Although EBHC is not new (for example, Briggs, 1972, called for nursing to be a research-based profession), it is currently considered to be the way forward towards achieving clinical effectiveness. Among the reasons for its current importance are (a) the failure of health professionals to make use of available research findings, (b) the variations in clinical practice, and (c) the need to justify interventions on the basis of cost-effectiveness.

In nursing, for example, there is considerable evidence about the treatment of leg ulcers, yet an audit revealed over 50 different treatments used (RCN, 1996b). The failure to make use of existing evidence is not restricted to nursing. In Chapter 16, more evidence is provided of the non-utilisation of research in nursing and other professions and disciplines.

It is not uncommon in the health service to find that different forms of treatment are offered for the same condition. The type of treatment often depends on the preference of the clinician and the part of the country where one resides. Research can help to evaluate the effectiveness of preventative, treatment and rehabilitation programmes in order to provide the best possible care to clients. In practising by trial and error, we are in effect 'experimenting' on clients. This has moral, legal, financial and professional implications. Nurses in the UK are accountable to the United Kingdom Central Council for Nurses, Midwives and Health Visitors (UKCC) to deliver the best possible care to their clients (UKCC, 1996).

The issue of rationing and prioritising health-care expenditure is one which faces health professionals, policy-makers and politicians at local, national and international levels. Peckham (1993), in an introduction to *Research for Health* (DOH, 1993a), points out that:

> The lack of information on cost-effectiveness, for example, is a real handicap to purchasers and providers of care. Even simple, inexpensive procedures that are widely and unnecessarily applied can consume huge resources. In the era of knowledge-based health care, diversity of approach in routine practice will be increasingly difficult to defend unless supported by a sustainable and convincing rationale.

The situation is no different in the US, where Coulter and Orsolits (1991) report that:

> Nurses are under tremendous pressure to identify and quantify their contributions to achieving positive outcomes and improving patients' functional health status. As resource dollars become more and more scarce, we must make better decisions for reallocating our health care dollars. We must know which nursing interventions and which nurse delivery systems are the most cost effective for our patients and provide the most therapeutic outcomes.

To achieve the goal of clinical effectiveness, 'a number of key initiatives and centres have been established at a national level', including 'The UK Cochrane Centre, the NHS Centre for Reviews and Dissemination, The Centre for Evidence-Based Nursing, the Centre for Evidence-Based Medicine, the National Centre for Clinical Audit and the UK Outcomes Clearing House' (RCN, 1996a).

The Cochrane Collaboration is part of an international network of researchers and reviewers, whose main task is to carry out systematic reviews (see Chapter 5) of RCTs and disseminate the findings. The aim of the NHS Centre for Reviews and Dissemination (CRD), based at York University, is to 'identify and review the results of good quality health research and to disseminate actively the findings to key decision makers in the NHS and to consumers of health care services' (CRD, 1996). The CRD takes a multidisciplinary approach; its 'purpose is to complement the work of the Cochrane Centre by commissioning reviews of available research beyond the area of controlled trials ensuring that the information is of good quality' (DOH, 1993a).

EBHC can be achieved by a multidisciplinary approach since health is a multifaceted concept. The scope of the nurses' contribution to multidisciplinary work is wide, and opportunities should not be missed if nurses want their voices heard and their efforts valued. However, since most of nursing practice is distinct from other practices such as medicine and physiotherapy, there is a need to develop evidence-based nursing as well. In 1996 the RCN launched its Clinical Effectiveness Initiative (RCN, 1996a), the objectives of which are:

1. To promote the nursing contribution to the development of evidence based health care in the UK and to the debate on clinical effectiveness.
2. To collaborate with a range of organisations to promote evidence based health care and education.
3. To develop methods to facilitate the dissemination, implementation and evaluation of evidence based nursing and health care.
4. To set up the infrastructure and marketing framework supported by the leadership of the RCN to promote the implementation of the Clinical Effectiveness Initiative.

One of the main strategies to facilitate the use of research and other evidence is the development, implementation and evaluation of clinical guidelines. The RCN, as part of the above initiative, wants, among other things, to 'establish a rolling programme of clinical guideline development' and 'to demonstrate links between clinical audit and clinical guidelines within a framework of clinical effectiveness' (RCN, 1996a).

Producing evidence from systematic reviews of existing research is one contribution towards achieving clinical effectiveness. Nurses need to continue to ask questions about their practice and seek answers. Research needs to be carried out in areas that remain unresearched or underresearched. In some areas in which findings are inconclusive, more research will be required. However, where much research has been carried out, it is our moral responsibility to make use of the findings and not to waste valuable resources in undertaking new studies.

RESEARCH AND PROFESSIONAL DEVELOPMENT

While research should address specific nursing practices, it could also contribute to the improvement of nursing practice in general by developing theories that can guide nursing actions. For example, White's (1984) study of 'client attrition in an obesity programme' not only helped to prevent drop-outs in this particular programme, but also made a contribution to the knowledge of patients' compliance with care in general. The health belief model (Rosenstock, 1966) and the theory of reasoned action (Fishbein and Ajzen, 1975) are just two of the theories which nurses have used to underpin their research, in return contributing towards their refinement.

Fawcett (1980) warned that unless research 'is guided by theory and unless theory is tested through research, both are in danger of being isolated and therefore trivial enterprises'. Nursing needs to develop its own theories and knowledge base. According to Fawcett (1980), 'the only way to generate, refine, or enlarge the knowledge needed by nursing is through scientific research'. Munhall (1990) comments that 'much of the scientific knowledge necessary to formulate rational nursing practice is lacking'. The relationship between theory and practice is further discussed in Chapter 6.

The accumulation of knowledge on different aspects of nursing constitutes a 'body of knowledge' that nurses and others can draw upon and contribute to. This body of knowledge is the sum total of nursing knowledge (theories, research findings, reflections on practice, and so forth) contained mainly in books, journals, reports, theses and other audiovisual forms. The progress made in the creation of nursing's body of knowledge can be gauged by the availability of books on different aspects of nursing and the number of nursing journals currently on the market compared with the early 1970s, when the number of books on nursing in the UK probably amounted to only a handful. The creation of a body of knowledge distinct to nursing is an important step in establishing nursing as a profession. One of the hallmarks of a profession is the possession of a body of knowledge based on research, and in the progress of nursing towards true professional status, the acquisition of a research basis for practice is essential (RCN, 1982). Nursing relies heavily on knowledge from other disciplines, such as biology, chemistry, sociology and psychology. While nursing will continue to draw upon, and contribute to, knowledge from these other sciences, it is imperative that it continues to create a body of knowledge to inform its own practice. Fawcett (1980) believes that the emergence of nursing as a profession can occur only when nurses 'identify a distinct body of knowledge about the individuals, groups, situations, and events of interest to nursing'.

The status of nursing as a profession will be enhanced when other professions recognise that nursing is not just common sense but is based on knowledge derived from research and organised in the form of concepts and theories. Aggleton and Chalmers (1986) point out:

> for nursing to develop as a set of practices autonomous from those of medicine and the paramedical professions, it must have its own research base. That is, it should cease to rely so heavily upon research findings generated in other areas of health-care activity, but should instead seek to develop and work with sets of understandings which relate specifically to nursing concerns.

The contribution of research towards the status of a profession is also recognised in physiotherapy. Sackley (1994) reported that 'physiotherapists in the UK have recognised the trend towards becoming research-based practitioners, ready to justify their techniques and procedures'.

The creation of a body of knowledge is the means by which parity with other professions can be achieved, and research is the process by which this knowledge can be developed and validated. Fawcett (1980) draws a parallel between the struggle for independence of underdeveloped countries and the struggle for nursing to be established as a fully fledged profession:

> Just as it is the case with an underdeveloped nation, nursing will not achieve fully developed status until is attains independence. And that means not relying on others for the knowledge that shapes our practice. The time has come to us to construct our own theories and test them in the real world of nursing. And the time has come for knowledge validated by research to be the primary determinant of nursing practice. Only when this goal is realized will nursing be able to declare its independence.

This was written in 1980. How far has nursing travelled on this road, since then, towards becoming a recognised profession in your country?

The Role of Nurses in Research

As explained above, nurses have an important role to play in creating a body of knowledge and using it to inform practice. However, what this role is depends partly on the education, training and position of the nurse. Everyone knows the famous quote from the Briggs report (Briggs, 1972) that 'nursing should become a research-based profession'. Twelve years later, Boore (1984) commented:

> In the years since the 'Briggs' report, nursing as a profession has not moved far in clarifying what is meant by 'a research based profession', or in identifying the specific attributes (in terms of research knowledge and skills) expected in a newly qualified nurse at the end of a 2 year, 3 year and 4 year exposure to nursing education.

Boore (1984) suggested three possible roles for the 'newly qualified professional nurse'. Firstly, she should question the scientific basis of her practice and have a sense of a need for research; secondly, she should be able to read research critically, with a view to using the findings in her practice; and finally, she 'should be able to carry out small scale research projects within the clinical settings where she is working' (Boore, 1984).

With the advent of the new Diploma in Nursing (Project 2000 courses) and the integration of nurse education into higher education, the debate on the role of the diplomates in nursing research continues. Anecdotal evidence suggests this has been interpreted differently by different institutions, with the result that some courses require students to carry out a literature review on a topic related to practice, while others expect students to formulate a research proposal or even carry out a small-scale project. While some courses may be expecting more from their students than others, the consensus in the nursing profession seems to be that qualified nurses should be able to read and use research critically and have a sense of the need for research to underpin their practice. The task of conducting research should rest with those who have acquired further education and training, especially in research methodology. Buckeldee and McMahon (1994) comment:

> Although research has become a central focus in both pre- and post-registration courses, the focus needs to be on identifying problems that require further investigation and on critiquing existing research so that its relevance in informing and changing practice can be assessed. We believe that the channelling of students' energies into the integration of research into practice would be more valuable than trying to teach them research skills which they are unlikely to use again.

In discussing the role of nurses in research, the impression can be wrongly given that research is somehow an 'extra' (Cang, 1979) to nursing practice. Far from being 'added on' or an option, 'a sense of the need for research should become part of the mental equipment of every practising nurse and midwife' (Briggs, 1972).

RESEARCH-MINDEDNESS

The term 'research-mindedness' is often used interchangeably with 'research awareness'. Clark (1987) describes the different 'roles of the "research-aware" nurse'. These are:

- raising problems and questions for research;
- cooperating with researchers in an informed way;
- seeking out and critically evaluating published research studies;
- using research findings; and
- communicating with others and sharing the task of keeping abreast of new developments.

The RCN (1982) explains what the term research-mindedness means to them:

> We understand the term 'research-mindedness' to imply a critical, questioning approach to one's work, the desire and ability to find out about the latest research in that area, and the ability to assess its value to the situation and apply it as appropriate. It also implies a recognition of the importance of research to the profession and to patient care, and a willingness to support nurse-researchers in their work.

It is clear the two terms are used in the same sense. Three main components of research awareness or mindedness are: the adoption of a questioning stance to one's practice, a knowledge of existing research, and the ability to use it. As Phillips (1994) has observed, 'questioning practice and not adhering to comfortable, familiar routines out of habit alone is an important aspect of research awareness'.

There is perhaps a sense in which research-mindedness is more than just research awareness. It is when a nurse adopts the thinking processes of a researcher and uses some of the basic research skills to improve practice. ...ham (1994) states that 'the basic skills of research, i.e. listening and ...vation, are also the basic skills of midwifery'. Nurses and midwives engage in problem-solving on a daily basis. They constantly collect and analyse data in the assessment and evaluation phases of the nursing and midwifery process. The basic skills of interviewing and observing can be sharpened through learning some of the research method skills.

RESEARCH EXAMPLE | Jackson (1994)
So much for common sense

It is current practice to note a woman's temperature, pulse and blood pressure when she is admitted in labour and to record the fetal heart rate. These information are normally then recorded at regular intervals throughout labour....

There is no research base to support the need for some of these observations in the first instance or to use as a basis for determining the frequency of others. Yet I, like many others, would be reluctant to abandon them. There does seem to be a logical explanation for performing the observations and I could, like all midwives, explain why they are thought to be necessary. On the other hand, I cannot recall ever finding a woman's temperature to be raised at the beginning of labour except in circumstances where a pyrexia would have been expected or anticipated. So why have I continued to take and record it? If I am honest, it's because I've never really thought about it before writing this piece (Jackson, 1994).

There are a number of triggers which can make you question your practice. These include:

1. When you carry out a task, although you have doubts about whether it is effective, harmful or even necessary, as illustrated in RE 1.
2. When you observe that the incidence of a particular problem is higher than would normally be expected. For example, you may observe there has been an increase in the number of patients falling or in the incidence of pressure sores. RE 2 shows how such an observation led to a research project.
3. When you compare your practice with what others do or when others question your practice. Different approaches may come to light during discussions with your peers while on a course. You may also discover these at conferences and other similar forums, or read about them in books, journals and other publications. RE 3 shows how one student nurse changed her practice.

RESEARCH EXAMPLE 2   Smith (1984)
A beginner's guide to research

The author explains why she decided to investigate the problem of constipation on her ward:

> I work as a senior sister in a mixed, 27 bed cardio-pulmonary medical ward. When the nth patient on the nth drug round asked me for 'something' for his bowel, I wondered, yet again, why was constipation so rife. I had long got rid of the 'bowel book', as I felt this made patients dwell on the fact that they 'hadn't been', when asked daily by a nurse about their bowel habits. I am also sure that a lot of nurses, like myself, think that patients have nothing better to do than to discuss their bowel habits all day long. I decided to approach our nursing research department with my thoughts and see if they would like to get involved in a research project.

RESEARCH EXAMPLE 3   Deacon (1986)
Does anyone read research?

The author emphasises the importance of questioning practice and describes how, as a first-year student nurse, she stopped using ring cushions in the treatment of pressure sores:

> It is essential to question current cli⋯ ⋯ see to it that what we do is backed up by scien⋯ ⋯ y to conform to what is the ward custom or the pr⋯ ⋯ the hierarchy than ourselves must be questioned. For instance, ring cushions are used because they are available and are used by others. Does availability of a product stop your questioning? I used ring cushions until discouraged by another student nurse who prompted me to realise that I could not justify my practice. Do you use ring cushions? Can you justify your practice?

On the other hand, one must be careful when adopting or rejecting particular practices on the basis of inadequate research evidence. In a review of the literature on ring cushions, Church and Lyne (1994) concluded:

> It appears that various authors' misgivings regarding the use of ring cushions in nursing and midwifery are not fully supported by empirical data in the literature. Thus present policy on their use rests on clinical judgement, rather than research findings. The case of the ring cushion is an example of how a tentative conclusion has been widely interpreted as definitive evidence, and thus extensively accepted.

RESEARCH UTILISATION

Being aware of research findings and the need for research is only the first step towards fulfilling the research role of nurses. Utilising research to underpin practice is the ultimate aim of nursing research. There are many ways in which research can be used. If we accept the notion of research as providing an insight into the phenomenon being studied, we are likely to increase our knowledge of it. For example, if the purpose of the study is to identify factors that contribute to health visitors' job satisfaction, we can acquire a knowledge of these factors. The findings can subsequently be used to promote such satisfaction. In a practice-based profession such as nursing or midwifery, the use of research is highly valued as it seeks to provide solutions to problems faced by practitioners.

However, the utilisation of research is more than the implementation of findings. Research also provides an insight into how a phenomenon is investigated. This process itself is enlightening and makes us think, even if we are not interested in the problem or do not believe the findings. The literature review, if properly carried out, can be quite illuminating. By discussing what is already known about a particular topic, the researcher provides us with valuable information as well as the different ways in which problems can be conceptualised. In the above example of factors contributing to the job satisfaction of health visitors, the researcher may not only inform us of research findings from similar studies, but also put the study in a theoretical context. Thus Maslow's theory of the hierarchy of needs may be used to categorise the various factors, such as recognition from peers, pay, support from managers, and so on. The literature review can widen the horizon of practitioners who perhaps previously did not perceive the issue from a number of different perspectives.

The way in which research is carried out – the identification of the problem, the definition of the terms used in the study, the decision-making process involved in the choice of design and methods, the analysis of data and their interpretation – are all useful exercises which can in themselves be fascinating to follow and useful to learn from.

The implementation of findings in nursing practice is discussed further in Chapter 16.

THE ROLE OF NURSES IN THE CONDUCT OF RESEARCH

Not every nurse is expected to carry out research, but for nursing to be research based, some nurses must be involved in conducting it. Fawcett (1980) believes that 'it is incumbent upon nurses to conduct investigations of nursing phenomena'.

Briggs (1972) proposed that 'the active pursuit of serious research must be limited to a minority within the profession', while Fawcett (1984), writing about the USA, suggests that registered nurses read research, share the findings with others and use them in their practice, and that those with a Masters or higher degree are expected to carry out research.

To carry out serious research, nurses need a fair degree of knowledge and skills, not usually attainable in basic training. The research training of undergraduate nurses varies in the UK, as explained earlier. Anecdotal evidence, as well as a perusal of the nursing literature, shows that more and more staff nurses in the UK conduct research, albeit small-scale projects, mainly as part of their courses. Many take part in projects led by doctors and other health-care professionals. In a study of practice nurses in the West Midlands, it was found that 12 per cent of practice nurses were assisting general practitioners with research projects (Greenfield, 1987, cited in Kenkre, 1994). Sixty-four per cent of a random sample of 550 midwives reported they had carried out research (Hicks, 1993). Mander (1995) commented, 'it may be that this large proportion merely reflects the large number of midwives who have been involved in others' (probably medical) research'. It is also possible that many of these projects were carried out as part of the requirement of a course (Mander, 1995).

Practising nurses are frequently asked to collect data for other researchers, be they nurse researchers, doctors, psychologists or others. Their clinical nursing experience can be valuable to the research enterprise. Nurses are in a position to identify problems that need investigation through research. On the other hand, the researcher can also bring her detached perspective to bear on the problem being researched. This can be illustrated by the following example.

A researcher was called upon to help to improve care in an elderly care ward through research. She had a hunch that constipation might be a problem in this group of patients. The ward sister did not think so until they both examined the kardex and found that 11 out of 19 patients were 'on' laxatives, some three times daily. While discussing each patient individually, the ward sister also observed that those who were not prescribed laxatives were also the most confused patients on the ward and would probably not have been able to ask for medication. Without clinical insight, the researcher would have missed this important observation. This highlights the important and unique contribution that nurses can make to the research enterprise in nursing. The research–practitioner collaboration is further discussed in Chapter 16.

The danger of leaving the conduct of research to a minority of nurses within the profession is that practitioners may not see research as integral to their practice. While there is some evidence from nursing journals of staff nurses conducting research, it is too much to expect first-level nurses to do so, even though many are very capable. Whether they conduct research or not will depend on their research training, their interests and their skills, as well as the presenting opportunities. In a study by Rizzuto *et al.* (1994), few nurses in the sample of 1217 employed at nine health-care agencies in the USA were interested in conducting their own research. More were interested in 'collaborating with others and in applying findings'. Although nurses should collaborate with others, they must seek to become full members of the research team. The opportunities to register for a higher degree must also be considered. Nurses have grown in confidence from the early days when they were mostly handmaidens to medical and other researchers, collecting data with little to show for it.

One important role of nurses relating to the conduct of research is ensuring that research carried out on patients does not cause the latter any harm; human rights have to be protected. Practitioners' priority is the patient and therefore they should act not only as gatekeepers to the patient population but also as guardians and advocates for their rights.

Funding Nursing Research

One common feature of the development of nursing research world wide is the lack of funding necessary for training researchers and for research to be carried out. Stinson *et al.* (1990) explain that in Canada:

> The paucity of research funding pertains not only to the design and conduct of investigations but as well to the support of such infrastructure as research training, university and health care agency based clinical researchers, seed money, research development programs in health care agencies, scientific travel, conferences and journals – and the development of research units.

They go on to point out that 'until the mid-1960s most Canadian nursing research was funded or minimally so', and 'although greater funding is more readily available' in the 1990s, it is not sufficient if nursing research is to have a positive impact on patient care. In the UK in 1990, central government retained responsibility for the funding of research studentships and postdoctoral fellowships, together with the provision of funding for research units at King's College, the University of London and Surrey University (Lelean and Clarke, 1990). Since then, the unit in Surrey has been closed. Although some funding is available from other sources, and nurses have been able to attract more funds in recent years, the RCN (1992) has stressed that the 'level of resources available for research in nursing does not recognise or reflect nursing's pivotal role within all health care settings'. The RCN would welcome the establishment of a funding strategy that had specific funds 'ring-fenced' for nursing research (RCN, 1992). Giving evidence to the House of Lords Science and Technology Committee in 1995, the RCN told the committee:

> nursing research continues to be perceived as illegitimate activity in the sense that it has no formally recognised funding structure sanctioning its work from region, through purchaser to provider level. (Doult, 1995)

In the UK, there is now a clear research and development (R&D) strategy (DOH, 1993a). The emphasis in on a multidisciplinary approach to health issues and problems, as reflected in this statement from *Research for Health* (DOH, 1993a):

> To accomplish its objectives, the R&D programme draws on research expertise and methods from diverse interests including hospital medicine, primary care, public health, dentistry, nursing, the professions allied to medicine, biological and physical sciences, epidemiology, statistics, economics and social sciences. It draws on the views of patients and the public.

In May 1993, *The Report of the Taskforce on the Strategy for Research in Nursing, Midwifery and Health Visiting* (DOH, 1993b) was published. It recommended, among other things, that the centrally commissioned programme of research be maintained at least in real terms and that the DOH undertake an internal appraisal to ensure that:

- there is a coherent and high profile approach to research in nursing, health visiting and midwifery;
- the nursing dimension is fully recognised and funded wherever it is relevant to a commissioned programme or project; and

● a nursing research dimension – especially relating to the evaluation of current and innovative practices and procedures – be firmly embedded in the re-focused resources which the Department devotes to research units, with each appropriate unit containing an identifiable element of nursing research.

Although the taskforce did not recommend separate funding for nursing research, it made recommendations to the NHS Management Executive, the Director of Research and Development, the Regional Health Authorities, the Special Health Authorities, the Medical Research Council (MRC) and the Economic and Social Research Council (ESRC) to take greater cognisance of nurses and nursing research when agendas for research are set, when funding is allocated and in research training programmes.

In the present research funding structure, nurses have to compete with the other health professions for funds. The potential for nurses to acquire grants from R&D programmes, the MRC, the ESRC and, indeed, the European Union must not be underestimated. According to Luker (1992), 'the challenge for nurses is to ensure that the nursing dimension in any multi-disciplinary project is clearly defined and is adequately funded'. Nurses' success will depend, in great part, on the quality of proposals (these will have to meet the criteria outlined in *Research For Health*: DOH, 1993a), the relevance of their topics to the R&D agenda and, to some extent, the multidisciplinary membership of grant-making bodies, whether statutory or voluntary. Apart from obtaining funds for research, 'there will be many opportunities for nurses to participate in shaping the strategy (R&D) through their professional organizations and regional authority networks' (Luker, 1992).

There will need to be a genuine recognition of methodologies other than RCTs. Currently, proposals for R&D funding should 'be designed so that the findings will be of value to those in the NHS facing similar problems outside the particular locality or context of the project' and should also 'follow a clear, well-defined peer-reviewed protocol approved, where necessary, by the Local Research Ethics Committee and any other relevant body' (DOH, 1993a). Clearly, in this context, qualitative approaches are at a disadvantage. This will affect in particular nurses and midwives, who (judging by the articles published in the UK's main academic and professional journals) are increasingly undertaking qualitative research studies.

Whether the DOH, MRC, ESRC and others take nursing research seriously will be gauged by nursing's success or otherwise, relative to the other health professionals, in obtaining funding from these sources and in contributing to the research agenda.

The formation of the National Institute of Nursing Research in the USA is an indication of the commitment to nursing research aspired to but so far unrealised by nurses in other countries.

Despite the bumpy road it has travelled and the hardships it has encountered on the way, nursing research in the industrialised countries has come far. This can be summed up in the words of Luker (1992) who, in a guest editorial of the *Journal of Advanced Nursing*, concluded:

> nursing research has made a substantial contribution to our understanding of nursing as a distinct discipline. It has also produced a sound knowledge base which has encountered problems diffusing into practice, and in cases where it has diffused it has contributed to improvements in patient care.

Lest we become complacent and conclude that the struggle is over, it is important to remember that many battles have still to be fought. Webb and MacKenzie's (1993) study of nurses employed in one health authority in England has shown that research-mindedness is far from being achieved.

Summary and Conclusion

Nursing research has come of age in some countries, while in others it is still in its infancy. The role of research-based knowledge in decision-making is crucial for effective practice, and the need to have a sound rationale for one's practice has increased over the last decade.

While nursing research must be carried out by nurses in order to create a nursing body of knowledge, a multidisciplinary approach is also required as nurses work with other health professionals and share the same goal. It is not incumbent on every nurse to carry out research, but all should be research-minded enough to value the contribution of research to practice, identify problems that can be explored through research, be aware of research findings, collaborate with others in research activities and protect the rights of patients with regards to their involvement in research projects.

The momentum created by nursing research must be maintained and increased if it is to contribute positively to patient care and achieve the recognition it deserves.

References

Aggleton P and Chalmers H (1986) Nursing research, nursing theory and the nursing process. *Journal of Advanced Nursing*, **11**:197–202.

Benner P (1984) *From Novice to Expert – Excellence and Power in Clinical Nursing Practice*. California: Addison-Wesley.

Benton D and Avery G (1993) Quality, research and ritual in nursing. *Nursing Standard*, **7**(49):29–30.

Boore J P R (1984) Nursing research – nursing education. *Journal of Advanced Nursing*, **9**(1):93–5.

Buckeldee J and McMahon R (1994) *The Research Experience in Nursing*. London: Chapman & Hall.

Briggs A (1972) *Report on the Committee on Nursing* (Briggs Report). Cmnd 5115. London: HMSO.

Cang S (1979) Nursing research: problems of aims, method and content. *Journal of Advanced Nursing*, **4**(4): 453–8.

Chick N P (1987) Nursing research in New Zealand. *Western Journal of Nursing Research*, **9**(3):317–33.

Church S and Lyne P (1994) Research-based practice: some problems illustrated by the discussion of evidence concerning the use of a pressure-relieving device in nursing and midwifery. *Journal of Advanced Nursing*, **19**: 513–18.

Clark E (1987) Research awareness: its importance in practice. *Professional Nurse*, **2**(11):371–3.

Clark J MacLeod and Hockey L (1979) *Research for Nursing – A Guide for the Enquiring Nurse*. Bucks: HM+ M.

Clark J MacLeod and Hockey L (1986) *Research for Nursing – A Guide for the Enquiring Nurse*. Chichester: John Wiley & Sons.

Coulter S J and Orsolits M A (1991) Strategies for establishing a nursing research program. *Aspen's Advisor*, **6**(4):1–8.

CRD (Centre for Reviews and Dissemination) (1996) *Undertaking Systematic Reviews of Research on Effectiveness*. CRD Report 4. York: CRD.

Crow R (1982) How nursing and the community can benefit from nursing research. *International Journal of Nursing Studies*, **19**(1):37–45.

Deacon L (1986) Does anyone read research? *Nursing Times*, **82**(32):57–9.

DOH (Department of Health) (1992) *Research and Development Strategy*. London: DOH.

DOH (Department of Health) (1993a) *Research for Health*. London: DOH.

DOH (Department of Health) (1993b) *Report of the Taskforce on the Strategy for Research in Nursing, Midwifery and Health Visiting*. London: DOH.

Doult B (1995) Nursing research is still undervalued. *Nursing Standard*, **9**(39):8.

Farrell M and Christensen B W (1990) Coming of age: nursing research in Europe. In Bergman R (ed.) *Nursing Research for Nursing Practice – An International Perspective*. London: Chapman & Hall.

Fawcett J (1980) A declaration of nursing independence: the relation of theory and research to nursing practice. *Journal of Nursing Administration*, June, 36–9.

Fawcett J (1984) Hallmarks of success in nursing research. *Advances in Nursing Science*, **7**(1):1–11.

Fishbein M and Ajzen I (1975) *Belief, Attitude, Intention and Behaviour: An Introduction to Theory and Research*. Reading: Addison-Wesley.

Flaherty M J (1990) Nursing research: cornerstone of nursing practice in Canada. In Bergman R (ed.) *Nursing Research for Nursing Practice – An International Perspective*. London: Chapman & Hall.

Getcliffe K (1993) Freeing the system. *Nursing Standard*, **8**(7):16–18.

Greenfield S, Stilwell B and Drury M (1987) Practice nurses: social and occupational characteristics. *Journal of the Royal College of Practitioners*, **37**:341–5.

Hicks C (1993) A survey of midwives' attitudes to, and involvement in, research: the first stage in identifying needs for a staff development programme. *Midwifery*, **9**:51–62.

Hunt M (1987) The process of translating research findings into practice. *Journal of Advanced Nursing*, **12**:101–10.

Jackson K (1994) So much for common sense. *British Journal of Midwifery*, **2**(3):131–2.

Jennings B M (1995) Nursing research – a time for redirection. *Journal of Nursing Administration*, **25**(4):9–11.

Kemp J (1988) Graduates in nursing: a report of a longitudinal study at the University of Hull. *Journal of Advanced Nursing*, **13**:281–7.

Kenkre J (1994) Is research for practice nurses? *Practice Nursing*, **5**(17):18–22.

Kenny C (1994) Nursing intuition: can it be researched? *British Journal of Nursing*, **3**(22):1191–5.

Kirkham M J (1994) Using research skills in midwifery practice. *British Journal of Midwifery*, **2**(8):390–2.

Lelean S R and Clarke M (1990) Research resource development in the United Kingdom. *International Journal of Nursing Studies*, **27**(2):123–38.

LoBiondo-Wood G and Haber J (1994) *Nursing Research: Methods, Critical Appraisal, and Utilization*, 3rd edn. St Louis: C V Mosby.

Luker K A (1992) Research and development in nursing (guest editorial). *Journal of Advanced Nursing*, **17**:1151–2.

Luker K A and Kenrick M (1992) An exploratory study of the sources of influence on the clinical decisions of community nurses. *Journal of Advanced Nursing*, **17**:457–66.

Lydon-Rochelle M and Albers L (1993) Research trends in the *Journal of Nurse-Midwifery* 1987–1992. *Journal of Nurse-Midwifery*, **38**(6):343–8.

Mander R (1992) See how they learn: experience as a basis of practice. *Nurse Education Today*, **12**:11–18.

Mander R (1995) Midwife researchers need to get their work published. *British Journal of Midwifery*, **3**(2):107–10.

Mangay-Maglacas A (1992) Nursing research in developing countries: needs and prospects. *Journal of Advanced Nursing*, **17**:267–70.

Marshall-Burnett S (1990) Nursing research in Jamaica: catalyst and partner in health policy. In Bergman R (ed.) *Nursing Research for Nursing Practice – An International Perspective*. London: Chapman & Hall.

Munhall A (1990) The contribution of the basic sciences to nursing practice research. *Journal of Advanced Nursing*, **15**:1354–7.

O'Brien D and Davison M (1994) Blood pressure measurement: rational and ritual actions. *British Journal of Nursing*, **3**(8):393–6.

Peckham M (1993) Introduction. In *Research for Health*. London: Department of Health.

Phillips R (1994) The need for research-based midwifery practice. *British Journal of Midwifery*, **2**(7):335–8.

Polgar S and Thomas S A (1991) *Introduction to Research in the Health Sciences*, 2nd edn. Melbourne: Churchill Livingstone.

RCN (Royal College of Nursing) (1982) *Research-Mindedness and Nurse Education*. London: RCN.

RCN (Royal College of Nursing) (1992) *Strategy for Nursing Research: Comments from the RCN to Department of Health Task Force on Research in Nursing*. London: RCN.

RCN (Royal College of Nursing) (1996a) *The Royal College of Nursing Clinical Effectiveness Initiative: A Strategic Framework*. London: RCN.

RCN (Royal College of Nursing) (1996b) *Clinical Effectiveness: A Royal College of Nursing Guide*. London: RCN.

Reed J and Procter S (1995) *Practitioner Research in Health Care*. London. Chapman & Hall.

Rew L (1986) Intuition: a concept analysis of a group phenomenon. *Advances in Nursing Science*, **8**(2):21–8.

Rizzuto C, Bostrom J, Suter W N and Chenitz W C (1994) Predictors of nurses' involvement in research activities. *Western Journal of Nursing Research*, **16**(2): 193–204.

Romney M L and Gordon H (1981) Is your enema really necessary? *British Medical Journal*, **282**:1269–71.

Rosenberg W and Donald A (1995) Evidence based medicine: an approach to clinical problem-solving. *British Medical Journal*, **310**(6987):1122–5.

Rosenstock I M (1966) Why people use health services. *Millbank Memorial Fund Quarterly*, **44**: 94–121.

Rundell S (1992) Research has shown…. *Nursing Times*, **88**(7):24.

Sackett D L, Rosenberg W M C, Gray J A M, Haynes R B and Richardson W S (1996) Evidence based medicine: what it is and what it isn't. *British Medical Journal*, **312**:71–2.

Sackley C (1994) Developing a knowledge base: progress so far. *Physiotherapy*, **80**(A):24A–28A.

Smith L N (1994) An analysis and reflections on the quality of nursing research in 1992. *Journal of Advanced Nursing*, **19**:385–93.

Smith S (1984) A beginner's guide to research. *Nursing Times*, **80**(22):64.

Stinson S M, Lamb M and Thibaudeau M F (1990) Nursing research: the Canadian scene. *International Journal of Nursing Studies*, **27**(2):105–22.

UKCC (United Kingdom Central Council for Nursing, Midwifery and Health Visiting) (1996) *Guidelines for Professional Practice*. London: UKCC.

Walsh M and Ford P (1990) *Nursing Rituals, Research and Rational Actions*, 2nd edn. Oxford: Heinemann Nursing.

Webb C and MacKenzie J (1993) Where are we now? Research-mindedness in the 1990s. *Journal of Clinical Nursing*, **2**:129–33.

White J H (1984) The relationship of clinical practice and research. *Journal of Advanced Nursing*, **9**:181–7.

2 KNOWLEDGE, SCIENCE AND RESEARCH

> We might have accumulated an immense amount of knowledge in what we regard as science but we have barely begun to understand what knowledge is. (DeMey, 1982)

INTRODUCTION

Science has evolved as a dominant and legitimate mode of knowledge production in modern societies, and research plays an important part in the scientific enterprise. This chapter examines the relationship between knowledge, science and research. It also distinguishes between the two main research paradigms in health and social research – positivism and interpretivism. This is followed by a brief introduction to grounded theory, ethnography and phenomenology. Many of the issues raised here will be discussed in more detail throughout the book.

THE NEED FOR KNOWLEDGE

Humans have always had a need for knowledge. Our prehistoric ancestors had to 'know' their environment in order to survive: to know what food to eat and where to get it. Knowledge brings with it a degree of power. Sometimes sheer force and numbers have not been enough to win battles; those with a superior knowledge of weapons and tactics often had the advantage. Authority and status are bestowed on people who possess knowledge. Those who appear on our television screens to display their knowledge on particular issues are referred to as 'experts'.

Professionals are highly regarded because they possess a body of knowledge in their particular disciplines. Although some knowledge is sought for aesthetic reasons, most of us need to 'know' in order to make decisions in our daily lives.

We have come a long way since humans felt at the mercy of the environment. As Sigerist wrote in 1943 in his classic book, *Civilisation and Disease*:

> We have created the means of lighting up the darkness and can heat our dwellings to the temperature of summer in the middle of winter. We have

learned to produce food in the quantity and quality desired, sometimes even in complete disregard of the seasons. (Sigerist, 1943)

Since then humans have invented the microchip and sent people to the moon.

We seek knowledge to change not only our environment, but also ourselves. Behaviour therapy and genetic engineering are but some of the products of this quest for knowledge, which began with our ancestors' need to know how to adapt to their environment in order to survive. In 1927 Freud wrote that the 'principal task of civilisation, its actual *raison d'être*, is to defend us against nature'.

The knowledge we have acquired seems to have put nature at our mercy. Indeed, a mark of modern civilisation is how nature is protected by and from humans.

BELIEF SYSTEMS

Knowing what happens only partly satisfies the thirst for knowledge; humans also need to know why things happen. For example, knowing how day follows night, that the tide comes in and goes out or that someone has abdominal pain is not enough. We need to know why these things happen. The first two phenomena can be explained by the movement of the planets, and the last could be food poisoning. However, the same phenomena would have been explained differently in the 10th century BC, in the Middle Ages or during the Renaissance. In the history of humans, different belief systems have provided the frameworks within which phenomena can be interpreted. These systems of belief have also provided rules governing what should or should not be questioned. Three belief systems that have been dominant in the West are the mythical or theological, the metaphysical and the scientific.

Mythical or theological beliefs

In primitive times, people predominantly believed that supernatural objects or beings had power over their lives. Thus gods, spirits, planets, mountains, rivers and trees were thought to possess magical powers, and everything that happened was determined by them. According to Sigerist (1943), 'primitive man found himself in a magical world, surrounded by a hostile nature whose every manifestation was invested with mysterious forces'.

Later, organised religions emerged and provided the framework for people to make sense of themselves and the world in which they lived. Judaism, Christianity and Islam seemed to have put some order into the mythical world by providing the notion of one supernatural being, God, instead of a number of gods or spirits, but they kept some of the elements of prereligious times (Sigerist, 1943).

Metaphysical beliefs

When people began to question and doubt the power of the supernatural and relied more on their own observation of the world around them, they began to put more faith in nature, which did not appear to be as threatening as they had previously thought. This was a time when armchair speculations were rife. Philosophers and others postulated theories to explain phenomena. One such theory, which illustrates the break from supernatural beliefs and the emphasis on the relationship between nature and human beings, is the theory of the four humors postulated by Hippocrates and later developed by Galen and the Arabs. As Sigerist (1943) explains:

> Each humor had elementary qualities. Thus blood was hot and moist like air; phlegm was cold and moist like water. Yellow bile was hot and dry like fire, and black bile was cold and dry like earth. Man was part of nature. Nature was constituted by the four elements, the human body by the four humors... When the humors were normal in quantity and quality... man was healthy... When, however, as a result of disturbances, one humor came to dominate in an abnormal way, the balance was upset... and the individual was sick.

Scientific beliefs

Metaphysical thoughts had elements of science and influenced earlier scientific theories, but they were limited because most of their explanations were based on speculation.

Polgar and Thomas (1991) place the origin of Western science in the metaphysical age:

> The beginnings of modern Western science are generally traced to the 16th century, a time in which Europe experienced profound social changes and a resurgence of great thinkers and philosophers. Gradually, scholars' interests shifted from theology and armchair speculation to systematically describing, explaining and attempting to control natural phenomena.

The next stage in the evolution of human thought was to put some of these theories to the test. We began to rely more on what we could observe in order to explain phenomena. However, casual observations were not enough: there was a need to observe systematically and rigorously so that the explanations offered could be verified by others. Experiments became the medium through which scientific knowledge was created, and this area of activity became known as research. The scientific age is characterised by the belief that nature can be controlled, that phenomena can be prevented and predicted. Epidemics were no longer thought to be a punishment for human transgressions of religious laws but were seen to be caused by the spread of infections. Therefore, by preventing the spread, the disease could be contained. In laboratory experiments, the infectious organisms could be identified, and the ways in which they were transmitted could be observed.

Belief systems and knowledge

The world is made up of more belief systems than can be described here. However, the three systems described above are believed to have dominated Western thought. Although they are presented here in chronological order, different belief systems have also coexisted throughout history. Scientists and philosophers worked and lived amidst primitive societies, and spiritual, religious and scientific beliefs coexist to this day. People are also eclectic in their beliefs. This means that they can borrow elements from different belief systems in order to make sense of their world. For example, some people who believe that AIDS is caused by a virus may believe at the same time that it is also a punishment for sin.

By contrasting these three belief systems – the mythical, the metaphysical and the scientific – a number of issues can be raised. Firstly, each system seems to have evolved from the failure of the dominant system at the time to satisfy the curiosity of human beings, science being the latest attempt to explain natural phenomena. Secondly, they each have their own interpretation of the same phenomena. For example, in the mythical age, disease was explained by spirit possession or punishment from God or other supernatural beings. Metaphysical philosophers thought that the balance between the sick person and nature was disturbed, while science attempts to identify the causal agents using microscopes, X-rays and other scanning devices. Thirdly, their sources of knowledge differ. In the mythical or theological age, knowledge was thought to be acquired through divination, revelations or dreams. Knowledge was invested in witchdoctors, healers, prophets and religious leaders. Metaphysical knowledge was obtained through speculation, inspiration and no doubt as a result of some forms of limited observation. Scientific knowledge, on the other hand, is derived mainly from research. Finally, each of these systems has rules for what should or should not be questioned or studied. The knowledge of spiritual healers or religious leaders was not to be questioned. There was a mystique concerning where this knowledge came from and how it was passed down. By and large, religions were concerned with souls and forbade the study of the human body.

The metaphysical age, which can be thought of as a transition between the other two periods, opened the way for people to question everything. Philosophers speculated on the soul as well as the body. Science, on the other hand, dictates that only what can be observed can be studied: the body, not the soul, is now the central focus of study.

Referring to the interpretation of disease, Sigerist, in 1943, summed up for us the place of science in relation to other beliefs:

> The scientific interpretation of disease is still very young. We still have enormous gaps, and we know that the truth of today may appear as an error tomorrow. Yet we may face the future with confidence because we fill the gaps of our knowledge not with religious dreams or philosophical speculations but with scientific facts. And when we make use of working hypotheses, as we have to do all the time, we know that they are assumptions and we are ready to discard them whenever new facts warrant it.

SCIENCE AND KNOWLEDGE

The term 'science' is derived from the Latin word *scientia* meaning knowledge. However, it is difficult to find one definition of science that is acceptable to all. Dawkin's (1989) definition of science as 'a communal enterprise in which truths are established by appealing not to authority or private conviction but to public evidence and shared logic' would be acceptable to many people, but the notion of science as searching for universal laws to explain and predict human behaviour would be challenged by many who do not believe that the scientific methods used in the natural sciences can be applied to the study of man.

The aim of science is to produce a body of knowledge that can enhance our understanding of phenomena, and, where possible, to predict, prevent, maintain or change them. Although scientific knowledge should ideally be used to benefit humanity, it can, as in the case of nuclear physics, be used to destroy as well as to enhance the quality of our life. How scientific knowledge is used depends on individuals and society.

SCIENCE AND RESEARCH

Scientists construct knowledge through the process of *induction* and *deduction*. Induction means that after a large number of observations have been made, it is possible to draw conclusions or theorise about particular phenomena. A theory, simply defined, is an explanation of why certain phenomena happen (see Chapter 7). The inductive method consists of description, classification, correlation, causation and prediction. The scientific study of plants (botany), for example, initially necessitated a description of the different type of plant species. The next inevitable step was to classify these, according to whether they were trees, flowers or grass, or whether they were edible or poisonous, for example. Through observation, it was possible to discover that the same plants grew better in certain conditions. After a large number of observations, scientists were able to theorise that some plant species thrived better with adequate light and water, a suggestion that could then be tested in experiments. Scientists were able thereafter to predict the conditions under which plants would thrive or wither. According to Bronowski (1960), 'science puts order in our experience'. Without descriptions, classifications and theories, we would be exposed to a mass of information about plants which we would find difficult to make sense of. Wilson (1989) reminds us:

> in the... natural sciences vast amounts of time and energy were – quite rightly – consumed in their early stages by way of simply observing and classifying and describing phenomena (think of zoology, for example): only much later, and with great difficulty, could scientists move toward anything like a theory.

While the inductive method has been in use in the natural sciences, it was Glaser and Strauss (1967) who made it popular in nursing and the social sciences with the publication of their book *The Discovery of Grounded Theory*.

Other scientists, however, formulate a theory or a hypothesis (a mini-theory) and then collect data in order to support or reject it. This approach to knowledge acquisition is called deduction. For example, if the proposed theory is that heat causes iron to expand, a large number of experiments will be carried out to put it to the test. This theory will be supported so long as no-one shows, in one or more experiments, that heat does not cause iron to expand. If this happens, the theory is falsified, and a new theory may emerge. The testing process has been termed 'falsification' by Popper (1969). According to him, theories formulated by researchers must be 'put to the test' by the scientific community. As Chalmers (1980) explains:

When an hypothesis that has successfully withstood a wide range of rigorous tests is eventually falsified, a new problem, hopefully far removed from the original solved problem, has emerged. This new problem calls for the invention of new hypotheses, followed by renewed criticism and testing. And so the process continues indefinitely. It can never be said of a theory that it is true, however well it has withstood rigorous tests, but it can hopefully be said that a current theory is superior to its predecessors in the sense that it is able to withstand tests that falsified those predecessors.

There is normally some form of generalisation from observations prior to the formulation of a theory. For example, casual observations made during the Napoleonic wars showed that injured servicemen left unattended for days were found to have higher survival rates if their wounds had been infested by maggots (*Sunday Times*, 1995). These observations, however unscientific, led to the hypothesis that maggots help wound healing. This could then be tested in laboratory type experiments.

What is research?

In our daily lives, we use deductive and inductive approaches in gathering information, drawing conclusions, or having a 'hunch' about something, and we look for evidence to support our beliefs. For example, you may find that, after taking a certain medication, some patients always look drowsy. You may conclude (after finding that this happened a number of times) that there is a connection between the drug and drowsiness. You have, therefore, used the inductive approach to collect this information. On the other hand, you may have a hypothesis or hunch that a particular form of treatment is ineffective. Subsequently, having found out that a number of patients who were given this treatment did not get better, you may conclude that your hypothesis is right. You have, therefore, used a deductive approach.

The 'scientific' research process consists mainly of formulating questions or hypotheses, collecting data using research methods such as observations, interviews or questionnaires and analysing data. You may be right in thinking that this is what we do all the time. We always have questions to which we seek answers; we either observe or talk to others in order to gather our information and we process this information and come to some conclusions. There are, however, crucial differences between the way in which non-researchers and researchers find out about phenomena.

Researchers are rigorous and systematic in their approach. Suppose, for example, that a researcher is studying the 'effects of authoritarian management on the job satisfaction of nurses'. A literature review will be

carried out to help her to arrive at definitions of 'authoritarian management' and 'job satisfaction' that are acceptable to others. It must be clear
that what is being measured or observed is actually job satisfaction and
not another concept. If, for example, the researcher observes nurses'
interaction on the wards rather than asking them questions about their
level of satisfaction, the data collected would not be valid because interactions in themselves do not tell us whether or not nurses are satisfied with
their jobs. A method is *valid* when it measures what it sets out to measure.

The people from whom data are eventually collected must represent
the population referred to in the research question. In the above
example, the researcher is studying the job satisfaction of 'nurses'.
Therefore she must draw a sample who will be representative of nurses,
be objective in her choice and avoid selecting her friends or only those
who volunteer to take part; she must be rigorous and systematic in her
selection of respondents. If the sample is biased, the data will not be
reliable because the answers may not reflect the views of those who did
not have a chance to be selected. Similarly, if some nurses in the sample
understand the questions differently from others, or have not all been
asked the same questions, the answers may not be reliable. *Reliability*
refers to the consistency of a particular method in measuring or
observing the same phenomena.

Once the data are collected, the researcher will analyse them systematically. She cannot reject answers that do not reflect her views. Thus,
the difference between lay people finding answers to questions in their
daily lives and a researcher studying a particular phenomenon is that
the latter is rigorous and systematic in her approach. She must not let
her prejudice influence the decisions and actions she takes. She must
describe in detail all the steps taken in order for others to follow what she
has done and to verify her findings, if they so wish, by replicating the
study. *Replication* refers to the process of repeating the same study in the
same or similar settings using the same methods with the same or
equivalent samples.

Research can be defined as the study of phenomena by the rigorous
and systematic collection and analysis of data. Research is a private
enterprise made public for the purpose of exposing it to the scrutiny of
others, to allow for replication, verification or falsification. This is one
definition of research which may not be acceptable to those who believe
that, while it must be rigorously carried out, it does have to be systematic. Some researchers do not need to ask the same questions to all
respondents, nor use large random samples, and do not subject their
data to systematic statistical analysis. They use a flexible approach
which they believe allows them to get closer to the truth or the essence of
phenomena. One can still argue that they develop their own 'systems'of

collecting and analysing data but that their systems are more flexible. The definition of research given above reflects the dominant approach in social and nursing research, although this is rapidly changing. This approach, or paradigm, has been termed the 'scientific method'.

PARADIGMS

The term 'paradigm' was coined by Kuhn (1970). Paradigms can loosely be described as schools of thought, although it will be clear later that they are much more than that. Smith (1991) describes paradigms as:

> different scientific communities [who] share specific constellations of beliefs, values, and techniques for deciding which questions are interesting, how one should breakdown an interesting question into solvable parts, and how to interpret the relationships of those parts to the answers.

From this description, it seems that paradigms influence:

- the types of phenomena that should or could be researched;
- the methods by which they can be studied;
- the techniques by which the data can be analysed and interpreted.

In any era, one paradigm is likely to be dominant. When this paradigm, also called normal science, is no longer effective and influential in addressing topical research problems, a crisis occurs (Kuhn, 1970). According to Kuhn (1970), a 'scientific revolution' takes place in which the dominant paradigm is replaced by a new science, which in turn becomes normal and dominant until it is in turn challenged and replaced, and so the process continues. An analogy from the field of music will serve to illustrate the notion of paradigms.

Classical music was the dominant form in the West until replaced by jazz; this was then followed by rock and roll and pop music, which is itself challenged by newer forms of music. While different types of music coexist, there is always a dominant form that emerges as a response to the failure of the previous dominant type to reflect the views or musical taste of those influential in the music industry. The dominant form of music provides not only the current definition of what constitutes music, but also how it should be played.

Positivism

One paradigm that has influenced much research in the health and social sciences is *positivism*, a movement that evolved as a critique of the supernatural and metaphysical interpretations of phenomena. The name 'positivism' derives from the emphasis on the positive sciences – that is, on tested and systematised experience rather than on undisciplined speculation (Kaplan, 1968). Developments in the natural sciences, especially physics and chemistry, led early sociologists (in the mid-18th century) to the belief that the methods of these sciences could be applied to the study of human behaviour. As Ayer (1969) explains:

> It was the belief of positivists [that] the empire of science was to be extended to every facet of man's nature; to the workings of men's minds as well as their bodies and to their social as well as their individual behaviour; law, custom, morality, religious faith and practice, political institutions, economic processes, language, art, indeed every form of human activity and mode of social organization were to be explained in scientific terms; and not only explained but transfigured.

Throughout history, mathematics was thought by philosophers to be the science potentially able to explain and predict human actions. Bertrand Russell (1971) pointed out that positivists regarded mathematics as the pattern to which other knowledge ought to approximate, and thought that pure mathematics, or a not dissimilar type of reasoning, could give knowledge as to the actual world.

The most important characteristic of positivism is *empiricism*, according to which only what can be observed by the human senses can be called facts. It is clear that such a definition of empiricism means that concepts such as anxiety, social support, satisfaction, well-being and so forth are therefore not amenable to empirical study – yet they have been empirically studied. This is because researchers have not used the term 'empirical' in its literal sense. Singleton *et al.* (1993) explain that:

> empiricism in science often takes the form of *indirect* observation, whereby instruments are employed that aid and extend the scientist's ability to observe. We might call this *sophisticated* empiricism to distinguish it from the kind of *naive* empiricism that relies on the unaided use of one's senses.

Thus weight can be measured according to the reading on a scale, and attitude according to the ratings of people on an attitude scale.

Positivists also believe in the notion of cause and effect (*determinism*) and look for explanations in empirical data. They adopt the *hypothetico-deductive* approach of physics and chemistry. This means that hypotheses or theories are put to the test by the deductive process during the course of experiments. Finally, positivists look to mathematics, more particularly, logic (a branch of mathematics), for the interpretation of data, hence the label of *logical positivist*.

The main criticism of the positivist approach is directed at the study of human beings as if they were objects. In physics, it is possible after a number of experiments to formulate laws relating to, for example, the expansion of metals when heated. From such laws, the amount of expansion that will occur in particular circumstances can be predicted. However, when a man loses his job and becomes depressed, it does not mean that he will be depressed each time he loses his job, nor can we say that everyone who loses their job becomes depressed. Therefore, not only does the same person not necessarily react the same way every time he is under the same pressure, but also different people may react differently when subjected to the same pressure. Apart from the loss of a job itself, there may be other factors, such as whether or not the man liked his job, that may precipitate or prevent the depression. Humans can also be affected by the fact they are being studied, and their actions cannot be understood without access to the thinking processes of the person. We do not always mean what we say nor do we always say what we mean, even when we are not lying or drunk. Sometimes we do not know if and why we behave the way we do. Therefore empirical observations only skim the surface of the behaviour being studied.

The intentions and motivations of the person needs to be examined if we are to make sense of a behaviour. Ayer (1969) pointedly asks:

> May it not be that there is something about the material on which these sciences have to work, something about the nature of men, which makes it impossible to generalize about them in any way comparable to that which has made the success of the natural sciences?

Interpretivism

Interpretivism has been put forward as an alternative to positivism. It 'is the belief that the social world is actively constructed by human beings' and that 'we are continuously involved in making sense of', or interpreting, our social environments (Milburn *et al.*, 1995). It is a blanket term for a collection of approaches broadly called 'qualitative', which share an opposition to the logical positivists' notion of studying humans as objects or particles. They share the philosophical belief that human behaviour can only be understood when the context in which it takes place and the thinking processes that give rise to it are studied. These approaches also recognise that researchers have preconceptions that must either be 'bracketed' (i.e. prevented from influencing the research process) or discussed in relation to their implications for the data. Beyond this, researchers following interpretivist paradigm use a variety of methods which mostly reflect the particular branch of the discipline they adhere to. Thus cognitive and Freudian psychologists, Marxist sociologists, symbolic interactionists, linguists and semioticians bring their own rules and meanings to the study of phenomena.

Atkinson (1995) argues that there is too much diversity in the qualitative approach for it to constitute one paradigm:

> If we confine ourselves just to the so-called qualitative paradigm, it is apparent that it is characterized by a great deal of diversity. There is no single set of theoretical or methodological presuppositions to underpin a qualitative paradigm, nor is there an uncontested collection of methods and research exemplars. On the contrary, any remotely comprehensive listing of qualitative studies will reveal at best a collection of assumptions, methods, and kinds of data that share some broad family resemblances. Together, they do not suggest the kind of coherence and consensus among researchers as to constitute a single paradigm.

The three approaches most commonly used in the interpretivist tradition are:

- ethnography
- phenomenology
- grounded theory.

Ethnography

Ethnography is an approach relying on the collection of data in the natural environment. The ethnographer is interested in how the behaviour of individuals is influenced or mediated by the culture in which they live. According to ethnography, human behaviour can only be understood if studied in the setting in which it occurs. Unlike the positivist who carries out experiments in a laboratory setting by controlling variables, the ethnographer aims to study how different variables in the natural environment interact, resulting in the observed behaviour. Stevens et al. (1993) identify structures in the natural environment which are the focus of ethnographic studies:

> Ethnographers place particular emphasis on studying groups and communities as a unified whole. According to them, individuals, groups, families, religions, ceremonies, social organisations, economic systems

interrelate to produce a cultural environment. No part can, therefore, be studied and understood on its own.

Ethnography is a holistic approach to the study of phenomena and has its roots in cultural anthropology. It was adopted by early anthropologists who went to live in and study tribal communities. They immersed themselves in the culture and adopted the manners and habits of the people they studied, as well as taking part in their rituals. Nowadays, ethnographic studies take place nearer home: in hospitals, schools, prisons, intensive care units and nursing homes.

Ethnography places emphasis on the cultural norms and social forces that shape human behaviour and other events. However, it is more a method or approach than a philosophy. In fact, the ethnographer who studies the points of view of her respondents as well as the way they interact with one another can make use of concepts from other disciplines. Mackenzie (1994) explains that 'sociologists have adopted ethnography in various ways depending on the perspective or school of thought, such as phenomenology, ethnomethodology or symbolic interactionism'.

Some would see the purpose of ethnography as simply describing people's interactions and experience in particular environments and reject the notion of using theories from other cultures or developing theories from ethnographic data. However, as Layder (1993) suggests:

> Descriptive ethnography of this type may co-exist with qualitative analyses which seek to develop theory and to employ systematic methods of study. There is no reason for the two to be seen as *competing* approaches.

Ethnography is further discussed in Chapter 8.

Phenomenology

Phenomenology as a research approach in the interpretivist tradition 'has its roots in philosophy' and was 'conceived by the German philosopher Husserl, at the beginning of the 20th century to investigate consciousness as experienced by the subject' (Baker *et al.*, 1992). It focuses on individuals' interpretation of their experiences and the ways in which they express them.

Unlike ethnography, which places particular emphasis on people's behaviour in relation to their cultural and social environments, phenomenology focuses on describing how the individual experiences phenomena.

Phenomenology as a philosophy stresses the notion that only those who experience phenomena are capable of communicating them to the outside world, and that the researcher's empirical observations are limited in understanding people's perceptions. Wittgenstein (in Rhees, 1975) succinctly illustrated this point when he wrote:

> Physics differs from phenomenology in that it is concerned to establish laws. Phenomenology only establishes the possibilities.... Science... tries to grasp the world by way of its periphery – in its variety and philosophy tries to grasp the world at its centre – in its essence. It is concerned with the 'lived experience' of its respondents.

The researcher's task is to describe phenomena as experienced and expressed. One of the main features of Husserlian phenomenology is the notion of 'bracketing'. Simply described, it means the 'suspension' of the researcher's preconceptions, prejudices and beliefs so that they do not interfere with or influence her description of the respondent's experience.

Phenomenology is also a method comprising a set of procedures and steps to guide the data collection and analysis processes (see Chapter 8).

A recent development in phenomenological research is the adoption of a Heideggerian hermeneutical approach to the study of nursing phenomena. Wilde (1992) describes hermeneutics as:

> an ancient discipline, originally involving the interpretation of religious texts. It was initially a method for finding out the correct interpretation from several differing versions of the same text.

Heidegger, a student of Husserl, did not believe that getting to know and describe the experience of individuals was enough. Instead, he stressed the importance of knowing how respondents come to experience phenomena in the way they do. As Orne (1995) explains, 'meaning, in a hermeneutic sense, refers to how a socially and historically conditioned individual interprets his or her world within a given context'.

Heideggerian phenomenology seeks to find out how individuals' personal history, such as their education and social class, past events in their lives and their psychological make-up, influences the ways in which they experience phenomena. Its focus is not on social structures, as is the case in ethnography, but on the individual's background.

According to Koch (1995), Heidegger focuses on the experience of understanding, while Husserl focuses on the 'experience' itself. An important difference between Heideggerian and Husserlian phenomenology is that the former rejects the notion of 'bracketing', because, as Koch (1995) puts it, 'one cannot separate description from one's own interpretation'. Both the researcher and the respondent have their own preconceptions and prejudices. Heideggerian phenomenology, far from rejecting or bracketing them, regards such preconceptions as essential to the understanding of how people experience phenomena differently. According to Gadamer (1990), who further developed the hermeneutical approach, a 'fusion of horizons' takes place as a result of the meetings of the preconceptions of the researcher and of the people she studies.

Grounded theory

An alternative to the hypothetico-deductive approach of positivism was formulated by Glaser and Strauss (1967), who coined the term 'grounded theory' to mean an inductive approach to research whereby hypotheses and theories emerge out of, or are 'grounded' in, data. Grounded theory itself is not a theory but a description of theories developed in this way. Strauss and Corbin (1990) provide a clear answer to the question of 'what is grounded theory?':

> A *grounded theory* is one that is inductively derived from the study of the phenomenon it represents. That is, it is discovered, developed, and provisionally verified through systematic data collection and analysis of data pertaining to that phenomenon. Therefore, data collection, analysis, and theory stand in reciprocal relationship with each other. One does not begin with a theory, then prove it. Rather, one begins with an area of study and what is relevant to that area is allowed to emerge.

Its strength lies in allowing researchers to start afresh and not be influenced by the present knowledge, thereby opening up the possibility of new perspectives on old problems. Grounded theory is also useful for studying phenomena for which little or no theory has been developed. Layder (1993) explains that, according to Glaser and Strauss (1967):

> theory generation had been stultified by an over-emphasis on the verification of extant theories... Such theories are generally 'speculative' in nature because they have not grown directly out of research, and thus remain ungrounded. As a consequence, these theories very often lack validity because they do not 'fit' the real world and thereby remain irrelevant to the people concerned.

The purpose of grounded theory is to generate hypotheses and theories, although, as Glaser and Strauss (1967) suggest, once hypotheses or theories have been formulated from observations, they can be tested deductively. Grounded theory, as a research approach, is particularly useful in nursing, an emerging science still seeking to clarify its concepts and to develop its own theories. Grounded theory is further discussed in Chapter 8.

What's in a name?

It is understandable that students of nursing research can be confused when the differences between these approaches are not as 'black and white' as they would like them to be. The similarities between them and the variations within each approach (see for example ethology, ethnomethodology and ethnoscience in Field and Morse, 1985), further exacerbate the problem.

Baker *et al.* (1992), commenting on 'method slurring' in qualitative research, explain that both grounded theory and phenomenology 'focus on the richness of human experience' and 'seek to understand a situation from the subject's own frame of reference' but that 'they are based on different intellectual assumptions and, flowing from these, have clear differences in purpose and methodological prescriptions'.

Just because the views of individuals are sought does not mean that the study is phenomenological. In the same way, studying individuals in their own environment does not necessarily make it an ethnographic study. Since all three approaches seek to study individuals' experiences and perceptions in the context of their natural environment, it is difficult to differentiate between them. However, if one understands what the focus is for each of these approaches, the difference between them may become clearer.

Phenomenology collects data on individuals' experiences and its focus is on individuals. In ethnography, individuals are studied as part of their environment, and the focus is on individuals not in isolation, but in relation to their institutions, organisations, communities, customs or policies. Both these approaches seek mainly to describe phenomena rather than to explain them. In grounded theory, the focus is on the generation of theories from data, and it therefore matters little if individuals are studied in isolation or as part of their cultural and social environment. In addition, both phenomenology and grounded theory have distinctive methods and procedures that researchers can follow to collect and analyse data.

THE INFLUENCE OF PARADIGMS

A paradigm creates its own cultural environment that regulates the behaviour of its followers and favours research conforming to its own rules. Rewards in the forms of funding and status go to those who carry out research within the dominant paradigm, and research articles that adopt the favoured paradigm have more chances of being published.

The dominant scientific paradigm in medical and nursing research sees the testing of hypotheses as the highest form of scientific research. This has implications for the granting of funds for research, as Daly *et al.* (1992) explain:

> the problem of methodological priorities also influences the way in which granting committees and funding bodies set their priorities and assess applications for funding. A practical illustration is that applications are commonly required to be submitted in a form designed with hypothesis-testing in mind and suitable for experimentally based biomedical research or clinical trials.

According to Daly *et al.* (1992), these forms are not appropriate for other types of research in health care.

The dominant paradigm can also define what are legitimate or accepted topics of enquiry. As explained earlier, religions in the past prohibited the study of human anatomy and planets. Although present-day scientists cannot impose such prohibitions, they can prescribe rules of scientific method, control the funding and publishing process and exclude other topics and modes of enquiry. For example, alternative therapies have been struggling to gain acceptance and recognition as 'science'. Advocates of these therapies believe that the 'usual protocols of investigation and publication in standard scientific journals' are too restrictive (Salmon, 1985).

Summary and Conclusion

In this chapter, we have looked briefly at the need of humans for knowledge, and we have examined the relationship between knowledge, science and research. We have seen that each of the three main belief systems not only interprets phenomena differently, but also has its own ways of 'knowing'. Science is the latest attempt to produce and organise knowledge, and research plays an important part in generating and testing theories, which remain the ultimate goal of scientific endeavours.

There is, however, no consensus on what research is and how it should be carried out. The two main paradigms in social, health and nursing research (positivism and interpretivism) have their own assumptions of how phenomena should be studied and of what constitutes scientific knowledge.

The nature of science and knowledge is such that no one school of thought can have a monopoly on the definition and the production of knowledge, although the dominant or favoured paradigm tends to influence what is researched and how. Dzurec and Abraham (1993) sum up succinctly the relationship between knowledge and research:

> All research is an effort to fulfill cognitive needs, to perceive, and to know. These needs emerge from curiosity about the world as expressed in a desire to understand it and from an incessant attempt to gain a sense of mastery over self and world. Consequently, if differences among researchers exist, it is not because they aspire to different ends, but because they have operationalized their methods for reaching those ends differently.

REFERENCES

Atkinson P (1995) Some perils of paradigms. *Qualitative Health Research*, **5**(1):117–24.

Ayer A J (1969) *Metaphysics and Common Sense*, 2nd edn. London: Macmillan.

Baker C, Wuest J and Stern P N (1992) Method slurring: the grounded theory/phenomenology example. *Journal of Advanced Nursing*, **17**:1355–60.

Bronowski J (1960) *The Commonsense of Science*. Harmonsworth: Pelican.

Chalmers A F (1980) *What Is This Thing Called Science?*, 2nd edn. Buckingham: Open University Press.

Daly J, McDonald I and Willis E (1992) *Researching Health Care: Designs, Dilemmas, Disciplines*. London: Tavistock/Routledge.

Dawkins R (1989) *The Selfish Gene*. London: Pelican.

DeMey M T (1992) Action and knowledge from a cognitive point of view. In Kallen D B P, Wagenaar H C, Kloprogge J J J and Vorbeck M (eds) *Social Science Research and Public Policy-Making: A Reappraisal*. Netherlands: NFER.

Dzurec L C and Abraham I L (1993) The nature of inquiry: linking quantitative and qualitative research. *Advances in Nursing Science*, **16**(1):73–9.

Field P A and Morse J M (1985) *Nursing Research: The Application of Qualitative Approaches*. London: Croom Helm.

Freud S (1927) *The Future of an Illusion*. London: Hogarth Press.

Gadamer H G (1990) *Truth and Method*, 2nd rev. edn. New York: Crossroad.

Glaser B and Strauss A (1967) *The Discovery of Grounded Theory*. Chicago: Aldine.

Kaplan A (1968) Positivism. In Sills D L (ed.) *International Encyclopedia of the Social Sciences*. New York: Macmillan/Free Press.

Koch T (1995) Interpretive approaches in nursing research: the influence of Husserl and Heidegger. *Journal of Advanced Nursing*, **21**:827–36.

Kuhn T (1970) *The Structure of Scientific Revolutions*, 2nd edn. Chicago: University of Chicago Press.

Layder D (1993) *New Strategies in Social Research*. Cambridge: Polity Press.

Mackenzie A E (1994) Evaluating ethonography: considerations for analysis. *Journal of Advanced Nursing*, **19**:774–81.

Milburn K, Fraser E, Secker J and Pavis S (1995) Combining methods in health promotion research: some considerations about appropriate use. *Health Education Journal*, **54**:347–56.

Orne R M (1995) The meaning of survival: the early aftermath of a near-death experience. *Research in Nursing and Health*, **18**:239–47.

Polgar S and Thomas S A (1991) *Introduction to Research in the Health Sciences*, 2nd edn. Melbourne: Churchill Livingstone.

Popper K R (1969) *Conjectures and Refutations*. London: Routledge & Kegan Paul.

Rhees R (1975) *Ludwig Wittgenstein – Philosophical Remarks*. Oxford: Basil Blackwell.

Russell B (1971) *Logic and Knowledge: Essay 1901–1950*, 5th edn. London: George Allen and Unwin.

Salmon J W (1985) *Alternative Medicines: Popular and Policy Perspectives*. London: Tavistock.

Sigerist H E (1943) *Civilisation and Disease*. Chicago: University of Chicago Press.

Singleton R A Jr, Straits B C and Straits M M (1993) *Approaches to Social Research*, 2nd edn. New York: Oxford University Press.

Smith H W (1991) *Strategies of Social Research*, 3rd edn. St Louis: Holt, Rinehart & Winston.

Stevens P J M, Schade A L, Chalk B and Slevin O D'A (1993) *Understanding Research*. Edinburgh: Campion Press.

Strauss A and Corbin J (1990) *Basics of Qualitative Research: Grounded Theory, Procedures and Techniques*. California: Sage.

Sunday Times (1995) Hospitals use maggots to heal infected wounds. 21 Jan, pp. 1, 20.

Wilde V (1992) Controversial hypotheses on the relationship between researcher and informant in qualitative research. *Journal of Advanced Nursing*, **17**:234–42.

Wilson J (1989) Conceptual and empirical truth; some notes for researchers. *Educational Research*, **31**(3):176–80.

3 QUANTITATIVE AND QUALITATIVE RESEARCH

It is easier to know man in general than to understand a
man in particular. (La Rochefoucauld, Maxims, 1665)

INTRODUCTION

'Quantitative' and 'qualitative' are two terms that frequently appear in
the nursing research literature. In this chapter, the two approaches will
be explored, compared and contrasted. To help the reader to distinguish
between them, a framework is proposed for their analysis. The value and
limitations of both approaches to nursing phenomena will also be
discussed, and the potential benefits and drawbacks of using quantitative and qualitative approaches in the same study will be examined.

DIFFERENTIATING BETWEEN QUANTITATIVE AND QUALITATIVE APPROACHES

As explained in Chapter 2, distinctions between different qualitative
approaches in the interpretivist paradigm are sometimes blurred (Baker
et al., 1992). Distinguishing between quantitative and qualitative
research, on the other hand, can also be problematic. The popular
notion that quantitative research deals with quantity and numbers and
qualitative research deals with quality and description is too simplistic
and unhelpful. According to Henwood and Pidgeon (1993):

> Part of this confusion comes from the narrow association of qualitative
> methodology either within particular modes of data gathering (typically
> interviews or fieldwork) or its non-numeric character (for example, verbal
> protocols, verbatim transcriptions of subjects' discourse....

Although quantitative researchers typically use large, probability
samples and qualitative researchers small, non-probability ones (see
Chapter 10), this is not always the case. It is not uncommon, however, to
find students differentiating between these two approaches on the basis
of the sampling method alone.

In assessing whether a study is quantitative, qualitative or a
mixture of the two, more than one aspect of the study should be

considered. To distinguish between quantitative and qualitative research, we can use the three constituent parts of a paradigm: philosophical assumptions, methods of data collection and techniques of data analysis, as a framework.

Philosophical assumptions

Quantitative research draws on the positivist paradigm, but it should not be mistaken for positivism. The latter relies on objective measurement of data, which can be obtained only through sensory observations. Quantitative research typically adopts a modified form of empiricism, as many of the concepts in health and social research are not amenable to objective measurements, but it also relies on subjective ratings by respondents. Norbeck (1987) gives us his example:

> in social support research, the typical measurement strategy is not to measure minutes of interaction, number of interpersonal contacts or counts of other commodities that transpire between people but to measure the individuals' perceptions of their social support. This measurement approach is based on the assumption that phenomena, like social support, are experienced and interpreted by individuals through their own meanings and past experiences.

According to Hammersley (1993), 'there are probably few social researchers today who would call themselves positivists, but the influence of positivism persists'. It certainly does in quantitative research, which adopts a reductionist approach. *Reductionism* means reducing complex phenomena to simple units that can be observed or recorded. For example, stress is a concept that cannot be observed by the human senses, although its signs and symptoms can. Thus Boore (1994) studied postoperative stress by measuring biochemical indicators of stress – '17 hydroxycorticosteroid excretion and sodium: potassium ratio in the urine'. Similarly, a concept such as patient satisfaction can be measured by responses to a number of statements on a patient satisfaction scale.

Quantitative research is also deterministic. Determinism is belief in the notion of 'cause and effect'. This is exemplified in experimental research, which is considered in the positivist tradition to be the highest form of research. Another characteristic feature of positivism that is present in some quantitative research is deductivism (hypotheses and theories are put to the test by collecting data to support or reject them). However, not all quantitative research is experimental or hypothetico-deductive. The survey, which is the most popular form of design in quantitative research, can collect descriptive data as well as test hypotheses (see Chapter 8).

As stated earlier, one assumption that seems to describe qualitative research is the belief that phenomena must be studied from the individual's perspective and in the context in which they happen. Thus, for the purpose of simplification, one can describe qualitative approaches as holistic as opposed to reductionist. The individual's description of the experience of stress and how it is mediated in the setting in which it occurs is believed to offer a more complete description of the phenomenon than does the objective observation of its signs and symptoms. Inherent in most qualitative approaches is the notion that phenomena cannot be studied objectively and that the researcher in some way influences the process of data collection and interpretation. The degree of interaction and involvement between researcher and respondents varies depending on the specific approach adopted.

The essential difference between quantitative and qualitative approaches therefore lies in their different philosophical assumptions, which in turn guide the data collection and analysis process. However, these assumptions are not always made clear or explicit. Thus one can turn to data collection techniques for clues that could indicate the approach.

Methods of data collection

Selecting methods of investigation is not a neutral, value-free or haphazard exercise. Instead, the choice reflects the particular beliefs and values of the researcher. Hughes (1980) claims:

> No technique or method of investigation... is self-validating: its effectiveness, its very status as a research instrument making the world tractable to investigation, is dependent, ultimately, on philosophical justification. Whether they may be treated as such or not, research methods cannot be divorced from theory; as research tools they operate only within a given set of assumptions about the nature of society, the nature of man, the relationship between the two and how they may be known.

Questionnaires, observation schedules and other measuring tools, such as scales to measure knowledge, skills and attitudes, and instruments to measure physiological and biochemical changes, comprise the main methods used in quantitative research. These are *predetermined* (constructed prior to the study), *structured* (the units to be studied are specified in advance, requiring little input from the respondent or researcher) and *standardised* (administering the same tools in the same way to all respondents). The samples and sampling method are also specified in advance and cannot be altered.

In qualitative research, the methods of data collection, such as unstructured interviews and observations (see Chapters 12 and 13), are more flexible and less structured. The questions are not always predetermined in advance nor are the same questions necessarily asked of all respondents. Samples are not necessarily selected in advance of data collection. Researchers may decide to include or exclude respondents at any time during the research process. While the researchers can use props (such as notepads or tape-recorders) to record data, she may herself be a tool of data collection. Her mind records, registers and processes some of the information during interviews and observations as well as thereafter. Often she records some of the observations and thoughts in her diary as 'field notes'.

Techniques of data analysis

An important feature of quantitative research is the 'measurement' of phenomena. Values and numbers are central to their understanding. For example, each statement on an attitude scale is given a value (1, 2, 3, and so on), and these are added to provide a score indicating the presence and strength of a particular attitude. Quantitative researchers carry out, wherever possible and appropriate, statistical tests to establish, among other things, the probability of certain phenomena occurring. For example, if the job satisfaction scores of male nurses are higher than for females, a statistical test may be performed to find out if these scores have been obtained by chance and what the chances of this happening are.

Although the main purpose of quantitative research is to measure, this is not always possible. Most studies attempt to 'describe', 'assess' or 'evaluate' the level, extent or degree to which certain phenomena occur. The aim, however, is to quantify.

Qualitative researchers, in general, do not subscribe to the notion of measurement and therefore do not attribute values to the concepts that they study. According to Jones (1988), the analysis of qualitative data:

> is a process of making sense, of finding and making a structure in the data and giving this meaning and significance for ourselves, and for any relevant audiences... the way we do this and the kind of structures we look for in the data depend on the purpose of enquiry and what we see as the underlying purpose of qualitative research.

From the nursing research literature, it is clear that qualitative researchers use different methods of analysis. The most common treatment of qualitative data is to structure them in themes or categories. It is not uncommon, however, to find that qualitative data are reported in the form of frequency and percentages. Although purists may frown on this practice, it is the importance that researchers give the numbers which indicates whether data analysis is qualitative or quantitative (this is discussed in Chapter 14). Table 3.1 lists the main characteristics of the two approaches.

Table 3.1 Contrasting characteristics of quantitative and qualitative approaches

Quantitative	Qualitative
It is reductionist and/or deterministic	It is holistic
Its methods are predetermined structured, standardised and inflexible	Its methods are semi- and unstructured and flexible
Its purpose is to measure	Its purpose is to describe and/or theorise

Authors of research reports and articles often confuse readers when they state that they have used one approach when in fact the other has been employed. Try using the framework above (philosophical assumptions, methods of data collection and techniques of data analysis) to find out for yourself whether a study is qualitative, quantitative or in some cases a mixture of the two. To start you off find out in RE 4 and RE 5 how this can be done.

THE VALUE OF THE QUANTITATIVE APPROACH TO NURSING

Until recently, quantitative research was believed to be the only scientific method capable of advancing nursing knowledge because it provides hard, objective facts that can be statistically analysed and interpreted. Those who support a quantitative approach point to the value of objective, systematic observations for nursing practice. Norbeck (1987) suggests that many of the questions nurses need to answer are consistent with this research perspective. As she explains:

> When we plan for groups of patients, assess the acuity of a unit in the hospital, develop predictive models for at-risk groups or search for causal explanations, we rely on systematically gathered, objective data drawn from relatively large numbers of individuals.

RESEARCH EXAMPLE **4**   Rukholm *et al.* (1991)
Needs and anxiety levels in relatives of intensive care unit patients

The abstract from this study reads as follows:

The purpose of this study was to explore the perceived needs and anxiety level of adult family members of intensive care unit (ICU) patients. The study was conducted over a 3-month period, on a convenience sample of 166 subjects selected from the total adult population of family members visiting an ICU in three Sudbury hospitals. Data were gathered using a self-report questionnaire, the Critical Care Family Needs Inventory (CCFNI) and Spielberger's State Trait Anxiety Inventory (STAI). Interviews were conducted in French or English according to the subject's preference. The major variables examined were: family needs; state and trait anxiety; on-site sources of worry; spiritual needs; level of knowledge of ICU from past experience or pre-surgery education; sociodemographic data. The Situational Anxiety Scale yielded a mean score of 45.24 and the Trait Anxiety Scale a mean score of 37.3. Inferential statistics demonstrated that family needs and situational anxiety were significantly related ($P < 0.0002$). Furthermore, worries, trait anxiety, age and family needs explained 38% of the variation of situational anxiety. As well, spiritual needs and situational anxiety explained 33% of the variation of family needs.

Comments

We can use the following three components of a paradigm (p. 39) to decide whether this study is quantitative or qualitative.

Philosophical assumptions: In this study, the philosophical assumptions on which the study is based are not stated but inferred. The authors are not interested in knowing what anxiety means to the respondents but rather what their level of anxiety is. The assumption made is that it is possible to *measure* the concept 'anxiety' and that this can be done by asking respondents to rate (from 'not at all' to 'very much') 20 items or statements on an anxiety scale (STAI). Thus a *reductionist* approach is used because anxiety is, in this case, 'reduced' to these 20 items.

Methods of data collection: The methods were predetermined, that is the questionnaires and scales (CCFNI and STAI) were developed prior to the study. They were also highly structured as respondents were required only to respond to items as a scale. The CCFNI, for example, contained 46 items, some of which are shown below. Respondents had to indicate whether they 'judged' each of these to be 'not important', 'important' or 'very important'. Part of the scale would have looked like this:

Statement	Not Important	Important	Very Important
To be assured of best care			
Honest answers			
To be called regarding changes			
To know the prognosis			
To know specific progress			
To feel hopeful			
To know medical treatment			
To know exact care			

The methods used in this study were also standardised, that is they were administered in the same way to all respondents with no variation (no changes were allowed).

Techniques of data analysis: Data were analysed statistically and presented in a quantitative form using percentages, scores and other statistical measures (see abstract above).

Together, these three components of a paradigm should indicate whether a study is quantitative or qualitative. In practice, however, many researchers use a mix of methods, which makes this task difficult but not impossible.

RESEARCH **5** Geissler (1990)
EXAMPLE **An exploratory study of selected female registered nurses: meaning and expression of nurturance**

The purpose of this study is to explore the meaning of 'nurturance' among a group of '14 female registered nurses who gave direct patient care' and their experience of nurturing. A qualitative approach was used because, according to Geissler 'little is known about the meaning and expression of nurturance in nursing practice'. This design 'was selected to uncover what is there, what meanings are attached to the discoveries by RNs and how the meanings can be organised into a description of the phenomena'.

A semi-structured interview schedule was used to ask three questions:

1.   What do you think is the meaning of the term nurturance?
2.   What behaviours do you think you use to express nurturance?
3.   Describe a situation in which you are expressing nurturance to your client. Tell it like a story describing what is occurring between you and your client.

The data collected through the interviews were transcribed and the four themes which emerged were:

*   enabling maximum potential;
*   providing physical and emotional protection;
*   engaging in a supportive interaction;
*   conveying shared humanity.

Comments
As in Research Example 4, the three components of a paradigm will be used as a framework to explain why this study is qualitative.

Philosophical assumptions: This study is based on phenomenological philosophy. As Geissler explains:

> The belief that reality is not an empirically derived reductionist determination, but rather a subjective individually formulated and interpreted judgement is inherent in this method. It does not explore reality, *per se*, but what reality is perceived to be.

Most qualitative researchers state whether their study is based on phenomenological, ethnographic, grounded theory or other qualitative approaches.

Methods of data collection: Semistructured interviews were carried out. Only broad questions were asked (see above). Respondents were able to formulate their responses in their own words. The researcher sets out to explore the meaning of nurturance. Although she may have her own ideas of what nurturance means, she is more interested in how respondents perceive and experience it. According to her, 'exploration can mean venturing into new territory for which there are no charted maps'. In contrast to Rukholm *et al.'s* (1991) study (in Research Example 4), where they had a list of 46 items that together represented family needs, Geissler (1990) wanted to know from her respondents how *they* perceive 'nurturance'.

Techniques of data analysis: Data were analysed using the phenomenological method. This consisted of reading the transcripts of the interviews and making sense of what respondents said. Forty-five codes (such as 'recognition of worth', 'advocate' and 'facilitate') were identified. These 45 codes were organised into four themes, as mentioned above. The data were reported in descriptive form.

As Geissler concludes:

> Thus what began with interviews, then extraction of codes or behaviours as exemplars and synthesis into themes, ultimately inductively produced an exhaustive description of the phenomenon.

Additional comments

1. A qualitative approach was used in this study because little was known about nurturance. However, this is not always the case. Sometimes even when there is a lot of knowledge on a phenomenon, researchers may want to 'start afresh' and obtain a different perspective.

2. The 45 codes and four themes produced inductively can thereafter be used to construct a quantitative tool, such as the CCFNI in Research Example 4, p. 55.

3. You may wonder why the design in this study is not described by the author as grounded theory, since concepts or themes were formulated inductively. This is partly because the technique of data analysis was based on that of Colaizzi (1978), a phenomenologist, rather than those of Glaser and Strauss (1967), who devised the grounded theory method. As explained in the text, there are many similarities between phenomenology, grounded theory and ethnography.

There are at least two sides to human phenomena: the objective reality as it is manifested and observed by others, and the person's subjective experience of the phenomenon. For example, our behaviour often appears to others different from our own perception of it. We may not feel angry but may convey the signs of anger. The behaviour as it is manifested to others is as important as how the person behaving really feels. It is the objective reality, the manifestation of phenomena, that the quantitative approach seeks to study. A patient has the same pressure sore whether nurse X disagrees with nurse Y over their assessment of it. This is not to deny that the patient's experience of the sore is real and important as well. Nurses treat patients with sores, rather than treating the sore isolated from the patient.

In studying the occurrence of pressure sores, a number of factors that put people at risk of sores have been identified. These include body weight, mobility, activity, incontinence, nutrition and mental status, factors common to most people at risk of developing pressure sores. Phenomena have unique and common characteristics. It is these commonalities which quantitative researchers seek to study.

There is an assumption in quantitative research that it is possible to study certain characteristics of groups of people rather than the individuals themselves. Mathison (1988) explains that 'in the quantitative sense of objectivity, an individual's view is considered to be subjective and the collective view of many individuals is an objective one'. For example, carefully constructed scales can give an indication of the presence and strength of particular attitudes among a group of people without interviewing each of them in depth. Opinion polls, despite some setbacks, have also been successful in 'feeling the pulse' of public opinion. Surveys are not meant to study a subject in any great depth. The Oxford Dictionary defines 'survey' as a 'general view, casting of eyes or mind over something'. Thus surveys provide a glimpse of rather than a window into human behaviour.

Quantitative methods are useful in studying nursing phenomena. Two of the most popular designs in quantitative research are experiments and surveys. In nursing, there are numerous examples in which experiments have shown to be of value. As early as 1979, a study by Measal and Anderson (1979) in the USA found that premature infants become more relaxed and could be tube-fed successfully if allowed to suck on a pacifier during and following each feed, leading to a readiness for bottle-feeding 3–4 days earlier than for those in the control group (Waltz *et al.*, 1991). In the UK, studies by Hayward (1994) and Boore (1994) have demonstrated the value of experiments in measuring the effects of information-giving to patients prior to surgery. In midwifery, Grant *et al.*'s (1989) experiment to compare glycerol-impregnated catgut with chromic catgut showed that, when the former was used, 'there was substantial increased risk of pain and discomfort, which was still detectable three years after suturing' (Chalmers, 1993).

The survey method, with large samples, can provide valuable data within a short period of time. Apart from demographic and epidemiologic data, surveys can explore links between variables, which can sometimes be tested further in experiments. Survey data are useful for planning, evaluation and comparative purposes. A large number of scales have been developed to measure various nursing concepts. Some of these concepts include the functional ability of elderly patients, individualised care, patient satisfaction with care, pain, confusion, hope, compliance, health beliefs and stress. Although according to Horsfall (1995), quantitative research may be appropriate for the study of issues related to the technical–clinical aspects of nursing, such as 'tube-feeding, pre-operative preparation of patients, cannula changing and catheterization', we can see that it also studies abstract phenomena, as identified above.

LIMITATIONS OF THE QUANTITATIVE APPROACH

Supporters of the quantitative approach have described it as the 'highest form of attaining knowledge that human beings have devised'; its critics 'have conceptualised it as a ghost requiring exorcism from nursing; as a barrier to nursing's "scientific quest"; and "as being non-congruent with nursing's philosophy"' (Bargagliotti, 1983). Those who reject quantitative research point to the limitations of empirical observations in understanding human phenomena. For example, when concentrating on the manifestation of behaviour, it is possible only to study what is observable. Therefore only a partial glimpse of the phenomenon is revealed. By reducing complex phenomena such as stress, anxiety or hope to what can be observed, it is not possible to have a complete understanding of what it means to be stressed, anxious or hopeful. Even those defending empiricism admit to the differences between physical and human phenomena and the difficulties in measuring the latter, but they still believe that measurement is possible, as Norbeck's (1987) comments show:

> The inanimate objects in the physical world can be measured, melted down, fractioned and recomposed in predictable and repeatable ways. In contrast, human behaviour is difficult to measure, multideterminant and highly variable. But such difficulties do not necessarily imply that human behaviour defies objective observation.

According to its critics, the quantitative approach yields useful but limited data and provides only a partial view of the phenomena it investigates. If these data were taken for what they are instead of what they pretend to be, quantitative research would probably not have suffered the barrage of criticism which it has since the 1970s. Data in themselves are not pretentious; it is the claim that they 'measure' some phenomenon or other, or that they provide 'hard evidence', which elevates the quantitative approach to a level far above others, a position highly contested by its critics.

THE VALUE OF THE QUALITATIVE APPROACH TO NURSING

Nursing's philosophy is congruent with qualitative approaches (Munhall, 1982). Apart from being technical, nursing is also patient centred, holistic and humanistic. Most qualitative approaches share some of these characteristics, which makes them eminently suitable for the study of nursing phenomena. Qualitative research, with its focus on the experiences of people, stresses the uniqueness of individuals. In nursing, each patient is a unique individual for whom a specific care plan is developed.

Qualitative researchers collect data from respondents, often in their natural environments, taking into account how cultural, social and other factors influence their experiences and behaviour. Nursing care should ideally be holistic in that the patient and her illness are treated, rather than the illness being targeted separately. The environment in which the patient lives, her partner and her family, should all be taken into account in the planning and delivery of care.

Qualitative approaches value respondents' views and seek to understand the world in which they live. Implicit in some approaches and explicit in others is the notion that respondents have experiences, wishes and rights that must be respected. As will be shown below, some researchers believe in the empowering potential of research for the participants. Nurses, too, can adopt a humanistic approach to their work, which entails not letting their personal prejudices influence their professional judgement, and respecting and promoting their clients' rights.

Qualitative research and empowerment

The interactive process of some qualitative approaches can also be compatible with nursing's aim of achieving better care through patient participation. According to Creswell (1994), researchers adopting a qualitative stance 'interact with those they study, whether this interaction assumes the form of living with or observing informants over a long period of time or actual collaboration'. Collaborative research in one form or another is on the increase. There is a movement in the interpretivist tradition which favours an approach to research aiming to empower the participants. According to Denzin and Lincoln (1994), 'more action activist-oriented research is on the horizon as are more social criticism and social critique'.

One approach that is becoming increasingly popular, especially in developing countries, is participatory action research (PAR). It consists of three elements – research, adult education and sociopolitical action. It is reminiscent of the chartist, utopian and other social movements of the 19th century and aims to help the oppressed in their struggle to change their condition (Fals-Borda and Rahman, 1991). There are other types of collaborative action research, such as 'co-operative inquiry' and 'action inquiry' (see Reason, 1994). Most approaches adopt a reflective stance to challenge and change the status quo. According to Fals-Borda and Rahman (1991), they operate from the premise that:

> science is not a fetish with a life of its own or something which has an absolute pure value, but is simply a valid and useful form of knowledge for specific purposes and based on relative truths. Any science as a cultural product has a specific human purpose and therefore implicitly carries these class biases and values which scientists hold as a group. It therefore favours those who produce and control it, although its unbridled growth is currently more of a threat than a benefit to humanity.

Because research produces knowledge, it empowers those who carry it out or commission it. Some sections of society benefit more than others. Some women in particular feel that research studies by men on women, considering topics chosen mainly by men, do not necessarily serve women's interests and in fact contribute to their domination. Thus feminist research emerged out of the failure of conventional research to address the issues of relevance and benefit to women. According to Seibold *et al.* (1994), 'feminist researchers share with critical theorists the need to make a difference through research; that is the desire to bring about social change of oppressive constraints through criticism and social action'. Seibold *et al.* (1994) cite M Duffy's (1985) typical checklist of what characterises feminist research:

> the principal investigator is a woman: the purpose is to study women and the focus of the research is women's experiences; the research must have the potential to help the subjects as well as the researcher; it is characterized by interaction between researcher and subject, non-hierarchical relations and expression of feelings and concern for values (one or all may be incorporated); the word feminist or feminism is used in the report; non-sexist language is used, and the bibliography includes feminist literature.

Although the qualitative approach, with its notion of interacting and collaborating with participants, is better suited to feminist research, there are those, like Oakley (1989, cited in Baum, 1995), who argue 'that methodologies derived from experimental research such as randomised controlled trials can be emancipatory in practice and can benefit both the women involved in research and women more generally'. Jayaratne (1993) also advocates the use of quantitative methodology in feminist research. Thus, while PAR is usually associated with qualitative approaches, its aims may also be achieved by other methodologies.

An example of feminist participatory action research comes from British Columbia, Canada, where Abbott *et al.* (1993) initiated a project 'on the lack of affordable opportunities for recreation for low income women'. Questionnaires were developed, distributed and analysed by the women themselves, the researchers merely facilitating the process. According to Abbott *et al.* (1993), 'one outcome of the research was that the group members prepared a proposal for funding to investigate and develop a list of recreational opportunities available to people on a low income'.

In the true spirit of empowerment:

> the project raised the general community awareness about the need for more accessible, lower-cost recreation, and has enhanced the confidence of low income families to speak out about their concerns. The women who

took part were empowered to address issues that make a difference in their lives by sharing knowledge, increasing their self confidence and learning skills such as dealing with the media.

LIMITATIONS OF THE QUALITATIVE APPROACH

The interactive nature of qualitative approaches, even without the overt political agenda of participatory action research, is considered, according to its critics, to be its main weakness. It is suggested that because researchers get so involved, they cannot be objective. The researcher as a tool of data collection and analysis in qualitative research is likely to be subjective in selecting which data to accept or reject. The interaction of one researcher with her subjects in a particular setting is a unique process, unlikely to be experienced by another researcher studying the same phenomenon.

Mays and Pope (1995) summarise the main criticisms of qualitative approaches thus:

> The most commonly heard criticisms are, firstly, that qualitative research is merely an assembly of anecdote and personal impressions, strongly subject to researcher bias; secondly, it is argued that qualitative research lacks reproducibility – the research is so personal to the researcher that there is no guarantee that a different researcher would not come to radically different conclusions; and, finally, qualitative research is criticised for lacking generalisability.

There is evidence in the nursing research literature of impression-istic accounts and biased qualitative studies. Using criteria from one paradigm to assess research in another, however, can be misleading. The purpose of quantitative and qualitative research is different. Quantitative researchers are expected to use large probability samples to generate data that can be generalisable to other settings. Qualitative researchers seek to describe people's experiences, which are considered unique, context related and not replicable. Many reject the notion of objectivity, replicability, generalisability, reliability and validity as understood by quantitative researchers. To them, it is similar to using the rules of one religion to judge the behaviour of people from another religion: certain behaviours can be seen as sinful or acceptable when viewed through the eyes of different religions. Qualitative researchers have devised their own terminologies, such as 'truth value', 'applica-bility', 'consistency' and 'neutrality' (Lincoln and Guba, 1985), and have developed their own strategies of ensuring rigour in their approaches. Mays and Pope (1995) suggest that this can be achieved by creating 'an account of method and data which can stand independently so that another trained researcher could analyse the same data in the same way and come to essentially the same conclusions' and by 'producing a plausible and coherent explanation of the phenomena under scrutiny'.

Both quantitative and qualitative approaches have an important contribution to make despite their limitations. In the next section, the terms 'objectivity' and 'subjectivity' as used in research, will be explored.

Objectivity and subjectivity

Objectivity in the quantitative sense means that the researcher 'stands outside' the phenomenon in order to study it. The ways in which data are collected and analysed are expected to be free from bias on the part of the researcher. Thus the selection of participants for a study is carried out by, for example, using a table of random numbers (see Chapter 10). In this way, the personal preferences of the researcher do not influence the selection process. Objectivity in the quantitative sense also means that, if exactly the same process is followed in the same circumstances by other researchers, more or less the same results should, in theory at least, be obtained.

Qualitative research is sometimes described as being subjective. This is because, in the collection of data, the researcher does not necessarily stand back but can instead interact with respondents in order to get close to what respondents think and experience. This type of interaction is very personal and cannot be replicated. Subjectivity is also present in the choice of participants in qualitative studies. One of the preferred methods is to select people whom researchers or their colleagues believe may be suitable for their studies by virtue of having knowledge or experience of the phenomena being investigated. Thus researchers use their subjective knowledge of respondents in their sampling method. Finally, the methods of data analysis are considered to be subjective since it is possible that other researchers may analyse the data differently and even obtain different results.

As explained above, quantitative researchers are expected to adopt an objective stance and make observations without allowing, as much as possible, their own prejudices to interfere with data collection and analysis. However, in deciding what and how to observe, researchers are influenced by their own views of how phenomena should be studied. Implicit in the quantitative approach is that the researcher 'knows' and simply wants to confirm her knowledge. For example, structured questionnaires offer people a range of responses, made up by the researcher, from which to choose. These responses often reflect the values and previous knowledge of the researcher. Lipson (1991) points out that 'even the most rigorously designed quantitative study can still be subjective in relation to the researcher's theoretical stance, questions asked, and interpretation of findings'.

The objective stance of the quantitative researcher also means that she does not get near enough to her respondents to take a close look at what she is studying. Therefore, while objectivity has the advantage of uniformity and consistency (administering the same tools to everyone in the same manner and in the same context), it also creates a distance between the researcher and the researched, which can result in a superficial understanding of the phenomenon.

On the other hand, qualitative researchers exploit the notion of subjectivity in order to collect useful data. However, they are aware that they also need to be rigorous in their approach. To do so, some adopt such strategies as describing their actions and thoughts in great detail, stating their values and beliefs about their research topic and involving others in the analysis of data (see Chapters 12 and 14).

MIXING QUANTITATIVE AND QUALITATIVE APPROACHES

Quantitative research seems to be the choice approach when large amounts of data are required (for example, on the knowledge of, and attitudes of nurses to, AIDS in one regional health authority); when it is desirable and possible to collect data empirically (for example, when recording verbal and non-verbal interactions, fluid intake or physiological measures); and when evaluating different forms of programme or treatment (for example, the effects of primary and team nursing on patient care).

Qualitative research is more appropriate when studying the experiences and perceptions of clients, nurses and others (for example, noncompliance with professional advice or the experiences of women who have had breast surgery), and when the interaction between people and their environment is complex (for example, the socialisation of student nurses in clinical areas or nurse–client relationships in a community setting).

There are some phenomena that clearly benefit more from one approach than the other. For example, the quality of life of abused children would gain more from a qualitative approach, while the effects of fluid intake on the incidence of constipation among elderly patients would be better studied by the quantitative approach. However, by distinguishing between phenomena that can be studied by one approach rather than another, we run the risk of denying some phenomena the opportunity of being explored by other approaches. Concluding a review of blood pressure research between 1980 and 1990, Thomas *et al.* (1993) remark:

> Our tradition of caring, compassionate service puts nursing in a unique position to lead in developing methods which examine physiological indicators such as BP [blood pressure] from dimensions broader than the traditional empirical model. We hope that the current review provides a stimulus for designing research on BP which captures its bio-psycho-social nature.

Different aspects of the same phenomena can be studied by either one or the other approach. For example, in studying 'non-compliance with professional advice', the quantitative approach can provide data from a large number of clients to explore links between variables such as gender, class, occupation or age, and trends such as how often, when and in what circumstances people do not comply. At the same time, it is possible to use the qualitative approach to explore the meaning and experience of non-compliance of some respondents in order to gain an understanding of their way of thinking, their priorities, their motivations and their beliefs. In this way, a more complete picture of non-compliance can emerge.

Sometimes the same aspect of a phenomenon can benefit from both approaches. This is known as 'method triangulation'. Denzin (1970, cited in Kimchi *et al.*, 1991) defines triangulation as the combination of two or more theories, data sources, methods or investigators in the study of a single phenomenon. Kimchi *et al.* (1991) list six types of triangulation:

- theory – an assessment of the utility and power of competing theories or hypotheses;
- data – the use of multiple data sources with similar foci to obtain diverse views about a topic for the purpose of validation;
- investigator – the use of two or more 'research-trained' investigators with divergent backgrounds to explore the same phenomenon;
- analysis – the use of two or more approaches to the analysis of the same set of data;
- methods – the use of two or more research methods in one study;
- multiple – the use of more than one type of triangulation to analyse same event.

Myers and Haase (1989), emphasising the importance of different data sources, suggest that in studies of bonding between mother and infant, 'the subjective descriptions of mothers' progressive ability to anticipate their infants' needs' can be 'contrasted with objective observations of the mother–infant interaction'.

Not everyone agrees, however, that approaches and methods can be mixed in the same study. Creswell (1994) has identified three schools of thought on the subject:

> The 'purists' said that paradigms and methods should not be mixed; the 'situationalists' asserted that certain methods are appropriate for specific situations; and the 'pragmatists' attempted to integrate methods in a single study.

Mixing methods without reconciling paradigms runs the risk that one paradigm will be considered more important than the other. Haase and Myers (1988) call for a reconciliation of paradigms and explain how this can happen:

> Qualitative and quantitative approaches share a common goal for research – understanding of the world in which we live. Considering this goal, the assumptions of each approach can be recognized as complementary, and the primacy of assumptions underlying one or the other approach can be eliminated as unproductive. Nurses can in this way value both approaches and begin to reconcile assumptions.

It is clear that some researchers would never let their actions override their beliefs, while others may be happy mixing paradigms and methods.

Using both approaches in the study of the same phenomenon does not necessarily mean that each provides data to complete the whole picture, in the way that jigsaw pieces do. The findings can be contradictory: people may show outward signs of satisfaction, yet may privately be disgruntled. Human nature is unpredictable and complex, and research methods are fallible. Far from being disheartened by contradictory findings, the researcher's understanding of the phenomenon and of research methodology can be enhanced. For example, the difference between what people reveal in groups and in personal interviews can give an insight into the way they think and behave. According to Hanson (1994), 'It is naive to presume that a single consistent picture will be obtained by the use of different methods'. The results from her own study of the world of the cancer nurse showed that, from her interviews, '80% of nurses in her sample were aware of the positive aspects of the psychological nursing process', yet this 'was not reflected in the completed kardexes'. Hanson (1994) concluded:

The use of methodological triangulation enabled a more holistic picture to emerge of the cancer nurses' world of stress amongst persons with cancer. The use of a single method would have led to a limited view of human behaviour, as it would have merely focused on one slice of reality.

There are a number of other ways in which one approach can be used to inform and enrich the other. As explained earlier, quantitative research, because of its reductionist approach, sometimes lacks validity. To counteract this, qualitative methods such as in-depth interviews, group interviews and unstructured observations are used to gather data, which can increase the content validity of tools such as questionnaires (see Chapter 11). Pope and Mays (1995) illustrate this with an example 'of qualitative research conducted to establish which sexual terms would be most appropriate to use in the "British National Survey of Sexual Attitudes and Lifestyles"'. As they point out:

> The meaning of many terms – 'vaginal sex', 'oral sex', 'penetrative sex', 'heterosexual' – was unclear to a sizeable enough number of people to threaten substantially the overall validity of response.

A more substantial contribution of qualitative to quantitative method is in the construction of tools. To ensure the validity of these research tools, items must represent the phenomena being measured. Qualitative methods such as interviews can be used to generate and validate ideas. For example, Stokes and Gordon (1988) developed an 'instrument to measure stress in the older adult' by first identifying stressors from a literature review and then conducting qualitative interviews with a sample of older people, before finally submitting the resulting list to two 'experts in gerontologic nursing'. Wilde et al. (1994) developed a 'patient-centred questionnaire based on a grounded theory model'. They carried out in-depth interviews with patients and followed the grounded theory method to code the data. Their questionnaire benefited from the fact that it was based on the patients' perspective and, because 'the wordings were inspired by the patients' interview responses', most patients found the questions easy to comprehend (Wilde et al., 1994).

When used in the preliminary phase of quantitative research, qualitative methods may be seen as subordinate to the 'superior', more 'scientific' quantitative approach. There has been a disproportionate emphasis on quantitative methodologies in the literature (Duffy, M E, 1985). Recently, it has been suggested that qualitative research has 'come of age' (Leininger, 1992), and this is borne out by the quality and quantity of papers, journals and books on or about qualitative research.

The adherence to one approach can seriously impede the development of a body of knowledge for nursing that clearly comprises biological as well as psychosocial and cultural elements. So far, quantitative research has drawn most of the funding and influenced the agenda of nursing research, although this is changing. It would also be a mistake to reject 'quantitative methodology as a legitimate and appropriate means of studying nursing' (Akinsanya, 1988). Researchers must realise that a 'phenomenon cannot be molded to fit the research tradition, rather the research tradition is selected to fit the phenomenon' (Bargagliotti, 1983). Both approaches have the potential to advance nursing practice. According to Delamont and Hamilton (1976), 'a knowledge of their deficiencies is as important for their successful use, as an appreciation of their potential' and 'neither is, nor can be a universal panacea'.

SUMMARY AND CONCLUSION

In this chapter, a framework derived from the definition of paradigms to differentiate between quantitative and qualitative approaches has been proposed. The value and limitations of both approaches to the study of nursing phenomena have also been discussed. While both have distinct and valuable contributions to make, the nature of nursing phenomena is such that they can benefit from both approaches provided the most appropriate methods are used and that the specific issues involved in mixing paradigms are recognised.

REFERENCES

Abbott K, Blair F and Duncan S (1993) Participatory research. *Canadian Nurse*, **89**(1):25–7.

Akinsanya J A (1988) Complementary approaches. *Senior Nurse*, **8**(5):20–1.

Baker C, Wuest J and Stern P N (1992) Method slurring: the grounded theory/phenomenology example. *Journal of Advanced Nursing*, **17**:1355–60.

Bargagliotti L A (1983) Researchmanship: the scientific method and phenomenology: toward their peaceful coexistence in nursing. *Western Journal of Nursing Research*, **5**(4):409–11.

Baum F (1995) Researching public health: behind the qualitative–quantitative methodological debate. *Social Science and Medicine*, **40**(4):459–68.

Boore J R P (1994) Prescription for recovery. In *Research Classics*, vol. 1. London: RCN.

Chalmers I (1993) Effective care in midwifery: research, the professions and the public. *Midwives Chronicle*, **106**:3–13.

Colaizzi P (1978) Psychological research as the phenomenologist views it. In R Valle and M Kings (eds) *Existential Phenomenological Alternatives for Psychology*. New York: Oxford University Press.

Creswell J W (1994) *Research Design*. California: Sage.

Delamont S and Hamilton D (1976) Classroom research: a critique and a new approach. In Stubbs M and Delamont S (eds) *Explorations in Classroom Observation*. London: John Wiley & Sons.

Denzin N K (1970) *The Research Act: A Theoretical Introduction to Sociological Methods*. Chicago: Aldine.

Denzin N K and Lincoln Y S (eds) (1994) *Handbook of Qualitative Research*. California: Sage.

Duffy M (1985) A critique of research: a feminist perspective. *Health Care for Women International*, **6**:341–52.

Duffy M E (1985) Designing nursing research: the qualitative–quantitative debate. *Journal of Advanced Nursing*, **10**:225–32.

Fals–Borda O and Rahman M A (1991) *Action and Knowledge – Breaking the Monopoly with Participatory Action-Research*. London: Intermediate Technology Publications.

Geissler E M (1990) An exploratory study of selected female registered nurses: meaning and expression of nurturance. *Journal of Advanced Nursing*, **15**:525–30.

Glaser B and Strauss A (1967) *The Discovery of Grounded Theory*. Chicago: Aldine.

Grant A, Sleep J, Ashurst H and Spencer J A D (1989) Dyspareunia associated with the use of glycerol-impregnated catgut to repair perineal trauma – report of a three year follow-up study. *British Journal of Obstetrics and Gynaecology*, **96**:741–3.

Haase J E and Myers S T (1988) Reconciling paradigm assumptions of qualitative and quantitative research. *Western Journal of Nursing Research*, **10**(2):128–37.

Hammersley M (ed.) (1993) *Social Research: Philosophy, Politics and Practice*. London: Sage.

Hanson E J (1994) An exploration of the taken-for-granted world of the cancer nurse in relation to stress and the person with cancer. *Journal of Advanced Nursing*, **19**:12–20.

Hayward, J (1994) Information – A Prescription against Pain. In *Research Classics*, vol. 1. London: RCN.

Henwood K L and Pidgeon N F (1993) Qualitative research and psychological theorising. In Hammersley M (ed.) *Social Research: Philosophy, Politics and Practice*. London: Sage.

Horsfall J M (1995) Madness in our methods: nursing research, scientific epistemology. *Nursing Inquiry*, **2**:2–9.

Hughes J (1980) *The Philosophy of Social Research*. London: Longman.

Jayaratne T E (1993) The value of quantitative methodology for feminist research. In Hammersley M (ed.) *Social Research: Philosophy, Politics and Practice*. London: Sage.

Jones S (1988) The analysis of depth interviews. In Walker R (ed.) *Applied Qualitative Research*, 2nd edn. Aldershot: Gower Publishing.

Kimchi J, Polivka B and Stevenson J S (1991) Triangulation: operation definitions. *Nursing Research*, **40**(6):364–6.

Kincheloe J L and McLaren P L (1994) Rethinking critical theory and qualitative research. In Denzin W K and Lincoln Y S (eds) *Handbook of Qualitative Research*. California: Sage.

Leininger M (1992) Current issues, problems and trends to advance qualitative paradigmatic research methods for the future. *Qualitative Health Research*, **2**(4):392–415.

Lincoln Y and Guba E (1985) *Naturalistic Inquiry*. Newbury Park, CA: Sage.

Lipson J (1991) On bracketing. In Morse J (ed.) *Qualitative Nursing Research: A Contemporary Dialogue*. Newbury Park, CA: Sage.

Mathison S (1988) Why triangulate ? *Educational Researcher*, March 13–17.

Mays N and Pope C (1995) Rigour and qualitative research. *British Medical Journal*, **311**:109–12.

Measal C P and Anderson G C (1979) Nonnutritive sucking during tube feedings: effects on clinical course in premature infants. *Journal of Obstetrics and Gynaecology*, **8**:265–72.

Munhall P L (1982) Nursing philosophy and nursing research: in apposition or opposition. *Nursing Research*, **31**(3):176–7.

Myers S T and Haase J E (1989) Guidelines for integration of quantitative and qualitative approaches. *Nursing Research*, **38**(5):299–301.

Norbeck J S (1987) In defence of empiricism. *Image: Journal of Nursing Scholarship*, **19**(1):28–30.

Oakley A (1989) Who's afraid of the randomised controlled trial? Some dilemmas of the scientific method and 'good' research. *Women Health*, **15**:25.

Pope C and Mays N (1995) Reaching the parts other methods cannot reach: an introduction to qualitative methods in health and health services research. *British Medical Journal*, **311**:42–5.

Reason P (1994) Three approaches to participative inquiry. In Denzin W K and Lincoln Y S (eds) *Handbook of Qualitative Research*. California: Sage.

Rukholm E, Bailey P, Coutu-Wakulczyk G and Bailey W B (1991) Needs and anxiety levels in relatives of intensive care unit patients. *Journal of Advanced Nursing*, **16**:920–8.

Seibold C, Richards L and Simon D (1994) Feminist method and qualitative research about midlife. *Journal of Advanced Nursing*, **19**:394–402.

Stokes S A and Gordon S E (1988) Development of an instrument to measure stress in the older adult. *Nursing Research*, **37**(1):16–19.

Thomas S A, Liehr P, DeKeyser F and Freidmann E (1993) Nursing blood pressure research, 1980–1990: a bio-psycho-social perspective. *Image: Journal of Nursing Scholarship*, **25**(2):157–64.

Waltz C F, Strickland O L and Lenz E R (1991) *Measurement in Nursing Research*, 2nd edn. Philadelphia: F A Davis.

Wilde B, Larsson G, Larsson M and Starrin B (1994) Development of a patient-centred questionnaire based on a grounded theory method. *Scandinavian Journal of Caring Sciences*, **8**:39–48.

4   THE RESEARCH PROCESS

INTRODUCTION

One of the first tasks in reading and evaluating a research study is to identify the actions and steps taken by the researcher in order to answer the research question. This chapter describes the research process in quantitative and qualitative research and points out the differences between them. There are ethical implications at every stage of the research process. An outline of the guiding principles to safeguard patients' rights and safety is given.

THE MEANING OF 'RESEARCH PROCESS'

The process of any activity is what happens from its inception to its end. The tasks and actions carried out by the researcher in order to find answers to the research question constitute the *research process*. Decisions are taken in choosing the tasks and the way in which they are carried out. A number of factors, including the researcher's beliefs and experience, ethical considerations or resources, may influence these decisions. The thinking processes of the researcher, the assumptions made and the theoretical stance are also part of the research process. According to Denzin and Lincoln (1994), there are:

> three interrelated activities which define the research process: the articulation of the researcher's individual worldview or basic belief system (in relation to the research domain), decisions on the theoretical perspective and strategies of enquiry, and decisions on methods of data collection and analysis.

Thus, although the research process is often described in terms of the tasks and actions undertaken, it also consists of the decisions and the thinking that underpins these decisions.

Whatever the type of research carried out or the approaches used, the research process invariably consists of three main components:

- the identification of the research question;
- the collection of data;
- the analysis of data.

To carry out these tasks, a number of other tasks may be performed. For example, in identifying the research question, a review of the literature and/or discussion with colleagues may be useful. Before data can be collected, a questionnaire or an interview schedule may have to be constructed. The research process, therefore, consist of all these tasks and the decisions made during the course of the project.

THE RESEARCH PROCESS AND THE NURSING PROCESS

A number of authors have compared the research process to the nursing process (Burns and Grove, 1987; Thomas, 1990). They are both problem-solving processes and both consist of a number of steps or stages. However, they differ in the goals they aim to achieve. The main purpose of the nursing process is to provide care to clients. In doing so, nurses gather information in order to assess the nursing problem and to evaluate the care given. The collection of such information is not expected to be as rigorous and systematic as is the case in research. For example, when assessing clients, nurses can ask questions but do not have to use a tool such as a questionnaire with established validity and reliability in order to do so (although some do). The aim of research, on the other hand, is to find solutions to research questions, which may or may not contribute to better care for clients. Data for research purposes must be collected systematically and rigorously. Table 4.1 shows the main components of the nursing process and the research process.

Table 4.1 Main components of the nursing and research process

Nursing process	Research process
Assessment	Identification of research problem
Planning	Collection of data
Implementation	Analysis of data
Evaluation	

THE PROCESS IN QUANTITATIVE RESEARCH

The research process is often described as having a number of stages and steps. Depending on the type of research, these stages are not necessarily linear (performed one after the other, in one direction only). There are important differences between quantitative and qualitative research in the way in which the research tasks are undertaken.

The systematic and inflexible nature of quantitative research means that the research proceeds in a logical and sequential manner. The stages of the process in quantitative research can be broken down in a number of steps. The number of steps varies according to textbooks. Polit and Hungler (1995) describe 16 major steps and Abdellah and Levine (1979) 12. The difference in the number of steps is not important provided the main tasks are carried out and explained. The main stages of experimental and survey research are described briefly below. The chapters that follow will provide more detail and discussion on these topics.

STAGES OF THE RESEARCH PROCESS

Identification and formulation of the research question

This is the first stage of a research project, when the researcher decides what is to be researched and formulates one or more questions. The next step is for the researcher to define the terms and concepts used in the research questions. A review of the relevant literature (see Chapter 5) helps to clarify issues, inform the researcher of how others have formulated similar research questions and define concepts. At the end of this stage, the research questions or hypotheses developed must be stated clearly and unambiguously.

Collection of data

A number of tasks will be carried out by the researcher before data are collected. Decisions will be taken in order to choose a design for the study and a conceptual framework (if appropriate), and to select or develop instruments to collect data (for example questionnaires, interviews or observation schedules). This may be followed by the testing (or piloting) of these instruments in order to refine them (sometimes the whole study is piloted on a small scale to find out whether the project is feasible). At this stage of the process, the researcher will define the population from whom the data will be collected, seek access to them and obtain ethical approval from the relevant ethical committee. When all these preparations have been completed, data are ready to be collected.

Analysis of data

In the final stage of the process, the researcher analyses, interprets and presents the findings. During the data collection phase, decisions about the type of analysis would have been taken. For example, when questionnaires are constructed, the researcher must decide whether and what statistical test should be carried out and code the question-naire accordingly.

When the data have been analysed, it is usual for the researcher to interpret the findings, discuss the limitations of the study, make recommendations for practice and further research, and present the study orally and/or in written form.

Steps of the research process

The stages described above are sometimes listed as a number of steps, as suggested below by Hek (1994):

- Identify the general problem or topic of interest.
- Critically review the relevant literature.
- Develop a theoretical framework.
- Refine the topic into a research question, aim or hypothesis.
- Plan the research design, research approach, population and sample selection, access to sample, ethical considerations, methods of data collection, data collection tool and methods of data analysis.
- Pilot study.
- Collect data for the main study.
- Process and analyse the data.
- Interpret the results.
- Identify the implications and limitations of the study.
- Produce recommendations based on the results.
- Write a report.
- Disseminate the results.

These steps represent the tasks undertaken by the researcher or by others on her behalf. In quantitative research, certain tasks must be carried out before undertaking others. For example, the research question or hypothesis must be clearly formulated before data are collected. The research questions cannot be modified during the data collection phase, and all data must be collected before analysis can start. Beyond this requirement, the research process in quantitative research can have a degree of flexibility. According to Arber (1993), 'although the research process can be represented as a series of discrete stages, in practice a number of activities are generally in progress at the same time, for example, you can select a sample while designing the question-naire and recruiting interviewers'.

THE PROCESS IN QUALITATIVE RESEARCH

The flexible nature of qualitative research is such that the research process takes on different forms. The stages of the research process may also differ from one qualitative study to another. As qualitative research comprises a variety of approaches and techniques, it is difficult to generalise about them.

Researchers using the qualitative approach may or may not define the research question prior to collecting the data. Often, a broad topic is identified and the phenomenon on which the researcher finally focuses is decided during the data collection phase. Sometimes a thorough review of the relevant literature is carried out before the data are collected, and at other times no literature review is conducted as the researcher may not want to be influenced by other people's perspectives. Regarding conceptual or theoretical frameworks, those using a grounded theory approach believe that hypotheses and theories are generated from the data collected. Therefore no attempt is made to use conceptual frameworks, although there are cases where this happens.

Instruments may or may not be constructed in advance of data collection. In qualitative research, although questions can be written and asked of respondents, the researcher is part of the instrument of data collection. Some questions may be thought of and formulated on the spot and new perspectives explored. The researcher is at liberty to alter questions or omit questions asked of previous respondents. The designs of qualitative studies are flexible enough to accommodate these and other changes. The research enterprise is moulded to suit the phenomena being studied.

In qualitative research, the researcher can begin to analyse data as they are collected. Although formal analysis takes place when data collection is completed, the researcher usually processes some of the data mentally or otherwise during fieldwork even before all the data are collected. After data analysis researchers can, and often do, go back to respondents to seek clarification and/or validation.

Do not be disheartened if at this stage you feel confused about some of the terminologies used. This chapter on the research process exposes you to the journeys (Hek, 1994) that researchers undertake. The new terms encountered are like places you will become familiar with on this journey. The rest of the book will clarify the terminologies and topics raised in this chapter.

UNDERSTANDING THE RESEARCH PROCESS

The research process is presented above as a framework for researchers to present their study and for readers to understand the reasons for the decisions taken and for the main tasks carried out. The research process is more than what is reported. For the purpose of articles or reports, the researcher breaks down the project into a number of parts or steps, which facilitates the reader's understanding of what was done. The final publication is often a sanitised version, purified of the difficulties and frustrations encountered during the process, and almost never gives an insight into the trials and tribulations faced by researchers. In Buckeldee and MacMahon's (1994) book entitled *The Research Experience in Nursing*, the research process is shown to be 'a messy and, at times, disorganized process, requiring creativity and reflection at all stages and that is not an ordered linear process implied by many research texts'.

While this applies mostly to quantitative research, Sapsford and Abbott (1992) point out that 'qualitative reports tend to display greater reflexivity: they reflect more on the process of research, on how the participants made sense of it, on their own preconceptions, and on how detailed events may have shaped the nature of the data'.

Publication conventions impose restrictions on how research studies are reported. Although, as pointed out earlier, some qualitative researchers do not consult or review the literature before collecting data, a literature review section invariably appears at the start of an article as if a review were carried out at the start of the research. Journals adopt formats which they believe facilitate the reader's understanding. Invariably, they require research articles to have the following structure or sections: an introduction (which introduces the topic and gives a rationale for the study), a review of selected literature, a description of the design, the main findings and a discussion of them. This extract from the *Nursing Times* (1994) Guide for Contributors illustrates this point:

> papers which are primarily about a research project should be presented with sections as follows:
>
> (a) Title;
> (b) Summary;
> (c) Introduction;
> (d) Materials and Methods;
> (e) Results;
> (f) Discussions;
> (g) References; and

(h) Tables and Figures.

As can be seen, this structure follows closely the stages of the research process in quantitative research. There is a challenge on the part of the author to shift through all the details of the process and to present an account as succinct and brief and yet as comprehensible and complete as possible and in a language that clarifies rather than obfuscates.

The research process has been summed up by Hek (1994) as:

> a systematic and logical way of trying to seek an answer to a problem. A commonly used expression is that undertaking research is like taking a journey rather than just arriving. There are various stages to go through on the journey, generally progressing in a certain direction, with the purpose of arriving at a destination. The journey can be made in a variety of ways and stops made, and more time spent in one place if necessary.

CRITIQUING THE RESEARCH PROCESS

One of the first tasks in critiquing a research article is to attempt to describe the actions and tasks undertaken by the researcher. If the process is well described, you will have little difficulty in doing this. However, in some cases, the structure of the article may be such that you will need to 'tease out' what was actually done. It is for the benefit of readers that the research process is reported in a neat version. There is always a desire on the reader's part to know more than what is reported. While it is not possible for the researcher to describe in detail everything that happened, you must not be left with major questions unanswered. For example, if only the size of the sample is given and you are not provided with an explanation of how the sample was chosen, this will limit the extent to which the data can be generalised to other settings (see Chapter 10).

Some details are important in assessing the validity and reliability of data, some are not. For example, there are few implications for the data if the researcher had to make 10 telephone calls to a nurse manager in order to gain access to the respondents, but it is vital to know whether the nurse manager 'hand-picked' the respondents, thereby creating the possibility of bias in the sample. When reading a research article or report, it is essential for you to distinguish between information that is and is not relevant.

ETHICS AND THE RESEARCH PROCESS

There are ethical implications at every stage of the research process, including the choice of topic to research, the selection of the design and the publication of the findings. Even the decision to research or not to research has ethical implications. By continuing to base practice solely on customs and traditions, consumers are denied the best possible care (Parahoo, 1991). Therefore, one can ask whether it is unethical *not* to examine one's practice.

Although this book is not about how to do research, nurses need to know the implications of research to be able to safeguard patients' rights and ensure their safety. These implications are discussed throughout the book. However, there are six ethical principles (ICN, 1996) that nurses and midwives can use to guard their patients or clients from harm. These are:

1. *Beneficence.* The research project should benefit the participating individual and society in general (by contributing to the pool of human knowledge). Sometimes the benefit of participation is access to a new treatment not yet available to others. Participants are also likely to receive more attention and human contact than they might otherwise receive. On the other hand, when this attention is suddenly withdrawn at the end of the study, it can cause a feeling of isolation, which can be potentially harmful.
2. *Non-maleficence.* Research should not cause any harm to participants. While the potential physical harm may be obvious, the psychological effects may not be as transparent.
3. *Fidelity.* This principle is concerned mainly with the building of trust between researchers and participants. For example, if during a study the researcher finds that participants are in some way at risk, they should not put the need to complete the experiment above the participants' safety. Research subjects entrust themselves to the researcher, who has the obligation to safeguard them and their welfare in the research situation (RCN, 1993).
4. *Justice.* This involves being fair to participants by not giving preferential treatment to some and depriving others of care and attention they deserve. Participants' needs must come before the objectives of the study. Researchers must ensure that participants are fairly treated and that the power relation is not unfairly tilted in their (the researcher's) favour.
5. *Veracity.* To build trust between participants and researchers, the latter must tell the truth, even if this may cause participants not to take part or to withdraw during the study. Being 'economical with the truth' can be a form of deception.

6. *Confidentiality.* The confidentiality of the information gathered from and on participants must be respected. Giving consent to participate in a study does not mean giving researchers the right to consult the subject's medical notes as well. Researchers often ask nurses and doctors, but not the participant, for permission. The presentation of the findings can potentially identify participants or participating institutions. Researchers must take care not to inadvertently reveal information that participants may want to remain confidential.

The above six ethical principles have been synthesised into four rights of subjects considering participation in research: the right not to be harmed, the right of full disclosure, the right of self-determination (subjects' right to decide to take part or to withdraw at any time) and the right of privacy, anonymity and confidentiality (ICN, 1996).

Nurses may not always have the necessary knowledge to decide whether a research study can be detrimental to the patients or clients invited to take part. Local ethics committees exist for the purpose of examining the ethical implications of such studies and for granting permission, when appropriate. The panel members usually have a range of expertise necessary to carry out this task.

Informed consent is the process by which researchers ensure that potential participants understand the potential risks and benefits of participating in a study; they are informed about their rights not to participate, and they are presented this information in a manner that is free from coercion (ICN, 1996). While it is the researcher's responsibility to seek informed consent, it is possible that an overzealous researcher may apply subtle pressure on participants, especially captive and vulnerable ones, or withhold information that may lead to a refusal to participate.

Where possible, nurses, as patients' advocates, are in a position to ensure that informed consent is what it means, that patients are able to understand the information given and that they are not under pressure to participate. When the nurse is the researcher, she must not use her position to recruit participants unfairly.

The ethical implications of research are discussed in relevant parts of the book, more specifically in relation to experiments, questionnaire design and use, interviews and observations (especially covert observation). Two useful publications on this topic are *Ethics Related to Research in Nursing* (RCN, 1993) and *Ethical Guidelines for Nursing Research* (ICN, 1996).

Summary and Conclusion

In summary, the research process constitutes all decisions and actions taken by the researcher. The process is normally reduced to a number of steps for the purpose of reporting. The stages and steps of the research process in quantitative research are more or less linear, while in qualitative research it is possible to revisit previous stages during the project.

Research has many ethical implications, and nurses must be vigilant to ensure patients' rights and safety. They can be guided by the six ethical principles outlined above.

Finally, it is important for researchers to describe the research process clearly to enable readers to make sense of the report.

References

Abdellah F G and Levine E (1979) *Better Patient Care Through Nursing Research.* New York: Macmillan.

Arber S (1993) The research process. In Gilbert N, *Researching Social Life.* London: Sage.

Buckeldee J and McMahon R (1994) *The Research Experience in Nursing.* London: Chapman & Hall.

Burns N and Grove S K (1987) *The Practice of Nursing Research: Conduct, Critique and Utilization.* Philadelphia: W B Saunders.

Denzin N K and Lincoln Y S (1994) Introduction: entering the field of qualitative research. In Denzin N K and Lincoln Y S (eds) *Handbook of Qualitative Research.* California: Sage.

Hek G (1994) The research process. *Journal of Community Nursing,* **8**(6):4–6.

ICN (International Council of Nurses) (1996) *Ethical Guidelines for Nursing Research.* Geneva: ICN.

Nursing Times (1995) Guide to Contributors. *Nursing Times,* **90**:11 (inside back page).

Parahoo K (1991) Politics and ethics in nursing research. *Nursing Standard,* **6**(6):36–9.

Polit D and Hungler B H (1995) *Nursing Research: Principles and Methods,* 5th edn. Philadelphia: J B Lippincott.

RCN (Royal College of Nursing) (1993) *Ethics Related to Research in Nursing.* London: RCN.

Sapsford R and Abbott P (1992) *Research Methods for Nurses and the Caring Professions.* Buckingham: Open University Press.

Thomas B S (1990) *Nursing Research: An Experiential Approach.* St Louis: C V Mosby.

5 THE LITERATURE REVIEW

INTRODUCTION

The purpose of research is to make a contribution, however small, towards understanding the phenomenon being studied and ultimately towards the total body of knowledge. Researchers can benefit from what has been done before and hope, thereafter, to offer something in return. Two questions they should ask are:

- What can the current literature contribute to their research?
- What can their research contribute, in particular, to the understanding of the phenomenon under investigation, and to knowledge in general?

This chapter will help readers to understand and evaluate a literature review. It will also describe the purpose and process of systematic reviews.

THE NEED TO REVIEW THE LITERATURE

Most researchers turn to the literature for ideas. Many of those who start constructing a questionnaire find that they very quickly run out of questions to ask. Some learn later, to their cost, that they have omitted asking relevant and pertinent questions. The greatest feeling of frustration is to discover afterwards that the same research has already been carried out, and that, had this been known, 're-inventing the wheel' would have been unnecessary. More importantly, researchers find that they could have benefited from reading other similar studies, had they known about them prior to starting their own. There seems to be a natural tendency to get on with the project and start collecting data instead of (what could be seen as) 'wasting time reading the literature'. Research dissertation supervisors often find that students start formulating questionnaire and interview items before making any attempt to search and review the literature.

A literature search and review serves to put the current study into the context of what is known already on the phenomenon. It should stimulate the researcher's thinking and can provide a wealth of ideas and perspectives. This is useful in helping to identify, refine and formulate questions. Research on the same or similar topics can, in many ways, be very informative and useful. These functions of a literature review will be discussed further later on in this chapter.

What is Meant by 'The Literature'?

People are generally familiar with terms such as English or French literature. In research terminology, 'the literature' refers mostly to any published material, although reference is sometimes made to radio, television or other audiovisual media, such as slides, photographs and songs. What normally constitutes literature, however, is mainly books, theses, journals, letters, newspapers, pamphlets and leaflets. Sometimes reference is also made to what was said at a conference or to personal communications (face-to-face or telephone conversations, and letters). Although the value of each of the different types of literature depends on what individuals derive from them, researchers place more value on some rather than others. The value of each type of publication varies according to the type and quality of information it contains. The credibility of each type of information itself depends on how objective or subjective it is and whether or not it is verifiable. Information from nursing and allied literature can be categorised as research, conceptual and theoretical, statistical, descriptive and personal opinion: categories derived from Polit and Hungler (1995).

Research information comes mainly from research studies. It relates to the topic being researched, the methods of data collection and the findings. This type of information is highly valued as it is usually systematically and rigorously collected and analysed, and, in the case of quantitative research, may be verifiable.

Conceptual and theoretical information is the backbone of all disciplines. It takes the form of the intellectual discussion of ideas. Although the views expressed are those of individuals, the arguments put forward must be structured logically and argued coherently for others to understand, contribute to and hopefully use. Theoretical frameworks should inform the practice of nursing. An example of conceptual information comes from an article by Burgener and Chiverton (1992). As the authors explain in the abstract:

> This article addressed a neglected area within nursing knowledge development: appropriate conceptual frameworks for guiding care of institutionalized, cognitively-impaired elders. Following a review of possible conceptual frameworks, psychological well-being, as defined by Lawton (1983), is

proposed as an appropriate framework for guiding knowledge development and care of this elderly population. Two aspects of psychological well-being, positive and negative affect, may be appropriate indicators of the concept in cognitively-impaired elders. Instruments for measurement of psychological well-being are also discussed. The implications of using psychological well-being as a conceptual basis for both research and nursing care are presented.

This summary then develops into a theoretical discussion. The authors did not collect data for the purpose of this paper. Instead, they discussed findings from previous research as well as ideas put forward by others.

Statistical information, when rigorously collected, is also objective, although it can be manipulated to support opposing arguments on the same issue. The credibility of statistical information depends on how, by whom and for what purpose the data are collected. An example of statistical information is the *World Health Statistics*, published annually by the World Health Organisation, and containing information on health and demographic data, causes of death and life expectancy for different regions of the world.

Descriptive accounts of nursing practice can be found in nursing journals, especially professional ones. Although they contain valuable information, they tend to be subjective. Nonetheless, where little information is available, descriptive accounts can be useful and informative. More importantly, they are vehicles for sharing experiences of practice between professionals and others. An example of descriptive information is from Peace (1995) who describes 'the experiences of one family caring for a relative with the condition':

> Mr Harris described his wife before the onset of Alzheimer's as a handsome woman who kept the house spotless. She was a regular church-goer, never smoked or drank and was always healthy. Now she's 'a different person in the same body'. He feels let down and questions why should this happen when he has worked hard for a good retirement.

Personal opinion. Policy, practice and professional issues are important to nurses, some of whom make their opinions known by publishing them. These opinions are subjective, although the authors may back their arguments by research and other evidence. Wright (1995), for example, argues that 'caring is cost-effective' and 'patients could in future demand hospitals with higher skill mixes and a higher nurse/patient ratio'. He bases his arguments on research evidence and the views of others. It is not a research study that shows 'caring is cost-effective' but a case put forward by the author based on, among other things, his convictions, beliefs, experience and the available 'evidence'. One research study whose findings he uses to support his arguments is that of Carr-Hill *et al.* (1992). This shows nursing care to be cost-effective when compared with the care delivered by others. The credibility of the information in a personal opinion article depends in part on how the arguments are developed and supported, and on the status of the author. The list of references or the absence of it is an indication of how personal the opinion is or how much effort the author has made to relate his views to available evidence.

There are many areas that remain unresearched or underresearched. Those reviewing the literature on such areas can only rely on anecdotes and personal accounts. The editor of the *Nursing Times* (1994), referring to the need for research to back up the use of complementary therapies, pointed out that:

> a worrying number of submitted papers on complementary medicine cite references as providing evidence for the use of a therapy that turn out to be introductory guidebooks offering no research to support the therapeutic claims contained within them.

PRIMARY AND SECONDARY SOURCES

The value of information also depends on whether it is reported first or second hand. Original publications are known as *primary* sources. Such publications as the Briggs Report (Briggs, 1972) and *Introduction to Nursing: An Adaptation Model* (Roy, 1976) are primary sources. *Secondary* sources are publications that report on the original work. *Callista Roy: An Adaptation Model* (Lutjens, 1991) is a secondary source because Lutjens reports on Roy's original work published in 1976. Besides reporting on the original work, the authors may explain, comment or discuss the original ideas. By doing so, secondary sources are sometimes useful in that they simplify and summarise the primary material. However, there is the possibility that the original work may be distorted, misinterpreted and selectively reported as the information is first filtered through the mind of someone else. Therefore, by reading secondary sources, the reader depends on a 'middle person' to accurately report what the original author(s) wrote.

It is not always possible to review primary sources because some of these are out of print or not easily accessible, or the material is too 'hefty' and time-consuming to read. Although secondary sources may shed some light on the original material, they convey the essence of the work and are not the work itself. When research projects are reported second hand, they can lack the details necessary to fully understand how the study was carried out. As far as possible, primary sources must be consulted. The reviewer has to make a judgement on how and when to use either of the sources. It is sometimes easier to quote Roy or the Briggs Report, for example, from a secondary source near at hand than to search for these quotes in the original works. However, if Roy's model is used as a conceptual framework in a study, it is inadmissible not to use the primary source. Reading the list of references at the end of a chapter or article will give you an idea of whether there is a reliance on secondary rather than primary sources.

ASSESSING THE VALUE OF PUBLICATIONS

Let us now evaluate each type of publication according to the type of information it contains and assess its value as a source of material for a literature review.

Books

There are different types of nursing books, such as, among others, textbooks, books that contain a number of research projects and specialist books (for example on stress or models of nursing). Books are good sources of material that can be used in a literature review. Textbooks provide some understanding of concepts and issues but are limited in that they may cover a wide range of topics. Some textbooks make extensive reference to research, while others do so sparingly. There are also books that report exclusively on one research project (for example Millman, 1976, *The Unkindest Cut*) or a number of projects (for example Wilson-Barnett, 1983, *Nursing Research: Ten Studies in Patient Care*). They provide useful information that can be used in literature reviews. It is worth noting, however, that by the time books are written, published and consulted, the research and statistical information they contain is already dated. Heavy reliance on books as sources of material for a review is a sign that the reviewer has not 'cast her net' widely enough to take into account what has recently been researched and written. Books are reviewed by 'experts' on the topic before publication. As such, they would be credible sources of information. Their value also depends on how well researched they are and on their academic status.

Journals

The main source of literature for researchers are journal articles, which are self-contained entities. This means that, unlike a chapter in a book, which should be read in relation to previous and later chapters, an article contains, in a few pages, all the messages the author wants to convey. Another advantage of articles over books is that they can be read quickly. Although on average it may take over a year from acceptance to publication, they are more 'fresh' than any other source of information on research and other issues, excluding perhaps conference papers.

A distinction is sometimes made between a scholarly/academic and a professional journal. Academic journals (for example *Image: Journal of Nursing Scholarship* and *Journal of Advanced Nursing*) contain articles of high intellectual calibre.These are written in a language and style that tend to appeal more to academics than practitioners but which can also obscure their lack of quality. They are read by both academics and practitioners. Professional or popular journals (for example *Nursing Times, Nursing Standard* and *Professional Nurse*) are written mainly for practitioners. They tend to be more descriptive, seeking to identify practice implications, while academic ones are more abstract and put more emphasis on theory and research. The popular journals have a useful contribution to make, as J P Smith (1996) explains:

> The popular nursing journals aim to keep their readers regularly informed about up-to-date and topical professional developments, trends in nursing care and practice, news about individuals and the profession, and by providing conference reports. They also provide a marvellous forum for novice writers to air their views and to develop their writing and critical abilities in the correspondence columns and book reviews sections.

Journal articles submitted for publication are normally refereed; that is, they are sent to 'experts' who advise the journal on the feasibility of publication. The 'experts' are normally other authors, which is why this practice is referred to as 'peer review'. It helps to maintain standards in publishing and gives credibility and value to the published material as unsuitable articles are either rejected or sent back to the author for revision. On average, an article is sent by the journal editor to two referees, although some journals may require only one, and others three or more. Referees are not normally made aware of who the author is. Thus a 'double-blind peer review' means that referees do not know who the author is nor does the author know who the referees are.

Theses

Doctoral and other postgraduate theses are useful and credible sources of information. They should not only contain a thorough review of concepts, theories and research studies, but also details of research processes and findings. Some doctoral theses are published as books (for example McKenna, 1994, *Nursing Theories and Quality of Care*) or monographs (for example Gott, 1984, *Learning Nursing*). The latter was published as one of a series of RCN monographs. Unfortunately, many theses remain unpublished, but they can be obtained from the particular libraries where they are kept. Theses are examined and the status of the information they contain is enhanced by this process.

Research reports

Although doctoral theses follow a more or less prescribed format, research reports come in different sizes and forms of presentation. They tend to have less literature review but focus instead on the findings, conclusions and recommendations. This is, perhaps, because sponsors, for whom research reports are primarily written, are more interested in the findings and their implications for practice than they are in the literature review. Many of these research reports are also published in the original forms or as research articles. Research reports do not as a rule undergo a peer review process before publication, although they are subsequently scrutinised by researchers, clinicians and others. These projects are normally carried out by experienced researchers. An example of a research report published for general consumption is *Diet, Lifestyle and Health in Northern Ireland* by Barker *et al.* (1988). This study was financed by the Health Promotion Research Trust, to whom the report was submitted.

Conference proceedings

The main reason to refer to, and review, conference proceedings is because the information is not available elsewhere in print. Conference proceedings are in fact abstracts or summaries of papers submitted to conferences, and, as such, they contain only brief information. Their value is mainly in being 'hot off the press'. They are limited in that not enough details are available for the reader to evaluate the project. For example, the Research Advisory Group (RAG) of the RCN organises an annual research conference and publishes summaries of all papers presented at these conferences. It is also possible to write to conference presenters for copies of their papers.

Newsletters, pamphlets, leaflets, newspapers and popular magazines

The value of newsletters, pamphlets and leaflets as sources of information is limited in that they are brief communiqués of news and comments. They can only present information with few opportunities for discussion and explanation. They also report much of their information second hand, although they have an advantage because they deal with topical issues. Leaflets and pamphlets from drug advertising companies do contain useful information, but they can also be selective in their evidence, which they may produce in order to sell their products.

Letters written to professional journals reflect the topical interests and concerns of practitioners and others, and express the subjective views of the authors on topics they want to draw attention to. Their value lies in the fact that they are often the expressions of practitioners who are working 'on the ground'. Without systematic research, however, it is difficult to know how representative these views are.

Newspapers and popular magazines also publish material related to health and nursing. They are interested in topical and sometimes 'sensational' issues and report the latest news on selected issues. Depending on the author of the article and the type of newspaper, the information can be one-sided and biased.

All these sources of information can form part of a literature review. The researcher should cast her net wide in order to 'feel the pulse' of the phenomenon she is studying. The uses to which different types of information are put depends on what the reviewer wants to achieve. For example, if the reviewer wants to show that there is controversy over the benefits of Roy's model for the care of older people, she may refer to letters in the *Nursing Times* or the *Nursing Standard* to illustrate the point. However, she would have to look for discussions of models, in particular Roy's model, in academic books and journals. She would also need to search and review previous research on this issue, information that can be found mostly in academic journals and possibly in postgraduate theses.

Reviewers must look for the most up-to-date, relevant and credible information they can find. In practice, this usually means relying more on academic/scholarly journals and books, research reports and theses than on professional journals, newspapers, leaflets and anecdotes.

LITERATURE SEARCH AND LITERATURE REVIEW

In order to review the literature, a search must first be carried out. A literature *search* simply means locating and identifying the most up-to-date and relevant material. A literature *review* involves the scanning and critical reading of the selected literature to find out how it can be useful to the current research. From the review, a case can be made for the importance of the current research and for justifying the design of the study. The scene is also set for comparing the current findings with those of similar studies. The review carried out by the researcher is much more than the written summary that appears in articles or than what is reported in theses and research reports. Much more literature is read and analysed than is discussed.

The literature review should perform the following functions:

- provide a rationale for the current study;
- put the current study into the context of what is known about the topic;
- review the relevant research carried out on the same or similar topics;
- discuss the conceptual/theoretical basis for the current study.

Provide a rationale for the current study

Those who eventually read the article or report may or may not be aware of the reasons why it was carried out. Therefore, researchers need to provide a rationale; in doing so, they can try to convince readers that the study is of sufficient importance. Some give as many reasons as possible, perhaps in an attempt to convince the journal's editor and referees that the current research is important. Sometimes the real reason for doing research is because of the requirement of a course or because of the pressure on academics and others to publish. Ideas for research projects come mainly from one's observation of practice and/or from the literature.

The most frequently cited reason for doing a study is the lack of research on the particular aspect of the topic being researched. For example, Duxbury (1994), in a study of 'Primary nursing and the administration of PRN medication', came to the conclusion, after embarking on a review of the literature, that there was a lack of studies on this topic. As she explained:

One striking feature that came to her [the author's] attention as a result of this initial review was that little work, if any, had addressed the topical issue of how primary nursing affects the attitudes of night nurses concerning their role in the administration of prn night sedation and how this might affect their practice when compared to nurses not using primary nursing.

The reduction of morbidity and mortality, the prevention of illness, and the economic and social costs of a particular disease or treatment are often cited as arguments for conducting research, as these quotes from Tettersell (1993), who carried out a study on 'Asthma patients' knowledge in relation to compliance with drug therapy', illustrate:

> The amount of morbidity and mortality associated with the condition is extensive. According to statistics by the British Thoracic Society (1982), the death rate from asthma has remained at 2000 per annum for over a decade.
>
> between 70% and 86% of deaths are potentially preventable.
>
> The cost of asthma, both in social and economic terms, to the individual and his family, society and health and social services is extensive.

Statistical data and research findings can provide valuable back-up for the arguments put forward by researchers for their studies.

Another reason often given as rationale for a study is to inform the debate on controversial issues. For example, while there is demand among women for greater choice in the type of maternity care they receive, there is also opposition to home birth on the grounds of safety (Woodcock *et al.*, 1994). To make a research contribution to this debate, Woodcock *et al.* (1994) carried out 'a matched study of planned home and hospital births in Western Australia'.

The ultimate goal of nursing research is to improve clinical practice, although this is implied but not always stated. Konopad *et al.* (1994) made clear the rationale for their experiment comparing 'different methods of temperature recording in intensive care patients with or without an oral endotracheal tube':

> Temperature monitoring is a nursing task which has been practised since the late 1800s... . Owing to the preference for using rectal rather than oral temperatures in intubated patients, and the lack of experimental data relative to a procedure which is so frequently used, it is important to examine OT monitoring in intubated, critically ill patients. Such research is needed to increase our knowledge and thereby improve the practice of temperature monitoring in orally intubated, critically ill patients.

Policy-related reasons are also given as a rationale for research studies. Researchers may set out to investigate professionals' reactions to policies or recommendations. For example, in carrying out a study on 'nurse teachers' feelings about participating in clinical practice', Baillie (1994) cites two reports, *The Education of Nurses* (Commission on Nursing Education, 1985) and *A Strategy for Nursing* (Department of

Health, 1989), which suggested that nurse teachers should retain clinical practice skills.

The need to evaluate the effects of particular aspects of policies, old and new, is frequently given as part of the reason for research being carried out. For example, Wade (1993) conducted a study of job satisfaction of community nurses in four NHS trusts. With the introduction of Trust status in the hospital, she wanted, among other things, to monitor over a 3-year period 'the impact of organizational change on the role and function of nurses working in the community' and 'the strategies adopted by different groups of community nurses and their managers in response to organizational change'.

In addition, researchers may simply want to replicate or follow up other studies. Whatever the reasons, the rationale for a study must be relevant, clear and convincing. It must be supported, where appropriate and possible, by research findings, statistical data and, in some cases, expert opinion.

Put the current study in context

The literature review must place the present study in the context of what is already known about the topic. It must also, where appropriate, explain or discuss the concepts, variables and issues relevant to the research problem being investigated. In a study of factors influencing the job satisfaction of hospital nurses, the researcher should discuss the concept of job satisfaction. It is likely that she will compare and contrast various definitions and descriptions offered by others who have grappled with the concept, and choose the meaning she will give to job satisfaction in her study. She will also look for previous research findings and other conceptual/theoretical literature relating to factors affecting job satisfaction. If there is little or no literature relating to hospital nurses, the researcher will draw on literature on community nurses. Failing this, she could consult relevant research and non-research material from other professions.

In reviewing the literature, the researcher will shed some light on what is known already about variables such as gender, expectation, the nature of the job or pay, which may influence job satisfaction. Although different researchers may approach this exercise in different ways, the key concepts, variables and issues must be explained, if not discussed.

Researchers have to be selective about what they present to readers. They cannot possibly write about everything known about the topic. They can only discuss material relevant to the case they want to make, but in doing so they must not only back up their arguments with evidence, but also present a balanced view in their discussions. Biases will be obvious when one-sided arguments are put forward, especially when readers are aware of counterarguments.

Among the issues discussed in the study by Duxbury (1994) on primary nursing and night medication are: sleep requirements and sleeplessness as a common problem for hospital patients; factors which affect sleep (such as noise, pain, temperature, discomfort and anxiety); the relationship between work organisation and disturbance; night nurses' role and attitudes in general; night nurses' role, relating to sleep and sleep problems, in particular; and primary nursing's effect on care at night. While putting her case for carrying out the study, the author presents a summary of what is known on relevant aspects of the topic and does so by referring to research and non-research literature.

Review relevant research

In reviewing the literature, the researcher tries to identify research previously carried out on the topic. By comparing, analysing and summarising their focus, methodologies and findings, she can come to some conclusions as to the state of research in this particular area. For example, Patterson (1994), studying 'perspectives of clinical teaching', found that 'much of the research pertaining to the thinking of clinical teachers has occurred in disciplines other than nursing'. She also observed that 'a great deal of the research in teacher thinking has focused on identifying the impact of teacher perspectives on students' learning'. This exercise informs the researcher of the main focus of similar studies and of aspects of the topic that have been overresearched or still remain to be investigated.

In the above study, Patterson's (1994) review also revealed that methodologies that have been used included 'ethnomethodology, phenomenology, case study, interview and participant observation'. Researchers can build on the strengths of previous methodologies or adopt other strategies. The pitfalls of previous research can also be avoided. Perhaps one of the major benefits is to be able to make use of other researchers' tools, such as questionnaires or other measuring instruments.

Comparing the findings of similar studies is an important exercise in understanding the phenomenon being studied. Similar results may reinforce their validity, while contradictory ones may raise questions about, among others, the data collection and analysis methods.

It is not important or necessary to discuss every previous research study in detail. How much the reviewer reports on or discusses depends on the particular points she wants to make. In literature reviews, the most common aspect of previous research reported is the findings.

When the findings from different studies are contradictory, a good reviewer should attempt to speculate on why this may be so. A close look at their methods, samples or data analysis would probably be required to explain the differences. For example, one study looking at the health of carers of spouses with cancer found that only 10 per cent of carers consulted a general practitioner about their own health. Another similar study found that general practitioner consultation was 23 per cent. There may be good reasons why these findings are different. It could be that these studies were carried out in different populations with different types of cancer. Cultural differences as well as different health-care systems may explain why consultation patterns vary. Alternatively, the explanation may also be found in the methods, response rates or data analysis. Whatever the reasons, the reviewer should not leave the reader to speculate on contradictory findings but must try to offer explanations, as it is the reviewer who has read these studies in detail.

By reviewing previous studies, the researcher can not only explain what has been achieved so far and what contribution her study proposes to make, but also learn from the achievements and mistakes of other researchers.

Discuss the conceptual/theoretical basis for the current study

The purpose of research is to contribute to the pool of knowledge, and, as we found in Chapter 2, knowledge is organised, among other ways, in the form of theories. The use of conceptual frameworks is a step towards this contribution. Not all research uses a framework. However, a review of the literature will inform the researcher of what frameworks are available and how others have used them. The use of conceptual frameworks in nursing research is the subject of the next chapter.

These functions of a literature review apply mainly to quantitative research. What is already known is then tested and built upon, which is why quantitative researchers, prior to starting their own research, need to know what has previously been done. In qualitative research, this information is not usually required since the researcher does not want to be influenced by previous knowledge. Nevertheless, she needs to know enough about the subject she is researching. For example, if an ethnographic study of the use of nursing models is carried out in a medical ward, the researcher must at least know what models are. She may not be interested, at the initial stage, in the findings of other studies, but may later want to compare hers with others.

In practice, it is unlikely that qualitative researchers do not read the literature. They may have to be selective and read enough to enable them to carry out the study without being unduly influenced by previous research. Qualitative researchers do not normally use existing conceptual frameworks or theories but instead try to formulate their own from the data they collect. Finally, in quantitative research, the literature is reviewed and completed prior to data collection, whereas in qualitative research there is more flexibility. In practice, many quantitative and qualitative researchers continue to read and review the literature at any time in the research process, right up to the completion of the report or thesis.

SYSTEMATIC REVIEWS

Literature reviews are performed in a number of ways depending on the purpose of the review. As part of a research study, a review of the research, and conceptual and other literature, may be carried out in the preparatory stage, mainly to explore the methodology used in previous studies, if any, to put the proposed study in a theoretical context and to narrow down a broad topic. The researcher, in this case, may be selective and does not necessarily undertake a systematic review of all the existing studies carried out over a period of time. Sometimes a literature review can focus only on the methodologies employed in research on a particular phenomenon. The purpose of this exercise varies. In general, it informs readers of the trends, strengths and limitations of methodological approaches and makes recommendations for future research. Another purpose of a literature review is to find answers to a particular issue or problem, clinical or otherwise. All available research studies on a particular topic are identified, analysed and synthesised, and a conclusion is reached.

This type of review produces the 'best available' evidence on which practice can be based. The purpose of the review, in this case, is to make recommendations for practice which can be used to develop clinical guidelines. Currently, the emphasis is on this type of review, which is called 'systematic review' because of the thoroughness and rigour with which the search for, and the evaluation of, studies is undertaken. Systematic review is referred to as 'an efficient scientific technique' by Mulrow (1994), who describes it as 'arduous and time consuming' but 'quicker and less costly than embarking on a new study'.

A systematic review makes research findings comprehensible to practitioners, who have little time to read the increasingly growing body of literature, let alone make sense of it. Systematic reviews are central to the drive for evidence-based health care. This is explained by Rosenberg and Donald (1995) who outline the four steps in evidence-based medicine, as follows:

- Formulate a clear clinical question from a patient's problem;
- Search the literature for relevant clinical articles;
- Evaluate (critically appraise) the evidence for its validity and usefulness; and
- Implement useful findings in clinical practice.

The process of systematic reviews can be laborious and requires much skill, both for searching and reviewing works, often in different languages. It involves manual and computer searches, spanning a number of years of publication. Thereafter, the located studies have to be sorted according to those which are relevant and those which are not, according to the criteria set by the reviewers. At this stage, 'it is important that this selection of articles is free from "selection bias"or "reviewer bias", which occurs when the decisions to include certain studies are affected by factors such as their results' (CRD, 1996).

Systematic reviews are also referred to as secondary research, since they involve a systematic and rigorous method that can be verified by others. According to Chalmers and Haynes (1994), 'systematic reviews of existing evidence, using meta-analysis when appropriate and possible, are examples of "advanced clinical research" '. Meta-analysis is 'the statistical analysis of a large collection of results from individual studies for the purpose of integrating the findings into a single, generalizable finding' (Lynn, 1989) (see Chapter 8 for meta-analytic designs).

There is a hierarchy of evidence according to the proponents of systematic reviews, with 'well-designed randomised controlled trials' at the top and 'opinions of respected authorities based on clinical experience; descriptive studies and reports of expert committees' at the bottom (CRD, 1996). This superiority of RCTs is not shared by those who believe that experiments are not the only or best way to research clinical issues. The emphasis on the quantifiable aspects of outcomes can seriously underscore the value of other approaches, as B H Smith (1996) explains:

> Forms of evidence allowable in evidence based medicine... remain heavily numerate. This encourages emphasis on the quantifiable and physical aspects of any clinical dilemma, which may be inappropriate. Denial of social and psychological aspects may be detrimental, and ignoring the less readily measured dimensions may be dangerous.

Systematic reviews have an important function in processing large volumes of existing research and making the results accessible and comprehensible to practitioners. Whether their findings are used will depend in great part on their credibility in the eyes of practitioners and their relevance to practice.

CRITIQUING THE LITERATURE REVIEW

While a literature review primarily benefits those conducting the study, you as a reader may want to know why the current study is important, what research, if any, has been carried out previously and what the researcher proposes to contribute. Books, theses and research reports give the authors ample scope to present extended literature reviews, while journal articles restricts them to a summary of the main arguments. The word-limit restriction should not, however, be used as an excuse for poor and inadequate reviews. The ability to present up-to-date, relevant information clearly, concisely and logically is crucial. The review should not be a collection of disparate, unconnected views or a series of quotes.

In critiquing a literature review, you may want to use the four functions described above as a framework to assess whether these four areas are covered. Is a rationale provided? If so, what is it? Sometimes more than one reason for the study can be given. How convincing are these reasons? For example, in a study of 'attitudes of undergraduate nurses towards mental illness', the author stated that nurses' attitudes and values are of considerable importance. However, the only reason put forward for this was 'they will be the leaders of tomorrow', undoubtedly a poor reason. Not only is the author making an assumption about 'undergraduates and leadership', but, more importantly; the relationship between 'attitudes and practice', which is more relevant, is not mentioned, let alone discussed.

Even when the rationale is convincing, the author needs to support it with such evidence as research findings, statistical data and, to a lesser extent, expert opinion. References to these need to be relevant and up to date. Although statistical data takes time to collect, analyse and publish, you must watch out for out-dated figures. For example, in one study it was stated that 'random controlled trials are rare in medicine'. This was backed up by a reference dated 1972, while the article was written in 1994: there would undoubtedly have been many such trials in the intervening years.

Does the author inform you of similar research carried out? You should not assume that no previous research exists when the author does not mention it. It is incumbent on the researcher to provide a brief critical overview of previous research. Making selective references to one or more studies whose findings may be favourable to her cause can only bring charges of bias against the author. Readers may be aware of the existence of contradictory findings or counterarguments.

A detailed critical review of all previous research may be boring and irrelevant. The author should guide you to make sense of the focus, methodologies and findings of other studies, rather than just describe them. Where necessary, inconsistent or contradictory findings must be explained. Prior to writing the review, it is the task of the reviewer to read, digest, compare and analyse most of the relevant material, and draw general conclusions.

If the current research study proposes to adopt approaches and methods different from those of previous research, you will be left wondering, if you are not told, which approaches and methods were previously used and why they have been discarded. When critiquing a literature review, you must identify information that is often omitted yet is crucial to your understanding of the review.

You must also find out whether important issues and concepts are dealt with adequately. It is unfair to expect the author to present a discussion of everything related to the topic. However, if for example, in a study considering 'health promotion strategies of health visitors', the concept of 'health promotion' is not explored, you may find it difficult to understand what constitutes health promotion for the author. You would also like to know what health promotion strategies are and, briefly, what the state of knowledge on them is.

As explained earlier, it is important to pay attention to the publication dates of the literature referred to in the review. It is difficult to generalise about what constitutes a 'dated' reference. If you read the nursing literature frequently, you will be aware of areas that are well researched. If you find that references are more than 5 years old, you can ask yourself whether there is more recent literature on the topic. It is up to the author to mention why the literature she refers to dates to earlier than one would expect. You must also take into account that it can take more than a year for an article, once accepted for publication, to be published. You should also question the author's reliance on secondary sources if this is the case.

Not every literature review fulfils the four functions mentioned above. In practice, the author focuses on one or more of these and pays little attention to the others. This choice depends on the case she wants to put across. Provided crucial information – such as a discussion of concepts relevant to the study and information about previous studies – is not omitted, the review may be adequate. You must also look out for assumptions and generalisations. In a study of 'psychiatric nurses' attitudes and behaviours towards patients in acute wards', the authors make the assumptions in the literature review that 'the management approach in acute psychiatric care needed to be changed' and that 'nurses working in these settings needed to have greater skills in rehabilitation and health promotion'. No evidence was offered to support either of these two statements. The study itself did not set out to investigate management approaches or the skills of psychiatric nurses.

It is unfair to be overcritical of literature reviews, especially in journal articles since the authors are limited for space. Not every issue, concept or research study can be discussed in depth. If the information is not there, you can ask yourself whether the lack of it affects your understanding of the study. If it does, this is a good indication that this information should have been included in the review. A good literature review provides you with essential, relevant information to put the current study into the context of present knowledge and research available on the topic.

SUMMARY AND CONCLUSION

The main purpose of a literature review is to show why the current study is needed and where it fits into the overall body of knowledge on the phenomenon being researched. Additionally, the review sets the scene by discussing the main relevant issues and concepts in, and related to, the research question, objectives or hypotheses. In designing their studies, researchers can draw upon the theoretical and research literature available. There are different types of literature, and the information they contain varies according to the type of publication. Researchers must as far as possible consult, and refer to, reliable and credible sources. This invariably means research-based literature, although there is other valuable information in the non-research literature as well. Primary sources should be consulted and reported where possible. Finally, it was proposed that a literature review can have four functions and that these can be used as a possible framework for critiquing reviews.

REFERENCES

Baillie L (1994) Nurse teachers' feelings about participating in clinical practice: an exploratory study. *Journal of Advanced Nursing*, **20**(1):150–9.

Barker M E, McClean S I, McKenna P G *et al.* (1988) *Diet, Lifestyle and Health in Northern Ireland*. Coleraine: Centre of Applied Health Studies, University of Ulster.

Briggs A (1972) *Report of the Committee on Nursing*. London: DHSS.

British Thoracic Society (1982) Death from asthma in two regions of England. *British Medical Journal*, **285**:1251–5.

Burgener S C and Chiverton P (1992) Conceptualizing psychological well-being in cognitively impaired older persons. *Image: Journal of Nursing Scholarship*, **24**(3):209–14.

Carr-Hill R, Dixon P, Gibbs I *et al.* (1992) *Skill Mix and the Effects of Nursing Care*. York: University of York Centre for Health Economics.

Chalmers I and Haynes B (1994) Reporting, updating, and correcting systematic reviews of the effects of health care. *British Medical Journal*, **309**:862–5.

Commission on Nursing Education (1985) *The Education of Nurses: A New Dispensation*. London: Royal College of Nursing.

CRD (Centre for Reviews and Dissemination) (1996) *Undertaking Systematic Reviews of Research on Effectiveness* (CRD 4). York: CRD.

DOH (Department of Health) (1989) *A Strategy for Nursing*. London: Department of Health, Nursing Division.

Duxbury J (1994) An investigation into primary nursing and its effect upon the nursing attitudes about and administration of prn night medication. *Journal of Advanced Nursing*, **19**:923–31.

Gott M (1984) *Learning Nursing*. London: Royal College of Nursing.

Konopad E, Kerr J R, Noseworthy T and Grace M (1994) A comparison of oral, axillary, rectal and tympanic-membrance temperatures of intensive care patients with and without an oral endotracteal tube. *Journal of Advanced Nursing*, **20**:77–84.

Lawton M P (1983) Environment and other determinants of well-being in older people. *Gerontologist*, **23**:349–56.

Lutjens L R J (1991) *Callista Roy: An Adaptation Model*. California: Sage.

Lynn M R (1989) Meta-analysis: appropriate tool for the integration of nursing research? *Nursing Research*, **38**:302–5.

McKenna H P (1994) *Nursing Theories and Quality of Care*. Aldershot: Avebury.

Millman M (1976) *The Unkindest Cut*. New York: Morrow Quill.

Mulrow C D (1994) Rationale for systematic reviews. *British Medical Journal*, **309**:597–9.

Nursing Times (1994) Dire need for data. *Nursing Times*, **90**(30):3.

Patterson B (1994) The view from within: perspectives of clinical teaching. *International Journal of Nursing Studies*, **31**(4):349–60.

Peace G (1995) Living with dementia. *Nursing Times*, **91**(45):40–1.

Polit D F and Hungler B P (1995) *Nursing Research: Principles and Methods*, 5th edn. Philadelphia: J B Lippincott.

Rosenberg W and Donald A (1995) Evidence based medicine: an approach to clinical problem-solving. *British Medical Journal*, **310**(6987):1122–5.

Roy C (1976) *Introduction to Nursing: An Adaptation Model*. Engelwood Cliffs, NJ: Prentice Hall.

Smith B H (1996) Evidence based medicine. Letter to *British Medical Journal*, **313**:169.

Smith J P (1996) The value of nursing journals (editorial). *Journal of Advanced Nursing*, **24**:1–2.

Tettersell M J (1993) Asthma patients' knowledge in relation to compliance with drug therapy. *Journal of Advanced Nursing*, **18**:103–13.

Wilson-Barnett J (1983) *Nursing Research: Ten Studies in Patient Care*. Chichester: John Wiley & Sons.

Woodcock H C, Read A W, Bower C, Stanley F J and Moore D J (1994) A matched cohort study of planned home and hospital births in Western Australia 1981–1987. *Midwifery*, **10**:125–35.

Wright S (1995) Sales pitch for nursing's softer side. *Nursing Management*, **2**(2):16–18.

Wade B E (1993) The job satisfaction of health visitors, district nurses and practice nurses working in areas served by four trusts: year 1. *Journal of Advanced Nursing*, **18**:992–1004.

6   RESEARCH AND THEORY

> Science is built up of facts, as a house is built up of stones;
> but an accumulation of facts is no more a science than a
> heap of stones is a house. (Henri Poincaré, 1905, Science
> and Hypothesis)

INTRODUCTION

In science, research is one of the main process by which data are collected
to support, reject or modify theories, or to develop new ones. Researchers
often use theories implicitly or explicitly to underpin their studies. Others
formulate their own hypotheses and theories from observations.

The development of any profession or discipline depends on the
accumulation of a body of knowledge. Theories play an important part
in this process by making the link between knowledge and practice. In
this chapter, we will explore the meaning of theory and examine its
relationship to knowledge, research and practice.

WHAT IS A THEORY?

The term 'theory' is often defined in relation to 'practice', as when, for
example, a teacher describes in the classroom the process of giving an
injection, as opposed to students actually giving injections to patients.
Theory, in this sense, means dealing with a topic (in this case the
administration of an injection) in an abstract form. Everyday conversations are full of theories. For example, people have their own theories
about who killed J F Kennedy, why working-class children are poor
achievers at school or why there is an increase in crime. These lay
theories (from non-experts) differ from scientific theories because the
latter must go through a process of falsification and verification before
they are accepted, at least for a while, before new data come to light to
modify or replace them with new theories. The theory that the earth was
flat was replaced when new observations caused scientists to think
again. Many scientific theories began life as speculations (see Chapter 2).
In the absence of empirical evidence (as observed by the human senses),
the best that people could offer was speculation. Even today, many of the
theories about 'space' and 'black holes' are speculations, even though
great strides have been made in astronomy.

Theories are merely interpretation of phenomena. They are not the
definitive explanation as they may in time be rejected or modified. There
may also be competing theories to explain the same phenomenon. For

example, the theory about the origin of man in the Bible's book of Genesis is different from Darwin's theory of human evolution.

Morse (1992) sums up the nature of theories thus:

> theories are not *fact*. They are not *the* truth. They are tools. They are merely abstractions, conjectures, and organizations of reality, and as such, are malleable, changeable, and modifiable. There are historical examples of theory adopted as doctrine that with the benefit of hindsight look ridiculous and even silly to our sophisticated eyes. As a theory is changeable, anyone has the privilege of making modifications, for on the day that theory is believed and accepted as fact, science will cease to advance.

DEFINING A THEORY

There are a number of definitions of a theory. At its most basic, theory explains the occurrence of phenomenon. To do this, it has to explain the relationship between variables or concepts. To borrow an example from the field of physics, 'an expansion in a bar of metal occurs when it is heated'. The phenomenon of expansion is therefore explained by the relationship between 'metal' (one variable) and heat (another variable). After a number of observations, it can be deduced that when heat is applied to a bar of metal it will cause the latter to expand.

According to Homans (1967), 'not until one has constructs (concepts) and propositions stating the relations between them, and the propositions form a deductive system – not until one has all three does one have a theory'.

In offering an explanation of why a phenomenon occurs, a theory must also predict that each time the variables happen to be in the same relationship, the same results will be obtained. In other words, the theory of metal expansion predicts that each time heat is applied to metal, the latter will expand. These explanatory and predictive functions of a theory are expressed in Kerlinger's (1986) definition:

> A theory is a set of interrelated constructs (concepts), definitions and propositions that present a systematic view of phenomena by specifying relations among variables, with the purpose of explaining and predicting the phenomena.

From these two definitions, it is clear that a theory is made up of a number of concepts which form not one but a set of interrelated propositions or hypotheses. Thus, from the above example, the theory of metal expansion comprises a number of propositions, mainly:

- Metals are made up of atoms.
- The structure of atoms is changed by heat.
- Heat causes atoms to expand.

In each of these propositions or hypotheses, there are a number of concepts (metals, atoms, heat and expansion). The relationship between concepts, propositions and theory can be explained in a simplified way by stating that a theory is made up a set of propositions, and each proposition is made up of concepts. Without concepts, there are no theories; this is why concepts are referred to as the 'building blocks' of theories (Waltz et al., 1991). Therefore, the importance of operational-ising concepts (see Chapter 7) for the development or testing of theories cannot be overemphasised.

Fawcett and Downs (1992) and Moody (1990) have expressed the view that such definitions as Homan's (1967) and Kerlinger's (1986) are too restrictive because they insist that a theory must state a relationship between concepts. Moody (1990) prefers Steven's (1984) definition of a theory as 'a statement that purports to account for or characterises some phenomenon' because 'it does not require that a theory states a relation-ship nor does it preclude statements of relationships', and because it 'does not require a theory to take more than one concept into account nor does it limit the theory to just one concept'.

TYPES OF THEORY

Moody (1990) identifies three types of theory: descriptive, explanatory and predictive. She refers to 'descriptive theories' as the most basic type of theory. According to her:

> They describe or classify specific dimensions or characteristics of individuals, groups, situations, or events by summarizing the commonalities found in discrete observations. They state 'what is'. Descriptive theories are needed when nothing or very little is known about the phenomenon in question.

While description and classification are important parts of the scientific process (as described in Chapter 2), they would not, according to positivists, constitute theories in themselves, because they do not seek to explain why phenomena occur. On the other hand, qualitative researchers do not see theories in the social sciences as necessarily having explanatory and predictive functions. They believe in the unique-ness of individuals and situations, and while they seek to find common-alties between different and similar situations, some are not concerned with explaining why things happen but what actually happens, from the respondents' perspectives.

Explanatory theory is described by Moody (1990), as one which specifies:

> relations between dimensions or characteristics of individuals, groups, situations, or events. These theories explain how the parts of a phenomenon are related to one another. These theories can be developed only after the parts of the phenomenon have been identified, that is, only after descriptive theories have been developed or validated.

It is clear that explanatory theories are seen as a 'step up' from descriptive theories in the scientific process of theory development. Few researchers would be content to know only what happens; most would probably want to know why these things happen, without necessarily seeking to find general laws to explain human behaviour.

Predictive theories, according to Moody (1990):

> move beyond explanation to the prediction of precise relationships between dimensions or characteristics of a phenomenon or differences between groups. This type of theory addresses cause and effect, the 'why' of changes in a phenomenon. Predictive theories may be developed after explanatory theories have been formulated.

This type of theory is normally developed in the natural sciences (where 'cause and effect', as for example between chemicals, is more easily established) and aspired to by positivists in the social sciences. It is likely, however, that most research in the social sciences falls within the first two categories: descriptive and explanatory.

LEVELS OF THEORY

Another way of describing and classifying theories is in terms of levels. Three levels – grand theory, middle-range theory and laws – will be described here.

Grand theory

These are broad and abstract ideas put together to give a vision of a phenomenon. Examples of 'grand theories' include Darwin's theory of evolution, Marx's theory of social structure and Freud's theory of human motivation. These theories are based on the synthesis of the theorist's own ideas and those obtained from other sources. They are examples of 'armchair' theorising, although, as in the case of Darwin and Freud, some experiments were carried out. Philosophers have for centuries formulated grand theories describing and explaining such phenomena as morality or human nature.

Grand theories tend to be all-encompassing of the phenomenon they describe. The Marxist theory of social structure comprises ideas, among others, about the relationship between those who produce (workers) and those who own the means of production (capitalists), the evolution and existence of social classes historically and cross-culturally, and ideology and its role in maintaining the *status quo*. Marx's theory is contained in many books and cannot be adequately described here. As can be seen, this type of theory comprises a multitude of other theories. Because they are broad conceptualisations, they have been termed also 'conceptual frameworks'.

Nursing theories tend to fall in the category of grand theories. Most of them offer broad conceptualisations of nursing. Fawcett and Downs (1992) describe nursing as having 'at least seven major conceptual models, including Johnson's Behavioural System Model, King's Interacting Systems Framework, Levine's Conservation Model, Neuman's Systems Model, Orem's Self Care Framework, Rogers' Science of Unitary Beings, and Roy's Adaptation Model. Walker and Avant (1988) believe that the grand theories of nursing 'have made an important contribution in conceptually sorting out nursing from the practice of medicine by demonstrating the presence of distinct nursing perspectives'.

Middle-range theories

Grand theories themselves cannot be empirically tested as they contain too many theories and propositions. Other researchers can take some of these propositions and develop smaller, more manageable theories with fewer concepts, and can be more specific about the relationship between them. These middle-range theories (Merton, 1967) fit the definition of scientific theories, as discussed in Kerlinger's definition given earlier. Layder (1993) explains that 'middle range theories describe the relations between empirically measurable variables... which can therefore be "tested" against empirically observed evidence'.

He also quotes Merton (1967) as stating that middle-range theory 'falls between the "minor working hypotheses" that are typical of earlier phases of research (and are not really much more elaborate than the hunches or insights that are ordinarily employed in everyday life) and the all-inclusive "grand" theories which aim to explain a wide span of social phenomena'.

Walker and Avant (1988) conducted an informal analysis of the content of six successive issues of the journals *Nursing Research* and *Research in Nursing and Health* and found that 'the clearest and most frequently used example of middle range theory' was the health belief model. Among the others identified were 'theories of coping, maternal role attainment and maternal attachment'.

Laws

Laws are the definitive type of theory to which scientists in the natural sciences aspire. As George (1985) explains:

> In other fields, especially the biological sciences, there are laws as well as theories. Laws are truly *predictable* and can be utilised with assurance because they provide a sound body of knowledge in which to function. For example, in chemistry, if one correctly places a salt and an acid in the same vehicle, one can predict the results.

As explained earlier, the purpose of theory in the view of positivists is not only to explain, but also to predict and control phenomena. Since nursing deals with human beings in a social and cultural context, it is unlikely that laws, in the way described above, can be developed. Instead, middle-range theories, clearly defined and tested, comprehensive and of value to practitioners, remain the goal to be aspired to, at least for the near future.

PRACTICE, RESEARCH AND THEORY

You may think at this point that all this is too 'theoretical' (i.e. abstract) or that theories are of interest and use only to academics. You may also wonder how theories in fact contribute to the accumulation of knowledge. Consider the following example. Suppose nurses in one hospital observe that patients rarely follow their advice on healthy eating. They may speculate or find out by reading the research literature that the following factors are associated with this type of behaviour: lack of motivation, lack of incentive and poor nutritional knowledge. Nurses in other hospitals, clinics or nursing homes may also have similar problems. They may find that this type of non-compliant behaviour is associated not only with lack of motivation, but also with the patients' age, social class or personality. Non-compliance with dietary advice is not restricted to one country or culture. Nurses in African or Asian hospitals may face similar problems. For them, a lack of nutritional knowledge, the influence of the family and local food customs may stand in the way of the implementation of a healthy diet.

Thus, casual observations, speculations and research findings together point to a multitude of factors that may be associated with non-compliance with dietary advice. These factors together constitute what can be called an accumulation of facts. A researcher may try to make sense of all these data by describing the non-compliant behaviour and by classifying these factors into, for example, individual factors (age, gender), psychological factors (motivation, incentive, personality), social factors (family influence, social class background, local customs) and economic factors (earnings, cost of food). Additionally, the researcher may compare this type of non-compliant behaviour with others, such as failure to act on advice on smoking, breast self-examination or the wearing of seat belts. The outcome of this process may be a descriptive theory describing and classifying non-compliant behaviours and the factors associated with them.

Researchers can also contribute by investigating more closely the relationship between some of these factors and non-compliant behaviour. Thus, not only has a large amount of knowledge been accumulated on non-compliant behaviours, but also attempts have been made to make sense of it. The researcher processes the mass of information available from various groups of people in different situations who experience the same phenomena. However, the researcher may not be content with explaining specific situations but is rather more ambitious and may seek to explain non-compliant behaviours in general. By moving from the specific to the general, the researcher becomes the theorist.

Having identified the problem in the first place, nurses all over the world can thereafter benefit from such a theory to guide their actions. Many nursing practices, such as choosing an injection site, rehydrating a patient, giving information to patients prior to surgery and helping people to quit smoking, are based on physiological, sociological or psychological theories.

Theories are not always invented in ivory towers. It is true that they can be formulated through the process of speculation, but most theories are based on observations by people in various situations and settings. The relationship between practice and theory is symbiotic, in that each one feeds on the other to their mutual advantage. The practice setting presents problems, while observations and theories help to make sense of these. Practitioners can thereafter apply them to their practice and, in so doing, help to provide information that can be used to support, reject or modify them; and so the process continues. Moody (1990) explains the relationship between theory and practice:

> Theorizing is not reserved for academicians – good practitioners are often some of the best theorists in that their hunches provide the basis for developing propositions that can be empirically tested.

Billings (1995), referring to Klaus and Kennell's (1976) bonding theory, explained that it would appear to be that 'it has several fundamental shortcomings that potentially limit the usefulness of the practical application of the theory to nursing'. Billings (1995) went on to say:

> Evaluative research and debate following in the wake of bonding theory has highlighted the following points: (i) that the theory appears to be insufficiently validated in research terms; (ii) that its narrow view fails to explain attachment behaviour in situations other than the immediate post-delivery period; and (iii) that its practical application has been shown conversely to be of detriment to the mother–child relationship.

This is an example of how a theory has been used to inform nursing and midwifery practice and how, in return, nursing and midwifery practice have questioned the value of the theory.

Some theorists may try to draw general principles from observations of non-compliant behaviours in order to predict and prevent such behaviours in the future. Others may see theories as only showing a range of possible factors associated with this type of behaviour, thereby increasing their understanding of this particular problem. Theories, in this case, are expected to guide nurses' actions rather than to prescribe them.

One theory used to explain non-compliant behaviours is the theory of reasoned action (Ajzen and Fishbein, 1980). Jemmott and Jemmott III (1991) point out that the theory 'has shown utility in the prediction of a broad range of health-related behaviours, including breast self-examination, smoking cessation, weight control, infant feeding, and contraceptive utilization'. They emphasise the need for theories to inform practice by stating that 'behavioural prevention efforts are likely to be most effective if they are based on a solid foundation of theory and systematic research'.

THEORY AND RESEARCH

Research is the process by which evidence is provided in order to support, reject or modify theories and develop new ones. Thus research has theory-testing and theory-generating potential. Science needs research (the process) to achieve its outcome – the production of theories. As explained in Chapter 2, there are two main routes by which research can make this contribution: deduction and induction. Theory-testing research adopts the deductive approach, while theory-generating research uses the inductive one.

Theory-testing research

Theory-testing research is mainly in the positivist tradition and is characteristic of middle-range theories. Layder (1993) explains how theory is tested in research through the deductive process:

> a testable hypothesis or proposition is logically deduced from an existing set of assumptions. The empirical data that is then collected either confirms or disconfirms the original hypothesis or propositions.

Only hypotheses or propositions drawn from a theory, and not the theory itself, can be empirically tested through research. For example, Skinner's theory of positive reinforcement (which occurs when a pleasant consequence follows a particular response, strengthening that response and therefore making it more likely to happen (Banyard and Hayes, 1994), is stated in an abstract form and has to be translated into real-life situations for it to be tested. An example of a proposition or hypothesis that can be derived from nursing practice based on Skinner's theory (Skinner, 1938) is 'there are fewer drop-outs among patients who are praised about their weight loss in the early sessions of a weight loss programme than among those who are not'. By collecting and analysing data to support or reject this hypothesis, a researcher is at the same time putting Skinner's theory to the test.

One proposition or hypothesis is hardly enough to test a theory. Many more from different situations would have to be drawn and tested. The theory of reasoned action, as mentioned above, is an example of a theory from which many hypotheses have been developed and tested relating to such phenomena as 'condom use among women' (Jemmott and Jemmott III, 1991), 'adolescents' use of seat belts' (Thuen and Rise, 1994) and 'exercise' (Blue, 1995). In a literature search of selected journals from 1980 to 1995, Blue (1995) found 16 studies using the theory of reasoned action in research on exercise alone. If data from these real-life situations do not support these hypotheses, the theory from which they are derived can be questioned.

Theory-generating research

If theory-testing research is firmly in the positivist domain, theory-generating research is characteristic of the qualitative approach. Much credit for pioneering the theory-generating role of research in the social sciences is given to Glaser and Strauss (1967). They pointed out that theory generation had been hampered by an overemphasis on the testing of existing theories, which were often limited in explaining reality as they were based not on observation but on speculation.

Glaser and Strauss (1967) saw the generation of theories from observation as a preliminary stage before they can be tested by quantitative methods later, thus acknowledging the dual functions of research as theory generating and theory testing. They, however, put more emphasis on the role of research in generating theories since, according to them, the inductive process is capable of producing more relevant theories. Glaser and Strauss (1967) also agreed with positivists that the role of research 'is to enable explanation of behaviour, prediction and control'. This view is not shared by all qualitative researchers, many of whom believe that the aim of research is 'to investigate and describe the social world as it really is beyond all presumptions and prejudices' (Hammersley, 1990, cited in Layder, 1993), rather than to explain, predict and control phenomena. Layder (1993) believes that there is a place, in qualitative research, for theory generation and for approaches that 'seek to develop theory' and 'employ systematic methods of study'. According to him, 'there is no reason for the two to be seen as competing approaches'.

Since it is believed that theories can be generated by the collection of data, many researchers feel the pressure to 'come up' with a theory each time they carry out a qualitative study. Theories do not grow on trees. They are the result of much intellectual and physical labour and patience. What most small research projects can hope to achieve is to describe and clarify concepts. This in itself contributes to knowledge and practice and is a worthwhile enterprise that can thereafter be built upon.

Finally, as explained in Chapter 2, few theories are formulated without some prior observations, conscious or unconscious, systematic or informal, made by the theorists or derived from the observations of others. Similarly, theories derived from qualitative data could somehow be influenced by the researcher's knowledge (of existing theories among others) and experience, despite the conscious effort not to allow these to influence the research process. As Morse (1992) aptly puts it:

> Although most researchers agree that a conceptual framework should not be used in qualitative research and that prior knowledge of the topic should be 'bracketed', we would be fooling ourselves if we thought that qualitative enquiry was divorced from established knowledge.

THEORETICAL FRAMEWORK, CONCEPTUAL FRAMEWORK AND CONCEPTUAL MODEL

These terms are sometimes used interchangeably in nursing research. They provide a framework within which research is sometimes conducted. The term 'theoretical framework' is perhaps more appropriate for research underpinned by one identified theory. For example, in

Jemmott and Jemmott III's (1991) study of 'condom use among black women', the theoretical framework was derived from the theory of reasoned action (Ajzen and Fishbein, 1980).

A conceptual framework draws on concepts from various theories and research findings to guide the study. The conceptual framework may or may not be stated. For example, in a study of the 'effects of dynamic exercise on subcutaneous oxygen tension and temperature', Whitney *et al.* (1995) do not mention the use of any particular theory, but make reference to physiological theories.

Conceptual models are the diagrammatic representation of concepts or theories, the purpose of which is to minimise the use of words. Wyper (1990), drawing from the health belief model (Rosenstock, 1974) for her study of 'breast self-examination', constructed the following model.

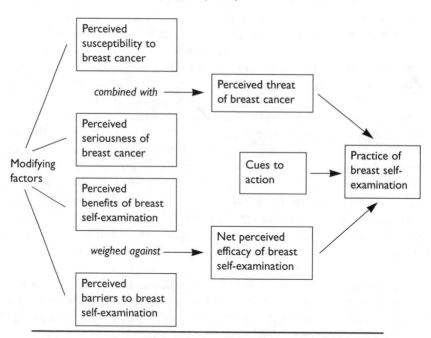

Figure 6.1 Major variables and constructs of the health belief model related to breast cancer and breast self-examination.

Although a distinction has been made between these three terms (theoretical framework, conceptual framework and conceptual model), researchers do not always differentiate between them in practice.

For the purpose of this chapter, 'theoretical framework' will be used interchangeably with 'conceptual framework' and 'conceptual model', in the sense that they are 'abstractions that may shape perception, reality, and inquiry' (Morse, 1992).

Instead of engaging in the exercise of finding out whether researchers have used the correct terminology, our effort can be better spent in identifying if and how concepts and theories have been used to underpin these studies.

The importance of the relationship between theory and research is stressed by Moody (1990), who states that, 'Progress in nursing science is best advanced when the researcher identifies the theoretical notions underpinning the research and attempts to formalise the link between theory and all phases of the research'.

In many research reports, there is no mention of theoretical frameworks, and in some cases where one is mentioned, there is little to explain how it guides the study design and how the data relate back to the theory or theories discussed earlier in the article. Downs (1994), in an editorial in the journal *Nursing Research*, makes the following comments:

> research without theory really does little to advance knowledge... The study that lacks a theoretical rationale lacks substance and fails to answer the 'so what' question. The findings just sit there, begging to be hitched to something. They are wagons stalled for lack of a horse. Perhaps the saddest thing about atheoretical studies is that they describe events in isolation from a context that allows the results to be generalized.

While some researchers may not consciously use a theoretical framework to guide their studies, the decisions they take are influenced by the beliefs they hold. These beliefs represent the world view of researchers. For example, in deciding to carry out qualitative interviews, the researcher holds the belief that it is important to listen to respondents rather than to ask them to place 'ticks' on a questionnaire to response categories (see Chapter 11) framed by the researcher. It signifies the value that the researcher places on the rights of respondents to formulate their own responses. Morse (1992) states that the choice of phenomenology, ethnography or grounded theory approach is itself influenced by the theories of Husserl and others (phenomenology), cultural theories (ethnography) and symbolic interactionism (grounded theory).

Similarly, those who decide to use structured observation (see Chapter 14) as a method of data collection are making the statement that it is possible to obtain valuable data using the positivist approach. Some researchers do not specify how they come to select items for inclusion in a questionnaire. However, their choice reflects their beliefs that these items are more important than others. We are not neutral beings. Our beliefs and knowledge are made up of assumptions about the world. Mitchell and Cody (1993) remind us, 'increasingly in the last few

decades philosophers have affirmed that all knowledge is theory-laden...
and that all methods are theory-driven'.

Conceptual Frameworks in Quantitative Research

Not all quantitative research is theory-testing. Often the purpose is to
find answers to particular localised problems. For example, a survey of
newly qualified midwives' knowledge of breast-feeding can be carried
out to identify gaps in their knowledge, with a view to improving
midwifery education in their school. Or patients can be interviewed to
discover their views about the care they receive in a particular hospital.
In both cases, researchers may only be interested in finding answers to
their specific research questions. However, the link with previous
knowledge (which includes theories, research findings, expert opinions
and descriptive accounts of practice) is important because researchers
can learn from it and, in return, contribute to it. Without reference to
existing knowledge, the study and its findings will exist in isolation from
other similar work or studies. To increase and enhance our understanding of phenomena, we must build upon our present knowledge.
One cannot, however, 'build upon' if one does not know what already
exists. Volumes have been written on phenomena of interest to nurses,
such as compliance, patient satisfaction, quality of life, social support,
patient teaching, stress, bereavement, physical development, and so on.
Some of these have more than one theory dedicated to them. By making
use of the relevant ones in their studies, researchers can help to test
them in practice.

You may have come across, while reading research articles, a
sentence stating that 'a conceptual framework is used to underpin this
study'. The Oxford Dictionary defines 'framework' as 'frame, structure,
upon or into which casing or contents be put in' and 'underpin' as
'support from below with masonry... strengthen'. This reference to
building and construction can equally apply to research. One can say
that the function of a conceptual framework is to provide a structure
that can strengthen the study. The nursing process is an example of a
conceptual framework; it has four components (concepts): assessment,
planning, implementation and evaluation. These components
represent the structure to which nurses attach the contents (such as
the information gathered in the process of assessing a patient). Thus,
the nursing process can be used as a conceptual framework in a study
of nursing care.

A conceptual framework for a research study can be derived from
conceptual definitions, models or theories. For example, in a study on
'student nurses' views of health', the researcher can use the WHO

(1946) definition of health as physical, mental and social well-being on which to underpin her study. These three components provide a guide to the researcher as to the areas of health on which to base her questions. She could have chosen Smith's (1981) 'progressive model of health which has four levels: clinical, role performance, adaptive and eudomonistic', on which Kenney based her study of 'the consumer's view of health' (Kenney, 1992). Our researcher could then base her questionnaire or interviews on each of these components. Alternatively, she could combine both definitions and provide her own conceptual framework.

An example of a conceptual framework derived from four theories comes from a study by Groër *et al.* (1992) on 'adolescent stress and coping'. As the authors explain, 'the conceptualization for the research was derived from developmental, stress/coping, gender and role theories'. The following propositions were developed from the conceptual framework:

- Life events are a source of stress.
- Adolescents adjust and adapt to stress by various coping strategies.
- Both developmental level and gender influence the degrees and types of life event stress and ways of coping.

By reviewing relevant theories, researchers can decide how they can approach their study. Groër *et al.* (1992) set out to collect data to support or reject their propositions. Thus these four theories provided a framework for their study. In return, the data collected could shed more light on the adequacy of these theories in explaining how adolescents cope with stress.

The nursing research literature reveals a number of ways in which researchers make the link between previous knowledge and their own studies. These range from studies making no mention of a conceptual framework to those with a sound theoretical base. Below are some examples.

Russell (1996) carried out a small study on 'knowledge and practice of pressure area care' among a group of 30 qualified nurses. No mention is made of a conceptual framework. However, it is implicit rather than explicit that the author makes use of previous knowledge. For example, one of the 20 questions she asked the nurses in her study is, 'what are the stages of pressure sore development?' She assesses their answer against Torrence's classification of pressure sores (Torrence, 1983). In doing so, she is making a link with previous knowledge, although, in this case, Russell is not trying to test or build upon Torrence's classification, but only wants to find out whether or not nurses are aware of it. Similar other questions, such as those on 'capillary pressure' and 'factors which increase the risk of pressure sores', are based on existing knowledge. However, it is not clear how Russell derives her questions for her questionnaire.

This study does not test any propositions and does not have an identified conceptual framework. As the author states, the aim is, among other things, 'to identify nurses' needs for education in pressure sore prevention in relation to assessing, planning, implementing and evaluating care'. While the findings provide a valuable insight into the knowledge and practice of these nurses, they remain relevant mainly to them, although, as the author states, others 'may wish to implement' her recommendations.

Another study that has no identified conceptual framework but which draws on existing literature, especially research findings, is that of Woodward (1995) on 'psychosocial factors influencing teenage sexual activity, use of contraception and unplanned pregnancy'. According to the author, findings from the literature search into factors that influence teenage sexual behaviour and the use of contraceptives formed the basis of her study. The link with previous knowledge is made clear. For example, in her literature review, Woodward discusses previous work by Bury (1986), who stated:

> contraception may be more effectively and consistently used in established teenage relationships. This may be due to the increased communication about sex and contraception that exists in stable relationships as well as the anticipation of when sexual intercourse will occur.

Woodward (1995) included a question based on Bury's proposal in her questionnaire in order to find out whether it also applied to her sample. Her findings did not support this claim.

Although she does not mention a conceptual framework, Woodward bases her questions on research findings. She is in fact testing some of the ideas or proposals put forward by others. The findings of her study on 61 teenagers were used to support, reject or make suggestions on what was previously known about the subject. She has thus placed her study in the context of a wider discussion on psychosocial factors influencing teenage sexual activity. Woodward's conclusion makes this implicit:

> The findings of this study demonstrate that there is no simple model of teenage sexual or contraceptive behaviour which would assist in developing strategies to stem the continuing rise of unplanned pregnancy in the teenage years. Further studies to investigate the effects of family discord, unemployment and perception of future life prospects on use of contracep-

tion and unplanned pregnancy in their teenage years emerged as important areas for future research.

As the questionnaire is based on the existing literature, Woodward's study enters the general debate on the phenomenon she investigates. In contrast, the questionnaire of Russell (1996) is specific to her group of nurses and therefore focuses the discussion on her sample.

An example of a study based on a sound conceptual framework is by Jemmott and Jemmott III (1991) on condom use among a group of 103 black women undergraduates in a US inner-city university.

As explained earlier, the theory of reasoned action was used as a conceptual framework in this study. This theory explains the relationship between attitudes, beliefs, intentions, subjective norms and behaviours. When a conceptual framework is used, it must guide the entire research process, from the literature review to the analysis of data. In this study, because the theory of reasoned action was selected to provide the conceptual framework, the authors reviewed the literature related to the main components of the theory, as well as other relevant research studies. The hypotheses proposed for this study are based on the selected theory. As Jemmott and Jemmott III (1991) explain:

> The present study tested the following hypotheses suggested by the theory of reasoned action. First, women who express more favourable attitudes toward condoms will report stronger intentions to use condoms than will women who express less favourable attitudes. Second, women who perceive subjective norms more supportive of condom use will report stronger intentions to use condoms than will their counterparts who perceive subjective norms less supportive of condom use.

The conceptual framework also guides the method of data collection. In this study, questions were developed for each of the components of the theory of reasoned action. For example, one of the questions measuring behavioural intention was 'how likely is it that you will decide to use a condom if you have sex in the next three months?' Similarly, questions were devised for attitudes, beliefs and subjective norms. To find out the relationship between these different components, Jemmott and Jemmott III (1991) had to carry out the appropriate statistical analysis of the data. Therefore, we can see how the conceptual framework guided the literature review, the formulation of hypotheses and the methods of data collection and analysis. Finally, to complete the circle, the findings of this study should, in turn, be used to test the effectiveness of the theory of reasoned action in predicting behaviour. Jemmott and Jemmott III (1991) concluded that their study provided strong support for the theory of reasoned action and 'that women who expressed more favourable attitudes toward condoms and those who perceived greater support for condom use among their significant referents reported stronger intentions to use condoms in the next three months'.

Jemmott and Jemmott III's study is an example of how a conceptual framework can be used optimally to guide every step of the process in quantitative research. It also makes a direct contribution to the body of knowledge by testing the theory itself.

CONCEPTUAL FRAMEWORKS IN QUALITATIVE RESEARCH

As explained earlier, qualitative research adopts the inductive approach. Therefore, conceptual frameworks have functions different from those in quantitative research. Researchers aim to develop their own concepts and theories from the data. For example, in a study of 'adolescent girls' experience of witnessing marital violence', Bennett (1991) formulates the following seven themes out of the data: 'remembering', 'living from day to day', 'feeling the impact', 'escaping', 'understanding', 'coping' and 'resolving'. These themes represent a description of the experiences of these adolescents. Other researchers can thereafter use them as a conceptual framework in a quantitative study.

It is also possible to derive questions or hypotheses from a conceptual framework using a quantitative approach and then collect data using qualitative methods such as unstructured interviews. This type of study would combine quantitative and qualitative approaches.

Another way in which a conceptual framework can be useful in qualitative research is when the researcher collects data qualitatively and tries to discover whether they support or reject existing theories. For example, Samarel (1992) used a phenomenological approach to 'describe patients' experience of receiving therapeutic touch', and her 'findings were examined in the context of Martha Rogers' conceptual system' of unitary beings. The author states that 'no specific model or theory was used to guide the entire study'. Samarel (1992) concluded that 'the findings were not entirely consistent with Rogers' conceptual system'. Thus, the findings of qualitative studies can be discussed in the context of existing theories.

The function of the inductive process in qualitative research is summed up by Morse (1992), who states:

> the inductive process of qualitative methods provides a powerful means for us to develop and to modify theory, to examine the conceptual basis of our discipline as well as our own beliefs, and to (cautiously) move the discipline forward. Because in qualitative research theory is developed from data (rather than from the library) and is verified, it is usually quite solid.

Sometimes, it is even surprising as new directions are identified and old concepts challenged.

NURSING THEORIES VERSUS OTHER THEORIES AS FRAMEWORKS FOR NURSING RESEARCH

The need to develop a body of knowledge specific to nursing has prompted the debate about whether nurse researchers should use nursing theories as frameworks for research or whether they should continue to import theories from other disciplines. The first view is illustrated by Michell and Cody (1993), who propose that:

> if nurses do commit to expand nursing's knowledge, then research requires a nursing framework that can appropriately specify the entire research process, including interpretation of findings. Interpreting research findings from within the bio-psycho-social tradition of borrowed theory will not contribute to the advancement of the discipline.

The second view is held by those who see theories from other disciplines as enriching the practice of nursing and contributing to the accumulation of nursing knowledge. This is expressed by Levine (1995):

> It is the marvellous complexity of the human condition that makes nursing such an exciting enterprise. It is not enough to know only 'physiology, psychology, sociology and education' in order to understand the patient. In confronting the wholeness of the individual, the more that can be known about each the better the understanding of the nursing task. There is a rich reservoir of knowledge in the many disciplines that contribute to understanding human life.

Levine (1995) also points out there is not a 'nursing theory which does not have a debt to the adjunctive disciplines, even those that claim otherwise'.

Some studies use a nursing and a non-nursing conceptual framework, as in Harrison *et al.*'s (1990) research on 'the effects of early parent touch on preterm infants' heart rates and arterial oxygen saturation levels'. As they explain:

> The study was based on a conceptual framework for analysing the meaning of touch that was developed by Weiss (1979)... Roy's (1984) adaptation model provided nursing conceptual framework for this study.

In an analysis of 720 research papers published during 1977–86, Moody *et al.* (1988) found the use of nursing theories in research increased from 8 per cent in 1977–81 to 13 per cent in 1982–86. Spearman *et al.* (1993) also reviewed all research articles in five major journals in the years 1986–91 to elucidate the degree to which Orem's self-care model was being empirically tested. Of the 31 studies they identified, only 4 (13 per cent) met the criteria of 'appropriately testing the theory'.

EVALUATING THE USE OF CONCEPTUAL FRAMEWORKS IN RESEARCH

You can start this exercise by identifying the links that the researcher makes with previous knowledge. This may not be made explicit, as explained earlier. If previous knowledge is used, you can find out whether or not reference is made to conceptual definitions, theories, models, research findings or other material. In some cases, the researcher may refer to some or all of these in the same study. More important, however, is how researchers use previous knowledge to guide their study. It often happens that one or more theories or research findings are mentioned without any indication of how (if at all) they are integrated in the study. For example, there may be no indication of how the research questions were derived. In some cases, a theory is mentioned to embellish the study and raise its 'academic status' without any intention of integrating it into the study.

When research findings, conceptual definitions or theories are used to underpin a study, the researcher must justify her choice. There is sometimes more than one theory to explain the same phenomenon. For example, researchers have a choice between the health belief model and the theory of reasoned action to explain patient compliance with health advice. Similarly, if there is more than one conceptual definition of 'stress', why does the researcher choose one as opposed to another? The choice must be objective and appropriate.

To justify the claim that a conceptual framework underpins a particular study, the framework must, as explained earlier, guide every stage of the research process from the literature review to the analysis of data. You must therefore find out how the framework is reflected in the research questions or hypotheses and in the data collection and analysis methods.

The study must also 'feed back' to the conceptual framework on which it is based if it is to contribute to knowledge in general. You should look for discussions on how the current findings relate to the conceptual framework or other theories (even when these were not discussed earlier in the literature review). Unfortunately, this is not a frequent practice among researchers. As Downs (1994) notes, from her experience as the editor of the journal *Nursing Research*:

> Once a theoretical statement has been made, it is never referred to again. The discussion of the findings may go on at some length, but not even a tip of the hat is made to what presumably formed the basis for the work.

An example of a study in which the research findings are discussed in relation to the theoretical framework is by Kenney (1992) on 'the consumer's views of health'. The theoretical framework was based on the work of Smith (1981), Laffrey (1986) and Woods *et al.* (1988). In her discussion, Kenney shows how the findings supported some claims and questioned others. She concludes that the findings from her study 'provide some support for each of Smith's levels independently, but do not support the premise of an exclusive hierarchy model of health'.

To contribute fully to existing knowledge, nurse researchers must, on the basis of their findings, make clinical, methodological and theoretical recommendations.

SUMMARY AND CONCLUSION

In this chapter, we have explored the meaning, types, levels and functions of theories. The relationship between knowledge, theory, practice and research has been further examined. We have also looked at some examples of how researchers make use of previous knowledge, especially research findings and theories, to underpin their quantitative studies. Those adopting a qualitative approach choose not to be influenced by existing knowledge but instead aim to generate their own concepts and theories. Nevertheless, they can still discuss their findings in the context of existing theories and research findings.

Not all research studies have an identified conceptual framework, and not all researchers believe they need one. For the frontier of knowledge to be pushed back, researchers must not only make use of what is already known, but also test it in practice. This deductive process, however, must not be at the expense of the efforts of others who seek to increase our understanding of phenomena by searching for new and fresh perspectives.

REFERENCES

Ajzen I and Fishbein M (1980) *Understanding Attitudes and Predicting Social Behavior*. Englewood Cliffs, NJ: Prentice Hall.

Banyard P and Hayes N (1994) *Psychology: Theory and Application*. London: Chapman & Hall.

Bennett L (1991) Adolescent girls' experience of witnessing marital violence: a phenomenological study. *Journal of Advanced Nursing*, **16**:431–8.

Billings J R (1995) Bonding theory – tying mothers in knots? A critical review of the application of a theory to nursing. *Journal of Clinical Nursing*, **4**:207–11.

Blue C L (1995) The predictive capacity of the Theory of Reasoned Action and the Theory of Planned Behavior in Exercise Research. An integrated literature review. *Research in Nursing and Health*, **13**:421–8.

Bury J (1986) Teenage and contraception. *British Journal of Family Planning*, **12**:11–14.

Downs F S (1994) Hitching the research wagon to theory. *Nursing Research*, **43**(4):195.

Fawcett J and Downs F S (1992) *The Relationship of Theory and Research*. California: Sage.

George J B (1985) *Nursing Theories – The Base for Professional Nursing Practice*. Englewood Cliffs, NJ: Prentice Hall.

Glaser B and Strauss A (1967) *The Discovery of Grounded Theory*. Chicago: Aldine.

Gröer M W, Thomas S P and Shoffner D (1992) Adolescent stress and coping: a longitudinal study. *Research in Nursing and Health*, **15**:209–17.

Hammersely M (1990) What's wrong with ethnography? The myth of theoretical description. *Sociology*, **24**:597–615.

Harrison L L, Leeper J D and Yoon M (1990) Effects of early parent touch on preterm infants' heart rates and arterial oxygen saturation levels. *Journal of Advanced Nursing*, **15**:877–85.

Homans G C (1967) *The Nature of Social Science*. New York: Harcourt and Brace.

Jemmott L S and Jemmott J B III (1991) Applying the Theory of Reasoned Action to Aids risk behaviour: condom use among black women. *Nursing Research*, **40**(4):228–34.

Kenney J W (1992) The consumer's views of health. *Journal of Advanced Nursing*, **17**:829–34.

Kerlinger F N (1986) *Foundations of Behavioral Research*, 3rd edn. New York: Holt, Rinehart & Winston.

Klaus M H and Kennell J H (1976) *Maternal Infant Bonding*, St Louis: C V Mosby.

Laffrey S C (1986) Development of a health conception scale. *Research in Nursing and Health*, **9**(2):107–11.

Layder D (1993) *New Strategies in Social Research*. Cambridge: Polity Press.

Levine M E (1995) The rhetoric of nursing theory. *Image: Journal of Nursing Scholarship*, **27**(1):11–14.

Merton R (1967) *On Theoretical Sociology*. New York: Free Press.

Mitchell G J and Cody W K (1993) The role of theory in qualitative research. *Nursing Science Quarterly*, **6**(4):170–8.

Moody L E (1990) *Advancing Nursing Science Through Research*. California: Sage.

Moody L E, Wilson M E, Smyth K *et al.* (1988) Analysis of a decade of nursing practice research: 1977–1986. *Nursing Research*, **37**(6):374–9.

Morse J (1992) The power of induction (editorial). *Qualitative Health Research*, **2**(1):3–6.

Rosenstock I M (1974) The Health Belief Model and preventive health behavior. *Health Education Monographs*, **2**:354–86.

Roy S C (1984) *Introduction to Nursing: An Adaptation Model*, 2nd edn. Englewood Cliffs, NJ: Prentice Hall.

Russell L (1996) Knowledge and practice in pressure area care. *Professional Nurse*, **11**(5):301–6.

Samarel N (1992) The experience of receiving therapeutic touch. *Journal of Advanced Nursing*, **17**:651–7.

Skinner B F (1938) *The Behavior of Organisms*. New York: Appleton-Century-Crofts.

Smith J A (1981) The idea of health: a philosophical enquiry. *Advances in Nursing Science*, **3**(3):43–50.

Spearman S A, Duldt B W and Brown S (1993) Research testing theory: a selective review of Orem's self-care theory, 1986–1991. *Journal of Advanced Nursing*, **18**:1626–31.

Stevens B J (1984) *Nursing Theory: Analysis, Application and Evaluation*, 2nd edn. Boston: Little, Brown.

Thuen F and Rise J (1994) Young adolescents' intention to use seat belts: the role of attitudinal and normative beliefs. *Health Education Research*, **9**(2):215–23.

Torrence C (1983) *Pressure Sores: Aetiology, Treatment and Prevention*. Beckenham: Croom Helm.

Walker L O and Avant K C (1988) *Strategies for Theory Construction in Nursing*. Connecticut: Appleton & Lange.

Waltz C F, Strickland O L and Lenz E R (1991) *Measurement in Nursing Research*, 2nd edn. Philadelphia: F A Davis.

Weiss S (1979) The language of touch. *Nursing Research*, **28**:76–80.

Whitney J D, Stotts N A and Goodson W H III (1995) Effects of dynamic exercise on subcutaneous oxygen tension and temperature. *Research in Nursing and Health*, **18**:97–104.

Woods N F, Laffrey S, Duffy M *et al.* (1988) Being healthy: women's images. *Advances in Nursing Science*, **11**(1):36–46.

Woodward V M (1995) Psychosocial factors influencing teenage sexual activity, use of contraception and unplanned pregnancy. *Midwifery*, **11**:210–16.

WHO (World Health Organisation) (1946) *Constitution*. Geneva: WHO.

Wyper M A (1990) Breast self-examination and the Health Belief Model: variations on a theme. *Research in Nursing and Health*, **13**:421–8.

7 Research Questions and Operational Definitions

Questions are at the heart of all research and the nature and quality of the evidence depends largely on how the question is asked. Information may be the starting point but understanding must be the goal. (Lydeard, 1991)

Introduction

The formulation of research questions is fundamental to the research process. It helps the researcher to clarify in her mind at least those questions which need to be answered. These can be formulated in a variety of formats, which often reflect the type of research carried out and the personal preference of individual researchers. Additionally, the terms and concepts used by the researcher must be defined in ways that can be understood by others who read the article or report. This chapter will help you to understand this important stage of the research process.

Formulating Research Questions

Research starts with a problem, which is often broad and multifaceted. For example, if there is an increase in the incidence of pressure sores on a particular ward, the nurse researcher faced with this problem may ask several questions, such as:

- Is there a relationship between nursing care and the incidence of pressure sores?
- Is there a policy on the prevention and treatment of pressure sores?
- Is this policy effective?
- How does the current prevention practice compare with a new form of practice on another ward with a similar group of patients?
- Do nurses have the necessary knowledge and skills to prevent and treat pressure sores?

It is not possible, especially in a small project, to address all these issues. The researcher may have to settle for one or two of these questions and focus on them. The literature review can play an important part in narrowing the problem down to manageable proportions. By reviewing what has been written on the topic and how others have approached similar studies, the researcher is more informed of what needs to be done.

122

The final choice of which aspect of the problem to focus upon depends on a number of factors, including the researcher's skills and interest, the lack of research on this particular topic and available resources.

The next step in quantitative research is for the researcher to state clearly what the purpose of the study is.

Purpose of the study

In most research articles or reports, the purpose or aim of the study is formulated so that readers are clear about what is being researched. Although the purpose of most research is ultimately to improve practice, the purpose of a study, in research terms, relates to the particular question(s) for which data can be collected. For example, the purpose of the above study could be 'to find out whether there is a relationship between nursing care and the incidence of pressure sores' on that particular ward. The long-term goal of a study may be to improve a particular practice, but the latter depends on more than research findings.

More often than not, the purpose of a study is stated earlier on in the article, but when this does not happen readers sometimes have to rummage through and look for it. RE 6 shows how some researchers have formulated the purpose of their study. As can be seen from these examples, the 'purpose' is itself broad and needs further explanation of how it is to be achieved. The purpose or main research question should be further subdivided into specific questions, objectives or hypotheses.

Questions

Research is about finding answers, and in order to do so questions must be posed. The purpose of a study is usually formulated as a statement which begs many questions. For example, in the work by Bullock and Pridham (1988) (see RE 6), the purpose of the study was further broken down into four specific questions:

1. What sources of information did mothers find helpful in building confidence or uncertainty regarding care for their young infants?
2. How did the sources change as the infants grew older and mothers became more experienced?
3. To what extent were the sources of information that contributed to confidence similar to or different from the sources that destroyed confidence?
4. How were the sources of confidence or uncertainty related to the mother's perception of competence in problem-solving issues of infant care?

RESEARCH EXAMPLE 6   **Examples of study purpose**

1.   Vaughan J A (1990) *Student nurse attitudes to teaching/learning methods*

The main purpose of the research was to find out the attitudes of student nurses towards a defined number of teaching/learning methods. The research was also concerned with assessing whether there was an association between students' expressed attitudes and the following variables: gender, age, the type of training the students were engaged in, the date training started, academic qualifications, parental occupation and training school.

2.   Bullock C B and Pridham K F (1988) *Sources of maternal confidence and uncertainty and perceptions of problem-solving competence*

This study explored the type of information on which maternal confidence is based and examined its relationship to perceived competence in problem-solving issues in infant care.

3.   Baillie L (1994) *Nurse teachers' feelings about participating in clinical practice: an exploratory study*

The aim of this small study was to explore nurse teachers' feelings about participating in clinical practice.

Comments

1.   These three examples show the different ways in which the purpose of the research can be expressed.
2.   In Vaughan's study, the author makes a distinction between the 'main' purpose and other aims.
3.   In Baillie's study, the term 'aim' is used in the abstract of the article, while in the text it is stated as the 'purpose'.
4.   The title may sometimes reflect the purpose of the study.
5.   A good abstract or summary should state the purpose or aim briefly and succinctly.

By asking specific questions, the researcher has given more details about what the purpose of the study is. However, the above questions are not exactly or necessarily the questions that mothers in the study will be asked. These questions only provide a basis from which further and final questions can be formulated in order to construct the tool of data collection as, for example, a questionnaire. In the above study, the final questions to mothers included, among others, the following:

How skilled are you in solving baby-care problems?

What things are most likely to make you feel confident regarding the care of your baby?

How well do you plan or think through how to deal with a concern? (Bullock and Pridham, 1988)

The broad research questions that emerge out of the purpose of the study must not be confused with detailed questions that the respondents are asked to answer.

Formulating the purpose of a study in the form of questions is useful in helping to clarify exactly what the study is about and sets the parameters of the research project. It focuses the researcher's and the reader's mind on the task in hand. In quantitative research, no deviation from the purpose of the study, as explained by the research questions, is possible.

Objectives

Another way of detailing the purpose of a study is in the form of objectives. Like research questions, objectives are set by the researcher in order to explain in some detail what the study is expected to achieve. Dealey (1991), who carried out a survey to find out 'the size of the pressure-sore problem in a teaching hospital', set the following eight objectives for her survey:

1. to identify the numbers of patients with pressure sores,
2. to identify the grade and position of the sores,
3. to discover the treatments being used,
4. to discover if the sores were improving, deteriorating or static,
5. to discover when the sores had occurred, i.e. prior to admission or on the ward,
6. to list any support systems in use,
7. to identify the degree of risk of pressure-sore development of all patients in the hospital, and
8. to identify any factors which are of particular relevance to tissue breakdown.

Dealey still had to ask specific questions in order to meet these objectives.

Hypotheses

Instead of asking questions or setting objectives, some researchers may go further in proposing what the answer to their main research question might be and then set out to look for evidence to support or reject their 'hunch'. In everyday life, people make educated guesses as to why certain things or events happen. For example, the increase in crimes by children is often blamed on violent behaviour in TV programmes. Nurses hypothesise about the phenomena they deal with. For example, they may attribute the high incidence of pressure sores in obese patients to their weight, or blame constipation in elderly patients on their lack of exercise. Some of these guesses may be influenced by their beliefs and experiences, and what they have read or heard.

Researchers, too, make educated guesses about the phenomena they investigate. However, unlike other people, they have to collect data in order to support or reject them. By surmising that there may be a relationship between pressure sores and obesity, the researcher is putting forward a hypothesis. By its very nature, a hypothesis is a tentative statement since the researcher is merely making an assumption before the data are collected. A *hypothesis* can be defined as a tentative statement, in one sentence, about the relationship, if any, between two or more variables. A *variable* is anything that varies or can be varied. An example of a hypothesis is 'lack of exercise causes constipation in elderly patients'. To be complete and comprehensive, a hypothesis must include three components: the variables, the population and the relationship between variables.

Variables

In the above example, exercise and constipation are the two variables for which a relationship is stated. In this case, it is a causal relationship because one (exercise) is assumed to cause the other (constipation). The variable 'exercise' can be varied (changed): elderly patients can take more or less exercise. The other variable, 'constipation', may vary according to the presence or absence of exercise. The variable causing the change is referred to as the *independent* variable, and the one which is changed is known as the *dependent* variable. One way to remember which is which is to view the dependent variable as the one that depends on the other to be changed. These and other types of variables are further discussed in Chapter 9.

The population

For a hypothesis to be complete, the population to which the phenomenon is related must be stated. For example, in the above hypothesis, the population is elderly patients. At this stage of the research process, more information or a definition of elderly patients (i.e. the age group, the clinical area in which they are cared for or their gender) is not required, provided that readers are able to identify the population to whom the hypothesis applies.

Relationship between variables

A hypothesis is a statement that normally specifies the relationship between variables. This relationship can *positive, inverse* or of *difference*. Here are some examples:

- *Positive* – the more food people consume the more obese they become.
- *Inverse or negative* – the more information given to patients preoperatively, the less anxiety they experience postoperatively.
- *Difference* – patients who exercise during the day sleep longer at night than those who do not.

Hypotheses can be stated in at least three main formats: the *null* or *statistical* hypotheses, the *research* hypothesis and the *neutral* or *associate* hypothesis. In the null hypothesis, the researcher states that there is no relationship between the variables. An example of a null hypothesis is:

Lack of exercise does not cause constipation in elderly patients.

The null hypothesis is often the preferred format in research for statistical reasons. The researcher can collect data to find out the likelihood that this statement can be rejected or supported. The research hypothesis is more positive in that it states there is a relationship, be it positive or negative, between the variables. An example of a research hypothesis is:

Lack of exercise causes constipation in elderly patients.

The neutral or associative hypothesis may simply state that there is a relationship but does not speculate what it is, as for example in:

There is a relationship between lack of exercise and constipation among elderly patients.

The choice of format often depends on the researcher. The neutral or associative hypothesis is sometimes more of an exploratory nature. The researcher may decide simply to carry out a survey to find out whether or not there is an association or correlation between two variables such as exercise and constipation. If the data show that there is a positive relationship, a positive hypothesis can be formulated and thereafter tested in an experiment.

Hypotheses can also stipulate the relationships between more than two variables. These complex hypotheses are stated because, in real life, a number of factors or variables work together in order to produce an effect. Although it is common knowledge that high-fibre diets can prevent constipation, other factors such as mobility and fluid intake can also be implicated. By controlling mobility and fluid intake in an experiment focusing solely on fibre, the researcher creates an artificial situation. To make the experiment more like real life, the researcher may decide to study a number of variables at the same time. A hypothesis for this study may read as follows:

> Lack of dietary fibre and low fluid intake cause constipation among elderly patients.

The independent variables are dietary fibre and fluid intake, and the dependent variable is constipation.

Finally, a hypothesis is either supported or rejected but not 'proven', because there may be many reasons or factors other than the independent variable that account for the results (see Chapter 9). Research findings must always be treated with caution.

OPERATIONAL DEFINITIONS

In formulating questions, objectives or hypotheses, a number of concepts are used. The next step in the research process is for these concepts to be defined so that readers (fellow researchers, practitioners and others) may be aware of the precise meaning of these terms and for them to assess the validity and reliability of these definitions.

Ambiguities arise in the use of concepts used in everyday language. Such familiar terms as 'happiness', 'love', 'coping' or 'human rights' give rise to a multitude of definitions depending on, among others, the person's gender, social class, cultural background and experiences. A common and agreed understanding of these and other terms that we use can greatly enhance communication.

Operational definitions in nursing practice

In nursing practice, too, we use terms that may have different meanings for different nurses. For example, when describing a newly admitted patient as 'a huge lady' to a fellow nurse, the latter was surprised to find she was (as she perceived) of 'normal' size. Reynolds (1988, cited in Waltz *et al.*, 1991) found that 'although health was believed to hold a central position of importance' in nursing, 'there was little agreement on its meaning'. Nursing practice and nursing research abound with concepts that need to be defined in order to facilitate communication and understanding between nurses. Grant and Kinney (1991) give the example of the concept of 'sleep disturbance', which can potentially be broken down into a number of characteristics such as 'interrupted sleep, tiredness, difficulty in falling asleep, difficulty in remaining asleep, restlessness, early/late awakening, listlessness, slow reaction, dark circles under the eyes and frequent yawning'. The meaning of these characteristics, in turn, needs to be conveyed in ways which can be observed and assessed by practitioners. Thus 'tiredness' can be identified through ' verbal expressions of feelings of tiredness, weariness, or fatigue' and 'frequent yawning' when the patient opens her 'mouth wide with a deep inspiration at least three times during a half-hour interval' (Grant and Kinney, 1991). The process of communicating precisely the meaning of a concept so that it can be observed and recorded is called *operational definition*.

Operational definitions in nursing practice can help to improve nursing diagnosis and evaluation, avoid ambiguities and lead to consensus in the use of concepts.

Operational definitions in nursing research

In research, as in nursing practice, defining concepts requires two steps: conceptual definition (also called theoretical definition) and operational definition (Waltz *et al.*, 1991). Burns and Grove (1987) define a conceptual definition as 'a broad, abstract meaning of a concept'. According to them, 'this definition is derived from a theorist's definition of a concept is developed by the research though concept analysis'. In a study of 'patients' satisfaction with nurses' caring during hospitalisation', Larson and Ferketich (1993) conceptually defined 'caring' as 'intentional actions that convey physical care and emotional concern and promote a sense of safeness and security in another'.

As can be seen, the concept of 'care' is explained in terms of further concepts such as 'intentional actions' and 'security'. In itself, the conceptual definition does not explain how 'caring' is to be measured. It only describes what constitutes 'caring' from the researchers' perspective. Conceptual definitions are important, because it stands to reason that researchers must be clear about what they mean by the concepts or terms they use before setting out to measure or assess them. A conceptual definition of caring, like the one offered above by Larson and Ferketich (1993), guides the researchers to areas (such as 'physical care' and 'emotional concern') that can be covered in questionnaires or interviews. Usually, the conceptual definition is derived from the researcher's own experience and/or from the literature review. Waltz *et al.* (1991) explain that theoretical (conceptual) definitions 'vary considerably in complexity' and that 'they may be derived from common usage of a term, "borrowed" intact from a pre-existing theory, or synthesized on the basis of literature and/or observation in the clinical or field setting'.

The researcher should explain how the conceptual definition of concepts central to the study is arrived at. For example, in a study of job satisfaction of community psychiatric nurses, the concept of satisfaction must be defined. This could be borrowed from an existing theory on job satisfaction, such as the one put forward by Herzberg *et al.* (1959). They explained job satisfaction as having 'motivation' factors (achievement, recognition, work itself, responsibility and growth) and 'hygiene' factors (supervision, physical working conditions, interpersonal relations, benefits, management and job security). Alternatively, the researcher could review what is written on the topic, including research findings. She will then synthesise (put together) the material and arrive at her own definition of job satisfaction.

Although conceptual definitions can shed more light on the use and meaning of a particular concept, it is not yet an operational definition as it does not specify what must be done in order to measure or assess it. Grant and Kinney (1991) explain that:

> An operational definition assigns meaning to a concept by specifying the activities or procedures necessary for measurement. In essence, operational definitions describe what is measured and how it is measured.

An example of how a concept is operationally defined is in the study of 'the size of the pressure-sore problem in a teaching hospital' by Dealey (1991). In it she defines a pressure sore as:

> damage to the skin caused by pressure, shear or friction or a combination of any of these.

As there are different types of pressure sores, she classifies them into five grades and defines each grade as follows:

- *Grade 1:* redness which does not fade and blanches under light pressure.
- *Grade 2:* redness which does not blanch, blistering or superficial break in the skin.
- *Grade 3:* break in the skin through to the dermis.
- *Grade 4:* sore down to the subcuticular layer.
- *Grade 5:* sore extends to other tissue, e.g. muscle, tendon or bone.

These operational definitions provide fairly clear details of how pressure sores were observed and recorded in the above study.

Some of the variables in the research questions, objectives or hypotheses are more easily operationally defined than others. For example, in a study by Campbell *et al.* (1994) of 'learning to nurse in the clinical setting', the following operational definitions were offered for the terms 'student', 'clinical instructor' and 'clinical setting':

Student:	a nursing student enrolled in any of years 1 to 4 of a baccalaureate nursing programme in the faculty of nursing of a large western Canadian University.
Clinical instructor:	a registered nurse with university preparation hired by the Faculty of nursing to supervise students in the clinical setting as they provide patient care.
Clinical setting:	a hospital or community agency where students have access to patients/clients in order to provide care.

Other concepts, however, are more difficult to define. Imagine that you are asked to operationalise (another term for 'operationally define') such concepts as 'job performance', 'job-related stress', 'social support', 'loneliness in adolescents' or 'level of functioning'. Do not despair. Researchers who set out to measure the above concepts have turned to tools developed for this purpose. For example, 'job performance' can be measured by the 'Six Dimension Scale of Nursing Performance' (Schwirian, 1978) and 'social support' by the 'Personal Resource Questionnaire' (Brandt and Wienert, 1981). Ready-made tools are not always available, and researchers have to offer their own operational definitions. RE 7 shows how the 'level of functioning' of oxygen-dependent patients with chronic obstructive pulmonary disease was operationalised.

In quantitative research, the purpose of operational definitions is to facilitate data collection on the concept being studied or measured. Such data can be objective or subjective. Taking the temperature using a thermometer is an example of objective data, and asking patients to report whether they feel tired produces subjective data because it involves a personal (hence subjective) judgement. Thus quantitative researchers collect both objective and subjective data.

EVALUATING OPERATIONAL DEFINITIONS

There are a number of criteria that can be used to evaluate the efficacy of operational definitions. The main ones (adapted from a list from Waltz *et al.*, 1991) include clarity, precision, validity, reliability and agreement/consensus.

Clarity

If the operational definition is not clear, it cannot be put into practice. The process of operational definition is precisely to reduce a complex or abstract concept into simple instructions that can be understood in the same way by everyone. Hall and Lanig (1993) gave the following definitions of spiritual care, spiritual activities, integration and comfort in their study of 'spiritual caring behaviours as reported by Christian nurses'. As they explained:

> The investigators defined spiritual care as those activities the nurse might use to meet perceived spiritual needs. The behaviors of talking about spiritual concerns, praying, and reading Scripture were selected as the most common spiritual activities that a nurse might use with a person to demonstrate care. Integration was defined as the harmonizing and inclusion of personal spiritual values into regular nursing activities. Comfort was defined as the degree of ease, readiness, and/or spontaneity the nurse experienced during these times.

While most of this is fairly clear, new concepts such as 'harmonising', 'spiritual values' and 'degree of spontaneity' are themselves abstract. To be fair, these researchers give an account of the questions they asked in the questionnaire they designed, thereby clarifying what they actually measured.

Precision

Operational definitions must be as precise as possible, so that a degree of consistency is achieved when put into practice. For example H S Wilson (1989), in a study of 'family caregiving for a relative with Alzheimer's dementia: coping with negative choices', defined a 'family caregiver' as:

> a member of the patient's informal support system (family/friend) who: (a) carried primary responsibility for providing a range of care to the patient at home, (b) was identified by a referral source as having ongoing responsibility for the patient's care, (c) was not financially reimbursed for caregiving activities, and (d) had been a caregiver for a *minimum* of 6 weeks not more than 3 months prior to the interview.

This can be compared with the definition of 'chief carer' in a study by Brocklehurst *et al.* (1981) on 'social effects of stroke', which read as follows:

> the person most totally involved in looking after the patient (if the patient was at home) or who seemed to be the person most likely to be involved in home care should the patient leave hospital in future.

The second definition may still serve the purpose of the study. However, by being precise and as detailed as possible, operational definitions offer readers a chance to compare whether the population in the study is similar to their own client groups, thereby increasing the applicability of the findings to their own settings.

RESEARCH EXAMPLE 7

Lee *et al.* (1991)
Effects of psychological well-being, physical status and social support on oxygen-dependent COPD (chronic obstructive pulmonary disease) patients' level of functioning

---

An example of operational definition:

In this study, the level of functioning was measured by an existing tool. As Lee *et al.* explain:

> The Sickness Impact Profile (SIP) (Gilson *et al.*, 1975) was used to measure level of functioning. It is a behaviorally based outcome measure that assesses the changes in usual activities and relationships individuals experience related to their health. The SIP consists of 136 quantitative statements that cover 12 categories: ambulation, mobility, body care and movement, social interaction, communication, alertness behavior, emotional behavior, sleep and rest, eating, home management, work, and recreation and pastimes. This is a scaled instrument with each item weighted to reflect the severity of disruption it represents in carrying out daily activities. To score each category, the scale values for the item checked within the category are summed and divided by the total possible score for that category. An overall score is obtained by ignoring the categories, summing the values of all items checked, and dividing by the total score possible on the scale.

Comments
1. The authors choose not to offer their own operational definition of 'level of functioning' and, in using Gilson *et al.*'s (1975) tool (the SIP), they agree with how the latter defined the concept. To construct such a tool, Gilson *et al.* defined 'level of functioning' as having 12 categories of daily activity (see above).
2. According to Grant and Kinney (1991), operational definitions in essence 'describe what is measured and how it is measured'. The SIP not only describes but also measures the level of functioning. By rating the items on a scale (according to how much or how little the activities are disrupted), the level of functioning is measured.

Validity

To be valid, the operational definition must represent what it is supposed to represent. There is the danger in translating a broad conceptual definition into a number of constituent parts that may not represent the concept being defined. One can ask whether, in fact, when a researcher sets out to measure a particular concept, she actually measures that concept or something else. As J Wilson (1989) explains:

> there is a logical gap between the concept with which the researcher begins and the subsequent research. To take an absurd (but, believe it or not, real life) example, researchers interested in what makes happy marriages decided to assess a marriage as happy if the partners called each other 'darling' more than a certain number of times a day. As many married couples know, one can say 'darling!' *con amore*, or through clenched teeth: as a candidate for a reasonable way of verifying, or explicating the concept 'happily married', this is a non-starter.

One of the common ways of operationalising such conditions as schizophrenia or depression is to rely on medical diagnosis. Although it saves the researcher the effort of providing her own definitions, using medical diagnoses as operational definitions is not without problems. If, in a study measuring the 'level of social support available to ME sufferers, the latter are defined as persons diagnosed by their general practitioner's as having ME', it is possible that some general practitioners may overdiagnose, underdiagnose or misdiagnose ME. Some people with ME may not even have consulted a general practitioner anyway. Therefore, in some instances, the validity of using medical diagnoses as operational definitions is questionable.

Another aspect of the validity of an operational definition is its appropriateness for the specific population for whom it is formulated. Concepts may have different meanings for different groups due to class, cultural, geographical, gender, age and social differences. Such a concept as 'touch' or 'bereavement' can be manifested differently in different cultures or even according to gender. Grant and Kinney (1991) explain that:

> although it may be appropriate to assess tiredness in adults who have a *sleep pattern disturbance* by asking whether they feel tired, weary, or fatigued, it would not be appropriate to use this method with infants or very small children. However, tiredness potentially could be measured in a population of 2–4-year-olds by focusing on behaviours such as rubbing or closing eyes frequently, irritability, crying, or holding a favourite object such as a blanket or teddy bear.

Reliability

The question to ask about the reliability of an operational definition is whether it will be consistently interpreted (in the same way) by all those who have to use it. Sometimes more than one researcher carries out observations in the same study; they must be able to interpret operational definitions in the same way. In the above example of a study on pressure sores, Dealey (1991) defined a grade 1 pressure sore as 'redness which does not fade and blanches under light pressure'. There are a number of concepts, such as 'redness', 'fading', 'blanching' and 'light pressure', which can be interpreted differently. Training and monitoring those who have to carry out observations can increase interrater reliability (i.e agreement between all those who make the observations and recordings). However, this is not always done. Dealey (1991) comments that a weakness in the methodology of her surveys was that 'there was no system for checking the accuracy of the information collected' and that 'previous studies had shown that there could be difficulty in recognizing grade 1 sores'. Misinterpretation of definitions could lead to the under- or overreporting of grade 1 sores, thereby giving inaccurate results on which subsequent decisions on nursing practice might depend. The fewer the number of persons required to make the observations, the more likely the findings are to be reliable. In Dealey's study, the nurses working on the wards or units carried out the observations.

It is not possible to offer absolutely perfect operational definitions, nor is it possible to offer further definitions of each of the terms that operational definitions generate. The problem with definitions is explained below by Bertrand Russell (1918):

> It is rather a curious fact in philosophy that the data which are undeniable to start with are always rather vague and ambiguous. You can, for instance, say: 'There are a number of people in this room at this moment'. This is obviously in some sense undeniable. But when you come to try and define what this room is, and what it is for a person to be in a room, and how you are going to distinguish one person from another, and so forth, you find that what you have said is most fearfully vague and that you really do not know what you meant.

Agreement/consensus

For some terms such as 'students' or 'patients', researchers can offer their own definitions to suit their studies. For example, some may define 'student nurses' as only those studying for a project 2000 diploma; others may also include undergraduate nursing students. No consensus or agreement is necessary for the term, provided that the researcher makes it very clear how the population is defined and that the definition is not absurd. On the other hand, there are concepts such as 'anxiety' or 'stress' for which there must be a consensus for their definitions, otherwise the validity of the findings will be seriously in question. To achieve consensus, operational definitions must reflect the concept in all its complexities and must be informed by the current state of knowledge on the concept. To gain consensus, researchers may provide a rationale for their definitions.

In some cases, researchers use operational definitions from previous studies. This allows for comparisons of the findings to be made and may lead to further refinement of the definition. The drawback of this is that sometimes no fresh contribution towards defining concepts is offered.

Operationalising concepts that figure in research questions, objectives or hypotheses is an important but often difficult part of the research process in quantitative research.

RESEARCH QUESTIONS AND OPERATIONAL DEFINITIONS IN QUALITATIVE RESEARCH

Different approaches within qualitative research mean that one cannot generalise about them. Purists, however, would see qualitative research as inductive rather than deductive. As the deductive approach involves the testing of hypotheses and theories, these have to be formulated and the variables they contain must be operationally defined. With the inductive approach, hypotheses and theories are expected to emerge out of the data. In phenomenological research, the researcher collects data from the respondent's perspective, and formulating questions or hypotheses at the start of the study is therefore not appropriate. However, in order to focus the study, some broad aims and even objectives are sometimes formulated. For example, in a qualitative study exploring 'the communication that takes place between nurses and patients whilst cancer chemotherapy is administered' (Dennison, 1995), the following objectives were set:

- to describe the content of the communication that took place between the nurses and the patients using meaningful categories;
- to describe the process of communication;
- to identify the environmental factors that may have influenced the conversations; and
- to identify those characteristics of the participants which may have influenced the conversations.

In a study of the problems experienced by patients moving from 'special hospital to regional secure unit', using a grounded theory approach (Skelly, 1994), the following aims were formulated:

1. to discover the extent of the problem of readmission within one special hospital;
2. to describe the nature of the problems experienced by this group of patients in RSUs; and
3. to generate a theory to explain why some patients experience 'failure'.

Although aims and objectives can be set, qualitative researchers tend to use these as broad areas on which to focus.

In some qualitative studies, however, broad questions are not set in advance, although researchers choose a starting point to focus on certain aspects of a phenomenon. During fieldwork (when researchers are out there collecting data), they may be more attracted to some aspects than others. In a study by Millman (1976) of the 'backrooms of American medicine', the broad area of study was 'features of the everyday world of the hospital that adversely affect the quality of patient care'. As she explains:

At first, my research interests were quite general. I soon found, however, that my attentions were drawn toward two intriguing issues. One was the variety of ways that doctors define, perceive and respond to medical mistakes – both their own mistakes and those made by hospital colleagues... The second major issue I came to focus on is the competing interests and conflicts among various groups of doctors within the hospital.

Millman (1976) carried out this ethnographic study of 'doctors and staff at work in a private, university-affiliated hospital'.

The ethnographic approach, which uses participant observation as its main data collection method (see Chapter 13), provides the opportunity for starting with a broad topic and thereafter focusing on particular aspect(s). In phenomenological studies, which use the unstructured interview method (see Chapter 12), it is also possible for researchers to select broad topic areas that they want to cover, but they may find their attention drawn to certain specific issues. Although the purpose of the study or broad questions are reported at the start of qualitative research articles, one cannot be certain that they were in fact the original aspects on which the researchers set out to focus.

In quantitative research, the measurement of concepts, whether in surveys or experiments, is central to the research process, and therefore these concepts require precise operational definitions. In qualitative research, the respondents' conceptualisation of the phenomenon is the essence of the study. Therefore, according to purists, operational definitions have no place in qualitative research. In fact, the researcher's conceptualisation of the problem is 'bracketed' to prevent it from influencing respondents. However, it is possible to find qualitative studies in which concepts are operationally defined. In a study on 'the process and consequences of institutionalising an elder', Dellasega and Mastrian (1995) offer these operational definitions of the following concepts: 'specific stressors', 'family members' and 'decision making/placement'. As they explain:

> In this study, *specific stressors* were defined as emotionally difficult events and feelings that were described by subjects in connection with the decision-making process, the placement process, or both. *Family members* were a spouse, a sibling, or a child of an elderly nursing home resident who was intimately involved in the decision-making or placement process and who consented to be interviewed. *Decision making/placement* was defined as considering alternatives and making choices that led to admission of an elder to a skilled nursing facility.

These definitions are broad and serve to explain the areas on which the researchers focused. They are not operational definitions in the 'quantitative' sense as they do not specify how these concepts are to be precisely measured; they merely delineate the areas of study.

In quantitative research, all questions must be decided in advance. This assumes that researchers know what questions to ask or the attributes of the phenomenon to be observed. However, it is possible that by just talking to or observing respondents, we come across new ways of thinking on certain topics. The view often taken by qualitative researchers is that not only do we not know the answers, but also we do not know what questions to ask.

Qualitative researchers work with the assumption that operational definitions fail to capture the essence of what is studied. For example, such a concept as 'intelligence' is reduced to being measured by a set of responses to a questionnaire called an intelligent quotient test. By defining the attributes or symptoms, we can miss the essence of the phenomena we seek to study.

The dilemma of operational definitions is aptly expressed by Bertrand Russell (1918):

> Everything is vague to a degree you do not realise till you have tried to make it precise, and everything precise is so remote from everything that we normally think, that you cannot for a moment suppose that is what we really mean when we say what we think.

CRITIQUING RESEARCH QUESTIONS AND OPERATIONAL DEFINITIONS

It is important to identify the purpose of the study, the research questions, objectives or hypotheses. Sometimes these are not reported under their respective headings; more often, readers have to tease out what they are. In one experimental study published in a reputable journal, the hypotheses were stated in the 'findings' sections. Readers cannot fully evaluate the methodology (and the literature review) that comes earlier in the article if they do not know what hypotheses or objectives are set.

Do not also be surprised if the objectives are presented as aims or the conceptual definitions as operational definitions, as frequently happens. Terminologies do not matter so long as researchers provide the relevant information clearly and precisely. It is essential for you to be clear about what questions are posed, how the variables are defined for the purpose of the study, what the researchers did to find answers to the questions and what the findings about these questions are. One useful exercise is to divide a page into three columns, and list the research questions in column 1, the method of data collection in column 2 and the findings in column 3. In this way, you can find out whether the purpose of the study, as expressed through research questions, objectives or hypotheses, has been achieved. It is not unusual to find that not all the research questions set at the beginning of an article are dealt with in the results and discussion sections. Sometimes new findings unrelated to the original research questions creep into the results and can surprise you.

To assess the value of operational definitions in quantitative research, you can use the five criteria discussed in this chapter: clarity, precision, validity, reliability and agreement/consensus. Although specific questions and operational definitions are not normally stated in qualitative research, the article or report must give a clear account of the broad area of study, the concepts investigated, the methods used and the findings.

SUMMARY AND CONCLUSION

In quantitative research, the formulation of the purpose of the study, research questions and operational definitions is a crucial part of the research process. These facilitate the readers' understanding of the nature and magnitude of the task undertaken by the research. They inform readers of what the study is about, and what is being measured, assessed or explored and how. Research is a private enterprise that is made public for it to contribute to existing knowledge. Reporting research questions and operational definitions facilitates the communication between researchers and those who subsequently read and use the report.

Most qualitative researchers only formulate broad questions or identify a broad area of study. During the study, questions emerge as the researcher learns more about the area and decides what to focus on. Concepts constructed from the data can thereafter be operationalised.

REFERENCES

Baillie L (1994) Nurse teachers' feelings about participating in clinical practice: an exploratory study. *Journal of Advanced Nursing*, **20**:150–9.

Brandt P A and Wienert C (1981) The personal resource questionnaire – a social support measure. *Nursing Research*, **30**:277–80.

Brocklehurst J C, Morris P, Andrews K, Richards B and Laycock P (1981) Social effects of stroke. *Social Science and Medicine*, **15A**:35–9.

Bullock C B and Pridham K F (1988) Sources of maternal confidence and uncertainty and perceptions of problem-solving competence. *Journal of Advanced Nursing*, **13**:321–9.

Burns N and Grove S K (1987) *The Practice of Nursing Research: Conduct, Critique and Utilization*. Philadelphia: W B Saunders.

Campbell I E, Larrivee L, Field P A, Day R A and Reutter L (1994) Learning to nurse in the clinical setting. *Journal of Advanced Nursing*, **20**:1125–31.

Dealey C (1991) The size of the pressure-sore problem in a teaching hospital. *Journal of Advanced Nursing*, **16**:663–70.

Dellasega C and Mastrian K (1995) The process and consequences of institutionalizing an elder. *Western Journal of Nursing Research*, **17**(2):123–40.

Dennison S (1995) An exploration of the communication that takes place between nurses and patients whilst cancer chemotherapy is administered. *Journal of Clinical Nursing*, **4**:227–33.

Gilson B S, Gilson J S, Bergner M *et al.* (1975) The sickness impact profile: development of an outcome measure of health care. *American Journal of Public Health*, **65**:1304–10.

Grant J S and Kinney M R (1991) The need for operational definitions for defining characteristics. *Nursing Diagnosis*, **2**(4):181–5.

Hall C and Lanig H (1993) Spiritual caring behaviors as reported by Christian nurses. *Western Journal of Nursing Research*, **15**(6):730–41.

Herzberg F, Mausner B and Snyderman B B (1959) *The Motivation to Work*. New York: John Wiley & Sons.

Larson P J and Ferketich S L (1993) Patients' satisfaction with nurses' caring during hospitalization. *Western Journal of Nursing Research*, **15**(6):690–707.

Lee R N F, Graydon J E and Ross E (1991) Effects of psychological well-being, physical status, and social support on oxygen-dependent COPD patients' level of functioning. *Research in Nursing and Health*, **14**:323–8.

Millman M (1976) *The Unkindest Cut*. New York: Morrow Quill.

Reynolds C L (1988) The measurement of health in nursing research. *Advances in Nursing Science*, **10**(4):32–7.

Russell B (1918) The philosophy of logical atomism. In Marsh R C (ed.) (1971) *Bertrand Russell – Logic and Knowledge*. London: George Allen & Unwin.

Schwirian P (1978) Evaluating the performance of nurses: a multi-dimensional approach. *Nursing Research*, **27**:347–51.

Skelly C (1994) From special hospital to regional secure unit: a qualitative study of the problems experienced by patients. *Journal of Advanced Nursing*, **20**:1056–63.

Vaughan J A (1990) Student nurse attitudes to teaching/learning methods. *Journal of Advanced Nursing*, **15**:925–33.

Waltz C F, Strickland O L and Lenz E R (1991) *Measurement in Nursing Research*, 2nd edn. Philadelphia: F A Davis.

Wilson H S (1989) Family caregiving for a relative with alzheimer's dementia: coping with negative choices. *Nursing Research*, **38**(2):947–58.

Wilson J (1989) Conceptual and empirical truth: some notes for researchers. *Educational Research*, **31**(3):176–80.

8 RESEARCH DESIGNS

INTRODUCTION

The next step in the research process after the literature review and the formulation of the research questions is the planning or designing of strategies for the collection and analysis of data. In practice, while the aims and objectives or hypotheses are being formulated, the researcher must also give prior thought to the possible design to be used to avoid setting unachievable objectives. The literature review should help the researcher to identify research designs and related issues in similar studies. Researchers have coined a number of terms to describe research designs in quantitative and qualitative research, with which you should become familiar if you are to fully understand the research process. Such terms as 'prospective', 'longitudinal', 'cross-sectional' or *ex post facto* may mean little at present; this chapter will explain these and other terminologies commonly used in order to enhance your interest in, and understanding of, research articles and reports.

RESEARCH DESIGN OR METHODOLOGY

The term 'research design' simply means a plan that describes how, when and where data are to be collected and analysed. It is sometimes used interchangeably with the term 'methodology'. The design or methodology of a study comprises the following aspects:

- the approach (qualitative, quantitative or both, with or without a conceptual framework);
- the method(s) of data collection;
- the time, place and source of the data;
- the method of data analysis.

The design also describes how the respondents are approached, informed and recruited. Therefore the researcher must explain in the 'design', 'methodology' or 'procedure' section of the article how ethical approval, if necessary, was obtained, how access was negotiated, what guarantees of confidentiality and anonymity were given and how these were achieved. These are important considerations as they may affect the reliability and validity of the data. For example, in one study on 'burn-out among nurses in a "care of older people" setting', respondents were asked to write their name on the questionnaire. It is likely that many would not admit to feeling 'burnt-out' for fear of losing their jobs if their employers got access to these data. Thus the reliability of these responses could be seriously threatened.

Sometimes readers confuse the terms 'methodology' and 'methods'. As explained above, methodology is a broad term involving all the strategies, including method or methods of data collection, adopted by the researcher to answer the research questions or test the hypotheses. Methods of data collection are described and discussed in Chapters 11, 12 and 13.

SELECTING A DESIGN

In order to meet the aims and objectives of a study, researchers must select the most appropriate design. In practice, the selection of the design depends largely on the beliefs and values of the researcher (she may, for example, place particular value on the quantitative approach), the resources available (cost, time, expertise of the researcher), how accessible the respondents are and whether the research is ethically sound. Resources often influence the choice of questionnaires over interviews. While such practices may be acceptable, readers must bear in mind that there is no short cut to knowledge. Making compromises and selecting strategies other than the most appropriate has implications for the validity and reliability of the data.

LEVELS OF RESEARCH IN QUANTITATIVE STUDIES

To understand the main research designs, we must refer to the various levels of research. You will recall from Chapter 2 that the steps of the inductive process comprise the following: description, classification, correlation, causation, prediction and control. One can group these steps into three levels: descriptive, correlational and causal (see Chapter 6 for levels of theories). At the descriptive level, the research is aimed at describing phenomena about which little is known. From the data, patterns or trends may emerge and possible links between variables can be observed, but the emphasis is on the description of phenomena. Descriptive research can be quantitative (RE 8) or qualitative (RE 9) or a combination of the two.

RESEARCH **8** Roe et al. (1994)
EXAMPLE **Nursing treatment of patients with chronic leg ulcers in the community**

A quantitative descriptive study

This survey describes the practice of 146 community nurses for their nursing treatment of leg ulcers, 'in particular the range of dressings, topical applications and bandages they used and their underlying rationale for choice'.

Roe et al. also reported that data were collected by a questionnaire and included biographical details, the length of time they had been qualified and/or practising as a community nurse, and professional issues, which included evidence of further reading about leg ulcers and courses attended. Information on cleansing, dressing products and bandages was also collected.

Comments

1. Descriptive studies tend to collect a wide range of data on the phenomenon being surveyed, as shown above. In contrast, correlational studies focus on two or three variables, as do experiments.
2. This a quantitative study because a questionnaire is used to collect this information. An attempt is not made to obtain in-depth understanding of the practice of dressing leg ulcers, but only to have a detailed description of the nurses, their practices, and the equipment used. The data are also analysed and reported quantitatively as in the following examples:

   Eighty-four respondents (58%) included non-adherence as a feature they would look for in a wound dressing; 69 (48%) patient comfort; 47 (32%) absorbency and 24 (16%) non-allergenic properties

   and

   The more recently qualified nurses were also significantly more likely (n = 44; 52%) to use a semipermeable film than nurses who qualified before 1981) (n = 16; 27%) (95% CI from 10 to 40%; P< 0.01).

3. This type of descriptive study is useful in informing nurses and others about their practice. Practitioners and policy-makers can base their decisions on data collected systematically and rigorously and do not have to rely on casual observations or anecdotes.
4. Descriptive studies can generate ideas that can be tested in experiments. Roe et al. (1994), in their conclusions, suggest this course of action when they report that their 'research illustrates that there is variation in practice in the management of leg ulcers and there is still a paucity of well-controlled research into the different modes of treatment'.

<table>
<tr>
<td>RESEARCH
EXAMPLE</td>
<td>9</td>
<td>Bluff and Holloway (1994)
'They know best': women's perceptions of
midwifery care during labour and childbirth</td>
</tr>
</table>

A qualitative descriptive study

> The aims of the study were to examine women's experiences of their labour and the birth of their baby. The use of the qualitative method ensured that the search focused on the perspectives of the participants. The purposive sample consisted of 11 women volunteers in a maternity unit of a general hospital. Unstructured, tape-recorded interviews provided an opportunity for the informants to express their thoughts and feelings.

Bluff and Holloway also explained that the purpose of unstructured interviews in their study 'was to obtain information in the participants' own words, to gain a description of the situation and to elicit detail'.

Comments

1. No predetermined, structured or standardised tools were used to collect data in this study. Instead, respondents could freely talk about their experience. In-depth information was obtained by 'an occasional probe' such as 'can you tell me a little more about this?'
2. The purpose of this study was to describe the women's experiences and perceptions, rather than to seek experiences, nor to seek correlation, nor to study cause and effect between variables.
3. In contrast to the quantitative descriptive study in RE 8, data were reported verbatim (in the respondents' own words). Here is an example:

> They've got an awful lot of experience, they know what they are doing. They know better than someone who has not experienced birth before.

> Using the grounded theory method, themes were developed during the process of data analysis.

Correlational studies (see RE 10) seek deliberately to examine or explore links between variables. The purpose is often to develop hypotheses that can be tested later in experiments. Sometimes the term 'exploratory' is used to denote descriptive or correlational studies. To some extent, all research explores phenomena.

RESEARCH **10** O'Brien (1993)
EXAMPLE **Multiple sclerosis: the relationship among self-esteem, social support and coping behaviour**

A correlational study

This study examines the relationship of self-esteem and social support to problem-focused coping behaviour of 101 individuals with multiple sclerosis, a chronic progressive disease.

The following research questions were developed:

1. What is the relationship between self-esteem and problem-focused coping in individuals with multiple sclerosis?
2. What is the relationship between social support and problem-focused coping in individuals with multiple sclerosis?
3. Are self-esteem and social support, when combined, predictors of problem-focused coping in individuals with multiple sclerosis?

Comments

1. If little was known of either self-esteem, social support or the coping behaviour of people with multiple sclerosis, descriptive studies exploring and explaining what they are, would have been useful. Here the author goes a step further and wants to focus on the relationship between these variables. Presumably, previous descriptive studies or clinical observations have hinted at such relationships. Therefore to have a clear picture of how these variables are interrelated, the author surveys 101 individuals and carries out statistical tests on the data to find whether there is a *correlation* between them.
2. This is not an experiment because O'Brien does not introduce any intervention (independent variable) and measure the effects (on the dependent variable). She simply administers three questionnaires to people with multiple sclerosis as they go about their daily lives.
3. The results showed 'a significant relationship between self-esteem and problem-focused coping: a nonsignificant relationship between social support and problem-focused coping; and that self-esteem and social support taken together did not contribute significantly to problem-focused coping'. 'Significant' and 'nonsignificant' here refer to 'statistical significance'.

Causal or experimental research (see RE 11) is concerned with cause and effect. It sets out to confirm or reject links between variables.

These three levels are developmental stages in the study of phenomena. For example, a descriptive study of postoperative stress may reveal how people experience stress, what factors they perceive as causing or relieving their stress and how they cope with it. Such a study may also give an indication that patients who are given information prior to surgery are less stressed afterwards. A correlational study can be carried out to collect data specifically to examine the connection between the two variables of information and stress. A questionnaire may be administered to a large number of patients to find out whether there is a difference in the self-reported levels of postoperative stress between those who received information and those who did not. Establishing a relationship between variables through correlational studies does not necessarily mean that such a relationship exists. For example, a survey may reveal that information given prior to surgery did not show a difference in stress levels, postoperatively. Questions may be raised about the content, structure and delivery of such information, among other things.

RESEARCH EXAMPLE ▌▌ O'Sullivan and Jacobsen (1992)
A randomized trial of a health care program for first-time adolescent mothers and their infants

An experimental study

O'Sullivan and Jacobsen used an experimental design to test 'the effectiveness of a special health care program for adolescent mothers (17 years old or younger) and their infants'. They allocated 243 pairs of mothers and infants randomly to two groups: an experimental and a control group. The latter received routine care while the experimental group received routine care as well as the special programme, which included health teaching and visits by social workers, paediatricians and nurse practitioners. The special programme was expected to lead to fewer repeat pregnancies, more mothers returning to school, more up-to-date immunizations for the infants and a reduced use of emergency room for infant care, in the experimental group than in the control group.

Comments
1. O'Sullivan and Jacobsen carried out this experiment to find out the cause-and-effect relationship between a number of variables. The cause, introduced by them, was the special health care programme, and the effect was measured by the number of repeat pregnancies, the rate of the mothers' return to school, the rate of immunization and the use of emergency rooms.
2. Experimental studies sometimes build upon findings from previous studies. O'Sullivan (1991) found 'a high rate of missed appointments at a well-baby clinic, yet a high rate of emergency room use for the infants, sometimes for care that could have been provided at home, or by telephone, or by a less expensive clinic'. This descriptive study, no doubt, provided food for thought for the above experiment.

Although correlational studies may seek to establish links between variables, no firm conclusions can normally be drawn as, for example, in the above study the researcher had no control over the information given and had to rely retrospectively on respondents' reports. To be able to make more definite statements about the relationship between preoperative information and postoperative stress, an experimental design may be used, in which the researcher controls or manipulates the information given and measures the level of stress while trying to control for other factors that may influence postoperative stress.

Descriptive and correlational studies, perhaps the most common forms of research in nursing, are no less important or difficult than experimental ones. All research studies require rigour, and all have a contribution to make which can be assessed by the 'added understanding' they bring to the phenomenon being investigated. Although research is described here as having three neat, distinct levels, studies may in practice combine elements from the different levels. It is not unusual, therefore, to find descriptive studies that are also correlational.

TYPES OF RESEARCH DESIGN

There is no consensus among researchers on the classification of designs (Castles, 1987); what seems to emerge is that, broadly speaking, there are three types of design:

- experimental (including quasi-experimental)
- survey
- case study.

Experiments examine and establish causal links between variables. In its basic form, an *experiment* consists of a researcher introducing and manipulating a variable (for example information-giving prior to surgery) and measuring its effects, if any, on another variable (for example postoperative stress), while making sure that there is no interference from other variables (for example drug intake or information from other sources). In quasi-experiments, the researcher has less control over certain variables than in a true experiment. The next chapter will discuss experimental and quasi-experimental designs.

A *survey* is designed to obtain information from populations regarding the prevalence, distribution and interrelationship of variables within those populations (Polit and Hungler, 1995). As such, the survey is appropriate for descriptive and correlational studies. Surveys are generally associated with the collection of a wide range of data from large, representative samples. Sometimes the entire population is surveyed, as in the case of a census, or a representative sample may be drawn. According to Polit and Hungler (1995), the central focus of a survey is very often 'on what people do: how or what they eat, how they care for their health needs, their compliance in taking medications, what types of family-planning behaviors they engage in, and so forth'. The main methods of data collection in surveys are questionnaires and structured and semistructured interviews, although observations can also be used, as in the case of a survey on dressing practices or pressure sores. Survey methods are discussed in Chapters 11 and 12.

Surveys are also a choice design for correlational studies. As explained earlier, links between variables suggested by data from descriptive studies can be followed up in correlational studies. Unlike experimental designs, where the researcher introduces a variable and measures its effect on another variable, correlational studies using the survey design aim to establish links without introducing an intervention. A survey can be carried out to find whether or not there is a link between lung cancer and people who smoke. The survey may comprise a large number of smokers and non-smokers. Data may show that indeed those who smoke have a higher prevalence of lung cancer. In this case, the researcher did not introduce 'smoking' to a group of people, but simply investigated the link after the smoking had taken place. Such a design is also known as *ex post facto* or 'after the fact' (Kerlinger, 1973). In correlational studies, researchers commonly collect demographic details such as age, occupation, gender and educational background and seek to establish links between these and other characteristics of respondents, such as their beliefs and behaviours. It is easy to see how surveys are suitable for descriptive as well as for correlational studies.

Case studies focus on specific situations. Using this design, the researcher studies individuals, groups or specific phenomena. Creswell (1994) explains that, in case studies, the researcher 'explores a single entity or phenomenon ("the case") bounded by time and activity (a program, event, process, institution, or social group) and collects detailed information by using a variety of data collection procedures during a sustained period of time'.

The type of data produced is mainly descriptive, although attempts are made to find correlations between variables. As a design, it lends itself well to both quantitative and qualitative approaches. For example, a researcher may evaluate a particular health promotion programme or find reasons why some women do not comply with advice from midwives at an antenatal class using the quantitative approach. Another researcher may carry out an ethnographic study of patient–nurse interactions on a particular ward.

The cases on which researchers focus need not necessarily be unusual; they can, and often are, typical of others. Using the case study approach, data can be collected in the past, present or future. For example, a researcher may investigate the events that led to the closure of hospital X in 1980 by interviewing some of those who were involved in the closure and by studying newspaper and television reports of what happened. A researcher can also 'follow' a group of mothers from the time they give birth to 18 months afterwards, to find out about infant feeding practices. While surveys involve large populations and use samples for the purpose of generalising their findings, case studies tend to be more specific, in-depth and holistic. The emphasis is on understanding the particular case or group of people, although the data gathered may be useful to other similar cases.

Experiments, surveys and case studies broadly describe the main research designs in social, health and nursing research. There are also different types of experiment, survey and case study, as will be shown later in this and the next chapter. Not all research fits neatly into this classification, as, for example, the Delphi technique or methodological research such as meta-analysis (discussed below). The purpose of classi-fication, however crude, is to simplify things and thus facilitate understanding. It has few implications for the reliability and validity of the data if a survey is wrongly described as a case study. What is crucial is for researchers to explain the research process in detail for readers to understand what was done. However, confusion can be created if appropriate terminologies are not used.

DESIGNS IN QUALITATIVE RESEARCH

Qualitative researchers do not carry out experiments as they aim mostly to describe phenomena. They do not normally use the term 'survey' to describe their research, although they study people's beliefs, attitudes, intentions, and so on, mainly perhaps because of the survey's association with structured methods, such as questionnaires. Some may describe their designs as case studies. In general, they do not subscribe to these terms but instead describe their approach as ethnographic, phenomeno-logical or grounded theory, and they go on to explain what they do.

ETHNOGRAPHIC STUDIES

As explained in Chapter 2, ethnography is concerned with under-standing human behaviour in the cultural and social context in which it takes place. This means that the ethnographer has to spend some time in the company of those being studied. This is what is often referred to as 'field-work'. As Hammersley and Atkinson (1983) explain:

> The ethnographer participates, overtly or covertly, in people's lives for an extended period of time, watching what happens, listening to what is said, asking questions; in fact collecting whatever data are available to throw light on the issues with which he or she is concerned.

The purpose of participating is to obtain a holistic view of respondents' behaviour. The ethnographer can not only ask questions, but also observe and, to some extent, share some of the respondents' experiences. The researcher's aim is to understand the way in which people live from their point of view (Spradley, 1980). Observations and interviews are the two main data collection tools. Hughes (1992) points out that question-asking, however, does not stand alone as a primary data-gathering tool, and direct questions are often ancillary to participant observation. According to Hughes (1992), 'the researcher uses the senses – vision, hearing, touch, smell, taste – as much as cognition as primary data-gathering tools to characterize important physical and social features of a given field of human behavior'.

Data from other sources, such as overheard conversations, case notes and information on notice boards, are all part of data collection. For example, in a study of the effects of 12-hour shifts on nurses, the researcher can carry out participant observation (see Chapter 13) on a number of 12-hour shifts and is thus able to ask questions, observe nurses' behaviour in the ward, canteen and social club, and, to some extent, perhaps experience the fatigue and loss of concentration that nurses may also experience.

In ethnographic studies, researchers are supposed not to impose their own interpretations in their attempt to understand and explain respondents' behaviour. In practice, researchers, as anyone else, need a framework in order to make sense of phenomena; they can only use their experience to do this. What differentiates ethnography and the hypothetico-deductive approach of quantitative studies is that in the former, the researcher is prepared to look at phenomena through the lenses of respondents, whereas in the latter, the researcher sets out mainly to test out her ideas.

It is not possible to generalise from data analysis processes in qualitative research, largely because the researcher analyses data during data collection as well as thereafter. While fieldwork notes and transcriptions can be systematically analysed and described, what happens during the interaction between researcher and respondent is a unique process that is generally difficult to convey to readers. The best that researchers can do is to offer their thoughts and reflections on aspects they perceive as influencing data collection.

Ethnographic data analysis, therefore, involves the researcher's analysis and synthesis of data during interviews and observations. Categories, concepts, themes, patterns, hypotheses or theories that may emerge during the early part of data collection are constantly compared, reviewed and explored further. Fieldnotes provide additional opportunities to continue this process of making sense of respondents' behaviour.

A number of computer programmes, such as TAP (Text Analysis Package), QUALPRO and The Ethnogaph (see Tesch, 1990) have been developed to facilitate qualitative data analysis. The analysis of data from qualitative interviews and unstructured observations is further discussed in Chapters 12 and 13.

Some of the limitations with ethnographic studies include the possibility that the researcher may immerse herself in the particular culture she studies to the extent that she is unable to have an objective view of the situation even after the fieldwork has been completed. Another problem is that it is not possible for the ethnographer to be in all places at the same time. She thus needs to be very enterprising to observe and experience as much as possible. The large amount of data that ethnographic studies may generate can make data analysis a laborious, time-consuming and challenging task. There are also ethical implications in collecting data on or from people without their awareness and consent. These are discussed in Chapter 13. An account of an ethnographic study is given in RE 12.

PHENOMENOLOGICAL STUDIES

While ethnography has its roots in cultural anthropology, phenomenology, as explained in Chapter 2, is based on the philosophy of Husserl (1962). The researcher is interested in how respondents give meaning to their experience, in other words how they perceive their world. As Koch (1995) explains, 'one of Husserl's directives to phenomenology was that it should be a descriptive psychology, which would "return things to themselves" and to the essences that constitute the consciousness and perception of the human world'. Phenomenology, as a research method, is especially suited to the study of clients' experience of illness and the care they receive. The client-centred approach requires nurses to take the perception of each client into acocunt. According to Beck (1994), 'phenomenology affords nursing a new way to interpret the nature of consciousness and of an individual's involvement in the world'.

The primary tool of data collection in a phenomenological study is the interview, during which the researcher seeks to gain insight into how respondents make sense of their experiences. The emphasis is on allowing or facilitating respondents to talk freely about the topic, and questions are asked in an attempt to seek clarification, illustration or further exploration. As explained in Chapter 2, the phenomenological researcher tries to bracket her own presuppositions about the phenomenon under study.

RESEARCH EXAMPLE 12

MacKenzie (1992)
Learning from experience in the community: An ethnographic study

Below is the author's summary of the study:

> This study seeks to gain an understanding of the learning experiences of district nurse students in the learning environment of the community, and to examine learning in the practice setting from the perspective of the student. Since the research depends upon the changing and differing interpretations of the individuals involved in the natural setting of the community, an ethnographic approach has been adopted. The experiences of students are monitored throughout the taught practice element of the district nurse course in both inner city and rural/urban locations. Data, collected through interview and observations, are analysed in the context of theory relating to adult learning and learning from experience. Three major categories are identified. Examples for these categories are identified and discussed. The categories are sequential and represent the learning process experienced by the students in the practice setting as they learn to fit into a new environment, test out their own ideas and compare the unreality of college with the reality of practice. Attention is drawn to the difficulties for students of fitting into new settings and trying out change, to the detrimental effect on learning of rigid practice routines and to the powerlessness of community practice teachers to exert a major influence on the learning environment.

Comments

1. Emphasis is placed on not only obtaining the perspective of the students, but also the clinical environment in which they learn, as MacKenzie explains:

   > Negotiating roles and changing perspectives are part of a process of interaction and can only be fully understood by investigation in the natural setting or social context.

2. The main method of data collection in ethnography is participant observation. The act of participating gives opportunities for the researcher to have conversations with or 'interview' people as she interacts with them. As is the case here, interviews can also be formally arranged at other times. In this study, MacKenzie carried out interviews and observations that were recorded in fieldnotes (an important 'prop' in ethnographic studies). Being an observer means that the researcher does not have to rely solely on what respondents say. This is an advantage of the ethnographic approach in that the ethnographer has some first-hand experience of the cultural and social environment of the respondents.

3. There are a number of similarities between ethnography and the grounded theory method. For example, both seek to study people in the context of their interaction with the environment. The crucial difference lies in their purpose. In grounded theory research, the aim is to generate concepts, hypotheses and eventually theories. Apart from generating hypotheses and theories, it *is* possible in ethnography, having collected data to simply discuss them in the context of existing theories. In this study, the broad questions that students were asked were considered in the light of significant theoretical ideas from the literature of adult learning and district nurse education.

As with ethnographic studies, phenomenological data can be analysed by searching for themes, patterns or trends. Findings are often presented in the form of verbatim quotes from respondents. A number of authors (Vankaam, 1966; Colaizzi, 1978; Giorgi, 1985) have developed their own methods to describe phenomenological data. Beck (1994) points out that there are differences in their approaches and disagreements over how data should be processed. According to her:

> Colaizzi is the only one who calls for a final validation to be achieved by returning to each participant. Only Vankaam requires intersubjective agreement be reached with other expert judges. In contrast to both of these phenomenological methods, Giorgi's analysis relies solely on the researcher.

Beck (1994) was referring to ways in which these phenomenologists validated the data they had collected. These disagreements suggest that there are different phenomenological methods. Colaizzi, Giorgi and Vankaam operate within the discipline of psychology, which explains why the focus is on individual's perceptions, while ethnography is the domain of anthropologists, who place emphasis on culture. While the subject of enquiry is the 'phenomenon', it is the standpoint from which they operate that distinguishes phenomenology from ethnography.

Many of the limitations of phenomenological studies are the same as those of qualitative approaches in general. Bracketing is not easy to achieve as it is not possible for people to suspend totally their presuppositions nor to account for all of them, especially if they are not aware that they are using them. The conduct of interviews requires skill and sensitivity, while the analysis of data requires a detached approach (see Chapter 12). See RE 13 for an example of a phenomenological study.

GROUNDED THEORY

The grounded theory method shares with ethnography and phenomenology the study of phenomena from the viewpoint of the respondents. As explained in Chapter 2, grounded theory adopts the inductive approach by relying on data in order to formulate hypotheses and theories. Essentially, grounded theory consists of a set of procedures that guide researchers using this approach. These procedures pertain mostly to the analysis of data and consist of three interrelated tasks as follows: organising information and identifying patterns, developing ideas, and drawing and veryfying conclusions (Singleton *et al.*, 1993). However, the data analysis process in grounded theory studies is ongoing, in that emerging hypotheses are constantly being reviewed during data collection.

Ericksen and Henderson (1992)
Witnessing family violence: the children's experience

A phenomenological study

A phenomenological study was conducted in order to describe the experience of children as they accompany their mothers who are leaving abusive relationships. Thirteen children were interviewed. The children describe their experience as having three components: living with violence, living in transition and living with Mom.

Comments

1. This study used a phenomenological approach, according to the authors, because data about these children's needs and behaviours had previously been collected in two ways: parental report and professional observation. As Ericksen and Henderson (1992) explain:

   While both of these approaches are important, the data are incomplete without the direct input of those most closely concerned – the children.

2. The authors also believe that the phenomenological approach is appropriate for studying people's experience from their own (people's) perspective. They pointed out that:

   The phenomenological method is an inductive, descriptive method which is appropriately used when concern is to understand the subjective perspective of the person who has lived the experience and the effect that perspective has on the individual's experience and behaviour.

3. Ericksen and Henderson (1992) conducted 'unstructured interviews' using 'an interview guide which focused the participants on the issue at hand, but which did not influence the formation of answers'. A quantitative method (questionnaire or structured interview) would have imposed the researcher's perspectives on the children. The areas covered in a questionnaire are chosen by the researcher and therefore reflect what she thinks is important. Phenomenological interviews allow respondents to talk freely, although the researcher may try to prevent them straying to other topics.

4. Data for this study were analysed using a method developed by Giorgi (1985). As Ericksen and Henderson (1992) explain:

   interviews were first transcribed and read, then read more closely for themes inherent in what the children were saying, followed by organisation of these verbatim themes into more abstract language, and concluding by making summary statements of the children's experience.

While the grounded theory method guides the collection and analysis of data, it does not prescribe the particular perspective which researchers need to adopt. Glaser and Strauss (1967) themselves used symbolic interactionism (a sociological theory) in their attempt to describe the hospital care of dying patients. It is possible for sociologists, psychologists or philosophers to use perspectives from their own disciplines to study phenomena using the grounded theory method as the latter is not 'discipline-bound' (Strauss and Corbin, 1990).

Bias can potentially be present at various stages of qualitative studies as, for example, in the researcher's focus on some aspects of the phenomenon rather than others, in the selection of respondents and in the analysis of data. Additionally, a researcher's inexperience and lack of skill may create awkward situations that may inhibit respondents from behaving as they normally would. The ability to ask the right questions on cue, analyse and synthesise information while seemingly engaged in a normal conversation is rarely required of a quantitative researcher. The strategies that qualitative researchers use to avoid bias and enhance validity are discussed in Chapters 12, 13 and 14.

RE 14 is an example of a study that uses the grounded theory approach.

VARIATIONS OF RESEARCH DESIGN

Not all experiments, surveys and case studies are the same. Some surveys collect data on one occasion only, others do so at intervals. Case studies can investigate current as well as past phenomena; some experiments may have only two groups, while others may have three or more. Research designs can be further classified according to their data sources (longitudinal and cross-sectional, retrospective and prospective) and their functions (evaluative or comparative). Other variations include the Delphi technique, action research and meta-analytic studies.

Longitudinal and cross-sectional studies

Some nursing phenomena evolve over time, and it seems appropriate that data should be collected at intervals in order to capture any change that may take place. For example, people coming to terms with the loss of a spouse may go through different phases. Collection of data at 3- or 6-month intervals from the time of bereavement up to 2 years afterwards would probably provide a better picture of the bereavement process, than would collection of data on only one occasion. Peoples' attitudes, beliefs and behaviours may change over a period of time. A researcher may be interested in studying the impact of patient education on the subsequent behaviour of post-myocardial patients. It is possible that a month after the infarction patients may be following nurses' advice, but there is no guarantee that this behaviour will be sustained.

RESEARCH EXAMPLE	**14**	Brydolf and Segesten (1996) **Living with ulcerative colitis: experiences of adolescents and young adults**

A study using a grounded theory (GT) approach

The abstract (summary) from the above study reads as follows.

The problems associated with ulcerative colitis and its treatment have effects on adolescents and young adults dissimilar from as well as more profound than those on older individuals. Adolescents are confronted with problems such as biological, psychological and social changes as well as role changes related to peers and family. This inductive study aimed to describe the adolescents' experiences of living with ulcerative colitis. A total of 28 subjects were asked about their experiences both at the present time and at the time their first symptoms appeared. Verbatim transcribed thematized interviews were analysed according to a method influenced by the constant comparative method for grounded theory. Eight categories were grounded in the data, forming a model which described the process from onset of disease to present time. The main variable identified was: reduced living space, a strategy to manage the new situation. Dependent on the reactions received from significant others, the outcome for the adolescents hovered between feelings of self-confidence and lack of self-confidence. If the adolescents experienced support, the living space was expanded again. The results might be of great value when caring for and assisting young persons with a chronic disease in general, and in particular when taking care of adolescents with a recently diagnosed inflammatory bowel disease.

Comments

1. The main purpose of the GT approach is to generate concepts from the data in order to formulate models, conceptual frameworks or theories. In this study, the following eight concepts emerged from the data: alienation, reduced living-space ('the central concept'), support, lack of support, confidence in self, disbelief in self, role as a child or patient and role as an adult. These concepts were used by the author to develop a model explaining how the onset of ulcerative colitis affected the adolescents and young adults in this study.
2. 'Verbatim transcribed thematized interviews' (see abstract) means that the informal interviews carried out in this study were tape-recorded and were later transcribed word for word (verbatim). The authors also looked for themes (hence thematized) or patterns from what the respondents said. For example, one of the patterns that emerged when the transcripts were read was that 'the participants described their experiences in two sequential components: first living in a state of transition, then a subsequently altered lifestyle.
3. Data were analysed using the constant comparative method (CCM) (see abstract). The CCM was developed by Glaser and Strauss (1967) and Strauss and Corbin (1990). It consists of a series of steps that can be followed in order for researchers to make sense of the data in grounded theory research.

Researchers who want to know whether the effects of patient education are durable will have to collect data at intervals over a period of time. Such a design is called *longitudinal* (see RE 15). It is appropriate for phenomena that change over time. The intervals at which data are collected must be justified and this should be on the basis that they are the most appropriate times to capture the phenomena under investigation. The term '*cohort*' is used to describe the same group of respondents who are 'followed' over a period of time. Thus, if your class of students takes part in a longitudinal study to find out how their careers progress over the next 10 years, your class constitutes a cohort.

RESEARCH EXAMPLE 15   Tulman *et al.* (1990)
Changes in functional status after childbirth

A longitudinal study

As the authors explained:

> The purpose of the... longitudinal study was to explore changes in and variables associated with role performance, in the form of functional status, during the first 6 months following childbirth.

Data were collected from a sample of 110 women at 3 weeks, 6 weeks, 3 months and 6 months postpartum, using a number of instruments.

Comments

1. The choice of a longitudinal design was justified on the basis that 'the postpartum is a time of considerable transition in the life of a woman'. Tulman *et al.* were interested in the changes *over time* in functional status.

2. They explained that they selected these intervals (3 weeks, 6 weeks, 3 months and 6 months postpartum) after a review of the literature and from data from a previous study indicating that 'these are the times when changes in functional status occur after childbirth'.

3. The attrition (drop-out) rate is relatively low in this study; '12 subjects withdrew, most often between the time of recruitment and three weeks postpartum'.

4. This study is also descriptive as well as correlational, as some of the findings show:

    Descriptive: by 6 months postpartum 6% of the women had not yet fully assumed the desired or required level of infant care responsibilities, nearly 20% had not yet fully resumed usual levels of household activities.

    Correlational: Statistical analysis revealed that different sets of health, and psychosocial, family and demographic variables were associated with functional status at each data collection point.

One of the main problems with longitudinal studies is that those supplying the data may drop out of the project. This is referred to as 'mortality' or 'attrition'. Respondents may actually die, but more often they withdraw or cannot be traced. This affects the original composition of the sample and may have implications for the generalisability of the findings. If the project lasts for several years, it is not unusual for the original researchers to cease to be involved in the project, often as a result of a career move.

Most research has the potential to influence the subsequent behaviour of respondents, although the extent to which this happens depends on the methods the researcher uses and the nature of the research. The effect of the observer on the observed is well documented (see Chapter 13). Surveys also can raise issues and trigger reactions among respondents. Longitudinal studies, because of their prolonged nature, are more likely not only to raise respondents' awareness, but also to give them time to change their attitudes and behaviours, thereby preventing researchers from studying behaviours as they would have been if there were no research interference. While studying 'the changing situations of a panel of family caregivers of elderly relatives in the home' using a longitudinal design, Collins *et al.* (1989) became 'increasingly aware of the unintended effects that study participation has had on the family caregiver'. They concluded from their study that:

> through the research process researchers actively influenced the experiences of many of the family caregivers in the study. Caregivers seem to have been stimulated to evaluate and change their appraisals of their care-giving situations and, at times, their use of external resources and patient management strategies.

Another problem with longitudinal studies is that they take time and are costly since they may span a number of years. To get round these problems to some extent, it is sometimes possible to survey a cross-section of respondents, who can provide data to describe the changing nature of the phenomenon. For example, instead of interviewing a group of people experiencing bereavement at 6 monthly intervals, the researcher can choose to collect data from people who are at different stages of bereavement. She will interview a group at 1 month after the loss, a group who are bereaving at 6 months and another group who are at the 1 year stage. All these data will be gathered only once from each group and together will provide an insight into the process of bereavement.

A *cross-sectional* design is one in which data are collected from different groups of people who are at different stages in their experience of the phenomenon. Its limitation lies mainly in the fact that the same group is not studied over time and that the various groups may not have similar characteristics. For example, various designs have been used to find out whether intelligence and problem-solving ability decline with age. Much of the research that supports the cognitive decline in aging hypothesis is cross-sectional, whereas longitudinal studies often report no decline or much more subtle effects (Robbins, 1991). In these studies, the performance of older people in intelligence tests and other problem-solving exercises were compared with that of younger people. However, comparing generations who had different upbringing, opportunities (especially educational) and stimulation (from toys, audiovisual media, and so on) is unlikely to yield valid results. A more appropriate design would be a longitudinal one in which the same person's level of intelligence is measured every 10 or 20 years. However, such a study, by its nature, has practical, financial and many other implications. This is why cross-sectional designs are preferred when researchers need answers now rather than in 10 or 20, let alone 60 or 70, years time.

Referring to studies on the career paths of nurses, Robinson and Marsland (1994) point out that cross-sectional studies have made important contributions. Nonetheless, they explain that:

> The development of strategies to reduce attrition and promote retention, however, requires an understanding of how individual careers develop over time and, in particular, which factors influence transitions in and out of different types of employment. Cross-sectional studies have a number of methodological and analytical limitations that restrict the contribution that they can make to an understanding of this process.

Retrospective and prospective studies

Phenomena that have already occurred have their explanations in the past. Researchers have to 'work backwards' and search for variables or factors to account for them. A wealth of valuable information resides in people and documents, which can help to shed some light on many current concerns. Records are kept for the purpose of describing, and accounting for, what people do. For example, health visitors' diaries contain information that can help towards the understanding of what they do. Patients' notes give information on the treatment and progress of their illnesses and a considerable number of demographic and other personal details. These were not collected for the purpose of research but can be used retrospectively to explain and inform current phenomena.

A *retrospective* design is one in which researchers study a current phenomenon by seeking information from the past. For example, Cheater (1993) carried out a retrospective document survey 'to investigate the extent to which urinary incontinence had been identified as a problem, and to examine the nature of its assessment and management'. As part of the survey, she examined '229 nursing and medical records of patients identified as incontinent of urine by the nurses-in-charge, in 14 acute medical wards and 26 health care of the elderly wards'. This study was mainly descriptive. However, a study can also be correlational, as when the researcher investigates a condition or illness that has already occurred and searches for variables in records or personal accounts that may be associated with it. For example, researchers have looked at upbringing, lifestyles and life events (information from the past) in an attempt to find causes that may be related to patients currently suffering from schizophrenia (i.e. which have already occurred).

Retrospective studies must be differentiated from historical studies. If one takes the view that everything that has gone before us is history, all retrospective studies can be termed historical. The crucial difference, in research terms, between the two is that retrospective studies aim to describe or explain a current phenomenon by examining factors that are associated with it or gave rise to it. A historical study, however, does not need to have a 'foot in the present'. It seeks to understand phenomena as embedded in that particular period in history. For example, a nurse historian may carry out a study of leadership styles of matrons in the 19th century or describe moral treatments that psychiatric patients received in asylums. Although some comparisons can be made with current leadership styles or psychiatric treatments, the aim of these studies is to focus on these events only as they happened at the time, with or without relevance or reference to what happens now. Below are some examples of historical research:

- An honourable calling or a despised occupation: licensed midwifery and its relationship to district nursing in England and Wales before 1948 (Fox, 1993).
- A pioneer for nursing (Grace Neill, 1846–1926, a founder of New Zealand's nursing profession) (Stodart, 1993).
- Tropical treatment (nursing in Malaya during the civil war of 1953) (Tomlinson, 1993).

One of the main drawbacks of retrospective designs is that the researcher relies on existing data that were, most probably, not collected for research purposes and therefore lack the rigour with which research is carried out. Description of past behaviour may be highly subjective. Records may be incomplete, or difficult to make sense of or even to decipher (see RE 16). Relying on respondents' memory also has its limitations. Apart from forgetting important details, respondents can be selective in how they view the past. Despite these shortcomings, retrospective studies have been useful in, for example, making links between lung cancer and smoking, and heart disease and fat intake.

RESEARCH EXAMPLE 16

Edéll-Gustafsson *et al.* (1994)
Nurses' notes on sleep patterns in patients undergoing coronary artery bypass surgery: a retrospective evaluation of patient records

A retrospective study

This study 'retrospectively evaluated nurses' documentation of sleep and sleep disturbances in the immediate postoperative period in records' of patients undergoing coronary artery bypass:

> A retrospective analysis was made of the nurses' documentation regarding sleep and wakefulness from 11.00 pm to 07.00 am during the first four postoperative nights ... An attempt was made to relate these findings to nurses' documentation for the night before surgery, and to the degree of alertness of the patient the following day. All patient records were analysed by one of the authors.

Comments

1. This was a descriptive, retrospective study. The results showed, among other things, that 'disturbances in the duration of sleep occurred on 103 occasions and in the quality of sleep, on 38 occasions', 'frequent awakening was common during all four nights' and 'continuous wakefulness was most common on the first night after surgery'. The findings also suggest relationships between sleep disturbances and other variables:

> The records showed that the most common health conditions which may have been potential causes of sleep disturbances were, in descending order, pain, nausea/vomiting, and coughing.

The links between these variables can be further investigated using a correlational or experimental design.

2. The fact that 'all patient records were analysed by one of the authors' prevents inter-subjective bias, which may occur if some records were analysed by one and some by another researcher. However, because one researcher may interpret the documents subjectively, another researcher could have sampled some of the records, compared their interpretations and resolved their differences. In this way, the reliability of records interpretation could have been enhanced.

3. Patients records were not in this instance compiled for research purposes. The authors found that:

> Nurses' description of sleep and sleep disturbances varied over a wide range, with a mixture of qualitative and quantitative expressions. On average, information on sleep or sleep disturbances was missing for about one-quarter of patients.

The lack of data in some cases and incomplete data in others points to the limitations of retrospective designs. In particular, it shows the lack of control that the researcher has over how data are produced, since she can rely only on what was already recorded. Nevertheless, this study shows that current problems (sleep disturbances) can be investigated retrospectively.

A *prospective* design is one in which researchers study a current phenomenon by seeking information from the future (see RE 17). Nurses may want to know the effects of their practices on patients' behaviour over time, or how the diagnosis of a condition such as breast cancer subsequently affects the lifestyle of its sufferers. Researchers using a prospective design can have control over whom they want to include in their study and how data are collected. To ensure that the lifestyle of the newly diagnosed cancer patients would not have changed anyway, another group of people without breast cancer can be studied at the same time. With this design, data are collected at one or more points in the future, as is the case in longitudinal studies. In fact, the two designs have a lot in common. The main difference between them is that longitudinal

---

RESEARCH EXAMPLE Kemp et al. (1990)
Factors that contribute to pressure sores in surgical patients

A prospective study

As the authors explained in their abstract:

> In this prospective study examination was made of whether (a) time on the operating table, (b) proportion of intraoperative diastolic hypotensive episodes, (c) age, (d) preoperative serum albumin, (e) preoperative total protein levels, and (f) preoperative Braden scores could identify those patients who do and do not develop pressure sores during elective surgery.

One hundred and twenty-five patients free from pressure sores before surgery were selected from operating schedules and assessed the morning of surgery and later during transfer from the operating table to the stretcher.

'Data were collected on post-operative days 1, 4, 7 and 10'. The results showed that time on the operating table, extracorporeal circulation, and age emerged as the best predictor correctly classifying 12 of 15 patients who developed pressure sores and 83 out of 110 patients who remained pressure sore free.

Comments
1. The design is prospective because the researchers started with the study in the present and went forward in time to collect data. They identified factors that might put patients at risk of pressure sores but had no way of knowing which, if any, would eventually be linked with the development of sores. They started with a problem in the present and looked for its causes in the future.
2. This study is also longitudinal as the data were collected on five separate occasions.
3. It is also a correlational study since the purpose was to find if there were statistically significant links between some of these factors and the occurrence of pressure sores.

studies can be both prospective and retrospective. Williams *et al.* (1994) used a prospective design to study 'early outcomes after hip fracture among women'. Outcomes were compared in three groups of formerly community-living women: 'those discharged home from the hospital, those discharged to a nursing home and staying there for more than 1 month, and those staying for less than 1 month.

Evaluative studies

In the era of evidence-based practice and client-centred care, evaluative studies assume great importance. According to Reid (1988), 'the evaluation of professional practice is central to every aspect of the organisation, delivery and quality of services'. Practitioners can evaluate their practice by reflecting on what they do. The difference between this and an evaluative study is that the latter is a systematic appraisal using research methods.

Evaluative studies tend to focus on a particular practice, policy or event. An evaluative study is normally carried out when the researcher wants to find out if, how and to what extent the objectives of particular activities have been or are being met. These activities could be the provision of service, a teaching programme or a series of therapeutic sessions. By focusing on these specific, well-defined activities, evaluative studies tend to take the form of case studies.

In Young's (1994) evaluative study of a community health service development, 'surveys of patients and staff in the health authority were conducted about a range of issues, defined by the original aims of the scheme'. The researcher may also decide to select aspects she wants to evaluate no matter what the original objectives were. However, if the purpose of the evaluation is to improve that particular activity or to be 'wiser the next time', it makes sense that the aims and objectives should provide the benchmark against which the success of the programme or activity can be measured.

In evaluative studies, researchers can use quantitative and/or qualitative methods. In Davis *et al.*'s (1994) study of 'nursing process documentation' in one hospital, the quantitative methods comprised 'a documentation Questionnaire, constructed and used by the researcher, and a self-administered Ward Manager Questionnaire, also constructed by the researcher'. On the other hand, Jennings (1994) used semistructured interviews in her study of 'hospital at home'. The main limitation of evaluation studies lies in the fact that they are aimed at understanding specific practices and policies. Their contribution to knowledge in general, and research methodology in particular, remains a secondary objective.

RESEARCH EXAMPLE 18

Davis *et al.* (1994)
Evaluation of nursing process documentation

An evaluative study

As the authors explain:

> Following the introduction of a nursing process and associated documentation in one hospital, an attempt was made to evaluate the effectiveness of the documentation as a record of the nursing process. Two questionnaires were developed, based on previous research in this field, one for the assessment of the documentation, and the other to assess the attitudes and practices of the ward sisters regarding its implementation.

> Before the questionnaire was constructed, a set of objectives was written to identify the main purposes of the nursing documentation... These key objectives formed the basis for the construction of the questionnaire, as did some of the strengths and weaknesses identified by the Report of the Nursing Process Evaluation Working Group (1986).

The evaluation showed among other things that:

> Approximately half the documents contained mostly legible material that was easy to understand. A few of the wards also appeared to display some evidence of specificity, continuity and individuality of the patient... However, the overall tendency was that individual care was not reflected in the documentation, despite using a structured approach.

Comments

1. In this study, a procedure or practice (nursing process documentation) was evaluated. At the same time, the researchers surveyed the attitudes and practices of the ward sisters regarding its implementation. This was necessary because, as Davis *et al.* explained, the two were linked and had 'implications for the extent to which individualised care was being implemented'.
2. Objectives set at the introduction of the nursing documentation constituted a benchmark against which the actual documentation could be assessed.
3. The evaluation took place in one hospital; therefore the findings relate to this specific setting, although the lessons learnt may be applicable elsewhere.
4. This was a retrospective evaluation since the documents were written before the start of the study. Davis *et al.* recognised the limitations of this retrospective approach when they pointed out that:

> Without observations of nurses actually at work and following through the decision-making aspects and the whole process, it is difficult to make criticisms with a high level of confidence from an analysis of the documentation.

There are many similarities and differences between audit and research (Closs and Cheater, 1996). Evaluative studies seem to be closer to audit than are any other research designs. This is mainly because both tend to address issues in specific settings. The data from both cannot readily be generalised to other settings. Both audit and evaluation research must use rigorous methods to collect and analyse data. Finally, the contribution of both audit and evaluative studies to the development of theory is rather limited.

One the main difference is that the research evaluation of a project can sometimes be an afterthought, although the original aims and objectives can be used as benchmarks. Audit, on the other hand, is a cycle that 'involves setting standards for practice, monitoring that practice, comparing actual practice with the standards set, if necessary making changes to practice and then remonitoring practice to see if the agreed standard is attained' (Closs and Cheater, 1996). This important practice element is not usually present in evaluative studies. RE 18 gives an account of an evaluative study.

Comparative studies

Many research designs involve some forms of comparison. Experimental studies compare results of experimental and control groups. Surveys collect data that allow comparisons according to such demographic factors as age, gender or class. The difference between these and comparative studies is that the purpose of the latter, at the outset, is to compare – whether it is people's characteristics, policies, practices or events.

As the main purpose of comparative studies is to compare, the rationale for this must be provided. In Suominen *et al.*'s (1994) study comparing 'patients' and nurses' opinions of nurses' role in informing breast cancer patients', a case is made by the authors for the need of such a study:

> Little is known about how patients with breast cancer perceive their informational needs and how they assess the information that they received. Ward and Griffin (1990) suggested that breast cancer patients' information needs are not adequately met. However, it is not clear whether this deficit is present because clinicians do not provide sufficient information, or because patients do not absorb information or whether it is due to an interaction of these two factors.

Comparative studies can be quantitative, qualitative or both. RE 19 describes a comparative study in which a quantitative approach is used. While and Wilcox (1994), on the other hand, used qualitative methods to explore 'the experience of children admitted to a day-case unit with that of children admitted to a general paediatric ward'. Their study 'aimed to provide an in-depth description of the experience' of the children. The methods used included non-participant observation,

RESEARCH EXAMPLE	19	Fielding and Weaver (1994) **A comparison of hospital- and community-based mental health nurses: perceptions of their work environment and psychological health**

A comparative study

This study compares hospital- (n = 67) and community-based (n = 55) mental health nurses in relation to their perceptions of the work environment and also their psychological health. Measures include: the General Health Questionnaire, the Maslach Burnout Inventory and the Work Environment Scale. The data, obtained from self-returned questionnaires, show that community nurses rated their work environments higher for the dimensions of Involvement, Supervisor Support, Autonomy, Innovation and Work Pressure. Hospital nurses saw their environments as being higher in (managerial) Control. There were no differences between the groups for the dimensions of Peer Cohesion, Task Orientation, Clarity or (physical) Comfort. Furthermore, there were no overall differences between the two groups in relation to psychological health, although the pattern of factors associated with emotional well-being differed. Finally, analyses of the community data revealed that those nurses with 'flexitime' arrangements evaluated their work environments less positively and showed higher levels of psychological strain than did those working 'fixed-time' schedules. The findings suggest that the hospital and community environments make different demands on nursing staff, and that this should be considered when organizing nursing services if stress is to be avoided.

Comments

1. The above abstract shows that the purpose of the research was to compare the two groups. They did not collect data from psychiatric nurses in a variety of settings, which incidentally showed differences between hospital- and community-based nurses.
2. Care must be taken to compare 'like with like'. In this study:

   in order to ensure that the two groups being compared were equivalent with respect to other major work variables, all participants met the following criteria: (a) they held professional nursing qualifications (SRN or RMN), (b) they were employed at grade 'H' (the top clinical grade) or below, and (c) they worked the equivalent of 37.5 hours per week.

   The differences in the data between groups can sometimes be due to the differences in their characteristics. You must pay particular attention to this aspect of the study when you set out to evaluate it.

   Sometimes the different conditions or settings in which the tools are administered or observations carried out can also produce different data. In this study, the response rate for community-based nurses was 72 per cent and for the hospital-based ones, 45 per cent. Fielding and Weaver suggest that it was likely that 'the lack of personal contact at the point of distributing the questionnaires for the hospital-based nurses is responsible for the difference in return rates for the two groups'.

3. Fielding and Weaver gave many reasons why this comparison was necessary. They relate to the NHS changes affecting the role and practices of both hospital- and community-based mental health nurses. As they explained:

    although both groups of nurses are likely to feel the impact of change and its resulting stress, the particular stressors (and means for their amelioration) may be quite different for each group.

4. A quantitative approach was used in this comparative study. The tools of data collection included: the Maslach burnout inventory, the general health questionnaire, the work environment scale and a questionnaire for personal and work-related details.

interviews and a diary. Comparative studies are a useful way of learning about people and practices. In health care, it is well known that there are different treatments and approaches to the same condition. While evaluation studies provide data on the effectiveness of particular treatments, comparative studies make it possible to compare different treatments. Since comparative studies adopt a variety of designs, such as experiments, surveys or case studies, they have the same strengths and limitations as these.

The Delphi technique

Another form of research, which is a variation of the survey design, is the *Delphi technique*. It consists of gathering the views of experts on a particular issue with the added agenda of seeking an agreement or consensus on the issue. This necessarily entails 'going back' to the experts until consensus is reached. There are many issues in nursing that some researchers believe can be enlightened by experts. For example, McKenna (1992) sought consensus among a number of nurse academics on the most appropriate model of nursing for long-stay psychiatric patients. He sent them a list and descriptions of each model without identifying the models by name. After analysing their responses, he posted another questionnaire summarising the data and asked them to reconsider their views. As he explains:

> This second questionnaire is returned to each subject and they are asked (in the light of the first round's results), to reconsider their initial opinion and to once again return their responses to the researcher. Repeat rounds of this process are carried out until consensus of opinion, or a point of diminishing returns has been reached.

The Delphi technique has been used to study such varied issues as clinical nursing research priorities (Bond and Bond, 1982), evaluation of professional practice (Reid, 1985), future trends in psychiatric nursing (White, 1991), and the features of primary nursing (Mead, 1992).

McKenna (1994) points out that 'contemporary nursing literature shows increasing evidence' of the successful use of the Delphi technique 'in a wide range of problem areas, including nurse education, research priorities, the management of patient care and the setting of standards'.

RESEARCH EXAMPLE 20

Crotty (1993)
The emerging role of the Bristish nurse teacher in Project 2000 programmes: a Delphi survey

---

A Delphi study

The following are extracts from the article:

> In order to explore the role of the nurse teacher as it emerges in the Project 2000 programmes, it was decided to utilize a Delphi survey followed by a qualitative approach, utilizing in-depth interviews for further exploration of the findings.

> The Delphi survey was undertaken within the colleges of nursing and midwifery in England which had implemented Project 2000 between September 1989 and April 1991. Of the 28 colleges, 25 agreed to participate in the study. All grade 2 nurse teachers working within these colleges who were teaching on Project 2000 courses were invited to join the panel of experts for the study. This resulted in a response of 201 nurse teachers, from the approximate total of 1000 teachers working within the 25 colleges. Three rounds of Delphi were utilized, and 151 (75%) of the respondents continued to the end of the third round.

Questionnaire

> In order to develop the first questionnaire, 10 teachers within the researcher's college were invited to give their views regarding the activities within their current role. The information was used to develop five main categories of activities under which a list of related areas were grouped. The questionnaire also contained requests for general information regarding the respondents, their college, and the preparation they had received for the activities within their current role.

> The collated and analysed data from the first round were used to develop the list of activities in the second questionnaire. The opinions of the participants were sought as to the importance, lack of importance, or of having no opinion in relation to each activity within their current and future role.

> In the third-round questionnaire, respondents were presented with responses they had made in round two. They were asked to agree or disagree with the importance of the activity within their current and future role.

Comments

1. In this study, there were only three rounds. The number of times the researcher 'goes back' varies, depending on the aims of the study, how soon these are achieved and whether further efforts do not prove productive enough.

2. The experts in Crotty's study were 'all grade 2 nurse teachers working within these colleges who were teaching on Project 200 courses'.

3. The Delphi technique was used to develop the list of activities for the second round, and to indicate their agreement or disagreement with the importance of each activity.

4. The response rate was 75 per cent by the end of the third round. Although one can agree with the author that the drop-out rate was not a problem in this case, one can ask whether the responses of those who dropped out would have made a difference.

5. The author pointed to one of the limitations of the study. As she explains:

By inviting all grade 2 nurse teachers in the 25 participating colleges to join the panel of experts, they were self-selecting and did not form a statistically representative sample. They represented approximately 20% of the total population of nurse teachers in the 25 participating colleges.

On the other hand, when in some studies the researcher selects the panel of experts, she is making a subjective judgement on who the experts are and by her knowledge of their existence and whereabouts.

6. Finally, Crotty found that 'overall, the use of the Delphi technique in this study was felt to be an efficient and reliable means of gathering expert information... on the role of the nurse teacher'.

The Delphi technique has the advantage of collating the views of experts using questionnaires without incurring the cost of getting the experts together. The fact that these people do not meet and are not aware of who the others are means that they do not have the opportunity of influencing one another, therefore allowing diverse opinions to be expressed. According to Reid (1988), 'the method removes the influence of the dominant personalities in achieving consensus'. The disadvantages include the subjective bias in the researcher's choice of 'experts' and the pressure on respondents to agree, thereby introducing the possibility of hasty decisions being taken. There is also the problem of low response rates, especially in the later rounds of the questionnaire, which casts doubt on the 'consensus' reached. Could it be that those who drop out do so because they do not want to change their initial views? The replicability of Delphi studies are also called into question (Reid, 1988). In RE 20 Crotty (1993) uses the Delphi technique to study 'the emerging role of the British nurse teacher in Project 2000 programmes'.

Action research

Action research, as the term suggests, has two main components – action and research. The purpose of conventional research is mainly to contribute to the body of knowledge. Some of this knowledge could eventually, but not necessarily, be used in practice. With action research, the emphasis is on 'action', and research methods are used to inform this action. Defining action research is problematic since there are a number of models (see for example Hart and Bond, 1995). In essence, it involves a collaboration between researcher and practitioner in:

- identifying a practice problem;
- using research methods to assess this problem;
- planning and implementing the change;
- evaluating the outcome.

And so the cycle continues. The number of steps depends on whose model one uses. There are four characteristics central to all forms of action research: collaboration between researcher and practitioner, the solution of practical problems, a change in practice and development of a theory (Holter and Schwartz-Barcott, 1993).

In its conventional form, research is normally carried out by outside researchers on practitioners and their practice to advance the researchers' cause. They use the practice setting to collect data, and rely on the goodwill of practitioners but give little back. In action research, there is more 'give and take' in the relationship between these two protagonists. With conventional research, findings are often couched in research terminologies that can remain incomprehensible to practitioners. Often the researcher's interpretation of practice phenomena does not coincide with the practitioner's perception of the same. Action research has the advantage that researcher and practitioner can enter into a dialogue, discuss their different interpretations and produce more valid findings by drawing from each other's special knowledge and experience. Research findings in conventional research can take up to 2 years before they are published. In action research, the emphasis is on the 'here and now'. Solutions to problems are immediately implemented and evaluated. There are, however, similarities between action research and conventional research, as Hovda and Kyle (1989) describe in relation to educational practice:

> both attempt to improve educational practice, one through the development of laws and principles, the other through understanding one situation as a basis for actions in the future. Also, each process begins with the identification of a problem. These problem areas, in each case, lead to questions, a choice of research design, the gathering of evidence, and conclusions and implications.

In Carr and Kemmis's (1986) model, action research has an emancipatory potential. They define action research as:

> a form of self-reflective enquiry undertaken by participants in social situations in order to improve the rationality and justice of their own practices, their understanding of these practices and the situations in which these practices are carried out.

There is little evidence that action research in nursing has realised the objective of empowering or emancipating its participants. Meyer (1993) explains that 'this type of research is by no means easy and that it should be noted that nursing action research studies in the past have not tended to address the practical issues and dilemmas that make this type of work problematic'.

Although action research is believed to have emerged through a rejection of the empiricist and interpretivist notions of science (Reason and Rowan, 1981, cited in Meyer, 1993), it incorporates research methods from both these approaches. Webb (1990) used a stress questionnaire and Senior Monitor, and Lathlean and Farnish (1984) adopted 'an interpretive approach in their evaluation of a ward sister development project' (Meyer, 1993).

Meyer (1993) points out some of the limitations of action research, which include the difficulty in reality of addressing the power relationship between research (expert) and other collaborators (mainly practitioners). Another limitation relates to the issue of informed consent. As Meyer explains:

> In action research, the change is usually dependent on the team pulling together and as such places individuals in a vulnerable position of forced co-operation with their colleagues. This is clearly at odds with the sentiment of action research which relies on willing and voluntary collaboration.

Overall, action research has the potential of closing the research–practice gap. It success depends on the degree and type of collaboration between researchers and practitioners. Examples of action research in nursing include the studies by Webb (1990), Armitage *et al.* (1991) and Titchen and Binnie (1993).

Webb (1990) used action research to help nurses to introduce team nursing in one care of the elderly ward (see RE 21). The main aims of Armitage *et al.*'s project were 'to implement primary nursing in two long-term psychiatric rehabilitation/continuing-care wards and to investigate the effects of the intervention on the quality of nursing care provision' (Armitage *et al.*, 1991). Titchen and Binnie (1993) were 'engaged in a 4-

year action research study of the development of patient-centred nursing' in an acute medical unit.

RESEARCH EXAMPLE 21 Webb (1990)
Partners in research

Action research

Webb (1990) used action research to introduce team nursing in one care of the elderly ward. At first she nursed alongside others in the ward in order to get accepted and win their confidence. Later, Webb 'changed her activities towards more formal data gathering'. As she explains:

> As well as the formative, qualitative research data which I would continue to gather through working with staff, I used Senior Monitor and a stress questionnaire to collect baseline measurements before considering any action. The plan was to repeat these measurements after the changes were implemented to evaluate them.

Meetings were organised weekly. Apart from teaching sessions led by the researcher (Webb), the meetings provided opportunities for discussing issues such as ' communication, care planning, handing over of information, and so on, as the need had arisen'.

Implementation took 6 months, during which time Webb worked the late shift on the day of the weekly meeting. At the end of 6 months, the project finally came to an end. As Webb explains:

> At this stage the stress questionnaires were repeated and we had a final meeting to evaluate progress and our feelings about the project and what we had discussed.

Comments

1. This project illustrates the stages of action research. The researcher identified a problem or need (the implementation of team teaching), used research methods (Senior Monitor and a questionnaire) to assess the problem, planned and implemented the changes and evaluated the outcome. Although the project came to an end, the action research cycle could have continued if required, using the evaluation data as the new baseline to implement further changes.

2. Action research uses research methods for assessment and evaluation purposes. Research methods can be both qualitative and quantitative, as explained above.

3. Action research can help to bridge the research–practice gap, and it has empowering potential. As Webb concluded:

> the project further consolidated my belief in action research as a valuable technique for introducing and evaluating change within a practice discipline, because it encourages an openness, self-criticism and reflexivity among all participants, and because it empowers participants to take control over their own work situations.

Meta-analytic studies

As the volume of nursing research grows, researchers are becoming interested in and drawn to methodological issues. In doing 'research on research', the most relevant studies on a particular topic are analysed and synthesised. The researcher can focus on one or more aspects of methodology, such as samples, methods or findings. This type of research enables nurses to find out about trends in nursing research and make recommendations for future studies. Meta-analysis is one form of research on research. In its pure form, it involves synthesising the results of studies (see Chapter 5). Lynn (1989) defines it as 'the statistical analysis of a large collection of results from individual studies for the purpose of integrating the findings into a single, generalizable finding'.

Meta-analysis helps researchers and practitioners to make sense of similar and contradictory findings on the same topic. However, by focusing exclusively on experimental research, the use of meta-analysis 'has not been maximized' (Reynolds et al., 1992). These authors suggest that the technique could be applied to descriptive research as well because for 'both experimental and descriptive studies, meta-analysis enables the researcher to draw conclusions about a body of literature, advance knowledge development, and facilitate the rapidity of practice innovations'.

The limitations of meta-analysis include the difficulty of identifying and accessing all studies on the particular topic of interest and the difficult task of integrating 'studies that have clearly different operationalizations or levels of quality' (Reynolds et al., 1992). For an example of meta-analytic study see RE 22.

SUMMARY AND CONCLUSION

In this chapter, some of the common terminologies used to describe research designs have been explained. Different levels and types of designs in quantitative research have been identified, as have the three most popular designs in qualitative research. To facilitate understanding, it was felt necessary to present each one as distinct and separate from the others. In practice, there is considerable overlap between, for example, descriptive and correlational studies. Experiments can be prospective, and a comparative study can be both descriptive and retrospective. What is important, however, is not what terminology is used but that the most appropriate design is selected and described in enough detail to make sense of what was done and to assess the reasons for such actions.

REFERENCES

Armitage P, Champney-Smith J and Andrews K (1991) Primary nursing and the role of the nurse preceptor in changing long term mental health care: an evaluation. *Journal of Advanced Nursing*, **16**(4):413–22.

Beck C T (1994) Phenomenology: its use in nursing research. *International Journal of Nursing Studies*, **31**(6):499–510.

RESEARCH EXAMPLE 22

Hyman *et al.* (1989)

The effects of relaxation training on clinical symptoms: a meta-analysis

A meta-analytic study

These researchers carried out a meta-analysis of experimental studies which looked at the 'effects of relaxation training on clinical symptoms'. They excluded pharmacological and mechanical assisted technique and included 'Benson's (1975) relaxation technique, Jacobson's (1938) progressive muscle relaxation (PMR), rhythmic breathing (RB), imagery, Lamaze, meditation, autogenic training, hypnosis, transcendental meditation (TM), yoga, and Zen'. Only studies after 1970 and which contained data that allowed statistical analysis were included. These studies were located following a computer search using the following key words: relaxation, hypnosis, biofeedback, meditation, yoga, zen, imagery, pain, hypertension and anxiety. Other sources consulted were: *Dissertation Abstracts International, Psychological Abstracts, Sociological Abstracts* and *Cumulative Index to Nursing and Allied Health Literature, Cumulated Index Medicus* and *World Nursing Research*. This 'resulted in a sample of approximately 100 studies, of which 48 fit the criteria for inclusion'.

Results indicated that 'relaxation techniques do affect some clinical symptoms' and that 'the treatments worked better for non-surgical than for surgical subjects'. Hypertension was the problem most positively affected by the relaxation techniques, 'with headache and insomnia also showing fairly consistent evidence of treatment effects'. Finally, Hyman *et al.* suggested that 'future studies be designed to test specifically whether the efficacy of specific relaxation technique varies depending on the symptom to be treated, on acute versus chronic problems, and/or in surgical versus non surgical settings'.

Comments

1. For meta-analytic studies to be useful, an extensive literature search to locate as many studies as possible must be carried out. This was the case in this instance, although it is still possible to miss a few important ones. Not all meta-analytic studies are as thorough.
2. Meta-analyses are mainly carried out on quantitative studies. In this case, only experimental ones were included; descriptive and correlational studies were not considered. This limits the generalisability of the findings to all studies, both experimental and non-experimental.

    The authors reported that only half of those studies obtained through the literature search were analysed as the rest did not meet the criteria set above. They admitted that this 'constitutes a limitation on the generalisability of the study results'.
3. One of the functions of meta-analysis is to identify new areas of research on the same topic. As can be seen above, Hyman *et al.* made suggestions for further (most probably experimental) studies.

Bluff R and Holloway I (1994) 'They know best': women's perceptions of midwifery care during labour and childbirth. *Midwifery*, **10**:157–64.

Bond S and Bond J (1982) A Delphi survey of clinical nursing research priorities. *Journal of Advanced Nursing*, **7**: 565–75.

Brydolf M and Segesten K (1996) Living with ulcerative colitis: experiences of adolescents and young adults. *Journal of Advanced Nursing*, **23**: 39–47.

Carr W and Kemmis S (1986) *Becoming Critical: Education Knowledge and Action Research*. London: Falmer Press.

Castles M R (1987) *Primer of Nursing Research*. Philadelphia: W B Saunders.

Cheater F M (1993) Retrospective document survey: identification, assessment and management of urinary incontinence in medical and care of the elderly wards. *Journal of Advanced Nursing*, **18**:1734–6.

Closs S J and Cheater F M (1996) Audit or research – what is the difference? *Journal of Clinical Nursing*, **5**:249–56.

Colaizzi P (1978) Psychological research as the phenomenologist views it. In R Valle and M Kings (eds) *Existential Phenomenological Alternative for Psychology*. New York: Oxford University Press.

Collins C, Given B and Berry D (1989) Longitudinal studies as intervention. *Nursing Research*, **38**(4):251–3.

Creswell J W (1994) *Research Design: Qualitative and Quantitative Approaches*. California: Sage.

Crotty M (1993) The emerging role of the British nurse teacher in Project 2000 programmes: a Delphi survey. *Journal of Advanced Nursing*, **18**:150–7.

Davis B D, Billings J R and Ryland R K (1994) Evaluation of nursing process documentation. *Journal of Advanced Nursing*, **19**:960–8.

Edéll-Gustaffson U, Arèn C, Hamrin E and Hetta J (1994) Nurses' notes on sleep patterns in patients undergoing coronary artery bypass surgery: a retrospective evaluation of patient records. *Journal of Advanced Nursing*, **20**:331–6.

Ericksen J R and Henderson A D (1992) Witnessing family violence: the children's experience. *Journal of Advanced Nursing*, **17**:1200–09

Fielding J and Weaver S M (1994) A comparison of hospital- and community-based mental health nurses: perceptions of their work environment and psychological health. *Journal of Advanced Nursing*, **19**:1196–204.

Fox E (1993) An honourable calling or a despised occupation: licensed midwifery and its relationship to district nursing in England and Wales before 1948. *Social History of Medicine*, **6**(2):237–59.

Giorgi A (1985) *Phenomenology and Psychological Research*. Pittsburg, PA: Duquesne University Press.

Glaser B and Strauss A (1967) *The Discovery of Grounded Theory*. Chicago: Aldine.

Hammersley M and Atkinson P (1983) *Ethnography: Principles and Practice*. London: Tavistock.

Hart E and Bond M (1995) *Action Research: A Guide to Practice*. Buckingham: Philadelphia.

Holter I M and Schwartz-Barcott D (1993) Action research: what is it? How has it been used and how can it be used in nursing? *Journal of Advanced Nursing*, **18**:298–304.

Hovda R A and Kyle D W (1989) Why action research? An emergent role in educational reform. *Irish Educational Studies*, **8**(2):24–37.

Hughes C C (1992) 'Ethnography': what's in a word-process? Product? Promise? *Qualitative Health Research*, **2**(4):439–50.

Husserl E (1962) *Ideas: General Introduction to Pure Phenomenology*. New York: Collier.

Hyman R B, Feldman H R, Harris R B, Levin R F and Malloy G B (1989) The effects of relaxation training on clinical symptoms: a meta-analysis. *Nursing Research*, **38**(4):216–20.

Jennings P (1994) Learning through experience: an evaluation of 'Hospital at Home'. *Journal of Advanced Nursing*, **19**:905–11.

Kemp M G, Keithley J K, Smith D W and Morreale B (1990) Factors that contribute to pressure sores in surgical patients. *Research in Nursing and Health*, **13**:293–301.

Kerlinger F N (1973) *Foundations of Behavioural Research*, 2nd edn. New York: Holt, Rinehart & Winston.

Koch T (1995) Interpretive approaches in nursing research: the influence of Husserl and Heidegger. *Journal of Advanced Nursing*, **21**:827–36.

Lathlean J and Farnish S (1984) The Ward Sister Training Project. In Meyer J (1993) New paradigm research in practice: the trials and tribulations of action research. *Journal of Advanced Nursing*, **18**:1066–72.

Lynn M R (1989) Meta-analysis: appropriate tool for the integration of nursing research? *Nursing Research*, **38**:302–5.

Mackenzie A E (1992) Learning from experience in the community: an ethnographic study of district nurse students. *Journal of Advanced Nursing*, **17**:682–91.

McKenna H P (1992) The selection and evaluation of an appropriate nursing model for long-stay psychiatric patients. Unpublished DPhil Thesis. Coleraine: University of Ulster.

McKenna H P (1994) The Delphi technique: a worthwhile research approach for nursing? *Journal of Advanced Nursing*, **19**:1221–5.

Mead D (1992) Innovations in nursing care, the development of primary nursing in Wales. Unpublished report. London: Department of Health.

Meyer J E (1993) New paradigm research in practice: the trials and tribulations of action research. *Journal of Advanced Nursing*, **18**:1066–72.

O'Brien M T (1993) Multiple sclerosis: the relationship among self-esteem, social support and coping behaviour. *Applied Nursing Research*, **6**(2):54–63.

O'Sullivan A L (1991) Tertiary prevention with adolescent mothers: rehabilitation after the first pregnancy. In Humenick S, Wilkerson N W and White N P (eds) *Adolescent Programs: Nursing Perspectives on Prevention*. White Plains: March of Dimes Birth Defects Foundation.

O'Sullivan A and Jacobsen B S (1992) A randomized trial of health care program for first-time adolescent mothers and their infants. *Nursing Research*, **41**(4):210–15.

Polit D F and Hungler B P (1995) *Nursing Research: Principles and Methods*, 5th edn. Philadelphia: J B Lippincott.

Reason P and Rowan J (1981) *Human Inquiry: A Sourcebook of New Paradigm Research*. Chichester: John Wiley & Sons.

Reid N G (1985) *Wards in Chancery? Nursing in the Clinical Area*. London: Royal College of Nursing.

Reid N (1988) The Delphi technique: its contribution to the evaluation of professional practice. In Ellis R (ed.) *Professional Competence and Quality Assurance in the Caring Professions*, 2nd edn. London: Chapman & Hall.

Reynolds N R, Timmerman G, Anderson J and Stevenson J S (1992) Meta-analysis for descriptive research. *Research in Nursing and Health*, **15**:467–75.

Robbins S E (1991) The psychology of human ageing. In Redfern S J (1991) *Nursing Elderly People*. Edinburgh: Churchill Livingstone.

Robinson S and Marsland L (1994) Approaches to the problem of respondent attrition in a longitudinal panel study of nurses' careers. *Journal of Advanced Nursing*, **20**:729–41.

Roe B H, Griffiths J M, Kenrick M, Cullum N A and Hutton J L (1994) Nursing treatment of patients with chronic leg ulcers in the community. *Journal of Clinical Nursing*, **3**:159–68.

Singleton R A, Straits B C and Straits M M (1993) *Approaches to Social Research*, 2nd edn. New York: Oxford University Press.

Spradley J (1980) *Participant Observation*. New York: Holt, Rinehart & Winston.

Stodart K (1993) A pioneer for nursing. (Grace Neill, 1846–1926, a founder of New Zealand's nursing profession). *Nursing New Zealand*, **1**(6):28–9.

Strauss A and Corbin J (1990) *Basics of Qualitative Research: Grounded Theory Procedures and Techniques*. California: Sage.

Suominen T, Leino-Kilpi H and Laippala P (1994) Nurses' role in informing breast cancer patients: a comparison between patients' and nurses' opinions. *Journal of Advanced Nursing*, **19**:6–11.

Tesch R (1990) *Qualitative Research: Analysis Types and Software Tools*. New York: Falmer Press.

Titchen A and Binnie A (1993) Research partnerships: collaborative action research in nursing. *Journal of Advanced Nursing*, **18**:858–65.

Tomlinson A (1993) Tropical treatment. (Nursing in Malaya during the civil war of 1953.) *Nursing Times*, **89**(1):40–1.

Tulman L, Fawcett J, Groblewski L and Silverman L (1990) Changes in functional status after childbirth. *Nursing Research*, **39**(2):70–5.

Ward S and Griffin J (1990) Developing a test of knowledge of surgical options for breast cancer. *Cancer Nursing*, **13**:191–6.

Webb C (1990) Partners in research. *Nursing Times*, **86**(32):40–4.

While A E and Wilcox V K (1994) Paediatric day surgery: day-case unit admission compared with general paediatric ward admission. *Journal of Advanced Nursing*, **19**:52–7.

White E (1991) *The Future of Psychiatric Nursing by the Year 2000: A Delphi Study*. Manchester: Department of Nursing, University of Manchester.

Williams M A, Obserst M T and Bjorklund B C (1994) Early outcomes after hip fracture among women discharged home and to nursing homes. *Research in Nursing and Health*, **17**:175–83.

Young K R (1994) An evaluative study of a community health service development. *Journal of Advanced Nursing*, **19**:58–65.

Vankaam A (1966) *Existential Foundations of Psychology*. Pittsburg, PA: Duquesne University Press.

9 EXPERIMENTS

Man is a cause-seeking creature; in the order of spirits he might be called the 'cause-seeker'. Other spirits conceive of things in relations different from us and incomprehensible to us. (Lichtenberg G C, 1764–99)

INTRODUCTION

In the previous chapter, we identified three levels of research in quantitative studies: descriptive, correlational and causal. The experiment as a research design corresponds to the third level. Its aim is to establish causal links between variables. It is the principal method in the natural sciences for testing hypotheses and theories, and it uses the deductive approach to data collection (hence the label 'hypothetico-deductive').

In this chapter, we will explore the meaning and purpose of experiments, the difficulties and limitations of using the experimental design in social and health research, the strategies that researchers use to enhance the validity and generalisability of their findings, the ethical implications of experiments involving humans as 'subjects', and the use and value of experiments in the study of nursing phenomena.

The current emphasis on systematic reviews of randomised controlled trials (RCTs) in itself warrants a closer examination of the experiment as a viable design in nursing research; this is why it is given a lengthy treatment here.

THE MEANING AND PURPOSE OF EXPERIMENTS

The term 'experiment' conjures up images of scientists mixing chemicals in a laboratory or observing the behaviour of rats in conditions induced by a researcher. Television adverts often show a man or woman in a white coat making such statements as 'test after test proves that' a particular brand of detergent or cat food is better than others. In everyday life, too, we also 'experiment'. A spice may be added to our usual recipe to find out whether it makes it taste better. Painkillers are taken to relieve headaches or sleeping tablets to induce sleep. The aim in each case is to attempt to produce a change (improve taste, relieve pain or induce sleep) by doing something (adding a spice, or taking painkillers or sleeping tablets). Whether or not we know it, we unwittingly carry out experiments, more often on ourselves, with the aim of making our lives more comfortable. Most people are particular about the type of painkiller they take for a headache. They have probably arrived at this choice by 'trying' out several brands. Some people with back pain will 'try' different forms of treatment, such as medication prescribed by a general practitioner, herbal medicine or the services of an osteopath. They know how they felt before and after each of these treatments and are thus able to make up their minds about its effectiveness. In 'trying out' these drugs or treatments, people have in fact engaged in a 'trial' or experiment.

Professionals, too, experiment during the course of their work. To enhance learning, teachers may 'experiment' with seminars, group discussions or lectures. Nurses may try a different type of dressing or introduce a different approach to the organisation of patient care, such as primary nursing or team nursing. If these do not produce the desired effect, they may try other approaches. By basing their practice on 'trial and error', some nurses unwittingly 'experiment' on their clients, and the negative implications of this can be serious.

In Chapter 2 it was explained that people need to know why things happen. A headache is explained by pressure at work, a hot summer may be attributed to global warming and an increase in child violence is often blamed on the type of TV programme they watch. Even when we cannot explain a phenomenon such as winning a lottery, we put it down to 'lady luck'. In fact, we are constantly preoccupied with 'cause and effect'. The relationship between cause and effect is the essence of an experiment.

RESEARCH EXPERIMENTS

The difference between the types of experiment that lay people and practitioners unwittingly carry out and 'research experiments' is that, in the latter, the researcher, systematically and rigorously, studies cause-and-effect relationships between variables, by taking steps to ensure that the results obtained (the effect) can only be attributed to the intervention (the cause).

Suppose a nurse observes that constipation is rife among patients on her ward. Having read in the literature that lack of fibre may be responsible for constipation, she decides to put this to the 'test'. After finding out that the amount of fibre in their current diet is in fact low, she increases it and observes whether there is a reduction in the incidence of constipation. However, a colleague may be sceptical and say that these results would have been obtained with or without an increase in fibre and that other factors, such as medication, mobility, age or nursing care, may be implicated. To rule out the possibility that the reduction in constipation would have happened anyway, the nurse can decide to have two groups of patients: one receiving the current diet, and the other the new diet. Additionally, she may 'control' the other factors by making sure that patients in both groups are, in general, similar in the amount and type of medication they take, in their degree of mobility, and in age, and that they are nursed by the same team of nurses. To avoid the possibility of bias in the selection of patients, the researcher can randomly assign them to either group. In so doing, she has carried out a research experiment. She has:

- put a hypothesis to the test (that a high-fibre diet reduces constipation);
- introduced an intervention (a new high-fibre diet) and measured the outcome (a reduction in constipation);
- compared the pre-test scores (the level of constipation before the experiment) with the post-test scores (the level of constipation after the experiment);
- compared the scores of the group of patients on whom she experimented (experimental group) with those of the group receiving the usual diet (control group);
- controlled other factors that may work for or against a reduction in constipation (by ensuring that both groups are similar in relevant factors except in the amount of fibre in their diets);
- randomly allocated patients to the two groups.

Our nurse has in effect met the three requirements of a true experiment: intervention, control and randomisation.

INTERVENTION

Without intervention, there is no experiment. A researcher has to do something to produce an effect or outcome. In the above example, the intervention is the introduction of a new diet, and the outcome is a reduction in constipation. In a correlational study, the researcher would not actively have intervened by introducing the new diet but instead could have, for example, carried out a survey of the fibre content of patients' diets and their bowel habits to find out whether or not there was a link between these two variables. Portsmouth *et al.* (1994) give us an example of a correlational study on the relationship between 'dietary calcium intake and energy intake of 113 eighteen-year-old university students in Western Australia'. They did not introduce any intervention but instead asked the students to record what they consumed over a period of 4 days. The analysis of these records showed that there was a strong positive association between these two variables (dietary calcium and dietary energy intake). In experimental studies the researcher attempts to make things happen, while in correlational ones she studies phenomena as they are. In health research, the term 'treatment' is often used instead of 'intervention'.

The experiment is the design of choice to test hypotheses and theories. In Chapter 7, a hypothesis was defined as 'a statement in one sentence, about the expected relationship between two or more variables'. In its simplest form, the hypothesis has two variables: *independent* and *dependent*. An experiment can have one or more hypotheses, for example, in Allen *et al.*'s (1992) study of the 'effectiveness of a preoperative teaching programme for cataract patients', the two hypotheses were:

> subjects who participated in the preoperative teaching programme would have higher scores on the knowledge and skill test and lower anxiety on their first postoperative home visit than those subjects who did not participate in the programme

and

> subjects who participated in the preoperative teaching programme would require fewer postoperative visits by the home care nurse and require less nurse's time than subjects who did not participate in the programme.

In this study, those who did not participate in the new programme received the 'routine teaching done by the ophthalmologist and hospital nurses' (Allen *et al.*, 1992).

In the first hypothesis, the independent variables (interventions) were a new preoperative teaching programme and the routine teaching. The dependent variables (the outcome) were knowledge, skill and anxiety. In an experiment, the researcher varies or *manipulates* the independent variables and measures their effects on the dependent variables. In this case, the teaching given to patients was varied, one group receiving the new programme and the other routine teaching.

The purpose of an experiment is to collect data to support or reject the hypothesis. Although experiments should have a formal hypothesis (Bond, 1993), you will find when reading research articles that many of them express the purpose of their studies in the form of questions. For example, Koh and Thomas (1994), in their study of patient-controlled analgesia (PCA), used an experimental design to collect data to answer questions such as:

1. Does PCA save nurses' time in pain control procedures compared to the traditional IMI method?
2. Given the time gain, are PCA patients more satisfied with nursing care than the patients in the traditional group?

3. Are there any differences in patients' satisfaction with nursing care between a ward that uses PCA and one that does not?

On the other hand, Hundley *et al.* (1994), in their study comparing 'midwife managed delivery unit' with 'consultant led care', formulated their research problem in the form of an objective which was:

> to compare care and delivery of low risk women in a midwife managed delivery unit with care and delivery in the consultant led labour ward in terms of four sorts of outcomes. As well as maternal and perinatal morbidity, reported here, we looked at expectations, experiences, and satisfaction of parturient women; the role, experiences, and satisfaction of midwifery staff, and costs of care.

One can see that the above questions and objectives have the potential of being translated into hypotheses such as 'PCA saves more nurses' time in pain control procedures than the traditional IMI method' or 'there is lower prenatal morbidity in midwife managed delivery than in consultant led delivery'. See how many hypotheses you can develop from the above questions and objectives.

Many authors do not state their hypotheses, questions or objectives. This does not facilitate the task of the reader, who has to piece together information from different sections of the article, including the results section, to find out what the author should have stated clearly in the first place.

CONTROL

Experimental and control groups

To make sure that the intervention which she has introduced is the only variable responsible for the outcome, the researcher can devise strategies to control *extraneous variables*. These are variables other than the experimental intervention that may also affect the outcome. Suppose that a researcher uses an experimental design to test the effectiveness of counselling in the treatment of a group of depressed patients. She may find that after a series of counselling sessions, their conditions have improved. She cannot be certain, however, that 'with the passing of time' they would not have got better anyway or that other factors such as the drug treatment they were also receiving or their nursing care did not contribute to their improvement. To find out whether the counselling sessions were indeed the only contributing factor, she could have compared her group of patients with another group receiving no treatment. However, in health-care settings it is likely that patients are receiving some form of treatment. She can, therefore, compare the group of patients receiving the counselling sessions with another group receiving the usual treatment. The group that is receiving the new intervention is called the *experimental group*, and the group with which the comparison is made is called the *control group*.

Because there is a possibility that some of the patients in one group may be more acutely ill or one group may have more women than men, for example, the researcher has to make sure that the two groups are similar in the major characteristics, such as age, gender, social class, type and duration of depression, that may affect the recovery from depression. In this way, she will have more confidence that her results are unaffected by these variables. She has, therefore, exerted control over these extraneous variables.

Matched pairs

One strategy that has been useful in ensuring that the subjects in the two groups are similar in the relevant characteristics is 'matching'. If a researcher requires an equal distribution of the following characteristics – women aged between 48 and 50, middle class and newly diagnosed with breast cancer – in her experimental and control groups, she will look for two subjects who meet these criteria and allocate one to each group until the required sample size is reached. This matched-pairs allocation technique is usually appropriate when the researcher knows in advance which variables to control. Also, as Dane (1990) points out, 'there is no end to the number of potential variables that may require matching, and therefore you can never be sure you have matched participants on all relevant characteristics'. Another limitation of this approach is that it can take a long time to find enough matched pairs for an adequate sample size. To partly overcome this problem, the researcher may try to match groups instead of pairs.

Between-subject design

By allocating subjects to either the experimental or control group, the researcher is making a comparison between the *two* groups of subjects. This type of control is known as between-subject design. Hauck and Dimmock (1994) conducted an experiment to evaluate the effect of an information booklet on breast-feeding duration. The experimental group of 75 breast-feeding mothers were sent a breast-feeding information booklet and a letter of introduction, and the control group of 75 breast-feeding mothers were sent only a letter of introduction.

Between-subject designs can have more than two groups. For example, in Sleep and Grant's (1988) study of 'the effects of salt and

Savlon bath concentrate post-partum', they allocated subjects to three groups. As they explained:

> One thousand eight hundred women recruited within 24 hours of vaginal delivery were randomly allocated to one of three 10-day bathing policies aimed at relieving perineal discomfort during the post-partum period. Six hundred mothers were asked to add salt, 600 to add Savlon bath concentrate and 600 not to add anything to the bathwater.

The number of groups depends on the purpose of the experiment. Sometimes researchers want to test the effects of a number of interventions in one experiment, as in McMahon's (1994) study of sub-mammary lesions (inflamed skin beneath the breasts of females) where five types of intervention were used in their treatment: talc, inserting gauze, applying Drapolene, a hydrocolloid patch and, for the control group, the application of plain soap and water.

Solomon four design

Sometimes the purpose of more groups is not to have more interventions but rather to have more control over extraneous variables. Earlier, it was explained that a pre-test and a post-test are normally carried out to find whether the independent variable (or intervention) has caused a change in the dependent one (outcome). It may happen, however, that the act of pre-testing may itself influence the outcome. For example, it could be that by assessing how depressed subjects are at the beginning of an experiment (pre-testing), some may become more aware of their condition and thereafter motivate themselves to get better. To avoid such influences, a *Solomon four* design can be used. This consists of four groups, of which two are control and two are experimental. Pre-tests and post-tests are carried out with one control and one experimental group only, and post-tests only for the other control and experimental group:

Experimental group 1	Pre-test	Intervention	Post-test
Control group 1	Pre-test	Usual treatment or no intervention	Post-test
Experimental group 2	No pre-test	Intervention	Post-test
Control group 2	No pre-test	Usual treatment or no intervention	Post-test

This type of design eliminates the effects that a pre-test may have on the outcome. By comparing the results of these groups, it is possible to discover whether such influences have indeed crept in.

Crossover or within-subject design

Despite the efforts of researchers to select subjects with similar characteristics for the experimental and control groups, the fact remains that
they are different groups of individuals and we can never be sure
whether or not some of their differences, however negligible, account for
differences, if any, in the outcome. To overcome this problem, the same
group of people can serve as both the control and experimental groups.
For example, if a researcher wants to find out whether aromatherapy
can induce sleep in patients with sleeping problems, she can select a
group of 20 patients, administer aromatherapy to 10 patients and give
the other 10 their usual sedatives for a period of 3 weeks. She then
changes this over, giving the first group their usual sedatives and the
other group the aromatherapy. By comparing the results for each
patient, the researcher can assess the effects of the new intervention.
This type of allocation is called a *crossover* or *within-subject design* as it
involves the same subjects 'crossing over' to the new intervention after
receiving their usual treatment and vice versa. An example of a
crossover design is in Roberts *et al.*'s (1994) study of Boomerang pillows
(U or V shaped) and respiratory capacity. As they explained:

> The design of the study was an experimental crossover design in which the
> vital capacity of well persons was compared at rest in a semi Fowler's
> position. Subjects were measured before and after a period of resting on a
> boomerang pillow and before and after a period of resting on straight
> pillows. Each subject was measured both in the control (straight pillows)
> and treatment (boomerang pillows) position and subjects therefore served
> as their own controls. This design minimized the possibility of differences
> between groups.

The main advantage of this type of design is that 'subjects are paired
with themselves and the influence of patient characteristics can be
eliminated' (Beck, 1989). One of the main problems with the crossover
design is related to the carry-over effect. This occurs 'when the effect of
the first treatment continues into the second treatment period' (Beck,
1989). In the above example of aromatherapy and sleeping problems, it
could happen that the aromatherapy that the first group of patients
received was so effective in relaxing them that its effects continued for a
while even after the therapy was discontinued. If this group were to have
their usual sleeping tablets immediately after the aromatherapy was
stopped, it would be difficult to assess whether their sleep was helped by
their usual drug therapy or by the carry-over effects of aromatherapy.
Researchers must pay particular attention to this problem and often

leave a time gap between the two interventions. Passmore *et al.* (1993) show in RE 23 how this can be done.

RESEARCH EXAMPLE 23
Passmore *et al.* (1993)
Chronic constipation in long-stay elderly patients: a comparison of lactulose and a senna–fibre combination

A crossover design

This multicentre study, conducted in long-stay elderly patients in hospitals or nursing home care (five hospitals and two nursing homes), compared the efficacy and cost-effectiveness of a senna–fibre combination and lactulose in treating constipation. As the authors explain:

> According to a randomised, double-blind, cross over design, patients (77) received active senna–fibre combination 10 ml daily with lactulose placebo 15 ml twice daily, or active lactulose 15 ml twice daily with senna–fibre placebo 10 ml daily for two 14-day periods according to a computer generated randomisation code.

Passmore *et al.* (1993) made sure that 'before entry into the first phase, and between treatments, subjects had a three to five day period free of laxatives'.

Comments
1. Each patient received two consecutive treatments: (a) active senna–fibre with lactulose placebo, and (b) active lactulose with senna–fibre placebo. The order in which they took them was determined by a computer.
2. Before crossing over to the second treatment, the researchers allowed a period of 3–5 days 'laxative free' to avoid any carry-over effect the first treatment might have had.
3. To avoid the possibility of the participants and researchers knowing which treatment was the senna–fibre combination and which was the lactulose, a placebo was used for each situation. Thus, the 'senna–fibre combination with lactulose placebo' would have been similar to the 'active lactulose and senna–fibre placebo', especially as the two were administered in the same doses. The term 'double blind' is explained later on.

While in the crossover design the same patient receives the two interventions consecutively, it is possible in some cases for the same patient to receive two interventions at the same time. In McMahon's study of submammary lesions, two interventions were carried out on the same subject at the same time (McMahon, 1994). For example, a subject was treated with Drapolene cream on one breast and soap and water on the other. This avoids the need for a control and an experimental group and ensures that extraneous variables are reduced to a minimum since it involves the same patient and almost the same type of lesion. However, there are very few cases where this type of experiment would be possible.

PLACEBOS AND BLIND TECHNIQUES

Two other strategies to control extraneous variables are the use of placebos and blind techniques in experimental designs.

Placebos

The idea of receiving a new form of treatment can itself make some people feel better. If some subjects in an experiment have high expectations of a new drug or other form of treatment being tested, this can affect the results of the study. To overcome the possible suggestive effect of the new intervention, a placebo – a substance that has no pharmacological or therapeutic property – can be administered to one group for comparison purposes. It is made, as much as possible, to resemble the new drug or treatment. Kleijnen *et al.* (1994) point out that:

> in any medical intervention there are placebo effects to some degree... these include perception of the therapist by the patient, the effect of the therapeutic setting, and the credibility of the medication itself (size, shape, colour, taste).

For an example of the use of placebos in an experiment see RE 23.

Single-blind and double-blind techniques

Being aware of which interventions the control and experimental groups are receiving may introduce bias on the part of the subjects and researchers. Patients may have a preference for a particular drug with which they are familiar or may have high expectations of the new therapy being tested. These may influence their assessment of the interventions. Researchers, too, may be biased in favour of the intervention being tested, and this may affect their observations and recording of data. To avoid these types of influence, it is possible, especially when two 'drugs' look and taste similar, as when placebos are used, not to let the subjects know whether they are in the experimental or the control group. For ethical reasons, their informed consent for taking part in the experiment must be obtained. A *single-blind* trial is one in which either the participants or the researchers are unaware of the allocation to groups. A design in which both the subjects and the researchers are unaware of which drug each group is receiving is called a *double-blind* trial. Dumas (1987) describes a triple-blind design as one in which 'persons other than the experimenters evaluate the response variables without knowing the group assignments of the subject'.

Cook and Campbell (1979) explain how the need for the placebo control group and double-blind experiments arose:

> In the earlier medical experiments on drugs, the psychotherapeutic effect of the doctor's helpful concern was confounded with the chemical action of the pill. So, too, were the doctor's and the patient's belief that the pill should have helped. To circumvent these problems and to increase confidence that any observed effects could be attributed to the chemical action of the pill alone, the placebo control group and the double-blind experimental design were introduced.

RANDOMISATION

Controlling extraneous variables with the use of a control group whose subjects are similar in the relevant characteristics to those in the experimental group does not necessarily ensure that biases are absent in the allocation of subjects to the two groups, and those more likely to respond positively to the new intervention may be assigned to the experimental group. The researcher may have 'hand-picked' subjects for the two groups. A random allocation can go some way towards removing any subjective bias that a researcher may show in selecting subjects. Earlier it was explained that 'matching' can be used to select equivalent groups but that there are practical difficulties in obtaining 'matched pairs'. In experimental terms, randomisation means that subjects have equal chances of being allocated to a particular group.

There are different ways in which randomisation can be carried out. If all eligible subjects are known in advance, it is possible, if the numbers are small, to pick names out of a box and allocate them alternately to groups. With large numbers, a computer package may be of assistance. More often, subjects are entered into an experiment at the time of admission to treatment. They can be allocated alternately to each group or the researcher may fill all the places in one group before allocating the rest to another group. A computer programme can also assist in the allocation of subjects as they enter the trial (see RE 24).

There is no guarantee with randomisation that subjects in the control and experimental groups are equivalent, especially when a small number of subjects is used. For example, if there are 4 men in a sample of 20 subjects, there is no guarantee that randomisation will allocate 2 to each group. However, large samples can have an equalising effect. In the study of the effects of salt and Savlon bath (mentioned above),

1800 women were randomly allocated to 3 groups (salt only, Savlon only and no additive) of 600 people each (Sleep and Grant, 1988). Descriptions of the groups at entry to the trial show that there were few differences in some of the relevant characteristics of the women in the three groups, which were similar with regard to maternal age and parity (Sleep and Grant, 1988). However, the number of assisted deliveries was 17.2, 21.4 and 15.7 in the three groups respectively; assisted deliveries may have an effect on perineal healing.

A *randomised controlled trial* (RCT) is an experiment in which subjects are randomly allocated to one or more control groups and to one or more experimental groups, depending on the number of interventions. It is a popular type of experiment for testing the effectiveness of drugs and other forms of therapies, and is increasingly being used to assess the effectiveness and cost-efficiency of other types of intervention (see Cupples and McKnight, 1994, in RE 24) and policies as well. The uses and limitations of RCTs are discussed later in this chapter.

SINGLE-SUBJECT EXPERIMENT

One of the problems of experiments involving people in health-care settings is finding large samples. Even when this is possible, it is difficult to allocate them into groups that are identical in relation to the relevant variables. The problem is further exacerbated when subjects, for various reasons, drop out of the experiments. A single-subject or single-case design, on the other hand, avoids these difficulties since it involves only one subject at a time. In its simplest form, it involves a pre-test followed by an intervention and a post-test. For example, a single-subject design could be used in an experiment to find out the effect of relaxation therapy on stress in one particular patient. Baseline measurements can be taken to find out how stressed the patient is before receiving relaxation therapy. A post-test measurement will then determine whether or not the therapy has been effective. Such a design is known as the AB design, where A is the pre-test, B the post-test and the intervention the middle.

It will, however, take more than just one intervention for a firm conclusion on the effect of relaxation therapy to be drawn. This will have to be repeated many times, especially on different days and if possible in different circumstances, to avoid other influences. Bithell (1994) points out that some researchers require data to be collected on at least ten occasions 'if statistical analysis is to be performed'.

Single-case designs give researchers the opportunity to focus on an individual and therefore pay more attention to details. It is particularly suited to the principle of patient-centred care, since the interaction between the individual and the treatment is unique, although lessons can be learnt which can apply to other cases as well. Riddoch and Lennon (1994) remind us that the single-case experimental method has been well established in psychology and educational research since the late 1800s and early 1900s. As they explain:

> Much of child psychology developed from the work of Piaget who based many of his theories on observations of his own children. In the field of learning, Skinner, Pavlov and Thorndike emphasised the importance of the intensive study of an individual in deriving an understanding of conditioning.

RESEARCH EXAMPLE 24 Cupples and McKnight (1994)
Randomised controlled trial of health promotion in general practice for patients at high cardiovascular risk

Randomisation

The objective of this study was 'to assess the value of health education for patients with angina in reducing risk factors for cardiovascular disease and lessening the effect of angina on everyday activities'.

According to the authors:

> Patients were identified from 18 group general practices in the greater Belfast area. General practitioners were asked to identify patients aged under 75 years who had had angina for at least six months and did not have any other severe illness.

After interviewing potential subjects and taking baseline measurements of their angina, smoking habits, exercise, diet, etc., a total of 688 patients were allocated to two groups: intervention (342) and control (346). The following procedure was carried out in order to randomise the participants:

> The health visitor opened an opaque, sealed and numbered envelope containing the allocation, which had been generated by a computer program using random permuted blocks.

Comments

1. Not all reports of experimental studies explain their randomisation method as is the case here.
   A computer programme was used to allocate subjects. Care was taken to prevent investigators from interfering with the method of selection by the use of 'opaque' envelopes. According to DerSimonian et al. (1982), 'carefully prepared sealed envelopes can work, but only if they are completely opaque even when held up to a strong light'.
2. Randomised controlled trials are normally associated with drugs and other therapies. However, in this study, the intervention consisted of giving 'practical relevant advice regarding cardiovascular risk factors'. The patients were also reviewed at 4-monthly intervals and given appropriate health education. The control group received no such input, and both groups were reviewed after 2 years.

One of the major limitations of single-case designs is that their findings cannot be generalised to similar populations, since they are individual cases. Bithell (1994) questions the scientific credibility of single-subject experiments. According to her:

> if we wish to demonstrate the general effectiveness of a treatment for patients with a particular problem, then a group study must be carried out with a representative sample drawn from that patient group. A series of case studies will not do.

Riddoch and Lennon (1994) disagree with Bithell's arguments and claim that 'a series of case studies may provide strong evidence for the efficacy of a particular treatment manipulation provided every attempt has been made to control for threats to internal validity'. Internal validity and external validity are explained below.

In RE 25 Beecroft (1993) uses a single-case design to study the effects of social skills training in adolescents on haemodialysis.

QUASI-EXPERIMENTS

For a number of reasons, ethical and practical, it may sometimes not be possible to carry out true experiments in nursing and midwifery. For example, if a researcher introduces a new model of nursing in a ward, it is not feasible to randomly allocate patients to two groups in the same ward or even to allocate them to different wards because of clinical, organisational and ethical considerations. The best she can do is to compare the ward introducing the new model with a similar ward in the same hospital. Although the researcher has a new intervention, she does not have a 'proper' control group but a comparison group as she cannot randomise subjects to each group. She has only partly met the criteria of a true experiment. In effect, she has carried out a quasi-experiment, a design that must have a new intervention but not necessarily a control group and has no randomisation (see RE 26 for a study using a quasi-experimental approach).

This type of experiment is appropriate in cases where the researcher seeks to introduce minimum disruption in a natural setting. Because in quasi-experiments researchers do not have the high degree of control over extraneous variables that are seen in true experiments, it is not possible to state with confidence that any new intervention is actually responsible for the effects measured. In other words, quasi-experiments cannot establish cause-and-effect relationships with certainty but it can establish strong links. However, because they take place in a natural setting, the findings are more generalisable than are those of true experiments.

RESEARCH EXAMPLE 25

Beecroft (1993)

Social skills training and cognitive restructuring for adolescents on hemodialysis

Single-subject design

The author carried out a series of single-subject experiments on adolescents with end-stage renal disease (ESRD). The purpose of the experiments was to give each adolescent (there were six in all) 'eight weekly training sessions' in social skills and 'cognitive restructuring'. These sessions were conducted by the researcher with each subject separately. Two of the three questions which the study addressed were as follows:

1. Do chronically ill adolescents undergoing hemodialysis and receiving cognitive restructuring and assertive skills training increase their perceptions of self-efficacy?
2. Is there an increase in the subjects' self-report of assertive skills from baseline to intervention phase after cognitive restructuring and assertive skills training?

Comments

1. The reason for choosing the single-subject design was, according to Beecroft, because of the 'great variability among adolescents with ESRD', especially in relation to 'gender, the age of disease onset, family support, disease severity, and individual personality'.

   The author also found it 'difficult to find a significant population of adolescents with ESRD at a single medical center' and 'random assignment of a sufficient number of subjects to treatment and non-treatment groups was impossible'.

2. Although six subjects took part in this study, they were not studied as a group but as individuals, that is there was a series of six single-subject design experiments. The subjects received individual training and did not commence the experiment at the same time.

3. Three of the six subjects dropped out of the study. The author concluded that:

   > it may not be possible to draw sweeping conclusions regarding implications for practice from the data provided by the study of 3 subjects; however, this study does provide sufficient information for another researcher to either replicate the study or design a succeeding study.

There are a variety of quasi-experimental designs. At the very least, the researcher can introduce a new intervention into a group and measure the outcome. For example, relaxation therapy may be introduced to a group of patients, and the researcher may want to find out whether they report a decrease in their level of anxiety. This is the weakest form of experiment since there are no baseline scores (pre-test) and no other groups with which to compare the final scores.

RESEARCH **26** Lima-Basto (1995)
EXAMPLE **Implementing change in nurses' professional behaviours: limitations of the cognitive approach**

A quasi-experiment

This quasi-experimental study sought answers to two research questions:

1. To what extent will an intervention, based on information processes, change nurse–patient interaction and the problem-solving approach to care?
2. Are there some cognitive-emotional factors associated with change in a group of nurses' professional behaviours?

Seventeen nurses from one cardiology unit of a general state hospital took part in this experiment. The intervention consisted of, among others, three group sessions, individual supervision and feedback, demonstration videos and individual tuition. Data were collected prior to the intervention, immediately after the intervention and 4.5 months later. Analysis of the data at this point showed 'limited change in professional behaviours'. Therefore the researcher decided to continue the intervention. Data were collected 2 months later and again, 1 month after that.

Comments

1. Only one group (experimental) was used in this study. As it lacks a control group (and therefore randomisation), the study meets only one of the three criteria of a true experiment (i.e. intervention). This is why it is a quasi-experiment.
2. One of the strengths of quasi-experiments is that they are carried out in the natural setting and therefore closely resemble the context in which people live and work. This also means that researchers have little control over extraneous factors. For example, in this study, to randomly allocate these nurses to two groups would have caused disruptions in the ward and would not have been feasible. In real life, too, practitioners do not always have control over factors that can influence what they do. In this study, the author is aware that several 'external occurrences' could have 'jeopardised' the internal validly of this experiment, but 'they were controlled as much as possible'.
3. Lima-Basto used a time-series design consisting of one pre-test and four post-tests. These series of tests on different occasions give a more accurate picture of changes over time.

The next step up is when a researcher measures the anxiety level prior to and after the introduction of relaxation therapy. This time, there is more confidence that a change has happened (if it has), although it is still difficult to establish with certainty that relaxation therapy is the cause, because a number of other factors may be implicated. To be more certain, the researcher may decide to have two groups: one experimental and one comparison. She measures the anxiety level on the experimental ward before and after the intervention. She also carries out the same measurements at the same time with patients on a similar ward (comparison group) who did not receive relaxation therapy. She can begin to have more confidence in her results. This last design is called a *non-equivalent groups* design. It may be that the subjects in both groups are similar in many respects but that the researcher did not have enough control over their selection and allocation to ensure that they were in fact equivalent. These three designs are depicted in Figure 9.1 below.

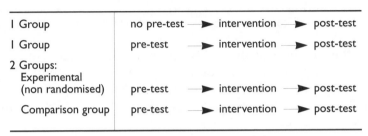

Figure 9.1 Quasi-experimental designs.

Another quasi-experimental design is the *interrupted time series* (ITS) (Cook and Campbell, 1979). This involves only one group (experimental) and a series of measurements before and after the intervention. This can be illustrated as follows (Polit and Hungler, 1983):

$$O_1 \quad O_2 \quad O_3 \quad O_4 \qquad X \qquad O_5 \quad O_6 \quad O_7 \quad O_8$$

O_1 to O_4 represent the four baseline measurements at time intervals selected by the researcher, X represents the time at which the new intervention takes place and O_5 to O_8 represent the four post-intervention measurements at time intervals selected by the researcher.

Suppose that a nurse wants to carry out an experiment by introducing primary nursing onto a ward to find out whether or not it increases patient satisfaction with nursing care. She can measure patient satisfaction on four occasions, monthly for 4 months, prior to the introduction of primary nursing, and can carry out four measurements at the same intervals afterwards. Her reason for the multiple measurements could be that one measurement may not be reliable since any event happening on that day or immediately prior to it might influence the results. By having four measurements at reasonable intervals, it is hoped that the same events may not be present each time. A better picture of patient satisfaction (which can fluctuate over time) can be obtained by more than one measurement. Multiple post-intervention measurements have similar functions. It can detect, among others, the 'novelty effect' of new interventions. Most of the phenomena with which nurses deal are dynamic and evolving and can be better studied over time.

There are a number of variations on the ITS (Cook and Campbell, 1979), including the two-groups design, depicted in Figure 9.2.

Experimental group:	O_1	O_2	O_3	O_4	X	O_5	O_6	O_7	O_8
Comparison group:	O_1	O_2	O_3	O_4	X	O_5	O_6	O_7	O_8

Figure 9.2 Two-groups interrupted time series.

One of the strengths of the ITS is that multiple measurements over a period of time give a more accurate representation of phenomena that fluctuate. Its main weakness is that the extended period of time required for multiple measurements increases the opportunity for extraneous variables to creep in.

INTERNAL AND EXTERNAL VALIDITY OF EXPERIMENTS

The purpose of experiments in nursing and health care in general is ultimately to contribute to better services. The usefulness of their findings, however, depends on their internal and external validity. *Internal validity* is the extent to which changes, if any, in the dependent variable can be said to have been caused by the independent variable alone. *External validity* is the extent to which the findings of an experiment can be applied or generalised to other similar populations and settings.

Internal validity

A number of unwanted factors internal to the study can, on their own or combined, interfere with the experiment and make it difficult to conclude with confidence that the findings reflect the true relationship between the two variables being investigated and nothing else. The purpose of control is precisely to eliminate or minimise these unwanted effects. Brennan and Croft (1994) ask two questions that can be used to assess the internal validity of an experiment:

1. To what extent might flaws in the study design have biased the study result?
2. If the result is thought to be free from bias, to what extent might other causes have confounded the observed association?

From these questions emerge two terms central to the understanding of internal validity: biases and confounders. Biases can be present at every stage of an experiment, from the admission of subjects to the experiment to the interpretation and reporting of findings. On the other hand, some factors in the study may work in the same or opposite direction to the independent variable and therefore affect the dependent variable. These factors or variables are known as confounders or *confounding* variables. The following hypothetical experiment gives an example of confounders.

A teacher carries out an experiment to investigate the effectiveness of a new study method: self-directed learning. She allocates 20 students to the experimental (self-directed learning) group and 20 students to the control group, who were exposed to their usual teaching method (lectures). The teacher then compares the students' knowledge at the end of the module and finds that those receiving lectures have a higher knowledge score than do the self-directed learning students. She had 'controlled' other variables such as age, gender and educational level to prevent these from influencing the results by making sure that, on average, both groups had students of the same age and educational level and had an equal number of males and females.

However, one variable of which she may have been aware but which she found difficult to control was the 'learning ability' of each student. It could be that the learning ability of those receiving lectures was higher than that of the other group. The researcher cannot state with confidence that the lecture is the better method of imparting knowledge, nor can she know whether the difference in the two groups' learning abilities is responsible for the difference in knowledge scores. In this experiment, 'learning ability' may be a confounding variable as it may be confounding, or confusing, the results. On the other hand, the researcher may also find that some members of the lecture group have also been exposed to a television programme on their module topic during the course of the experiment. She was powerless to do anything to prevent this as she learnt about it after the experiment was completed. Therefore 'exposure to the TV programme' is a confounding variable. Researchers may be aware of such variables and unable to control them, or be unaware of them. Their task is to speculate on the effects of all possible confounders as they are more familiar with their study than are those reading the report.

The random allocation of subjects should remove possible confounders by making the groups more or less similar in relevant characteristics, but it does not always do so. It may happen, for example, that by randomly allocating patients with the same type of illness to two groups, one group ends up with some patients who are more acutely ill than the other group. The severity or acuteness of the illness can therefore constitute a confounding variable. It has the potential to affect the results, especially if a drug or therapy is the subject of an experiment. It is sometimes possible to make allowance for such effects when data are analysed and interpreted. However, such undesirable interference from confounding variables can and must be avoided. According to Brennan and Croft (1994), samples in clinical trials can be made as large as necessary 'to ensure that imbalances in randomisation are extremely unlikely'.

Biases and confounders threaten the internal validity of experiments, hence the term 'threats to internal validity'. Cook and Campbell (1979) have identified a number of factors that can affect study findings. Some of these will be used here to assess the internal validity of experiments. These are history, maturation, testing, instrumentation, selection and mortality.

History effects

A history effect is produced whenever some uncontrolled event alters participants' responses (Dane, 1990). In the above experiment on teaching methods, the uncontrolled event is the TV programme that was shown during the time the experiment took place. According to Dane (1990), the event is a commonplace event, not necessarily a 'truly historical' one. It may not come to the attention of the researcher and thus its effects may remain unknown, but it may not confound the results if both groups are exposed to it. An example of a historical effect comes from a study by Berg *et al.* (1994) on 'nurses' creativity, tedium and burnout', in which the authors speculate that the 'results may have been affected by factors of an individual or social type'. As they explained:

> there was a large organizational change in the public sector during the intervention which meant that both wards were completely reorganized from the county council to the community. Also Sweden, in general, is facing increasing unemployment.

Instrumentation effects

The measuring process itself can be biased. Operational definitions of independent and dependent variables can be subjective (see Chapter 7). The choice of data collection methods may also reflect the researcher's preference and may not be the most appropriate for the study. For example, Allen *et al.* (1992), in their study of 'the effectiveness of a preoperative teaching programme for cataract patients', admitted that the questionnaire they had developed had some limitations. They explained:

> the areas of knowledge tested may not be the most important ones despite a content review by ophthalmic nurses and ophthalmologists. A true–false

format was perceived by the researchers to be the most appropriate for elderly subjects. Although subjects did not have difficulty in answering this kind of question, it may be that another format would be more appropriate.

The measuring process can also undergo changes that can bias the results. Smith (1991) points out:

> Observations, questionnaires, and interviews are commonly used in experimentation as measuring instruments. Observers and interviewers are particularly subject to changes in instrumentation – they learn, in the process of observing or interviewing, how to make different measurements, and their temporary motives (hunger, fatigue) may change the measurements. To the extent that they unwittingly make measurement changes during pretests and posttests, they contribute to instrumental invalidity.

A common problem with measuring tools is that they are sometimes not sensitive enough to measure the small differences between experimental and control group scores. A study by Martin *et al.* (1994), comparing patients receiving the 'home treatment team' nursing care and those receiving 'appropriate conventional community services', found that:

> The assessment scales chosen may have been insufficiently sensitive. If patients who benefited were those at the threshold of managing at home, a smaller change than we could detect with this study might nevertheless have resulted in a favourable outcome.

Selection effects

There are at least two points in the choice of participants at which bias can 'creep in'. Although the experimenter can set inclusion criteria (such as patients of a certain age group and not seriously ill), she still has to make a judgement of whom to include or exclude. Assessing the severity of illnesses is not as straightforward as it seems: it involves a degree of subjectivity. The allocation of subjects to groups can also give rise to bias. The more objective the allocation of subjects, the less likely it is to be biased. In quasi-experiments, researchers often have to 'work' with the people who are available. These may comprise, in the words of Smith (1991), 'volunteers, hypochondriacs, scientific do-gooders, those who have nothing else to do, and so forth'.

In true experiments, randomisation is expected to result in the equalisation of groups but, as explained earlier, this may not always be the case. While the three groups in the study of the 'effects of salt,

Savlon bath concentrate post-partum' by Sleep and Grant (1988) were similar in most other characteristics, they differed in their mode of delivery. Adjustments had to be made to take into account this potential source of bias in the sample.

Mortality effects

Researchers take care in allocating subjects so that groups are as far as possible similar in all the important characteristics. When subjects drop out, either because they die, cannot tolerate treatment or simply want to stop taking part, it can create an imbalance between the groups. The loss of participants to a study is known as *mortality* or *attrition*. Not only do groups become smaller in size, but they may also become dissimilar in the relevant characteristics. In fact, the benefits of randomisation can be undermined by mortality, especially in cases where drop-outs are not even between groups. The reasons why subjects fail to complete the experiment must be made clear and must be taken into account in the analysis of data.

Internal validity is the crucial test that every experiment should pass. As Cook and Campbell (1979) explain:

> Estimating the internal validity of a relationship is a deductive process in which the investigator has to systematically think through how each of the internal validity threats may have influenced the data. Then, the investigator has to examine the data to test which relevant threats can be ruled out. In all of this process, the researcher has to be his or her own best critic, trenchantly examining all of the threats he or she can imagine.

Your task as a reader is to assess the extent to which the researcher does this and to think of possible biases and confounders that may have been overlooked but which may have affected the findings.

Internal validity is not an all-or-nothing issue. It is more a question of the extent to which an experiment has internal validity, as it is not possible to be aware of, or eliminate the effects of, all biases and confounders. The validity of the findings is determined by checks on biases and extraneous variables. The list of all possible confounders must be exhausted before a causal relationship between the variables under study can be established.

External validity

The internal validity of a study is a necessary but not sufficient condition for its findings to be generalisable to other similar populations and settings;

it must also have external validity. An experiment takes place in a particular setting with a specific group of people at a particular time. Together,
these factors contribute to make the experiment a unique happening. The
question to ask is 'can its findings apply readily to similar populations in
different settings?' For this to be possible, the population and setting of the
experiment must closely approximate the population and setting where
the findings are to be used. For example, if a study shows that giving
relevant information prior to surgery relieves postoperative stress, does
this mean that giving information to preoperative surgical patients in
hospitals other than where the experiment was carried out would also
relieve their postoperative stress? Does information-giving have the same
effect in a ward where the atmosphere is relaxed and nurses are attentive
to patients' concerns as in another ward where the atmosphere is tense
and the nurse–patient relationship leaves a lot to be desired?

The main threat to external validity comes from the selection and
allocation of subjects. Randomisation in experiments means the random
allocation of *available* subjects to groups. It does not mean that the
samples are representative of the target populations (see Chapter 10).
Subjects in experiments are typically recruited at the time of diagnosis or
of admission to hospitals. They can be described as accidental samples
and are convenient, since the potential subjects happen to present
themselves at the time of recruitment. Seldom are sample frames
available from which representative samples can be drawn. RCTs also
recruit volunteers, who are then randomly allocated to groups.

In Cupples and McKnight's (1994) study of health promotion in
general practice for patients at high cardiovascular risk, 'letters were
sent to 1431 patients'. Those who responded and were eligible were then
randomly allocated to the control or experimental group using a
computer programme. This example shows that the sample starts by
being 'volunteer' and therefore not necessarily representative of people
at 'high cardiovascular risk'. The target population of people at high
cardiovascular risk consists of people of different gender, class,
educational background, lifestyle and personality. Some may be more
positive towards health promotion than others. It may be that by taking
subjects who are available or who volunteer, most of those who come
forward are from an educated, middle-class background and see the
experiment as an opportunity to do something about their health. What
randomisation does is simply to allocate randomly those who come
forward, for the purpose of having equal groups. The generalisation of
the findings to everyone at high cardiovascular risk is therefore limited.

Not all those who are available or who volunteer are recruited to an
experimental study. The researcher normally selects a sample by
specifying inclusion or exclusion criteria. In this way, the sample is

'cleaned of undesirables'. For example, Koh *et al.* (1994) describe those who were excluded in their study of the effect of a mental stimulation programme on the mental status of elderly patients with dementia as:

> below 55 years of age, or were noisy, violent or irrational, on medication such as sedatives and tranquillizers, known to have marked impairment of vision or hearing, severely incontinent or insufficiently mobile, i.e. unable to walk 50 yards to the room where the sessions were held.

The sample is further 'sanitised' when those who cannot complete the experiment drop out or are withdrawn. The findings of studies such as Koh *et al.*'s (1994) may not be generalisable to all elderly patients with dementia. In real life, many of these patients are 'noisy', 'insufficiently mobile' and receiving medication. Studies of 'sanitised' samples can only have external validity for people who meet the criteria set by the researchers for inclusion in the experiment. Cook and Campbell (1979) ask:

> In which categories of persons can a cause–effect relationship be generalized? Can it be generalized beyond the groups used to establish the initial relationship – to various racial, social, geographical, age, sex, or personality groups?

The limitations and dangers of using narrowly defined samples are spelt out by Newell (1992):

> Exclusions should not be too restrictive, as strictly speaking the results of the trial are applicable only to the population from which the patients/ clients were selected. In practice, if a treatment is shown to be effective, some extrapolation to a somewhat wider group will be made, but this can be hazardous, as in the extrapolation of 'allergic rhinitis' to 'upper respiratory infection', which led to the widespread ineffective use of antihistamines in the treatment of the common cold.

Oldham (1994) puts the issue of internal and external validity of experiments in context:

> Maximising internal validity by exerting a high degree of control may, however, provide an artificial situation reducing the external validity of the results. In the clinical environment, it is often necessary to reach a compromise between the two or ensure that the studies are replicated in a new setting and with different subjects. Much greater confidence can be placed in the findings if the results can be replicated in differing environments.

When evaluating an experiment, you can use the different aspects of internal and external validity discussed here as a 'checklist'. You will find that not all authors provide enough information on their experiments for you to carry out an evaluation effectively. One of the common omissions is information related to the intervention received by the control group. While a detailed description of the new intervention may be provided, the control group's intervention is simply described as the 'current treatment'. Some researchers forget that while they may be familiar with the 'current treatment', many readers are not. For example, in one study on the effect of an educational programme on the knowledge and attitude of patients to a particular topic, the teaching methods, the content and the duration of the programme that the experimental group received were described in detail. No such information was available about the control group. When no significant difference in knowledge and attitude was found, the researcher was at pains to explain why this was so. Attempts were made to explain what the control group 'would have received' rather than what they 'actually' received. In this and other studies, it is not clear how much attention researchers give to finding out what the control groups were exposed to. It is difficult to assess the internal validity of an experiment that sets out to compare two interventions when information on one intervention is not adequate.

Information about randomisation is also often lacking. According to Fetter *et al.* (1989), 'randomisation, a key element, is one of the least reported aspects of clinical trials'. Readers must be made aware of the precise method of random allocation and its implication for the internal or external validity of the findings.

ETHICS OF EXPERIMENTS

A number of ethical issues raised here apply equally to non-experimental research. Because experiments involve interventions by the researcher, they have more potential for causing physical and mental harm. There is an unequal distribution of power between the experimenter and the subject, more power resting with the former. Dane (1990) makes this point when he states that 'the power differential between researcher and participant is often greater in experimental research than in other research methods, if for no other reason than the experimenter can manipulate some aspect of the participant's environment'. The researcher also has power over whom to enter into the experiment and who should receive the current or the new treatment, except where randomisation is used. This unequal power relationship is evident in the fact that researchers possess information about the experiment and its implications, and control how much is given to participants.

There are, however, rules of ethical conduct which, if followed, can to some extent prevent abuse on the part of researchers. Ethical research committees exist for the purpose of ensuring, at least on paper, that participants' rights and well-being are protected. Many would like such committees to have a policing role as well. Clinicians and managers can and should also act as gatekeepers in order to protect the interest of patients.

Often when ethical issues of research are discussed in articles and reports, the main aspects dealt with are anonymity and confidentiality. While these are undoubtedly important, researchers must also be concerned with the physical and mental harm that can be done to participants in experiments. Causing them to worry is stressful enough. As regards clinical trials, Fetter *et al.* (1989) ask 'three central questions': 'is experimentation with human subjects justified?', 'do the possible benefits of conducting the study outweigh the potential risks?' and 'has informed consent been respected?' Let us now look at each of these questions.

Is experimentation with human subjects justified?

Clinicians 'do things' to people all the time without being fully aware of their effectiveness. As explained earlier in this chapter, this form of trial and error is itself a form of 'back-door' and uncontrolled 'experimentation'. At least research experiments are more in the open, with the result that participants' rights can be more protected. The purpose of clinical trials is to assess the effectiveness of particular treatments and to learn more about them for the benefit of more people than those included in the experiment. However, according to Pocock (1983, cited in Fetter *et al.*, 1989), 'where feasible, laboratory and animal experimentation should precede study with humans, particularly on subjects who might be highly vulnerable to treatment effects'. Those concerned with animal welfare may not agree with this statement.

Experiments should only be carried out when necessary. Just because patients are a captive population does not mean that they should be used by anyone wishing to 'prove' anything. Newell (1992) raises doubts also about the ethical implications of using a small number of subjects in experiments. As the author explains:

> The ethical aspect of sample size is that if a trial is of insufficient size to detect (for the benefit of future patients) a better treatment, it can hardly be ethical to include a patient in the trial, particularly as this will often involve discomfort, disturbance or some small element of risk to the patient.

Do the possible benefits of conducting the study outweigh the potential risks?

If clinical trials are carried out to assess the effectiveness of particular drugs or other therapies, it stands to reason that in cases where this information is already available, there is no need for the experiment unless the evidence is inconclusive and the intention is to replicate the study. No experiment can be justified if patients are denied the best available treatment for the purpose of experimentation. Freedman (1987, cited in Fetter *et al.*, 1989) also explained that the term 'equipoise' is used to describe cases where there is no identifiable definitive advantage of the new intervention over the usual (best available) treatment. In such a situation, experiments can be justified. According to Freedman (1987), 'subjects should also have equal opportunity for assignment to the treatment or control group'.

Has informed consent been respected?

Patients entering trials are often in a vulnerable position as well as being a captive population. They may be in a confused state, especially if they have just learnt that they have an illness. One can also ask whether or not they are in a position to refuse to take part in an experiment, especially in cases where the clinicians treating them are also the researchers involved in the study. As Silverman (1994) observed:

> many patients (often the majority of those eligible) refuse to participate in a trial in which the treatment is to be decided by the play of chance. In some instances, it was noted, patients enrol only because an exciting new form of treatment is not available outside the trial. Consequently, these patients may be disappointed, less co-operative, and more likely to drop out before completing the assigned regimen if they are randomly allocated to receive the treatment alternative they do not prefer.

Thus, while researchers may believe that randomisation is a fairer way to allocate subjects to control or experimental groups, some patients want to have a choice of groups. It also shows that patients are not as 'passive' as one might think. However, there is no doubt that some may feel obliged to take part for one reason or another.

People approached to take part in a study should be fully informed of its implications and of their rights to refuse or withdraw at any time during the experiment. Their informed consent should be sought prior to the study, and this consent must be offered free from pressure of any kind. Researchers have a vested interest in recruiting participants to their study. Giving information on the negative implications of the experiment may lead to refusal to participate. Where the number of potential participants is large, this may not be an issue, but when participants are hard to recruit, it must create a tension between the obligation to provide 'balanced' information and the need to recruit.

In the case of single- or double-blind experiments, the question of telling patients which treatment is the placebo negates the purpose of blindness in the study. However, giving a tablet of no pharmacological property or an injection of sterile water in an attempt to deceive patients into thinking that they are real treatments is an infringement of their rights. Researchers must, however, tell patients that a placebo is used and leave it to them to accept or refuse to take part. Fetter *et al.* (1989), explaining that no definitive answers exist for many of the above concerns, state:

> Study participants must be informed of potential risks and benefits, but detailed descriptions of randomization techniques and protocols may compromise the trial. Investigators need to present full justification for any deception and provide a post-trial debriefing plan which includes full disclosure.

Beside the possibility of withholding information from patients, researchers may be tempted to 'lean on' them. McMahon (1994) describes the dilemma that he and the other researchers in his study faced between recruiting fairly and using persuasion:

> Both my researcher associates and I had the experience of patients who refused to take part whom we felt that if we had 'pushed' would have consented. The issue of how persuasive one ought to be is not often discussed and this may be affected by whether one feels that the patient has a moral obligation to participate (Sim, 1991). Our experience demonstrated to us how easy it would have been with a largely elderly and vulnerable sample to, in our view, break the rules for the personal gain of having adequate numbers in the study.

Debriefing participants can help to bring them back to earth. However, one can still question the ethics of intensive monitoring of patients during the period of the experiment, only to leave them alone feeling abandoned once the data are collected. The security afforded during their interactions with researchers is suddenly removed at the end of the experiment.

No experiment is more important than the right of individuals to privacy and safety. Researchers must examine their own conscience and motives when taking decisions that can affect the participants' well-being. The role of ethics committees, practitioners and managers as gatekeepers and advocates for patients and others who take part in experiments is of the utmost importance.

PROBLEMS IN CONDUCTING EXPERIMENTS

Setting up, and conducting, an experiment requires rigorous standards that are not easy to attain. One of the problems frequently mentioned in the literature is the recruitment of subjects to trials (Jack *et al.*, 1990; Daly *et al.*, 1992; McMahon, 1994). Silverman (1994) reports on comments made at a workshop held at the UK Cochrane Centre in Oxford by some participants who argued that randomisation 'is often responsible for poor recruitment'. According to them, 'many patients (often the majority of those eligible) refuse to participate in a trial in which the treatment is to be decided by the play of chance'. McMahon (1994) experienced a number of difficulties in recruiting subjects for his experiment. He was concerned particularly with the possibility that researchers may compromise their obligation to seek informed consent free from pressure in favour of the need to recruit. Drawing from his own experience, he recalls that in his study:

> recruitment to the trial became a major issue. It is at this point, when the researcher begins to see his or her project running into difficulty, that I believe the elements of rigour and ethical conduct in the design of the study must be strictly upheld, at the cost of the project if necessary.

The difficulty of recruitment is further exacerbated when subjects drop out or are withdrawn during trials. Although some of the problems caused by subject mortality can be taken into account in the analysis of data, they by and large pose a threat to the rigour of experimentation, not least because researchers can be tempted to treat drop-outs as incidental and may not discuss the implications for the findings.

Blindness in clinical trials poses methodological problems, apart from the ethical implications discussed earlier. The researcher can never be sure that those who should be 'blind' in trials are necessarily so. In Ormiston *et al.*'s (1985) study comparing 'cadexomer iodine to a standard dressing for chronic venous ulcers' using a crossover, single-blind design, 'traces of the dressing could often be seen', thereby allowing researchers to know which treatment the subjects were receiving. Dale and Cornwell (1994), in their study 'of the role of lavender oil in relieving perineal discomfort following childbirth', found that, of the three interventions used, 'the GRAS compound' was distinguishable from the other two. As they explained 'in a "perfumery" sense the GRAS compound did not smell as "pleasant" as the lavender and synthetic lavender oils'. These and other clues negate the intended effects of blindness in experiments and pose a threat to internal validity.

The study of human subjects presents particular challenges to researchers because they can react to the controls imposed on them. Wilson-Barnett (1991) reminds us that 'not only are human beings seen to be particularly unpredictable and difficult to observe, but their critical behaviour and responses often seem to defy definition and measurement'. These problems are not exclusive to the experimental approach. However, the laboratory condition that researchers seek to create in the experimental study of human beings gives the impression that people are passive recipients of interventions, instead of seeing them as thinking, feeling and perceptive human beings, interacting with researchers and others in their environment. Researchers have devised strategies to diminish the effects of their presence and actions which can threaten the internal validity of experiments.

Ethical objections, recruitment and mortality problems, difficulties in achieving blindness, the dilemma between seeking informed consent and putting pressure on people to participate, and the reactions of subjects when being studied are some of the challenges that researchers face in trying to achieve their objectives, maintain rigour and keep within ethical boundaries all at the same time.

RANDOMISED CONTROLLED TRIALS IN NURSING

To conclude this chapter, we will briefly discuss some of the issues related to the use of experiments in nursing research, in particular how compatible they are for the study of nursing phenomena, their limitations and their potential benefits. For a more detailed, comprehensive and in-depth discussion of some of these issues, see Wilson-Barnett (1991) and Bond (1993). RCTs are true experiments, and these two terms will be used interchangeably in this section.

Nursing is a dynamic process, holistic and client centred. Nursing phenomena are dynamic and are thus difficult to control for the purpose of experimental study. Concepts such as healing, stress, coping or quality of life are not easily isolated and controlled. McNabb (1989) argues that the double-blind RCT is a 'completely inappropriate method when applied to a dynamic process such as labour'. She gives as an example a study on the effects of movement and position in childbirth. She explains that the researchers:

> randomly allocated women in 'upright' and 'recumbent' groups. But during the trials some of those in the former group (inevitably) expressed a desire to change position. In consequence, the 'upright' group ended up containing

women who remained 'up and about' and women who returned to bed and were 'nursed' in a sitting protocol and treated those women as if they had all remained 'upright', even though some had in fact changed position.

Most experimental designs typically comprise only one pre-test and one post-test, which may be limited in their assessment of phenomena such as pain or anxiety as they may vary between these two measuring periods. They present problems to the researcher, who must decide the times and intervals at which measurements should be carried out in order to capture these phenomena in their changing manifestations. Multiple pre-tests and post-tests can to some extent offset this limitation.

Nursing care is holistic. Diseases and illnesses are the product of the interaction between, among others, physiological, psychological and social factors. The experiment, on the other hand, is factor isolating. Only a small number of variables can be studied at any one time; the others are held constant. For example, when Hauck and Dimmock (1994) studied the effect of an information booklet on breast-feeding duration, they did not include 'single mothers, women from non-English speaking backgrounds, lower socio-economic groups and women with lower levels of education' in their sample. By excluding those variables, they could isolate the variables they wanted to study: the giving of information and breast-feeding duration. Although the interaction between education, social and cultural and other factors would influence breast-feeding duration, they had to be controlled for during the experiment. In real life, phenomena have multiple, interactive causes. However, the nature of a true experiment is such that the type of causal relationship it seeks to establish between variables can only be studied if these variables are isolated. The experiment is effective as a research design in cases where only a few variables are involved. Daly and McDonald (1992) explain:

> The randomised trial is of undoubted value in assessing the effectiveness of a drug or other therapeutic intervention. The clinical circumstances surrounding the administration of a drug are relatively simple so that the necessary controls can be instituted. In a clinical trial of a surgical intervention, confounding variables are more difficult to control and the results are correspondingly difficult to interpret.

Finally, nursing is patient centred; each patient is a unique individual. The experiment, on the other hand, seeks to study individuals in order to generalise to a larger group. As explained earlier, there is sometimes little similarity between the individuals studied in a controlled situation and the population to whom the findings are applied in real life.

The strongest argument for experimentation in nursing relates to the issue of evaluation. Much of what nurses, doctors and other health professionals do remains unevaluated. According to Bond (1993), 'nurses are in the business of making interventions, whether in offering information to allow patients to decide on the best course of action or in taking direct action where patients are unable to do so for themselves'.

The experimental design is one of the many approaches that can be used in evaluation, but it is the only one which, despite its limitations, seeks to establish cause and effect. The information produced by experiments is useful in providing the basis for guidelines to practice (Wilson-Barnett, 1991). Bond (1993) also argues that 'the information produced by experiments places individuals in a better position to be able to make a decision, so long as the facts produced are valid'.

Wilson-Barnett (1991) gives some examples of the contribution of experiments in health-related fields. Quoting from her own work (Wilson-Barnett, 1988), she points out that experimental evidence enhanced our understanding of 'the role of psychological and physical rehabilitative interventions in aiding adaptation and recovery after major illness'. She also quotes from the work of Paykel and Griffith (1983) and Marks (1985) on 'the effects of psychiatric nurses' care compared to "usual treatment" for patients in the community'. Other well-known experiments in nursing include those by Boore (1994) and Hayward (1994), measuring the effects of information-giving to patients prior to surgery.

This chapter has provided examples of the variety of phenomena that nurses and midwives have studied using experimental designs.

The prevalence of experimental research in nursing is low. Jacobsen and Meininger (1985) analysed all the articles in three American refereed journals (*Nursing Research, Research in Nursing and Health* and *Western Journal of Nursing Research*) in the years 1956, 1961, 1966, 1971, 1976, 1981 and 1983. They classified designs broadly as experimental (including quasi-experimental) and observational (where no deliberate intervention was made by the researcher). The results showed that of the 362 research articles, 73 per cent were observational and 27 per cent experimental. Moody *et al.* (1988), in a similar exercise, analysed 720 nursing practice research articles from *Nursing Research, Research in Nursing and Health, Journal of Advanced Nursing* and *Heart and Lung* between 1977 and 1986. They reported that 70 per cent were non-experimental. Of the rest, 6 per cent were true experimental and 24 per cent quasi-experimental. Lydon-Rochelle and Albers (1993) examined some of the feature articles that were published in the *Journal of Nurse-Midwifery* (an American journal) between 1987 and 1992. Of the 69 articles analysed, only 7 per cent were experimental and quasi-experimental. Lydon-Rochelle and Albers (1993) concluded:

As the nurse-midwifery profession continues to evolve, the predominance of descriptive studies will likely be balanced by a comparable proportion of analytic/hypothesis testing studies.

Bond (1993) performed an analysis of 'the contents of two UK-based nursing journals (*Journal of Advanced Nursing* and *International Journal of Nursing Studies*) in 1990, and found that the percentage of experimental/quasi-experimental studies (in relation to other types of research articles) in the *Journal of Advanced Nursing* was 13 per cent, and in the *International Journal of Nursing Studies* 21 per cent. Will the future trend in nursing research be towards more experimental studies? It is possible that the current emphasis on the evaluation of practice may prompt it to make that shift sooner rather than later.

PUTTING EXPERIMENTS INTO CONTEXT

There are different views on the value of experiments. The first sees the experiment as the *sine qua non* of scientific research and the RCT as the only way to evaluate health-care practices (McDonald and Daly, 1992). This school of thought believes that the experiment is the highest form of research performing the useful function of testing theories. The opposing view perceives it as limited in producing any kind of data that can contribute to the understanding of human experience and behaviour. The experiment is charged with being positivist and reductionist. Some feminists believe that women in particular have been victims of this research approach, used by doctors, who are mainly male, who study women as objects, thereby ignoring their needs and experiences.

Oakley (1989) argues that, far from rejecting RCTs, women can benefit from them. She explains that RCTs can help to provide data to support their cause. Oakley (1989) points out 'the frequency with which doctors impose on patients experiments of an uncontrolled nature has been one of the strongest objections to professionalised medicine made by the women's health movement over the last twenty years in Europe and North America'. RCTs have the potential to evaluate these medical, nursing and other health-care practices.

Wilson-Barnett (1991) suggests that 'the sensitive use of the experimental approach need not be contradictory to the values and purposes of nursing and nursing research'. Oakley (1989) is also in favour of a methodology that treats individuals with sensitivity and respect, and points out that there should be 'no division between this ethical requirement and other requirements of the method'.

The quasi-experiment, which studies individuals in their natural setting and does not require randomisation, has a potentially useful role in contributing to the understanding of, and evaluating the effects of, professional practices.

However, those who hold the purse strings can influence which type of research is carried out. It so happens that they also favour hard, quantitative, tangible data, the kind produced by surveys and experiments. Wilson-Barnett (1991) observes that 'at present, it seems there can be advantage from adopting quantifying and experimental approaches to research' and that 'policy makers and research funders may encourage this type of work in order to monitor change from established baselines'.

McMahon (1994) suspects that his project (an experiment) was successful in securing funding because the panel of consultants who interviewed him could identify with the project, while a colleague of his was unsuccessful because his study was ethnographic – 'a methodology which by definition is alien to scientists'.

This is one reason why the experiment is seen to have an unfair advantage over other methodologies. It may unwittingly cause some researchers to reject experiments to the degree that they are not prepared to consider some of their strengths.

Clearly, proponents of either school are firmly entrenched in their ideological and methodological bunkers and refuse to see knowledge produced by the other camp as useful. The quasi-experimental approach is to some extent seen as a compromise in the study of certain types of phenomena.

EVALUATING EXPERIMENTS

When evaluating a research study, the first task is to make sense of the information provided in the article or report. In the case of experimental studies, it is vital to look for the hypothesis (or hypotheses) or objectives and identify the independent and dependent variables. The next step is to find out how they are operationally defined. If the experimental hypothesis is that 'the use of an information booklet will lead to an increase in knowledge', readers must be clear about what the 'information booklet' consists of, how the participants 'use' it and how 'knowledge' is measured. Does a list of questions adequately measure participants' knowledge? In health research, the criteria for measuring outcomes can reflect professional prejudices. For example, if the hypothesis is 'dressing A is more effective than dressing B in the treatment of leg ulcers', the 'effectiveness' outcome can be measured by the time each type of dressing takes to heal the wound. However, other criteria, such as the side-effects of, or the degree of comfort of patients with, the dressing would give a more accurate assessment of effectiveness. Cartwright (1988) goes further and states that:

Measurements of morbidity and mortality are inadequate on their own. Assessments of treatment should also take account not only of physical side effects but of the social costs of attending for treatment, and the possible anxieties created.

The population taking part in experiments must be clearly defined: readers need to know what the inclusion criteria are. As DerSimonian *et al.* (1982) explain :

> If the selection criteria are not clearly stated, a reader is uncertain about who the subjects were and how they were selected. It is difficult to generalize the findings of such a trial to groups other than the subjects themselves.

A description of subjects in each group with reference to the relevant variables must be given. It is not enough to say that the groups are similar in important characteristics such as age, gender or educational background. Figures must be provided to allow readers to decide for themselves whether this is the case. Not all crude data can or should be made available. However, data on the profile of subjects in each group are important because any of their characteristics could be a confounding variable. An important piece of information often withheld is the illness condition of subjects in both groups. Without knowing how similar or different the groups are, it is difficult to decide with certainty that severity of illness is not a confounding factor.

As explained earlier, researchers often omit to give adequate information about the treatment of control groups. Readers need to know whether both groups received the same attention and care apart from the experimental drug or intervention. Could it be that in testing 'the effects of information giving on anxiety levels', the fact that those in the experimental group had someone to talk to was enough to reduce their anxiety? Did those in the control group receive the same amount of attention from the experimenters?

The allocation of subjects to experimental and control groups can in itself be biased. Many reviewers would simply not bother to read about an experiment if it were not randomised. When subjects are randomised, the precise method of allocation must be described for readers to decide whether there was a possibility that bias may have crept in. Randomisation comes in different forms, some of which have more bias than others. As DerSimonian *et al.* (1982) explain:

> Some methods of random allocation are sure and straightforward. Others may be effective but are uncertain in actual use, and others may appear to be random but actually have serious weaknesses... Flipping coins, tossing

dice, or drawing cards may tempt investigators to interfere with the process, and such procedures also cannot be checked. Randomization by the use of alternate cases, odd and even birthdays, or hospital record numbers has similar weaknesses.

Researchers must also explain clearly who were 'blind' in the experiment and how this was achieved. The difficulty in maintaining blindness has been discussed earlier. You must look for assurances from the researcher that adequate measures were taken to ensure blindness. For example, in a ward where some patients are given the experimental intervention and others the usual one, how can the experimenter be sure that the subjects did not talk to each other?

Those who left or were withdrawn from the experiment must be accounted for: it could be that the new intervention did not work for them. In any case, subject 'mortality' must be taken into account in the analysis and interpretation of data and should not be ignored.

The precise method of data analysis must also be described clearly and the findings stated unambiguously. To evaluate the validity and reliability of the findings, the factors identified in the previous section, such as history, instrumentation, selection and mortality effects, must be considered. Researchers must identify the limitations of their study. In practice, it is rare that experimenters do not suspect confounding variables of having interfered with the experiment. Therefore those who do not discuss the possible effects of confounders run the risk of taking their findings at face value. Finally, you must assess whether the findings, if valid and reliable, are applicable to your own clinical situation.

SUMMARY AND CONCLUSION

In this chapter, we have explained the meaning of 'experiment' and identified the main characteristics of a true experiment as intervention, control and randomisation. Different types of design, such as between-subject, within-subject and single-case, have been highlighted, as have the main differences between true and quasi-experiments.

In nursing, the number of experiments remains low relative to other designs such as the survey or case study. Nonetheless, there are numerous examples of the valuable contribution of experiments to nursing practice.

We have shown that experiments have strengths and weaknesses, as do other approaches. The methodological problems and ethical implications can, to some extent, be managed. Together they do not merit the total rejection of the experiment as a research approach. Such an action would be tantamount to 'throwing out the baby with the bathwater' (Downs, 1988).

Quasi-experiments, RCTs and other research designs can all contribute towards the pool of nursing and human knowledge. The experiment does not deserve the mystique that often seems to surround it (McMahon, 1994), nor does it merit the indifference with which some researchers regard it.

REFERENCES

Allen M, Knight C, Falk C and Strang V (1992) Effectiveness of a preoperative teaching programme for cataract patients. *Journal of Advanced Nursing*, **17**:303–9.

Beck S L (1989) The crossover design in clinical nursing research. *Nursing Research*, **38**(5):291–3.

Beecroft P C (1993) Social skills training and cognitive restructuring for adolescents on hemodialysis. *Clinical Nursing Research*, **2**(2):188–211.

Berg A, Hansson U W and Hallberg I R (1994) Nurses' creativity, tedium and burnout during 1 year of clinical supervision and implementation of individually planned nursing care: comparison between a ward for severely demented patients and a similar control ward. *Journal of Advanced Nursing*; **20**:742–9.

Bithell C (1994) Single subject experimental design: a case for concern. *Physiotherapy*, **80**(2):85–7.

Bond S (1993) Experimental research in nursing: necessary but not sufficient. In Kitson A (ed.) *Nursing: Art and Science*. London: Chapman & Hall.

Boore J R P (1994) Prescription for recovery. In *Research Classics*, vol. 1. London: Royal College of Nursing.

Brennan P and Croft P (1994) Interpreting the results of observational research: chance is not such a fine thing. *British Medical Journal*, **309**:727–30.

Cartwright A (1988) *Health Surveys in Practice and in Potential*. London: King Edward's Hospital Fund for London.

Cook T D and Campbell D T (1979) *Quasi-Experimentation: Design and Analysis Issues in Field Settings*. Boston: Houghton Mifflin.

Cupples M E and McKnight A (1994) Randomised controlled trial of health promotion in general practice for patients at high cardiovascular risk. *British Journal of Medicine*, **309**:993–6.

Dale A and Cornwell S (1994) The role of lavender oil in relieving perineal discomfort following childbirth: a blind randomized clinical trial. *Journal of Advanced Nursing*, **19**:89–96.

Daly J and McDonald I (1992) Introduction. In Daly J, McDonald I and Willis E (eds) *Researching Health Care*. London: Tavistock/Routledge.

Daly J, McDonald I and Willis E (1992) (eds) *Researching Health Care*. London: Tavistock/Routledge.

Dane F C (1990) *Research Methods*. California: Brooks/Cole.

DerSimonian R, Charette J L, McPeek B and Mosteller F (1982) Reporting methods in clinical trials. *New England Journal of Medicine*, **306**(22):1332–7.

Downs F S (1988) On babies and bathwater (editorial). *Nursing Research*, **37**(1):3.

Dumas R (1987) Clinical trials in nursing. *Recent Advances in Nursing*, **17**:108–25.

Fetter M S, Feetham S L, D'Apolito K *et al.* (1989) Randomized controlled trials: issues for researchers. *Nursing Research*, **38**(2):117–20.

Freedman B (1987) Equipoise and the ethics of clinical research. *New England Journal of Medicine*, **317**:141–5.

Hauck Y L and Dimmock J E (1994) Evaluation of an information booklet on breastfeeding duration: a clinical trial. *Journal of Advanced Nursing*, **20**(8):836–43.

Hayward J (1994) Information – a prescription against pain. In *Research Classics*, vol 1. London: Royal College of Nursing.

Hougart M K and Rushton C D (1989) Randomized clinical trials: issues for researchers. *Nursing Research*, **38**(2):117–20.

Hundley V A, Cruickshank F M, Land G D *et al.* (1994) Midwife managed delivery unit: a randomised controlled comparison with consultant led care. *British Medical Journal*, **309**:1400–4.

Jack W J L, Chetty U and Rodger A (1990) Recruitment to a prospective breast conservation trial: why are so few patients randomised? *British Medical Journal*, **301**:83–5.

Jacobsen B S and Meininger J C (1985) The design and methods of published nursing research: 1956–1983. *Nursing Research*, **34**:306–12.

Kleijnen J, de Craen J M, Van Everdingen J and Krol L (1994) Placebo effect in double-blind clinical trials: a review of interactions with medications. *Lancet*, **344**:1347–9.

Koh K, Ray R, Lee J, Nair A, Ho T and Ang P C (1994) Dementia in elderly patients: can the 3R Mental Stimulation Programme improve mental status? *Age and Ageing*, **23**:195–9.

Koh P and Thomas V J (1994) Patient-controlled analgesia (PCA): does time saved by PCA improve patient satisfaction with nursing care? *Journal of Advanced Nursing*, **20**:61–70.

Larsson G and Berg V (1991) Linen in the hospital bed: effects on patients' well-being. *Journal of Advanced Nursing*, **16**:1004–8.

Lima-Basto M (1995) Implementing change in nurses' professional behaviours: limitations of the cognitive approach. *Journal of Advanced Nursing*, **22**(3): 480–9.

Lydon-Rochelle M and Albers L (1993) Research trends in the *Journal of Nurse-Midwifery*, 1987–1992. *Journal of Nurse-Midwifery*, **38**(6):343–8.

McDonald I and Daly J (1992) Research methods in health care – a summing up. In Daly J, McDonald I and Willis E (eds) *Researching Health Care*. London: Tavistock/Routledge.

McMahon R (1994) Trial and error: an experiment in practice. In Buckeldee J and McMahon R, *The Research Experience in Nursing*. London: Chapman & Hall.

McNabb M (1989) The science of labour? *Nursing Times*, **85**(9):58–9.

Marks I (1985) *Psychiatric nurse therapists in primary care*. RCN Research Series. London: RCN.

Martin F, Ayewole A and Moloney A (1994) A randomized controlled trial of a high support hospital discharge team for elderly people. *Age and Ageing*, **23**:228–34.

Moody L E, Wilson M E, Smyth K, Schwartz R, Tittle M and Cott M L V (1988) Analysis of a decade of nursing practice research: 1977–1986. *Nursing Research*, **37**(6):374–9.

Newell D J (1992) Randomised controlled trials in health care research. In Daly J, McDonald I and Willis E (eds) *Researching Health Care*. London: Tavistock/Routledge.

Oakley A (1989) Who's afraid of the randomized controlled trial? Some dilemmas of the scientific method and 'good' research practice. *Women and Health*, **15**(4):25–59.

Oldham J (1994) Experimental and quasi-experimental research designs. *Nurse Researcher*, **1**(4):26–36.

Ormiston M C, Seymour M T J, Venn G E, Cohen R I and Fox J A (1985) Controlled trial of Iodosorb in chronic venous ulcers. *British Medical Journal*, **291**:308–10.

Passmore A P, Wilson Davies K W, Stoker C and Scott M E (1993) Chronic constipation in long stay elderly patients: a comparison of lactulose and a senna-fibre combination. *British Medical Journal*, **307**:769–71.

Paykel E S and Griffith J H (1983) *Community Psychiatric Nursing for Neurotic Patients*. RCN Research Series. London: RCN.

Pocock S (1983) *Clinical Trials: A Practical Approach*. Chichester: John Wiley & Sons.

Polit D and Hungler B (1983) *Nursing Research: Principles and Methods*, 2nd edn. Philadelphia: J B Lippincott.

Portsmouth K, Henderson K, Graham N, Price R, Cole J and Allen J (1994) Dietary calcium intake of 18-year old women: comparison with recommended daily intake and dietary energy intake. *Journal of Advanced Nursing*, **20**:1073–8.

Riddoch J and Lennon S (1994) Single subject experimental design: one way forward. *Physiotherapy*, **80**(4):215–18.

Roberts K L, Brittin M, Cook M A and deClifford J (1994) Boomerang pillows and respiratory capacity. *Clinical Nursing Research*, **3**(2):157–65.

Silverman W A (1994) Patients' preferences and randomised trials. *Lancet*, **343**:1586.

Sleep J and Grant A (1988) Effects of salt and Savlon bath concentrate post-partum. *Nursing Times* (occasional paper), **84**(21):55–7.

Smith H W (1991) *Strategies of Social Research*, 3rd edn. St Louis: Holt, Rinehart & Winston.

Wilson-Barnett J (1988) Patient teaching or patient counselling? *Journal of Advanced Nursing*, **13**:215–22.

Wilson-Barnett J (1991) The experiment: is it worthwhile? *International Journal of Nursing Studies*, **28**(1):77–87.

10 SAMPLES AND SAMPLING

INTRODUCTION

One of the important decisions in designing a study is what data to collect and from whom. When the study population is too large, as is often the case, researchers have to resort to strategies to obtain the same information from a smaller group of people. In this chapter, we will explore the meaning of samples, identify a number of sampling techniques and discuss their strengths and limitations. In particular, we will explore the use of samples in quantitative and qualitative research.

SAMPLES AND POPULATIONS

One of the crucial tasks in designing a research project is to decide on the number and characteristics of the respondents who will be invited to take part in the study. It is not always possible to include the entire population in a study, not least because of the costs involved. Having more respondents means that researchers spend more time in collecting and analysing data, so the lifespan of the project itself is, therefore, increased. It is also easier to collect more, and in-depth, data from a smaller than a larger number of people. For these reasons, researchers sometimes select a proportion of the total number of potential respondents from whom to collect data. A proportion or subset of the population is known as the *sample*. A carefully selected sample can provide data representative of the population from which the sample is drawn.

A *population* can be defined as the total number of units from which data can potentially be collected. These units may be individuals, organisations, events or artefacts. In a study on the use of nursing models by staff nurses in medical wards in the UK, all staff nurses (individuals) working in this type of ward in the UK constitute the population under study. If a study is to find out which types of dressing are used in surgical wards in a particular health district, the population is all surgical wards (organisations) in that district. All the dressings would also constitute a population of artefacts. In a study of psychiatric patients' aggressive behaviour at meal times over a period of 3 months in one hospital, all the

218

meal times (events) during the 3 months period make up the population. And in a historical study of how nurses were portrayed in newspapers in the 19th century, all the newspapers (artefacts) during this period make up the population. In layman's language, 'population' is mainly used to describe people, but in research terms it has a wider meaning. For the purpose of this chapter, the individuals, organisations, events and artefacts that make up a population will be referred to as 'units'.

It is sometimes important to use the entire units of a population in a study. For example the decennial Census of Population, undertaken by the Office of Population Censuses and Surveys (OPCS) comprise data from all households in the UK. Professional organisations, for example the UK's Community Psychiatric Nursing Association (CPNA) carries out quinquennial surveys of its members.

In theory, all the units of a population (also called the theoretical population), could potentially take part in a study, but in practice this may not be possible for various reasons. A researcher asking questions of patients with Alzheimer's disease in a geriatric ward will quickly realise that not all patients are able to take part. She may decide to include only those who are at an early stage of the disease. Additionally, she may exclude those who are restless and aggressive. In stipulating the inclusion criteria (early stage of disease) and exclusion criteria (restlessness and aggressive behaviour), the researcher has defined the *target* population, that is the population to be studied or, as it is commonly referred to, the study population.

The units of a population are never totally homogeneous (i.e. sharing the same characteristics). Although all staff nurses in medical wards work in the same type of clinical setting, they are not a homogeneous group because they differ in such variables as age, gender, years of experience and practice or qualifications. Depending on the research question and the resources, the researcher may want to include only full-time day staff nurses with 3 years' experience and may exclude those who are educated at graduate level. In practice, researchers must have good reasons for including and/or excluding units of population and must also clearly define these criteria. For example, 'patients in the early stages of Alzheimer's disease' needs to be operationally defined.

The target population, once defined, becomes the population of interest from whom the data can potentially be collected. In fact, the target population is a subset of the theoretical population. Sometimes all the units in the target population are included in the study, but more often a sample or subset of the target population is selected. When this happens, it is to the target population rather than the theoretical population that generalisations may be made. RE 27 shows how two researchers defined a target population for their study.

RESEARCH
EXAMPLE **27** Nyqvist and Sjödén (1993)
**Advice concerning breastfeeding for mothers
of infants admitted to a neonatal intensive
care unit: the Roy Adaptation model as a
conceptual structure**

Target population

The criteria for subject selection were that infant was a full-term singleton, admitted within his first day of life, discharged within 6 days, not treated with intensive care (by CPAP, ventilator or total parental nutrition), did not have any congenital malformation or severe disease such as chromosomal abnormality, and that the mother could speak Swedish. All children born in the catchment area of the University Hospital (viz Uppsala County) during 1 year, from September 1989 to August 1990, were included.

Comments

1. Although the reasons behind some of the criteria for inclusion seem to be self-explanatory, the authors could have made them explicit.
2. The target population consisted of 178 infants and their mothers.
3. It is to this population, as defined by the authors, that any generalisations can be made and not to all mothers whose infants are admitted to that neonatal intensive care unit where the study was carried out. For example, the findings may not apply to infants whose mothers could not speak Swedish.
4. In this study, data were collected from entire units of the target population. No sample was drawn.

Sample frame

A list of all the units of the target population provides the frame from which a sample (if required) is selected. Therefore the sample frame contains the same number of units as the target population. There are some ready-made sample frames. For example, if a researcher decides to explore the learning styles of current nursing undergraduates at one university, the sample frame would be a list of the names of all nursing undergraduates who are currently studying there. The researcher would simply cross out the names of those who did not meet the inclusion criteria. Examples of ready-made lists that may potentially be used as sample frames are the UKCC register, the general practitioners list of patients and the electoral register. Sometimes two or three lists may be combined to form a sample frame. For example, in Woodcock *et al.*'s (1994) study of 'planned home and hospital births in Western Australia (WA) 1981–1987', the cohort of all WA planned, singleton home births 'was identified from the Midwives' Notification System, together with midwives' home birth records and Health Department of WA Transfer forms'. These three lists were combined to provide a sample frame from which samples were selected. There are some drawbacks in using existing registers or lists as they may be incomplete, biased or not up to date.

It is not always possible or desirable to construct sample frames. For studies on sensitive issues such as sexually transmitted diseases, drug addiction or crime, ready-made lists are, understandably, not available. Participants are often recruited by means of newspaper adverts and newsletters, from support groups or by word of mouth. Sample frames are necessary when the researcher seeks to draw representative samples and thereafter to generalise from the data. It is important to note, however, in that qualitative research the concept of generalisation has a different meaning than it does in quantitative research, and that sample frames are rarely used by qualitative researchers. This will be discussed below.

Selected and achieved samples

A sample is defined as a subset of the target population. When all the units of the target population cannot be studied, the researcher may decide to select a small proportion of this population from whom to collect data. The selection method or procedure is called sampling. The most common example of the use of samples is in the opinion polls taken prior to elections. A sample of potential voters is carefully selected whose views, the pollsters believe, would represent those of the rest of the voting population.

The units in the sample selected by the researcher are the ones invited to take part in the study. However, not everyone invited is available, willing or able to take part, although the researcher will have laid down inclusion and exclusion criteria. People change addresses and cannot be traced; others are too busy or are uninterested. Whatever the reasons, the selected sample, through non-participation or through non- or part-completion of questionnaires or other tools, loses some units and becomes the achieved sample. Although the achieved sample is normally smaller than the selected sample, some researchers may exceptionally decide to replace units in the original sample that did not take part by other units from the target population.

RE 28 shows one instance of how a selected sample was reduced to an achieved sample.

RESEARCH **28** Anderssen (1993)
EXAMPLE Perception of physical education classes
among young adolescents: do physical
education classes provide equal opportunities
to all students?

Selected and achieved samples

A sample of 1195 students was initially asked to participate. Refusals from parents (N = 222), refusals from students (N = 46), exclusion of students with inconsistent answers (N = 11) and exclusion of students with missing values on items used to calculate the dependent variable (N = 21) resulted in the sample of 895 students (491 boys and 404 girls) used in the present analyses. This represents 74.9% of the initial sample asked to participate.

Comments

1. The author is rigorous in deciding whose responses are to be included in the achieved or final sample. Not all researchers would exclude 'inconsistent answers' (whatever this means).
2. The selected sample was 1195, the achieved sample 895 and the response rate 74.9 per cent.

The *response rate* is the percentage of the selected sample that actually takes part in the study. It is calculated as follows:

Response rate = $\dfrac{\text{Achieved sample} \times 100}{\text{Selected sample}}$

Example: If the achieved sample numbered 45 and the selected sample 60, the response rate is

$$\frac{45}{60} \times 100 = 75\%$$

Types of sample

There are two basic types of sample:

- probability
- non-probability.

In a *probability* sample, every unit in the target population has a more than zero chance (usually known in advance by the researcher) of being selected. For example, if a sample of 10 students is to be selected from a target population of 50, each student will have a 1 in 5 or 20 per cent chance of being selected. However, it is not always the case with probability samples that all units have an equal chance of selection. If the target population has 40 men and 10 women and the researcher selects a sample of 10 men and 5 women, it is clear that each woman has a 1 in 2 chance of selection, while each man has a 1 in 4 chance. Therefore a probability sample does not mean that each unit has an equal chance, but rather that it has a *known* chance of selection.

The main characteristic of a probability sample is that it is randomly selected from the target population. The term 'random', in the layman's sense, usually means haphazard, as when an interviewer picks out people as they come out of a general practitioner's surgery. Those who look approachable to the interviewer or those who do not seem to be in a hurry may be chosen. Apart from being subjective, this method of sampling has no sample frame. Therefore the chances of all those attending surgery on that particular day, of being selected, is not known. In research terms, the random selection of units for a sample is carried out according to a specified objective method, such as giving each unit a number, putting all the numbers in a box and picking out blindly one number at a time until the required size of the sample is drawn (there are more 'scientific ways' to do this, as explained below). The aim, in quantitative research, is to select a sample representative of, and the data from which can therefore be generalised to, the target population.

Non-probability samples are made up of units whose chances of selection are not known. In the example of people leaving a doctor's surgery, those who were available before the researcher arrived had a zero chance of selection, whereas the chances (of being selected) of those who were interviewed are not known, as the potential number of all those who could have been interviewed is also not known.

Qualitative researchers often use non-probability samples because, according to them, the purpose of qualitative research is to contribute to an understanding of phenomena. They therefore choose the sample which can best provide the required data, whatever the sampling method is. In fact, qualitative researchers sometimes substitute the term 'sampling' by 'recruitment'. The use and nature of samples in qualitative research is further discussed in a later section.

The decision to choose probability or non-probability samples is guided by two factors: the specific research question and the type of data required (Annandale and Lampard, 1993). Other factors that researchers take into consideration include the availability of, and access to, potential participants and the resources allocated to the study. In quantitative research, decisions about samples and sampling are not taken after the research question and the methods of data collection are known: all three must be considered at the same time as they depend on each other. Sampling also has implications for the analysis of data. For example, inferential statistics (see Chapter 14) are based on the assumption that random samples of populations have been used to generate data (Barhyte *et al.*, 1990). In qualitative research, the researcher is a tool of data collection and analysis. As Walker (1985) explains, 'decisions regarding the composition of the sample for a qualitative study emerge from the objectives and are modified by considerations governing choice of method and the scope of the study'. According to the author, 'the rigorous sampling procedures used in quantitative research are inappropriate to the nature and scale of qualitative work'.

Decisions about samples and the sampling method can be taken both prior to and during the data collection stage.

Types of probability sample

There are four types of probability sample:

- simple random
- stratified random
- systematic random
- cluster random.

Each of these sampling procedures requires a sample frame before a random selection can be drawn.

Simple random sample

The most common form of random sampling is one in which each unit in the sample frame is given a number, these are then put into the proverbial hat and numbers are drawn one at a time until the size of sample, specified in advance, is reached. Each unit has an equal chance of being selected. *Simple random sampling* is so called because once a number is given to each unit, it then takes only one step: picking numbers. This method of sampling may be appropriate for small sample frames. With large samples, a table of random numbers or a computer package can be used to draw samples. There is also a view that points out that once a number is taken out of the hat, the chances of those remaining are altered from what they were at the start of the process. For example, if a researcher decides to draw a sample of 10 from a population of 50, the chance of selection of each unit at the start of the operation is 1 in 5. After 5 units have been selected, the chance of each of the 45 units remaining in the hat being selected is altered to 1 in 9. For this reason, some researchers prefer to use a table of random numbers or a computer package.

Simple random sampling is mostly suitable for a population that is more or less homogeneous and from which any sample drawn is unlikely to be seriously biased. An example of a homogeneous sample can be found in a study of undergraduates by Ashley (1994). The sample consisting of 125 students:

> was homogenous with regard to age, race and gender. The sample ranged in age from 21 to 23 years. All respondents were female and 98% of the sample was white.

However, when the population has varied characteristics (i.e. is heterogeneous), it may be unwise to rely on simple random sampling to obtain a representative sample possessing the main variables being studied. For the purpose of this chapter, a simple experiment was carried out to discover how representative a small random sample of 10 units would be of a target population of 50 (40 women and 10 men). Each person was given a number from 1 to 50. The encircled numbers represent the men in the sample. These numbers were put in a box, and 10 numbers were drawn consecutively. This exercise was repeated five times and the following random samples were drawn (Table 10.1).

Table 10.1 Simple random sampling

Sample frame of 50 units

1	(2)	3	4	5	6	7	(8)	9	10
11	12	(13)	14	15	16	(17)	18	19	20
21	22	23	(24)	25	(26)	27	28	29	30
31	32	33	(34)	(35)	36	37	38	39	40
41	(42)	43	44	45	(46)	47	48	49	50
Sample 1: 3	4	6	16	22	28	29	38	41	48
Sample 2: 3	6	16	21	23	27	36	38	49	50
Sample 3: 1	7	25	30	31	37	39	48	49	50
Sample 4: 4	11	19	20	22	23	(24)	40	(42)	45
Sample 5: 7	(8)	14	18	20	21	(35)	36	47	50

As can be seen from the above figures, the first three samples do not have a single male representative, while the proportion of men in the last two samples are exactly the same as in the sample frame. To guarantee representation, this method of sampling may not be the most appropriate as much depends on chance.

The same experiment was repeated using a table of random numbers, and the same biases were noted. One way to increase representation is by drawing a larger sample. In the above experiment, three more samples of 10, 20 and 30 units were respectively drawn as follows:

Sample of 10: ②, 4, 11, 12, 14, 28, 31, 33, 49, 50
Sample of 20: 3, 4, 5, 7, ⑧ 9, 11, ⑬ 19, 20, 21, 22, ㉔ 30, �35 39, 40, 43, 45, ㊻
Sample of 30: 1, ②, 5, 6, 9, 11, 12, ⑬ 14, 15, 19, 21, 22, ㉔ 25, 27, 31, 32, 33, �34
37, 38, 39, 40, 41, ㊷ 44, 45, ㊻ 47

Although the representation of males increased with the size of sample, it did not increase proportionately.

Stratified random sample

When the sample frame contains units that vary greatly in variables such as age, gender, education, experience or illness condition, it is possible that simple random sampling may not be the most appropriate form of sampling in order to achieve representation. If one or more of these variables are important for the study, it is wise not to trust the selection process to chance. As shown earlier, there was no guarantee, in the example given, that with simple random sampling males would be represented in the final sample. There are reasons why variables should sometimes be assured of representation. For example, some illness conditions are more prevalent in one gender than another. Myocardial infarction is more common in men and breast cancer in women. Any sample of patients with either condition must be stratified if gender representation is important for the study. *Stratified random sampling* consists of separating the units in the sample frame in strata (layers) according to the variables the researcher believes are important for inclusion in the sample, and drawing a sample from each strata using the simple random sampling method.

For example, in a study of patients' satisfaction with spiritual care, if the sample frame of 300 patients comprises 228 Christians, 66 Muslims and 6 Hindus, the researcher must seek the views of patients of each of these three religions if the findings are to be generalised to the target population. A simple random sample may by chance under- or overrepresent one or more of these groups, or may not even include any representative of one of the minority groups. To ensure representation, the sample frame of 300 patients is divided into its religious composition before a proportionate sample from each group is drawn. The sampling method involves three steps as follows:

Step 1   Stratify the sample frame into its constituent group

    e.g.   Christians 228 or 76%
              Muslims 68 or 22%
              Hindus 6 or 2%

Step 2   Decide on a sample size and the proportion for each stratum

    e.g.   Total sample size $= 50$

$$\text{Sample size of Christian stratum} = \frac{76}{100} \times 50 = 38$$

$$\text{Sample size of Muslim stratum} = \frac{22}{100} \times 50 = 11$$

$$\text{Sample size of Hindu stratum} = \frac{2}{100} \times 50 = 1$$

Step 3   Draw a simple random sample of the required size from each stratum

    e.g.   Christian sample $=$ 38 out of 228
              Muslim sample $=$ 11 out of 66
              Hindu sample $=$ 1 out of 6

In this example, a proportionate stratified random sample of each stratum was drawn. This means that each unit from each of the strata had the same chance of selection (1 in 6). However, if the size of the Christian and Muslim samples is large enough to represent Christian and Muslim patients, a single Hindu may represent only the views of the individual. In this case, the researcher may decide to increase the size of the Hindu sample to two or three in order to increase their representation. The sample then becomes a disproportionate random stratified sample.

If gender as a variable is also important for this study, the sample frame would have to be stratified into male Christians, female Christians, male Muslims, and so on before a proportionate or disproportionate random sample could be drawn from each stratum. The heterogeneity of the target population is not in itself a good reason for stratification. The decision to stratify depends on the research question and the variables of interest to the researcher. RE 29 examines a study where stratified random sampling was used.

Systematic random sample

Systematic samples are drawn by choosing units on a list at intervals prescribed by the researcher in advance. The most basic system is choosing every nth number on a list until the required sample size is reached. A researcher may decide to interview the occupants of every third house on a street to find out about their health beliefs, or a teacher may pick out every fifth student on the register to ask about their views on the organisation and delivery of the course.

RESEARCH EXAMPLE 29   Dolan (1987)
The relationship between burnout and job satisfaction in nurses

Stratified random sampling

This study was carried out to find out whether there was a relationship between burnout and job satisfaction in psychiatric and general nurses. The all-female random sample 'comprised 30 psychiatric (PS) staff nurses, 30 general (GE) staff nurses, and 30 administrative (AD) staff, the latter acting as a control group'.

Comment

1. Clearly the author wanted each group to be represented and therefore chose an equal number (30) from each. This suggests that the sample is a stratified random sample but not a proportionate one. However, this cannot be inferred until we know the size of each the three sample frames from which these are drawn.

For a systematic random sample to be drawn, there must be a sample frame and every unit on the frame must have a chance of being selected. If a systematic random sample of 10 is to be drawn from a sample frame of 50, every 5th number (50 divided by 10) on the list is chosen. To avoid starting with number 1 each time, the researcher can pick a number at random between 1 and 5 and proceed to choose every fifth number from it. Say number 4 is picked at random as the starting number, every fifth number (9, 14, 19, 24, 29, 34, 39, 44, 49) will be selected until a sample size of 10 (including the starting number, 4) is obtained. One of the limitations of this type of sampling is that lists may have biases of their own. It is possible that every fifth name on a list is male and that they could by chance be selected, therefore creating a gender bias in the sample. One way to offset this drawback is to rearrange the names on the list and therefore break any periodic cycles it may contain. RE 30 illustrates the use of systematic sampling.

Cluster random sample

A cluster is defined in the *Oxford Dictionary* as 'a group of similar things'. Sometimes the units of a study population are already in the form of clusters. For example, each district has a number of hospitals. Each hospital is a cluster of health professionals, and within hospitals each ward is also a cluster of nurses. When the population already exists in clusters, it is sometimes more practical and cost-efficient to sample the clusters first and then sample the units from the selected clusters.

RESEARCH EXAMPLE 30

Millette (1993)
Client advocacy and the moral orientation of nurses

Systematic sampling

Sample selection
In the first portion of the study, 500 registered nurses in Western Massachusetts were surveyed by mailed questionnaires. Random selection was made from a list provided by the Board of Registration in Nursing of RNs from the four counties of Western Massachusetts. The 8662 RN population listed was divided by 500, resulting in the number 17. A table of random numbers provided the number 5, which directed that the fifth name on the list was the first selected. Thereafter, every 17th name on the list was selected, up to a total of 500. If a questionnaire was returned as undeliverable, a replacement was made from the list using the same procedure.

Comments
1. The lists from the four boards of registration constituted the sample frame for this study.
2. To avoid starting with the first name on the list, the author used a table of random numbers to pick out a number between 1 and 17. The number drawn was 5.
3. It is not clear whether the author changed the order of the names on the lists to break any periodic cycles that may have been present.

Suppose that the aim of our study is to find out the knowledge of, and attitude to, primary nursing among nurses in general hospitals in Wales. A simple random sampling will involve listing all staff nurses working in all the general hospitals in the country. When the sample frame is ready and a simple random sample of staff nurses is drawn, it is possible that some hospitals will be overrepresented and others under-represented. Researchers may have to travel to hospitals where two or three nurses have been selected. The whole exercise can be demanding, time-consuming and costly. A stratified random sample would ensure that each hospital is proportionately represented in the sample, but the cost of compiling a sample frame and travelling to all the hospitals can still be enormous. However, stratified random sampling is necessary if the purpose is to study differences between hospitals. Cluster random sampling, on the other hand, involves randomly sampling the hospitals before drawing a random sample of nurses from each of the selected hospitals or using the whole population of the randomly selected hospitals. In the above example, if there are 20 general hospitals, a sample of 8 hospitals could be drawn. The next steps will be to construct a sample frame of all staff nurses working in the 8 hospitals before a simple random sample is drawn. In doing so, a more in-depth study can also be carried out with less cost. Cluster random sampling is appropriate when the clusters are more or less homogeneous and when the final number of clusters selected is not small. For example, choosing a random sample of 2 hospitals out of 10 may decrease the viability of generalising the findings to the 10 hospitals. Therefore cost alone should not be the deciding factor in choosing this type of sampling.

A combination of stratified and cluster sampling can also be used. In the above example, if psychiatric, mental handicap and geriatric as well as general hospitals were included in the study, these hospitals could be divided into strata representing each specialty before a cluster random sample of each strata was drawn.

Cluster random sampling is also called multistage sampling because it can involve many stages. The use of cluster sample is illustrated in RE 31.

Types of non-probability sample

There are five types of non-probability sample, which can be divided into two broad and overlapping categories: purposive or judgemental, and convenience. The first involves judgement and choice on the part of the researcher, thereby giving her a degree of control over the composition of the sample. With convenience sampling, on the other hand, the researcher chooses according to who or what is available. In practice, this distinction is not rigid since both may involve a degree of judgement and convenience.

The five types of non-probability sample are:

- accidental
- purposive
- volunteer
- snowball
- quota.

Accidental sampling

In accidental samples, only those available have a chance of being selected. Interviewing shoppers outside a supermarket on their health beliefs is one way to select an accidental sample. Only those visiting the supermarket at that time and on that day will have a chance of being selected. In this type of sampling, there is no sample frame.

There are occasions when accidental sampling is appropriate. For example, if a researcher wants to find out the patients' views on the information they receive on admission to hospital, she may decide to interview the first 50 consecutive patients following admission. She does not have a sample frame as she does not know who will be admitted. No-one outside the first 50 patients will have a chance of selection. By accident, the sample may comprise mostly those with minor problems or of a particular social class.

RESEARCH EXAMPLE 31 | Coyle and Sokop (1990)
Innovation adoption behaviour among nurses

Cluster sampling

Ten hospitals were randomly selected from The American Hospital Association listing of all medium-sized hospitals (250–500 beds) in North Carolina. Due to the mixed reports on the effect of organisational size on innovation adoption... only medium-sized hospitals were included in this study in order to control for this variable. Two hundred registered nurses, 20 from each institution, were randomly selected from lists provided by Directors of Nursing in each of the participating hospitals. To be included in the study, the nurses had to be employed full-time on the day, evening, or rotating night shift, with direct patient care responsibilities on adult medical–surgical or intensive care units.

Comments

1. The sample frame is The American Hospital Association (AHA) listing of all medium-sized hospitals. A cluster sampling of these hospitals was carried out. The researchers did not, however, state from how many hospitals the sample of 10 was drawn.
2. The size of the selected sample of registered nurses was 200 (20 from each of the 10 hospitals). If the same size of sample were to be drawn from more than 10 hospitals, that is from the total number of hospitals in the AHA list, it is clear that the number of nurses selected from each hospital could have been very small indeed.
3. To ensure representation of all 10 hospitals, the authors carried out stratified random sampling to select 20 nurses from each hospital.

Accidental sampling can have implications for the data. For example, waiting at street corners to interview people about satisfaction with health services in the area could mean that only pedestrians will be chosen. Those who have cars, and who may perhaps be more affluent, may be excluded. With accidental sampling, there is degree of subjectivity involved in the selection, as the researcher does not always choose everyone who happens to be available.

Purposive or judgemental sampling

This method of sampling, used mainly but not exclusively in qualitative research, involves the researcher deliberately choosing who to include in the study on the basis that those selected can provide the necessary data. Thus if she wants to investigate the leadership styles of hospital general managers, she can deliberately choose managers with different styles in order to study the concept of leadership from different perspectives. For this, she may have to rely on her own judgement and/or that of those she believes can help her to make the choice. In this study, generalising the findings to the target population of managers is not the main concern of the researcher. Instead, she is seeking to contribute to the understanding of leadership styles. The sample is deliberately chosen by the researcher on the basis that these are the best available people to provide data on the issues being researched.

RESEARCH EXAMPLE 32 Roe et al. (1994)
The assumption of caregiveing: grandmothers raising the children of the crack cocaine epidemic

Purposive, volunteer and snowball sampling

The community advisory group played a central role in the construction of a rich and varied sample. Initial sampling identified differences in caregiving experience based on age, number of dependent grandchildren, sources of financial support, marital status and social support. Later sampling enabled comparisons based on factors such as employment, health status, and additional caregiving responsibilities.

Potential respondents were identified through health and social service providers, a dense network of community contacts, an invitational flyer, and snowball referrals from study participants. The latter two strategies were particularly effective in finding women who were without telephones, were not well connected to health and social services, and were in other ways likely to be overlooked by more traditional sampling methods.

Comments

1. This is an example of the use of flexible sampling methods, which is common in qualitative research.
2. The use of purposive or judgemental sampling is indicated by the involvement of the community advisory group in sample selection. A judgement had to be made by the researchers and the group on who to select.
3. The 'invitational flyer' was used to recruit volunteers to the project.
4. Snowball sampling was resorted to in order to recruit women who were 'likely to be overlooked by the more traditional sampling methods', which depend greatly on the existence of lists or records.

In choosing a purposive sample, the researcher must be guided by her research question and not be tempted to choose samples out of convenience or leave it to others to make the selection. The use of purposive samples in qualitative research is discussed further in this chapter. RE 32 shows the use of purposive sampling.

Volunteer sampling

Perhaps the weakest form of sampling is one in which people volunteer to take part and are therefore self-selected. It is a sample of convenience over which the researcher has little control, instead being dependent on the sample volunteering to take part. There are two categories of volunteer. Firstly, there are those who offer to take part in a study before coming into contact with the researcher or her associates. An example of this is when people respond to a notice board or newspaper advert asking for subjects to take part in a study. The researcher exerts little or no influence on the prospective subject except perhaps when financial or other inducements are offered. The second type of volunteer is those who are part of a captive population, either as patients in a hospital or students on a course. It is more difficult to know whether these groups really volunteer and whether their actions are what van Wissen and Siebers (1993) term 'uncoerced voluntary participation'. How 'voluntary' this type of participation is in reality is the question that the researcher and the readers of the subsequent report or article must ask. There are a number of reasons why a captive population may 'volunteer' to take part in a study:

- moral obligation – they may feel that the research will be of benefit to other patients;
- gratitude – in return for the care they receive;
- fear of reprisals – if they refuse they think they may be punished;
- fear of being labelled as uncooperative;
- the need to conform.

For these reasons, the validity of the data could be seriously questioned, especially if, in addition, the volunteer may not trust the confidentiality and anonymity of the data.

Volunteering is itself an act of cooperation and reflects the personality of those more likely to volunteer. They may be conformists and traditional in outlook and could thus bias the sample. Those who are self-selected may show more interest and motivation than those who do not. Therefore volunteer samples are limited because we know little or nothing of those who do not take part in the study. RE 32 shows how volunteers were recruited in one study.

Snowball sampling

In simple terms, this means that a respondent refers someone they know to the study, who in turn refers someone they know, until the researcher has an adequate sample. Sometimes it is difficult for the researcher to identify people who could take part in a study because of the sensitivity of the topic or because the researcher may not have ready access to a sample. For a sample of drug takers or petty criminals, the researcher may depend on initial contacts to direct them to others who may be willing to take part. However, snowball sampling is not used exclusively when sensitive topics are being researched or when potential participants are scarce. In qualitative research, the number of units in the sample is often not decided in advance. As the fieldwork progresses, the researcher may come across other potentially useful participants and enlists them as she goes along. One of the major drawbacks of snowball samples is that participants may refer people of similar backgrounds and outlook to themselves. Walker (1985) warns against the indiscriminate use of snowball sampling:

> Interviewers must not recruit their friends; nor as a rule are they allowed to 'snowball', i.e. to use people already recruited as a source of other people to approach as this would lead to groups in which participants know each other and are likely to have similar views.

As with other forms of sampling, the researcher must have good reasons for choosing a snowball sample. Mason (1994), who carried out a study on 'Maternal and child health needs in Northern Ireland and Jamaica', found that 'population lists were unavailable' in Jamaica and she could not therefore draw random samples. Being a stranger to the field, she had to rely on snowball sampling. As she explained:

> In this situation, snowball samples were appropriate. Initial introductions were made in each area by community health aides to two or three mothers, who were then interviewed... . Respondents were thereafter nominated by informants, and willingness to participate increased along with local familiarity with the researcher.

The use of snowball sampling is shown in RE 32.

Quota sampling

Quota sampling involves elements of purposive and stratified sampling without random selection. In this type of sampling, the researcher recognises the need for different groups in the sample to be adequately represented. In a survey of students' views on the resources and support they receive in a nursing department of a university, there are a number of groups that should be represented in the sample. These could include full-time and part-time students, students on all the courses offered, school leavers and mature students, and males and females. Thus the researcher may allocate 20 to each group. Depending on the aim of the research, proportionate or non-proportionate samples can be used. In accidental sampling, it is left to chance who is included in the sample. In quota sampling, the researcher allocates places in advance.

RESEARCH 33 EXAMPLE Fawcett and Weiss (1993)
Cross-cultural adaptation to cesarean birth

Quota sampling

The target population was cesarean-delivered women who represent three of the major ethnic groups in the west coast region of the United States. The sample consisted of 45 women who experienced cesarean childbirth, with 15 representing each of three cultures: White Caucasian, Hispanic, and Asian. The sample size was sufficient for an exploratory study. All the Hispanic women were originally from Mexico and spoke Spanish. The Asian group was made up of Vietnamese (n = 8), Laotian (n = 3), Cambodian (n = 1), Chinese (n = 1), Korean (n = 1), and Filipino (n = 1) women, all of whom spoke English.

The women were recruited from the postpartum unit of a large metropolitan hospital in a west coast city.

Comments

1. We are not told what the target population of each ethnic group is or whether the 15 respondents in each group were randomly selected from their respective sample frames. Had random sampling of each stratum been carried out, they would have been stratified random samples.
2. The use of quotas for each ethnic group is justified on the basis that this is a cross-cultural study.

Quota sampling involves two stages. In the first stage, the quota allocation is decided. For example, in a study of nurses' attitude to primary nursing, 20 places could be allocated to each of the following grades of nurses – A, B, C, D and E – making a total of 100 nurses. Or the researcher could allocate the 100 places according to the proportion of each grade. The second stage involves selecting the sample. If there is a sample frame of nurses and a random sample of 20 in each grade is drawn, the quota sampling becomes a stratified random sampling, or after deciding on quotas, the researcher can purposefully choose 20 nurses whom she believes will provide the data for the project. She can also wait at the exit of the nurses' canteen and interview those who are available until the quota for each of the grades is met.

In quota sampling, the overriding concern of the researcher is to have various elements represented. However, the sampling procedure remains a non-probability one because there is no recourse to random selection. In the above study, while the researcher is interested to find out the views of nurses in each grade, these nurses would not necessarily be representative of the rest of the nurses in the hospital mainly because no random sampling was effected. The study by Fawcett and Weiss (1993), outlined in RE 33 makes use of quota sampling to achieve its objectives.

It is not unusual for a researcher to use a mixture of sampling methods. RE 34 shows three types of sampling in the same study.

SAMPLING IN QUANTITATIVE AND QUALITATIVE RESEARCH

It is generally believed that, in quantitative research, the samples are large and probability sampling is frequent, while the qualitative researchers use small, non-probability samples. Although this is a fair description as far as sample size is concerned, it is not unusual to observe from research journals that many quantitative researchers use convenience samples and some qualitative ones resort to random selection. Convenience samples are probably the most frequently used of all types of sample in both types of research. Moody *et al.* (1988) reviewed 720 articles in six 'major refereed journals in nursing' (*Nursing Research, Research in Nursing and Health,* the *International Journal of Nursing Studies,* the *Journal of Advanced Nursing, Heart and Lung* and the *Western Journal of Nursing Research*) and found that 'convenience sampling was used more often (74 per cent), followed by purposive, 10 per cent; random, 9 per cent; and systematic, 6 per cent'.

In quantitative research, the data from randomly selected samples are generalised to the target population and sometimes beyond, to similar populations and settings. The purpose of research is not only to study the specific but to draw general principles and conclusions in order to apply them to similar situations outside the particular population and setting being studied. The degree to which the results of a study can be generalised to settings or samples other than the ones being studied is known as external validity (Polit and Hungler, 1995).

On the other hand, qualitative researchers believe that the phenomena they study are culture specific, and time-bound and that their findings are a result of the interaction between the researcher and the researched. This means that although the same phenomena may exist in other cultures, they are manifested and experienced differently in different cultures or settings. Also since the findings were obtained at a specific point in time (that is time-bound), the study cannot be replicated and the findings cannot be generalised to other settings.

RESEARCH EXAMPLE 34 Dalgas-Pelish (1993)
The impact of the first child on marital happiness

Mixture of sampling methods

Four cross-sectional groups of 25 couples who were childless, in the third trimester of pregnancy, had 5-month-old children or had 24-month-old children were invited to participate in this study. These four groups were selected to see if there were significant differences as the child aged, assuming that the pregnant couples were fantasizing about their child soon to be born, the 5-month-old child's parents might be still at the honeymoon stage of infant enjoyment, and the 24-month old child's parents would be at the busy toddler stage. Childless couples served as a comparison or reference point for the other groups of prospective or young parents.

One group was drawn from couples who participated in Lamaze childbirth classes for their first child. From the childbirth classes, couples who were at the third trimester of pregnancy with their first child were asked to volunteer. Couples with 5-month-old infants and couples with 24-month-old children were randomly selected from birth records at local hospitals and were telephoned regarding study participation.

To obtain the control group of couples who did not have children the three groups of parents were asked to volunteer the names of friends who might be interested in participating but who had not started their family and were not pregnant at the time.

Comments

1. The three types of sampling used in this study are :

   - Volunteer – couples from the childbirth classes were asked to volunteer.
   - Random – couples were randomly selected from birth records at local hospitals.
   - Snowball – couples were asked to volunteer the names of friends who might be interested in participating.

2. It was not specified whether the random sampling was simple, systematic or stratified.

Sampling for the purpose of generalising to other populations and settings is, and remains, anathema to purists in the qualitative tradition, although, as Schofield (1993) pointed out, 'a consensus appears to be emerging that for qualitative researchers generalisability is best thought of as a matter of the "fit" between the situation studied and others to which one might be interested in applying the concepts and conclusions of that study'. The purpose of selective sampling in quantitative research is to draw a representative subset of the population and collect data from them. The purpose of theoretical sampling in qualitative research is to recruit the respondents most likely to contribute to the understanding of what is being researched, even if they are not representative of the population from which they come. The difference between selective and theoretical sampling is clearly explained by Becker (1993):

> Selective sampling, as described by Schatzman and Strauss (1973), involves a calculated decision about who and where to sample prior to the onset of data collection. It implies that the problem is well defined and the researcher is confident that a selected sample will answer the questions regarding the problem. Theoretical sampling, on the other hand, is an ongoing process of data collection and is determined by the emerging theory and therefore cannot be predetermined.

The researcher in qualitative research is not rigidly bound by the sample drawn prior to data collection. Instead, the inherent flexibility of the approach 'allows sampling for the later stages of the project to be guided by the initial findings'. Quinn (1993), in a study of 'nurses' perceptions about physical restraints', gives two examples to illustrate how emerging concepts and questions guided sampling decisions:

> Early data analysis revealed that nurses made a distinction between initiating physical restraint and continuing restraint that was initiated by a previous caregiver. As sampling progressed, participants were selected to provide a sufficient number of incidents of both restraint initiation and continuation. Theoretical sampling was also used when it was noted that several participants identified time of day as a factor in restraint use. To develop categories related to issues of time, nurses who had cared for restrained patients during all three hours of duty were interviewed.

In my fieldwork on infant mortality in Mauritius (Parahoo, 1985), I came across a belief early on in the project that diarrhoea and vomiting in infants were caused by the eruption of a mythical 'robber tooth' in the infants' mouth. To learn more about this, I interviewed, through a snowball sample, people who knew about this belief. Thus my original sample of mothers increased in order for me to gain an in-depth understanding of this phenomenon.

To understand why qualitative researchers do not place emphasis on the generalisability of their findings, we must look also to the historical roots of qualitative research. Anthropologists, the early qualitative researchers, were interested in the exotic and the unusual. Each tribe they studied was different from the others and therefore the question of generalising their findings did not arise, although comparisons between tribes were made. They set out to describe to the outside world the culture of the people they studied. With the increasing realisation of the limitations of quantitative approaches in health and social studies, researchers began to use the anthropologist's methodology to study phenomena closer to home. Today the qualitative approach is widely used in such fields as sociology, psychology, education and nursing.

According to Schofield (1993), there has been an increasing use of qualitative approaches in evaluation and policy-oriented research. In the field of market research, the contributions of researchers to developing qualitative techniques have been substantial (Walker, 1985). It is clear that qualitative researchers have moved into areas where they never ventured before and are now funded from sources previously closed to them. The changes in the setting, subject matter and patrons of qualitative research have, to some extent, led researchers to consider seriously the utility of their efforts. It is also possible that since qualitative research has a large number of new recruits (some of whom were converted from the quantitative tradition), they have brought with them their concerns about objectivity and external validity. The increasing use of the mix of methods and approaches has led to different forms of sampling in the same study.

Stake's (1978) notion of 'naturalistic generalisation', which involves the use of the findings of one study in order to understand similar situations, is a useful one. For the findings of qualitative research to have wider implications than for the specific population and setting they emerged from, there is a need to study the 'typical' instead of the 'unusual' (Schofield, 1993). In her qualitative study of life in the backrooms of medicine in several American hospitals, Millman (1976) was concerned that what she researched was not unusual. She writes:

> The reader may wonder whether the incidents I describe are typical or unusual. My own research and that of others indicate that the situations I have portrayed are commonly found in American hospitals.

Therefore the issue of how the results of qualitative studies can be of use in understanding other similar phenomena is of more interest to qualitative researchers than is the notion of 'generalisability' in the quantitative sense of the word. This is why purposive and snowball sampling are commonly used in qualitative research. In summary, the choice of samples and sampling must be guided more by the research questions and less by convenience.

CRITIQUING SAMPLES AND SAMPLING

Although qualitative researchers may not claim that their data are generalisable to other settings, it is important for them to describe their samples and sampling method adequately for the reader to assess whether they are useful to other settings. Smith (1994) analysed all research articles published in the *Journal of Advanced Nursing*, the *International Journal of Nursing Studies*, the *Journal of Clinical Nursing* and the *British Medical Journal* in 1992, and found that the following occurred:

It could not be ascertained how a particular sample was accessed

it was not specified whether the sample was one of convenience or a random sample

and

the types of samples (e.g. patients, carers, nurses, public) were not always specified.

The components of a study – including the units of analysis, concepts generated, population characteristics and settings – must be sufficiently well described and defined in order for other researchers to use the results of the study as a basis for comparison (Goetz and LeCompte, 1984).

In quantitative research, the purpose of sampling is to collect valid and reliable data from a subset of the population that would be representative of the whole population. These findings are often expected to be generalisable to other similar populations and settings. The representativeness of the sample and the generalisability of findings depend on at least four factors: the size and the characteristics of the sample, the method of sampling, the setting where the study was carried out and the response rate.

Size of sample

According to Polit and Hungler (1995), 'the larger the sample the more representative of the population it is likely to be'. Small samples in quantitative research are also unlikely to yield results of significance. In fact, academic journals may refuse publication of research projects in which small samples have been used, except if little research exists on the topic. Clearly a sample size of 10 out of a student population of 300 is unlikely to be representative, even if the sample is one of probability. The degree of representativeness will increase with a sample of 50 and above. Equally important is the degree of 'fit' between the sample and the population from which it is drawn. This means that the sample must be similar in characteristics to the population. For example, if in a study of stress among hospital nurses, the composition of the target population is state registered nurses 50 per cent, state enrolled nurses 30 per cent, and nursing assistants 20 per cent, the sample must more or less reflect a similar proportion of these three groups. Certain variables, such as gender or age, may be more important in one study than in others; therefore the samples must reflect the target population in these key variables. The more homogeneous the target population, the more representative the sample is likely to be. Samples for heterogeneous population need to be large and carefully selected. Stratified random sampling is often the answer.

In general, qualitative studies use small samples, but it is a misconception to think that 'numbers are unimportant in ensuring the adequacy of a sampling strategy' (Sandelowski, 1995). However, size is not the starting point. It is the purpose for which the sample is required which should decide how many respondents are recruited. In in-depth studies, the sample is unlikely to be large. There have been cases where a sample of two or three respondents has been studied. It is possible, although unlikely, that such a sample size could yield a range of different perspectives if this is what the researcher is seeking. On the other hand, if researchers carry out qualitative interviews with 100 respondents, it is possible that saturation of data could be reached very quickly. The time and effort required to interview all of them could be better spent in more in-depth interviews with for example 50 of them, with the option of interviewing some of the same respondents more than once. The more varied the population from whom the data are required, the larger the sample size should be.

In quantitative studies, the focus is on how particular views or beliefs are distributed in a population. In qualitative studies, researchers are interested in the range of their experiences in order to obtain as complete an understanding of the phenomenon as possible. If these experiences are suspected to vary greatly in a population or if the population that possesses these experiences themselves vary in terms of demographic variables such as age, race, gender or social class, it makes sense that the sample should take this into account.

The flexible and enquiring nature of qualitative research makes hard and fast rules inappropriate. According to Sandelowski (1995), researchers have to make their own judgements. She explains that:

> Numbers have a place in ensuring that a sample is fully adequate to support particular qualitative enterprises. A good principle to follow is: An adequate sample size in qualitative research is one that permits – by virtue of not being too large – the deep, case-oriented analysis that is a hallmark of all qualitative inquiry, and that results in – by virtue of not being too small – a new and richly textured understanding of experience.

In considering the feasibility of applying the findings of a study to your own practice, you must assess how similar or different the studied sample is to 'your' population. For example, it may not be appropriate to apply the findings of a study on stroke patients with an average age of 50 to a group of patients with an average age of 65. Tornquist *et al.* (1993) explains what the reader must look for in samples:

> To evaluate methods, ask these questions about the study: who was in the study sample? Were these individuals unique in some way, or were they typical of people for whom the intervention or study results should apply? Examine carefully the sample characteristics that are most important for deciding on the applicability of the results to others. The key characteristics depend on the topic selected.

Sampling method

Although probability samples are likely to be more representative than non-probability samples, representativeness is not necessarily assured with random selection. The decision on which form of random sampling to use depend on, among other things, the availability of lists and the composition of the population and the research questions. Whatever the sampling methods, these must be described in enough detail for you to decide whether the sample has any bias. Just stating that a random or a convenience sample was drawn, without explaining how, is not helpful. It is important for researchers to say who selected the sample. Often this is left to managers and practitioners, resulting in researchers having little control over who is included in the study.

The setting

To generalise findings from research in one setting to another requires careful consideration of how similar or different they are. The findings of a study of support to informal carers of people with dementia in the USA may not be applicable to carers in the UK. Statutory voluntary services as well as social networks are likely to be different in the two countries. Far from rejecting the results, they could serve as a basis for comparisons, thereby enhancing one's understanding of support for carers in general. The setting in which data are collected can also introduce bias into the findings. Researchers must provide you with adequate details of the context in which research is carried out. The responses from a 'captive' population of patients (in hospitals receiving care) may not be the same as when they are interviewed in their own homes. The social and cultural factors in the environment in which research takes place must be taken into consideration.

Response rate

Another aspect of sampling that you need to monitor is the response rate. The lower the response rate, the less representative the achieved sample is likely to be of the target population.

Those who do not respond may have characteristics different from those who do. In a study of attitudes to homosexuality, it is possible that non-respondents are not interested in the topic or that they are homophobic and are so 'disgusted' that they do not take part. Some people may see non-responding as a form of protest.

It is difficult to define an acceptable response rate. Researchers usually compare their response rates with the 'norm' in similar studies. What is more important is for researchers to attempt to explain non-responses and their possible implications for the data.

The design of a study and, in particular, the method(s) of data collection can affect the response rates. Clarke and Rees (1989), cited in Barriball and While (1994) referring to studies on 'continuing professional education in nursing', pointed out:

> the views of nurses who have had minimal or no experience of continuing professional education may be little known because these nurses are unlikely to perceive the relevance of a questionnaire about continuing professional education to themselves and are, therefore, unlikely to have the motivation to respond.

Summary and Conclusion

In this chapter, we have looked at some of the common terminologies used in relation to samples and sampling. The uses, strengths and limitations of the main sampling methods in nursing research have been discussed. Samples are the sources of research data and as such must be carefully selected and soundly justified. Researchers must provide readers with adequate information on the composition of target population and sample, as well as the sampling method, to enable them to evaluate the representativeness of the sample, the usefulness and possible generalisability of the findings.

References

Anderssen N (1993) Perception of physical education classes among young adolescents: do physical education classes provide equal opportunities to all students? *Health Education Research*, **8**(2):167–79.

Annandale E and Lampard R (1993) Sampling in non-experimental research. *Nursing Standard*, **7**(28):34–6.

Ashley J (1994) Study groups: are they effective in preparing students for NCLEX-RN? *Journal of Nursing Education*, **33**(8):357–64.

Barhyte D Y, Redman B K and Neill K M (1990) Population or sample. Design decision. *Nursing Research*, **39**(5):309–10.

Barribal K L and While A (1994) Collecting data using a semi-structured interview: a discussion paper. *Journal of Advanced Nursing*, **19**:328–35.

Becker P H (1993) Pearls, pith and provocation. *Qualitative Health Research*, **3**(2):254–60.

Clarke J and Rees C (1989) The midwife and continuing education. *Midwives Chronicle*, **102**:288–90.

Coyle L A and Sokop A G (1990) Innovation adoption behavior among nurses. *Nursing Research*, **39**(3):176–80.

Dalgas-Pelish P L (1993) The impact of the first child on marital happiness. *Journal of Advanced Nursing*, **18**:437–41.

Dolan N (1987) The relationship between burnout and job satisfaction in nurses. *Journal of Advanced Nursing*, **12**: 3–12.

Fawcett J and Weiss M E (1993) Cross-cultural adaptation to cesarean birth. *Western Journal of Nursing Research*, **15**(3):282–97.

Goetz J P and LeCompte M D (1984) *Ethnography and Qualitative Design in Educational Research*. Orlando: Academic Press.

Mason C (1994) Maternal and child health needs in Northern Ireland and Jamaica: official and lay perspectives. *Qualitative Health Research*, **4**(1):74–93.

Millette B E (1993) Client advocacy and the moral orientation of nurses. *Western Journal of Nursing Research*, **15**(5):607–18.

Millman M (1976) *The Unkindest Cut. Life in the Backroom of Medicine*. New York: Morrow Quill.

Moody L E, Wilson M E, Smyth K, Schwartz R, Tittle M and Cott M L V (1988) Analysis of a decade of nursing practice research: 1977–1986. *Nursing Research*, **37**(6):374–9.

Nyqvist K H and Sjödén P-O (1993) Advice concerning breastfeeding for mothers of infants admitted to a neonatal intensive care unit. The Roy Adaptation model as a conceptual structure. *Journal of Advanced Nursing*, **18**:54–63.

Parahoo K (1985) The organisation, delivery and uses of health care in Mauritius. Unpublished PhD Thesis: Keele University, Keele.

Polit D F and Hungler B P (1995) *Nursing Research: Principles and Methods*, 5th edn. Philadelphia: J B Lippincott.

Quinn C A (1993) Nurses' perceptions about physical restraints. *Western Journal of Nursing Research*, **15**(2):148–62.

Roe K M, Minkler M and Barnwell R S (1994) The assumption of caregiving: grandmothers raising the children of the crack cocaine epidemic. *Qualitative Health Research*, **4**(3):281–303.

Sandelowski M (1995) Sample size in qualitative research. *Research in Nursing and Health*, **18**:179–83.

Schatzman L and Strauss A L (1973) *Field Research: Strategies for a Natural Sociology*. Englewoood Cliffs, NJ, Prentice-Hall.

Schofield J W (1993) Increasing the generalisability of qualitative research. In Hammersley M (ed.) *Social Research: Philosophy, Politics and Practice*. London: Sage.

Smith L N (1994) An analysis and reflections on the quality of nursing research in 1992. *Journal of Advanced Nursing*, **3**:385–93.

Stake R E (1978) The case-study in social inquiry. *Educational Researcher*, **7**:5–8.

Tornquist E M, Funk S G, Champagne M T and Wiese R A (1993) Advice on reading research: overcoming the barriers. *Applied Nursing Research*, **6**(4):177–83.

van Wissen K A and Siebers R W L (1993) Nurses' attitudes and concerns pertaining to HIV and AIDS. *Journal of Advanced Nursing*, **18**:912–17.

Walker R (ed.) (1985) *Applied Qualitative Research*. Aldershot: Gower.

Woodcock H C, Read A W, Bower C, Stanley, F J and Moore D J (1994) A matched cohort study of planned home and hospital births in Western Australia 1981–1987. *Midwifery*, **10**:125–35.

11 QUESTIONNAIRES

When you don't know the answer question the question.
(Anonymous)

INTRODUCTION

This chapter will take a close look at the questionnaire as a method of data collection in nursing and nursing research, in particular its value and limitations and the advantages and disadvantages of different modes of questionnaire administration. The strategies that researchers can use to ensure and enhance the validity and reliability of questionnaires are examined, and some of the ethical implications of this popular method of data collection are explored and discussed.

USE OF QUESTIONNAIRES IN NURSING

The questionnaire is by far the most common method of data collection in social and health research. However, it is not useful for research purposes only. We have all, at some time or other, been asked questions or to fill in a form, for example, when attending a general practitioner's surgery or an accident and emergency department. Nurses have a number of forms to complete as part of their work. The hospital admission form itself is a questionnaire seeking information such as the name, date of birth, next of kin, previous admission, family medical history and any previous illness of the patient. Clinical specialties may have their own forms asking specific questions. For example, a 'pre-operative screening chart' in one hospital asked questions about 'allergies, general health (hypertension, diabetes, cardiac disease), skin problems, dental problems and social habits'. Opposite is an extract from a 'clinical' questionnaire administered to patients at a fracture clinic.

Most of these forms or questionnaires that nurses administer to clients serve two main purposes: diagnostic and record-keeping. The information gathered provides the basis for any subsequent diagnosis and treatment. It is useful for assessing clients' needs and helps in the formulation of care plans. Other general information is routinely kept by health centres and hospitals for administrative, accounting and planning purposes. It provides indicators of admissions, discharges, morbidity, mortality, resource allocation, uptake of services, deployment of personnel, and so on.

These questionnaires were not designed primarily for the collection of research data, although patients' notes, care plans and other records are valuable sources of data for researchers conducting retrospective studies. Many of these questionnaires would not withstand a rigorous validity and reliability test, but they are usually useful for the purpose they serve, that is they provide the necessary information on which clinical and policy decisions can be made. There are, of course, ethical and legal issues involved in the use of information from patients' notes for research purposes. The UK Department of Health has issued guidelines for the protection and use of patient information (DOH, 1996).

Q5	Any past illnesses?	☐ Yes	☐ No
Q6	Do you have blackouts or faint easily?	☐ Yes	☐ No
Q7	Do you get breathless easily, i.e. asthma?	☐ Yes	☐ No
Q12	Do you have transport to and from hospital?	☐ Yes	☐ No
Q13	Do you live alone?	☐ Yes	☐ No
Q14	Do you smoke?	☐ Yes	☐ No

Stone (1993) sums up the use of questionnaires by pointing out that they:

> are not the exclusive preserve of academics. They have many uses, including screening, audit, administration, and public relations, as well as their more familiar role in research.

WHAT IS A QUESTIONNAIRE?

A *questionnaire* can be described as a method that seeks written or verbal responses from people to a written set of questions or statements. It is a *research* method when it is designed and administered solely for the purpose of collecting data as part of a research study. It is a quantitative approach since it is predetermined (constructed in advance), standardised (the same questions in the same order are asked of all the respondents) and structured (respondents are mainly required to choose from the list of responses offered by the researcher).

Questionnaires can be used in descriptive, correlational and experimental studies. In descriptive studies, they may not only provide data that facilitate understanding of the phenomena being investigated, but can also generate data from which concepts and hypotheses can be formulated. Thus they contribute to the production of knowledge *inductively*.

In correlational studies, questionnaires can provide data to support or reject hypotheses and thereby contribute *deductively* to the production of knowledge. In a study by Palmer *et al.* (1991) on 'risk factors for urinary incontinence one year after nursing home admission', the following hypothesis was formulated: 'individuals with detectable cognitive impairment, problems with adjusting to the nursing home, and impaired mobility would be at greater risk for being incontinent than those without these characteristics'. This hypothesis was put to the test by the administration of three questionnaires to residents over the age of 65.

In experiments, too, the questionnaire is a useful data collection tool, either on its own or with other methods. In Allen *et al.*'s (1992) experimental study of 'the effectiveness of a preoperative teaching programme for cataract patients', the pre-tests and post-tests consisted of 'a 20 item self-report inventory' and a 'knowledge and skill test' that comprised '10 true–false questions'. The 'subjects' ability to instil medicine properly' was assessed by observations carried out by nurses.

The questionnaire is, however, most frequently used in survey designs. In fact, the term 'questionnaire' is often used interchangeably with 'survey'. A distinction needs to be made between them. A survey is a research design (see Chapter 8) that can comprise one or more methods of data collection. Questionnaires can be used on their own or in conjunction with interviews and/or observations. For a survey on the dental health of school children, data can be collected by asking questions (by means of either questionnaires or interviews) and by observing the presence or absence of dental caries in these school children. Some surveys can be carried out almost entirely by observations, as in the case of a 'survey on food intake', when the food intake is observed, weighed and analysed.

QUESTIONNAIRES IN NURSING RESEARCH

The little evidence which is available suggests that the questionnaire is the most widely used method of data collection in nursing research. Brown *et al.* (1984) found that the questionnaire was the most common instrument used when they analysed a sample of 137 studies published in four international nursing research journals (*Nursing Research, Research in Nursing and Health*, the *Western Journal of Nursing Research* and the *International Journal of Nursing Studies*) in 1952–53, 1960, 1970 and 1980. In a similar exercise, Jacobsen and Meininger (1985) examined all 434 articles in three journals (*Nursing Research, Research in Nursing and Health* and the *Western Journal of Nursing Research*) in 1956, 1961, 1966, 1971, 1976, 1981 and 1983. Overall, questionnaires comprised 36 per cent of all data collection methods – 54 per cent if standardised tests (which accounted for 18 per cent) were counted as questionnaires. Observations and interviews constituted 15 per cent and 13 per cent respectively. Jacobsen and Meininger (1985) also reported that, in every year studied, questionnaires were used most frequently.

Smith (1994) carried out a meta-analysis of articles in four journals published in 1992 (the *Journal of Advanced Nursing*, the *International Journal of Nursing Studies*, the *Journal of Clinical Nursing* and the *British Medical Journal*). She reported that both professional groups (nurses and doctors) used a variety of research methods. Those writing in the *British Medical Journal* were 'far more likely to employ the use of records, often involving large data bases and to use laboratory-based tests', while nurses were 'more likely to employ self-design questionnaires and interview' (Smith, 1994). The total number of articles with question-naires was 86, compared with 46 for interviews and 20 for observations.

The questionnaire is potentially the quickest and cheapest, and a relatively confidential and frequently anonymous, method of collecting large amounts of information from a large number of people scattered over wide geographical areas. They are efficient in providing data on the attributes of clients and staff, and are employed in the evaluation of practice and policy and in the assessment of the needs of clients and staff. They have also been increasingly used in the measurement of concepts and constructs as varied as, for example, empathy, burn-out, social support, pain, coping, hope, stress and quality of life. There are, of course, other methods that are equally, if not better, suited to the study of these phenomena. Researchers must always choose the most appropriate data collection method or methods in order to answer the research question, while taking into account the resources available, including funding and time.

Questionnaires have been used mainly to collect information on facts, attitudes, knowledge, beliefs, opinions, perceptions, expectations, experiences and the behaviour of clients and staff. The most common factual data collected by questionnaires are demographic ones, such as age, gender, occupation, social class and qualifications. These are very useful for constructing profiles of clients and staff and in exploring their correlation with other attributes, such as personality, attitudes or expectations. Other facts related to practice include physiological measures, such as temperature, pulse, respiration or blood pressure, and other occurrences, such as the amount of fluid intake, attendance at outpatient departments and frequency of bowel movements.

The attitudes, knowledge and beliefs of clients are studied because they can influence, among other factors, how people regard their health and illness, how and which services they use, how compliant they are with nursing and medical treatment and advice, and what actions they generally take to promote their health. The attitudes, knowledge and beliefs of health professionals can also influence their practice. For example, their knowledge of, and attitudes to, research may determine whether and how they utilise research.

The opinions, views, perceptions, expectations and experiences of clients and practitioners are legitimate areas of inquiry because nursing is about meeting the needs of the client. The self-report of the client and the objective assessment of the nurse can combine to give an expert service sensitive to individual needs.

Although behaviour is best studied by observation, it is sometimes not feasible or practical to do so, as in the case of sexual practices and behaviours of dubious legal or moral status. Past behaviour, unless captured on film, cannot be studied by observation, nor can behavioural intentions. The questionnaire, on the other hand, can ask respondents to report on past, actual and potential behaviours, as perceived by them.

All the above phenomena that are commonly studied by means of questionnaires are important in helping professionals to better organise and deliver care and treatment in institutions and in the community. The data produced can also be useful in promoting health, preventing illness and disability and contributing to effective rehabilitation. Figure 11.1 gives some examples of the use of questionnaires in nursing research.

QUESTION FORMATS

Researchers have developed a range of question formats to collect valid and reliable data efficiently and to analyse them quickly. These are strategies designed to facilitate respondents in providing the necessary and relevant information in a short time and in a relatively painless way. The choice of question format depends mainly on the type of data that researchers want to collect. If they set out to elucidate from respondents which factors affect their job dissatisfaction, they could ask a type of question that is open enough to allow them to formulate their own responses. On the other hand, if researchers want to compare the degree to which staff are satisfied with their job, they may offer respondents a number of categories to choose from, such as 'very satisfied', 'satisfied', 'neither satisfied nor dissatisfied', 'dissatisfied' and 'very dissatisfied'. Common question formats in questionnaires include: closed, open-ended and rating scales.

Nolan (1995) **A comparison of attenders at antenatal classes in the voluntary and statutory sectors: education and organisational implications**

As the author explains, 'a questionnaire consisting of 14 items asking for basic demographic details including age, marital status, ethnic group, educational qualifications, occupation, distance travelled to classes and kind of transport used was designed'.

These and other data formed the basis of a discussion on the education and organisational implication of antenatal classes in the voluntary and statutory sectors.

Hicks (1995) **A factor analytic study of midwives' attitudes to research**

The author constructed a scale comprising 13 items to measure midwives' attitudes to research. She believes that while the reasons given by midwives for not publishing, such as lack of time, confidence and skills, are valid, these may be 'manifestations of a set of underlying attitudes to research in midwifery'. This is why she carried out a 'national survey of 397 midwives' to 'establish their attitudes to research'.

Tettersell (1993) **Asthma patients' knowledge in relation to compliance with drug therapy**

Postal questionnaires were used in this study, and it was found that the level of respondents' knowledge 'had no significant effect on compliance to drug therapy'. Another useful finding was that 'the level of patient knowledge appears to influence a patient's ability to manage an asthma attack'.

Sikorski et al. (1995) **A survey of health professionals' views on possible changes in the provision and organisation of antenatal care**

Questionnaires were sent to 251 midwives, including community midwives, 50 obstetricians and 438 GPs. The rationale for studying the views of these health professionals was given as follows:

> when the provision and organisation of antenatal care is in a state of flux, it is important to establish how the providers of antenatal care feel about possible changes in service provision. Indeed, it is now recognised that ascertaining the views of maternity care providers is an essential, but hitherto largely neglected, area of study.

Carr and Kazanowski (1994) **Factors affecting job satisfaction of nurses who work in long-term care**

The authors explain that a questionnaire (developed by them):

> was sent to 1000 nurses in various speciality areas. It was used to assess degree of job satisfaction, reasons for dissatisfaction, and the relationships of the work setting and sociodemographic data.

This is an example of a study using a questionnaire to collect data on the nurses' experience (job satisfaction) and perception (reasons for dissatisfaction as perceived by nurses) and on the correlation between demographic factors and working conditions.

Sharp (1990) **Relatives' involvement in caring for the elderly mentally ill following long-term hospitalization**

Questionnaires were used to collect data on the behaviour of relatives (as reported by them) and on staff perceptions of these behaviours. Although observation of these behaviours may have yielded more valid data, the task of observing relatives' involvement in the care of elderly mentally ill, even on a small scale, can be quite daunting, if not impractical.

Figure 11.1 Examples of phenomena studied with the use of questionnaires.

Closed questions

According to Henerson *et al.* (1987), there are several kinds of question format that are used in constructing closed response questionnaires, the four most common being:

- two-way questions
- checklists
- multiple-choice questions
- ranking scales.

Two-way questions, as the term suggests, offer a choice between two responses, as shown below.

Male ☐   Female ☐   (please tick one box)

A true/false or an agree/disagree as well as a yes/no option can also be offered, as in the following example:

		Please tick one box	
Q6	The reliability of an instrument is the degree to which it measures what it is expected to measure.	True ☐	False ☐
Q8	A knowledge of nursing models is essential for the practice of nursing.	Agree ☐	Disagree ☐
Q20	Do you think that every nurse should learn how to do research?	Yes ☐	No ☐

Checklists provide respondents with a list of responses from which to select. They can 'tick' as many items or statements as they think are applicable. An example of a checklist question comes from Reid's (1985) study of 'nurse training in the clinical area'.

Q13(b) Please tick any of the following learning aids which are available to students on the wards:

1. Text books ☐

2. Specially prepared charts or books ☐

3. Charts or other aids provided by commercial concerns ☐

4. Space available for study ☐

5. Access to patients' casenotes ☐

6. Other (please specify) ☐

Multiple choice is another format used in questionnaires. This offers respondents a list of responses, normally in the form of statements, from which they can select the one most applicable to them. Fretwell (1982) provides the following example of a multiple-choice question from her study on 'ward teaching and learning'.

Ring one letter:

Q7 a. Clinical teachers taught frequently on this ward.

    b. Clinical teachers sometimes taught on this ward.

    c. Clinical teachers hardly ever taught on this ward.

    d. Clinical teachers never taught on this ward.

Sometimes researchers want to know how respondents prioritise their needs, whom they consult most or least for health advice or what interventions they find most or least useful. To obtain rapid answers, they ask respondents to rank from a list of responses. The following is an example of a *ranking* question on school children's knowledge of, and attitudes to, mental illness.

Q10 Where did you get information on mental illness from? Please rank the items below by putting 1 to 6 in the boxes provided (*1 = most information, 6 = least information*).

   School teacher

   Television

   Books

   Magazines

   Parents

   Friends

Closed questions are asked when researchers consider that they know all the potential answers and only require respondents to select the one or ones that apply to them. Such questions are appropriate for demographic data and in cases where there are a more or less fixed number of alternatives. For example, a researcher can ask a closed question such as that shown overleaf:

By which route do you normallly administer medication X?

Orally   ☐   **Please tick one box**

Intramuscularly   ☐

Intravenously   ☐

when medication X can only be given via these three routes. Closed questions yield data that allow for comparison between respondents as all the responses are in the same format. They can be precoded, thereby making analysis a relatively easy task.

The main problem with closed questions is that the researcher may omit an important response and thereby obtain a result different from that had the response been included. For example, if in the above ranking question the researcher omitted 'magazines' from the list, the school children in the survey would rank what is on offer and therefore provide different data to those obtained if 'magazines' had been included. Another example of forced choice is when a respondent is asked to rank in order from 1 to 6, when in reality he or she may want to rank two items at number 1. Researchers constructing closed questions must make sure that all possible choices are included, yet at the same time respondents may be confused if they have to choose from too many categories.

The list of responses offered by the researcher may give the respondents an idea of what is normal. For example, by asking respondents to choose from a list of journals that nurses read, they may think that nurses *normally* read these journals, and that perhaps they should indicate that they do so as well. Therefore, checklists and multiple choices may unwittingly reveal to respondents what the norm is and thereby encourage what they perceive as socially desirable answers.

These limitations can be offset to a large extent by careful and skilful construction of the questionnaire, by paying particular attention to the categories offered to respondents and by including questions in appropriate formats.

Open-ended questions

When researchers do not have all the answers and/or want to obtain respondents' views, they can formulate an open-ended question, as in the example below.

> **Q3** Please indicate below the main factors that contribute to your job satisfaction.
>
> . . . .
>
> . . . .
>
> . . . .
>
> . . . .
>
> . . . .

It is also possible to ask an open-ended ranking question in a different way.

> **Q7** Please list, in order of importance, 4 factors that contribute to your job
> satisfaction (*1 = most important, 4 = least important*).
>
> 1. . . . .
>
> 2. . . . .
>
> 3. . . . .
>
> 4. . . . .

Open-ended questions suit the interview style better than the questionnaire. The greater the number of closed questions, the more highly structured the questionnaire is. Tall (1988), commenting on the use of open-ended questions, wrote:

> These questions are essential, but can cause considerable difficulty. Too many and the questionnaire seems to take for ever to answer (and the response rate will be appropriately small), none and the questionnaire designer is effectively saying: 'I know the right questions to ask and the range of possible answers. Be a good 'boy/girl' and just tick the right answer – your insight into the issue is not really wanted'.

Open-ended questions give respondents the opportunity to participate in, and interact with, the questionnaire in a way in which closed questions do not. Lydeard (1991) describes open-ended questions as 'easy to ask, difficult to answer, and even more difficult to analyse'. An open-ended question must be clear and unambiguous, or different respondents will interpret it differently. For example, in a questionnaire on job satisfaction, the researcher who wants to know the types of clinical area where respondents work (that is medical, surgical or care of the elderly) may ask 'which type of ward do you work in?' The answers could be 'a 25-bedded ward', 'a mixed ward', 'a care of the elderly ward', 'an open ward' or 'a chaotic ward'. There is always the possibility with open-ended questions that the researcher understands the question differently from some respondents. The responses given above would not be useful to the researcher, as they do not answer the question in the way and form in which she wants it.

Responses to open-ended questions can also vary in length. Some respondents continue their answers on the back of the questionnaire, whereas others give a response in a few words. The space provided for responses is sometimes an indication of how long the researcher expects them to be. However, some respondents have larger handwriting than others. A bigger problem may be in deciphering what is written and in making sense of what is said. Analysis of responses from open-ended questions can be time-consuming and difficult since responses are rarely made using the same terminologies, unlike the case in closed questions. The analysis of questionnaire data is further discussed in Chapter 14.

Open-ended questions do not make a questionnaire a qualitative method, as some people believe. As I have explained elsewhere (Parahoo, 1993):

> questionnaire data are treated at face value; there is no opportunity to unravel the real meaning of each individual response. What people say and what they *mean* can be different, and several interviews with the same person are sometimes necessary to collect meaningful data.

Open-ended questions are valuable in that they give respondents some freedom in expressing themselves rather than their being constrained by the 'straitjacket' style of closed questions.

Researchers face a dilemma in choosing between closed and open-ended questions. Lydeard (1991) offers the 'semiclosed' question as a compromise combining both types of question. Below is an example of a semiclosed question from the Ward Sister Questionnaire (Reid 1985).

Q24   How often do you visit the school?   *(Tick as appropriate)*

Never	. . . .
Once a year	. . . .
Several times per year	. . . .
Monthly	. . . .
More than once a month	. . . .

If any category except 'Never':

Give details of visists, including person or group visited, purpose of visit, etc.

. . . .

. . . .

. . . .

Both closed and open-ended questions have their place in question-naires. Researchers must use them judiciously and appropriately, and as much as possible use the strength of one to offset the limitation of the other.

RATING SCALES

You may have come across a questionnaire in a popular magazine or newspaper in which readers are asked to 'tick' the appropriate boxes and add up their scores to find out how 'sexy', 'romantic' or 'intelligent' they are. If you have indulged in such an activity, you have in effect filled in a rating scale. If you have not, here is an extract from a scale in the *Daily Mail* (17 July 1995) entitled 'Are you hot on gossip?'

---

1. After the party I like talking about how others there looked

   AGREE   A . . . ☐   DISAGREE   B . . . ☐

6. I usually skip the gossip columns in newspapers

   AGREE   B . . . ☐   DISAGREE   A . . . ☐

10. The saying 'There is no smoke without fire' is often wrong

   AGREE   B . . . ☐   DISAGREE   A . . . ☐

There were 10 items in all and readers were asked to add up their number of As and Bs. Those who scored 8 or more As were described as:

> You are so interested in gossip that you often prefer rumour and speculation about others than the hard truth

If their score was two As or fewer, they were described as:

> You probably prefer your own company to groups, and also realise that there are usually more mundane explanations for the events which grip and promote gossips.

While this may be light-hearted fun, the same principles apply to the construction of rating scales used in research and clinical practice.

Rating scales are sometimes referred to as questionnaires. There are, however, crucial differences between the two, especially with regard to their structure, design and purpose. Questionnaires, on the whole, contain a set of questions mostly in closed and open-ended formats.

Responses to each of the questions are treated on their own and analysed separately, although researchers seek to correlate and cross-tabulate variables. Together, responses from all the questions provide an answer to the research question or hypotheses. Rating scales are made up of statements or items that respondents are required to rate. Each rated statement is given a score and the total score, as shown in the 'gossip scale', is given an interpretation.

Researchers designing questionnaires carefully select questions that reflect attributes of the concept or aspects of an issue or topic being studied. For example, for a questionnaire on job satisfaction, a researcher will make sure that the main components of job satisfaction, such as autonomy, pay, working environment, promotion prospects and good working relationships, are represented in the questionnaire. She can ask questions on these aspects in checklist, open-ended, multiple choice or ranking format. A rating scale is normally constructed by collecting a large number of statements on the phenomenon being rated and, through an elaborate process, weaning them down to a smaller number that can be administered to respondents. Henerson *et al.* (1987) explain how an attitude rating scale can be developed. They propose the following steps:

1. Accumulate a large number of clearly favourable and clearly unfavourable statements about the attitude you wish to measure (approximately 60).
2. Ask 50 or more people to respond to these statements as a pilot run.
3. Score responses by assigning them from one to five points – five for most favourable, one for least favourable.
4. Compute a score for each respondent by totalling the points corresponding to his or her responses.
5. Identify high scores (top 25 per cent) and low scores (lowest 25 per cent).
6. Analyse each statement according to how high and low scorers responded to it.
7. Retain those items (approximately 20) which provided good discrimination between high and low scorers.
8. Construct the scale by listing the retained statements in random order.
9. Administer the instrument.
10. Compute a score for each respondent by totalling the scores corresponding to his or her responses.

This is not an attempt to teach you how to construct a scale but rather to show you the complexity of the exercise and the difference between this type of scale and other 'pseudo-scales' (when a few statements are quickly put together to look like a scale but not systematically constructed).

The type of scale described by Henerson *et al.* is called a Likert scale after Likert (1932) who developed it to measure attitudes. Using this technique, people were asked to respond to a series of statements using a 5-point scale ranging from 'strongly agree' through 'don't know' in the middle to 'strongly agree' at the other end (Banyard and Hayes, 1994).

The purpose of questionnaires is normally to explore, describe, assess or evaluate phenomena but not necessarily to measure them. Rating scales, on the other hand, represent researchers' attempts to measure phenomena such as attitudes, pain, illness behaviour, social dysfunction and quality of life. The overall score is a measure of the phenomenon, for example, how severe the pain or how dependent the patient is.

Not all rating scales are designed in the same way as the Likert attitude scales. Items for scales measuring nursing and health phenomena are mainly derived from the literature. For example, Quinless and Nelson (1988), for their scale measuring 'learned helplessness', developed a pool of 50 test items from the literature that reflected the attributes of helplessness, before submitting these to a panel of three experts, with a view to reducing them to 20.

Some of these scales were developed for research and clinical purposes. McDowell and Newell (1987), drawing on their experience as research consultants, state that 'researchers and clinicians are often unaware of the wide variety of measurement techniques that are available for use in health services research'. Clinicians can make use of scales primarily designed for research purposes and thus contribute towards bridging the research–practice gap. McDowell and Newell (1987) also point out that 'the development of health measurements has so far been an uneven process with deficiencies in some areas of measurement, while others show a proliferation of methods which vary only in minor detail'.

Semantic differential scale

The semantic differential (SD) scale originally developed by Osgood *et al.* (1957) is another technique or method that has been developed to measure an attitude or feeling towards a concept or phenomenon. Henerson *et al.* (1987) describe the SD scale as consisting of:

> a series of adjectives and their antonyms listed on opposite sides of the page with seven 'attitude positions' in between. At the top of the page, the attitude object is named as the heading. The attitude object may be stated as a word, a phrase, or it may even be a picture.

This extract from a SD scale is taken from Falicki and Monieta (1984). It sets out to measure feelings towards love.

Love							
sorrow	I_____2_____3_____4_____5_____6_____7_____ joy
despair	I_____2_____3_____4_____5_____6_____7_____ gaiety
sensitivity	I_____2_____3_____4_____5_____6_____7_____ indifference

An SD scale has three components: a stem, steps and anchors. In the above example, the *stem* is 'love'; it can also be expressed as a statement. The *steps* are the seven gradations to choose from. According to Waltz et al. (1991), the SD scale can have between five and nine steps. The *anchors* are the adjectives on each side of the lines. Respondents are instructed to put a 'X' or a '✓' in the space provided as quickly as possible. They are advised not to ponder or think rationally, but to give their immediate reactions, as it is their attitudes, feelings and emotions that are being measured. Such scales are used with the assumption that 'meanings often can be or are usually communicated by adjectives' (Waltz et al., 1991). The total score obtained by each respondent is an indication of their attitudes or feelings. The score is calculated by 'assigning a 1 to responses indicating the most negative response, a 7 to the most positive response, and scoring intermediate responses from 2 to 6 accordingly' (Henerson et al., 1987). These scores can then be subjected to statistical analysis.

According to Bowles (1986), the semantic differential model 'is a highly acceptable and frequently used measure of attitude and it lends itself to statistical techniques for validation purposes'. Henerson et al. (1987), on the other hand, find that the 'semantic differential yields only general impressions without information about their source' and are therefore ' not often worth the effort expended'.

Examples of phenomena in nursing research studied using SD scales include 'attitude toward menopause' (Bowles, 1986) and 'perception of stress' (Rosenfield and Stevenson, 1988).

Visual analogue scales

Another attitude-measuring instrument, similar to the semantic differential format, is the *visual analogue scale* (VAS). The main difference between the two is that with the SD technique respondents have a series of steps or graduations (from 5 to 9) to choose from. On the other hand, with the VAS, the response is recorded on a line representing a continuum between two points or anchor, thus allowing more freedom to respondents to put their 'X' in any position in the line. Cline *et al.* (1992) give a clear description of the VAS:

> Operationally, the VAS is a vertical or horizontal line, 100 mm in length, anchored by terms that represent the extremes of the subjective phenomenon the researcher wishes to measure. Subjects are asked to indicate the intensity of a sensation by placing a line across the VAS at a point that represents the intensity of the sensation at that moment in time. Responses are scored by measuring the distance between from the lowest anchor point to the subject's mark across the line.

An example of horizontal and vertical VAS is given below in Figure 11.2.

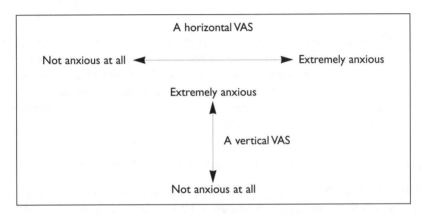

Figure 11.2 A horizontal and a vertical VAS.

The line can be of different lengths although the popular length is 100 mm: Heim *et al.* (1972, cited in Waltz *et al.*, 1991) used a 160 mm line to measure dyspnoea. The vertical VAS is also preferred because it is more 'directly analogous to the "more" (high, top) and "less" (low, bottom) ends of the continuum of degree or intensity commonly measured by the VAS', and because it 'eliminates difficulty with problems in left–right discrimination and adds to the sensitivity of the scale without altering its validity' (Waltz *et al.*, 1991).

The VAS is useful in clinical practice as well as in nursing research. Waltz *et al.* (1991) comment that VASs are 'ideal measures for clinical use because they can be administered quickly and easily and are suitable for most populations in the clinical setting'. Cline *et al.* (1992) observe that 'much current nursing research is focused on the measurement of subjective feelings, perceptions, sensations and symptoms' and that the VAS has been commonly used for this purpose. Examples of phenomena that have been measured by the VAS include pain, anxiety, nausea, fatigue, dypsnoea and hunger (Cline *et al.*, 1992).

The advantage of the VAS is that it is easy to administer and simple for the subject to understand (Cline *et al.*, 1992). The language is uncomplicated, and the scale takes little time to complete. It can also chart changes over time in the feelings or attitudes being measured. Its disadvantage is that people with visual impairment or psychomotor disability may find it difficult to make their mark on the line. The concept of a line measuring feelings may not be as easily understood by some respondents as it is by researchers.

The VAS has been, and continues to be, a popular and instant method of measuring feelings and attitudes. Aitken's conclusions of 1969 about the use of the VAS in measuring depression still seem to be valid today:

> The use of a Visual Analogue Scale for the assessment of mood in depressed patients has been shown to be practical, reliable and valid. It is particularly suitable for the measurement of change, and observation of its significance. Its limitations are no more than in the use of any language to communicate feelings from the patient to the observer; in our opinion, its limitations are less than for other available methods.

ADVANTAGES AND DISADVANTAGES OF QUESTIONNAIRES

These depend partly on the mode of questionnaire administration. Questionnaires can be self- or researcher administered. A *self-administered questionnaire* is one in which respondents write their responses on the questionnaire without the researcher helping in anyway. Normally the latter is not present, but there are cases when the researcher is in the same room or in the vicinity. The questionnaire can be delivered personally or posted, hence the term 'postal questionnaire'. Alternatively, the researcher can read the questions and record the responses on the questionnaire. This can be either 'face to face' or over the telephone. This type of 'face-to-face' encounter is more like a structured interview (described in Chapter 12). Questionnaires can also be administered to a group of people, for example students in a classroom. Telephone surveys are becoming increasingly popular in the social and health sciences, and questioning by telephone is extensively used in market research. An example of a telephone survey in nursing research is Hash *et al.*'s (1985) study of the educational needs of nurses.

The main advantage of questionnaires is that they can reach large numbers of people over wide geographical areas and collect data at a lower cost than can other methods such as interviews and observations. Because they are structured and predetermined and cannot as a rule be varied, both in their wording and in the order in which they are answered, they have a fair degree of reliability. The data collected from all respondents are in the same form, and comparisons can be made between them without great difficulty. Closed questions and rating scales can be precoded and can thereafter be easily and quickly analysed, especially if computer packages, which are becoming increasingly more efficient, are used. Self-administered questionnaires have the advantage of keeping the respondents anonymous except in cases where the researcher deliberately uses a code to identify non-responders for follow-up purposes. They also allow respondents to answer in their own time and at their own convenience. They can have the time to check records, especially when they answer factual questions.

One of the major advantages of self-administered questionnaires is the absence of interviewer effect. Dockrell and Joffe (1992) analysed data from their study of young people and HIV/AIDS and concluded that, while face-to-face interviews gave them insight into the behaviour of the respondents, the latter were often uncomfortable in discussing their sexual activities. According to them, the question-naire, with fixed choices, might be more appropriate and could lead to a more accurate reporting of such activities (Dockrell and Joffe, 1992). In the case of telephone questionnaires, the interviewer effect can be less than in 'face-to-face' encounters, due to the physical absence of the person asking the questions.

Finally, the questionnaire designer can improve the instrument by piloting it many times before administering it to respondents, thereby increasing its validity and reliability. It can also be useful for other researchers to borrow and adapt for use in replication studies.

The main disadvantage with the self-administered questionnaire is that there is no opportunity to ask respondents to elaborate, expand, clarify or illustrate their answers. Respondents themselves have no opportunity to ask for clarification. They may understand questions differently from researchers, thereby not inspiring confidence in the validity of questionnaires. They are not easy to construct and it can often take as many as 8–12 drafts before a reasonable one is ready for use (Crossby et al., 1989); even after all this effort, some questions can still be ambiguous.

Questionnaires tell us little about the context in which respondents formulate their responses. In interviews, researchers can read the body language and take it as a cue to probe further, if appropriate. As Nay-Brock (1984) explains, it is difficult 'to take into account any reluctance or evasiveness on the part of the respondent because the non-verbal responses of the respondents cannot be observed'. The data collected from questionnaires are sometimes superficial and can only be taken at face value (Parahoo, 1993). They are devoid of the context which gives rise to them and, although they may attempt to measure important contextual variables, they typically separate the measured behaviour from its particular historical, social and cultural contexts (Mechanic, 1989).

Questionnaires do not suit everyone, in particular those who have difficulty in reading and comprehension and in articulating written responses. This may lead some respondents to confer with others or ask them to complete the questionnaires. The implications of this for knowledge and attitude questions are obvious.

Another serious problem with questionnaires is low response rates. There are a variety of reasons why people may not respond to questionnaires. One of these is referred to as 'respondent burden', which is described by Sharp and Frankel (1983) as the 'presumed hardships entailed in being a survey participant'. Respondents' time is precious, especially for those busy at work in an office, a factory or the home. Health professionals, in particular, can be prone to questionnaire fatigue caused by being subjected to a battery of questionnaires from researchers. Respondents are requested to fill them in on top of other 'paperwork'. A study by Sharp and Frankel (1983) showed that the burden of filling in questionnaires was perceived as low when the respondents believed in the usefulness of surveys and when they did not see the questionnaire as invading their privacy. Various strategies can be used to increase response rates, including making respondents feel that their responses are valuable and ensuring that the questionnaire is easy to respond to, not too lengthy, and well structured and presented.

Some of the above disadvantages are inherent in the method, in that the questionnaire is by its very nature limited to collecting certain types of data, but many of the other disadvantages can be overcome through skilful construction. The questionnaire's popularity as a method of data collection suggests that, to many people, the advantages outweigh the disadvantages.

VALIDITY AND RELIABILITY OF QUESTIONNAIRES

For questionnaires to be of use to practitioners and policy-makers, they have to produce valid and reliable data. The validity of a questionnaire is the extent to which it addresses the research question, objectives or hypotheses set by the researcher. For example, if a questionnaire is designed to assess patient satisfaction, it must 'assess' rather than 'explore' patient satisfaction with nursing care; all the questions, together, must also reflect fully the concepts of 'patient satisfaction' and 'nursing care'. It can happen that the questionnaire only addresses physical care and ignores other aspects, such as psychological, social and spiritual care. Therefore such a questionnaire can hardly be said to assess satisfaction with 'nursing care'. Two questions can be asked when assessing the validity of a questionnaire:

1. Does the questionnaire answer the research question?
2. Do the questions adequately represent the different attributes of the concepts or the different aspects of the issues being studied?

The reliability of a questionnaire refers to the consistency with which respondents understand, and respond to, all the questions. For example, if a question such as 'what type of accommodation do you live in?' is put to respondents, would all of them interpret the terms 'type', 'accommodation' and 'live' in the same way? Do all respondents use the terms 'house', 'flat' and 'studio' in the same sense? Some may reply that they live in 'comfortable' or 'cheap' or 'council' accommodation. Others may 'live' in more than one accommodation. It is clear, therefore, that responses to this question will not be consistent if respondents interpret it differently. Two questions that can be asked when assessing the reliability of a questionnaire are:

1. Are the questions or statements clear and unambiguous enough for a respondent to understand and to respond to them in the same way each time they are presented to him (except where respondents have different answers to give), and for the respondent to understand them in the same way as others do?
2. Do all respondents interpret the instructions given by the researcher in the same way?

A questionnaire can be reliable without being valid, but it cannot be valid if it is not reliable. In the above example of a questionnaire assessing patients' satisfaction with nursing care, if the questions and instructions are interpreted in the same way by all respondents but the questionnaire content does not represent all the different aspects of nursing care, the questionnaire is reliable but not valid. If some respondents interpret the questions differently from others, their responses are not reliable and cannot also be taken as a valid assessment of 'patients' satisfaction with nursing care' as a result of the confusion over the meaning of some questions. Therefore reliability is a necessary but not a sufficient condition for validity.

Earlier in this chapter, we looked at the type of phenomenon, such as facts, knowledge and attitudes, that nursing research questionnaires describe or measure. However, they present a number of difficulties to researchers. In theory, facts are believed to be the easiest type of data that questionnaires can collect; in practice, it may be quite different. Mechanic (1989) points out that 'respondents misreport even the simplest items, such as age'. People can also be 'economical with the truth' for various reasons; facts can be 'coloured' to make responses more socially desirable. For example, some people who cannot afford two meals a day may not want the world to know about it. Lydeard (1991) explains that 'prestige bias, social desirability, ego, or practical/ethical standards, all are different names for the same phenomenon i.e. responders are modest/social drinkers that rarely smoke, brush their teeth with alarming frequency and never allow their children to watch dubious television programmes'.

Answers can also be exaggerated to protest or support particular causes. The context in which questionnaires are administered can affect the reliability and validity of the data. Researchers in the health field often have to deal with captive populations such as patients in a ward or clinic. Robinson (1996) gives the following example from the National Birthday Trust's (NBT) study of pain relief in labour (Chamberlain *et al.*, 1993) to show that 'questions answered before discharge are answered differently from the same questions asked later'. In the NBT's study, '70% of women questioned after delivery said they had been free to choose their method of pain relief', but when questioned 6 weeks after delivery, this had 'fallen to 55%' (cited in Robinson, 1996).

Memory distortion, memory-gaps and selective memory can all be responsible for inaccuracies in self-reporting. Memory distortion can happen when, for example, a past event is seen to be worse or better than it was because the 'passing of time' has put a different perception to it. Memory-gaps simply refer to the forgetfulness of events of little significance to respondents, especially if they happened a long time ago. With selective memory, respondents choose to remember certain events, for example joyful ones, and repress others that are painful.

Events and activities that require respondents or researchers to make an assessment, as in the case of the 'amount of fluid intake' or the 'frequency of bowel movements', can be under- or overreported as these involve a subjective judgement. These difficulties in and limitations of collecting reliable factual information must be borne in mind when evaluating data. They do not in themselves undermine the usefulness of questionnaires in the collection of such data. As Mechanic (1989) points out, 'poor reliability is not inevitable; if the investigator makes the effort and takes the time to ask questions in detail and in a precise way, reliability can be much improved'.

Measuring attitudes is a complex and challenging task. According to Henerson *et al.* (1987), 'an attitude is not something we can examine and measure in the same way we can examine the cells of a person's skin or measure the rate of her heartbeat'. They illustrate the complexity of attitudes with the example of racial prejudice:

when we attempt to measure an attitude such as racial prejudice, we find it is blurred by peer group pressures, the desire to please, ambivalence, inconsistency, lack of self awareness.

It is sometimes surprising to find that questionnaires are designed to measure a particular attitude using only two or three questions. This shows a lack of understanding of the complexities of measuring and assessing such concepts.

Measuring respondents' knowledge by questionnaire is a less challenging task than is measuring attitudes. However, there are particular problems that can threaten the reliability and validity of the responses. For example, self-administered questionnaires, as explained earlier, give opportunities for respondents to confer with others or consult other sources. Mulliner *et al.* (1995) pointed out in their study 'exploring midwives' education in, knowledge of and attitudes to nutrition in pregnancy' that it was 'considered unrealistic to expect midwives to respond to a postal questionnaire attempting to assess their nutritional knowledge'.

For interviewer-administered questionnaires, researchers often make an appointment with respondents and disclose in advance the remit of the questionnaire, thereby possibly giving them the opportunity to 'brush up' on the topic. Assessing the knowledge of health professionals, no matter what method is used, can be threatening to them even when the promise of confidentiality is offered. The response rate may understandably be low, and the number of partially completed questionnaires is often high. It is difficult to ascertain whether a non-response to a question means that the respondent did not know the answer, did not understand the question or simply chose to ignore it.

People often give an opinion when asked even if they have little or no knowledge of the topic or have not thought seriously about it. Multiple-choice and checklist questions offer the opportunity for guesswork. Many of the questions asked in a questionnaire can only be answered conditionally. According to Mechanic (1989):

> Although most people will respond to one of the structured response categories, they often know that the correct answer is 'it depends'. Survey researchers have learned that this is a response alternative that one never offers because respondents will typically choose it.

Studying behaviour and behavioural intention with the use of questionnaires can also be particularly difficult. Earlier, we mentioned some of the problems with self-reporting, including memory distortion, memory-gaps and selective memory. Behavioural intention is the 'nut' that policy-makers, planners and opinion pollsters would dearly like to 'crack'. Mechanic (1989) reminds us that there is 'an extensive literature on the gap between measured attitudes and intentions and subsequent behavior'. According to him, 'intentions may not result in expected action because statements of intention fail to take account of social pressures, environment barriers, and motivations that affect implementation'. Sparrow (1993) conducted recall interviews to find out why opinion polls failed to predict a Conservative victory in the 1992 UK general election. His study revealed that some people who told interviewers they would vote for a particular party decided on the last day to vote differently, and that there was 'a group of people who were unwilling to say who they would vote for in the original poll, but gave details of their voting behaviour in the recall interviews'.

The reliability of questionnaires depends largely on question wording and questionnaire structure. Lydeard (1991) explains that 'it is difficult enough to obtain a relatively unbiased answer even from a willing, alert individual who has correctly understood the question but the task becomes virtually impossible if hampered by poor question wording'.

The importance of question wording is illustrated in an example cited in Robinson (1996). As she explains:

> When the General Household Survey was collecting data on chronic illness, they asked ' Do you suffer from any disability?' The response rate was far lower than researchers expected. Next time they asked 'Do you HAVE any disability? and got a more accurate response. Many people had disabilities, but did not consider they suffered from them or perhaps were unwilling to say that they did.

Some of the threats to reliability come from questions that are *ambiguous, double-barrelled, leading, double negative* and *hypothetical.* Question order and the length of the questionnaire can also affect responses.

Fowler (1992) took seven questions from questionnaires used in national health surveys, and subjected them to a 'special pretest procedure' and found that they contained poorly defined terms. When they were clarified and administered, they yielded significantly different results. Terms like 'often', 'sometimes' or 'happy' can mean different things to different people. Schaeffer (1991) gives this interesting illustration:

> In the movie *Annie Hall*, there is a scene with a split screen. On one side Alvie Singer talks to his psychiatrist; on the other side Annie Hall talks to hers. Alvie's therapist asks him, 'How often do you sleep together?' and Alvie replies, 'Hardly ever, maybe three times a week'. Annie's therapist asks her, 'Do you have sex often?' Annie replies, 'Constantly, I'd say three times a week.

As the author says, the fact that frequency can be reported in different ways is a source of concern for researchers. Below are examples of the types of question that can affect the reliability and validity of questionnaire data.

Double-barrelled:

Traditional nurses are more realistic and concise in formulating care plans than degree nurses:

Agree ☐   Disagree ☐

Leading:

In the UK 30 000 people die each year from smoking-related diseases. Indicate your reaction to this statement by marking an X on the line below.

◀──────────────────────────────────────▶

Very concerned   Apathetic

Double negative:

	Yes	No
Are you not taking the sleeping tablets as prescribed?	☐	☐

Hypothetical:

	Yes	No
Would you like free dental care?	☐	☐

Lengthy and uninteresting questionnaires not only affect response rates, but can also lead respondents to take them lightly. Self-administered questionnaires that are time-consuming to complete may cause fatigue and lack of concentration, especially to people who are not accustomed to reading and writing. The order of the questions, the way in which they are grouped and their sensitivity (or lack of it) can all affect responses. Mechanic (1989) points out that, 'we have many relevant methodological studies, and some solutions, to such problems as acquiescence, social desirability effects, format biases, recall difficulties, and many more, but the complexity of these issues means that in the average study most of these cautions are acknowledged but ignored'.

The reliability and validity of questionnaires can be greatly enhanced by careful preparation and skilful construction, paying particular attention to the needs and circumstances of potential respondents and anticipating how they would react.

One thing to remember is that, despite all the efforts made to construct and administer a reliable and valid questionnaire, there will always be some respondents who will interpret terms or questions differently. Large samples can, to some extent, accommodate minor individual inconsistencies, but as Fowler (1992) explains, 'if the ambiguity systematically leads respondents to err in one direction, by definition, estimates based on these answers will be biased'. There are a number of strategies that researchers can use in order to reduce bias and ambiguities and ensure the validity and reliability of questionnaires.

ENHANCING VALIDITY

There are a variety of validity tests that can be applied, the main ones described here being content validity, criterion-referenced validity and construct validity.

Content validity

This type of validity refers to the degree to which the questions or items in the questionnaire adequately represent the phenomenon being studied. If the questionnaire sets out to measure staff nurses' nutritional knowledge in relation to the care of diabetic patients, a content validity test would ensure that there are enough relevant questions covering all the major aspects of the nutritional knowledge that nurses are required to have for nursing this particular group of patients. Therefore, an assessment of content validity 'typically involves an organized review of the questionnaire's content to ensure that it includes everything it should and does not include anything it should not' (Henerson *et al.*, 1987). Content validity can be illustrated by the example of a teacher setting questions on an examination paper for a particular module. All the questions together must address the whole content of the module.

To assess content validity, the questionnaire is submitted to a panel of judges with experience and knowledge of the topic, who can make suggestions for the adequacy and relevance of the questions. Liukkonen and Laitinen (1994) describe how they ensured the content validity of their questionnaire on 'reasons for uses of physical restraint' in geriatric nursing:

> The questionnaire was developed on the basis of the results of an earlier study (Liukkonen, 1991), which approached the phenomenon of physical restraint from inductive premises. Those results were used for purposes of conceptual elaboration and for writing the pre-set alternatives for this questionnaire. The objective of the earlier study was to improve the validity

of the measure. Content validity of the questionnaire was evaluated by a panel of experts composed of four gerontological nurses. Their suggestions were incorporated into the final draft of the questionnaire.

There is no statistical test for content validity, although an index of content validity can be calculated based on the degree of agreement of the panel members.

Content validity is sometimes referred to as '*face validity*' (Smith, 1991). Frank-Stromborg (1992) also describes the latter as 'a type of content validity'. In effect, face validity involves giving the questionnaire to anyone, not necessarily an expert on the subject, who can 'on the face of it', assess whether the questions reflect the phenomenon being studied. Greater or lesser weight may be given to face validity since, according to Litwin (1995), 'face validity is based on a cursory review of items by untrained judges, such as your sister, boyfriend, or squash partner'. Face and content validity are the ones most frequently reported in the literature.

Criterion-related validity

Another way to find out about the validity of a questionnaire is to compare its findings with data collected on the same phenomenon by other methods, such as another questionnaire or clinical observations. The data from these other sources become the criteria with which data from the present questionnaire can be compared. If the data are similar, the questionnaire can be said to have criterion-related validity. There are two types of criterion-related validity: *concurrent* and *predictive*.

Concurrent validity refers to other current criteria (hence concurrent) with which comparisons can be made. For example, for a questionnaire measuring pain to have concurrent validity, the data from the questionnaire must correspond to other data, such as nurses' observations relating to requests for painkillers and other behaviours. If the questionnaire is able to distinguish those who have pain from those who do not, data from other sources, including nurses' observations, must tell a similar story about the same patients. If this happens, the questionnaire can be said to have concurrent validity.

Predictive validity refers to data available in the future that will confirm whether or not data from the present questionnaire are valid. For example, a questionnaire that can distinguish between those who have positive and those who have negative attitudes towards people with a learning disability will have predictive validity if their future behaviours are consistent with the findings of the questionnaire. The difference between predictive and concurrent validity, then, is the difference in the timing of obtaining measurements on a criterion (Polit and Hungler, 1995).

Construct validity

This is the most difficult type of validity for a questionnaire to achieve. It refers to how well a questionnaire or scale measures a particular construct. The latter is defined as an abstraction or concept that is deliberately invented (constructed) by researchers for a scientific purpose (Polit and Hungler, 1995). Examples of constructs are self-esteem, burn-out, social support and empathy. Each of these constructs is difficult to define, let alone measure. Researchers have to resort to the theoretical and research literature before they can break down each construct into attributes, which can thereafter form the items or questions on a scale (see Chapters 6 and 7). Henerson *et al.* (1987) describes the construct validity of an instrument as, 'the extent to which you can be sure that it represents the construct whose name appears in its title'. It is difficult for a newly constructed questionnaire to achieve construct validity as it has to be tested in a multitude of settings and with different populations over a number of years.

Groer *et al.* (1992) used the adolescent life change event scale (ALCES) to measure adolescent stress and coping. They explained that the ALCES was 'theoretically grounded in research literature that suggests that life changes and social adjustments occurring within a given period produce stress and may predict illness'. They also pointed out that the instrument had been used to study life changes in relation to suicide or illness, and with male and female, rural, urban and suburban adolescents. Each new study using this instrument contributes towards assessing its construct validity.

There are different ways in which the construct validity of a questionnaire can be tested, the two main methods being the multitrait–multimethod approach (Campbell and Fiske, 1959) and the known-groups technique (Polit and Hungler, 1995). Fitz-Gibbon and Morris (1987) explain the principle behind the multitrait–multimethod approach:

> The idea is that if a construct exists it should be possible to measure it in more than one way. For example, self-concept might be measured with a paper and pencil self-report scale, a rating made by others and a projective test, or a clinical interview. The correlation among these different measures of the same thing should be strong and positive.... Moreover, if the same methods are applied to measure some other construct – for example, verbal ability – the results should not correlate highly with measures of self-concept.

The known-groups technique is simply to administer the instrument to a group of people who are known to possess the trait in a construct and to another group who are known to possess it less, and see whether or not the instrument is able to detect a difference in their scores. For example, an instrument measuring 'self-esteem' should be able to discriminate between the scores of a group of people who are depressed and those who are not, since it is widely agreed that those with depression have low self-esteem.

ENHANCING RELIABILITY

A number of reliability tests have been devised to find out the consistency with which questionnaires collect data. Among the well-known ones are test–retest, alternate-form and split-half.

Test–retest

The test–retest simply involves administering the questionnaire on two occasions and comparing the responses. For example, an 'attitude towards mental illness' questionnaire can be administered to a group of chemistry students. The same questionnaire can then be readministered to the same group 3 weeks later. The second set of responses from each individual should not differ unless something has happened to change their attitudes. If a group of student nurses were given the same questionnaire on two occasions and had visited a psychiatric hospital in the interval between the two administrations, a difference in results could be explained. If nothing has happened in the period between the two administrations which might change their attitudes, the scores must be the same; the questionnaire thus passes the test–retest and can be said to be reliable.

Alternate-form test

The alternate-form reliability test (also known as equivalence) is carried out by asking the questions in two different forms. Sometimes the order of the categories can be altered. For example, if we take a question from Fretwell's (1982) 'Rating Questionnaires for Learners', we can carry out an alternate-form reliability test by changing the order of her original categories A into a new form B as shown below.

A Original Version	B New Version
a. I learnt little on this ward	a. (d) I learnt very much on this ward
b. I learnt quite a lot on this ward	b. (c) I learnt a lot on this ward
c. I learnt a lot on this ward	c. (b) I learnt quite a lot on this ward
d. I learnt very much on this ward	d. (a) I learnt little on this ward

Another way of testing alternate forms of reliability is to substitute the wording of the question by equivalent terms without altering the meaning of the question. Litwin (1995) offers the following example, in which version A can be changed to version B.

Version A

During the past week, how often did you usually empty your bladder?

1 to 2 times per day......................	1
3 to 4 times per day......................	2
5 to 8 times per day......................	3
12 times per day.........................	4
More than 12 times per day	5

Version B

During the past week, how often did you usually empty your bladder?

Every 12 to 24 hours	1
Every 6 to 8 hours	2
Every 3 to 5 hours	3
Every 2 hours...........................	4
More than every 2 hours	5

Split-half test

This test involves dividing or splitting the instrument into two equal halves and finding out whether or not their scores are similar. For example, for an attitude rating scale with 10 statements, the researcher will take the total score of the first five and compare it with the score of the last five. If the scores are similar, the statements or test items are said to be homogeneous. No item has a greater value than any other in assessing an attitude. This means that all the items are designed to make the respondent react consistently in the same way if they possess a particular attitude. If this happens, the test shows high internal consistency.

The split-half test can only be carried out with questionnaires that measure a concept or phenomenon, and applies only to instruments for which there is a total score. Most questionnaires that set out to describe or explore particular phenomena do not fall into this category.

There are other tests for validity and reliability; only those most frequently reported in the literature are described here.

To sum up, the validity of an instrument is established mainly by comparing its responses or scores with the scores of other sources (other research instruments, clinical observations or other records). On the other hand, the reliability of an instrument is tested mainly by comparing its own responses or scores (on different occasions, with different wordings or structure, and between items).

PILOT TESTING THE QUESTIONNAIRE

Even before validity and reliability tests are carried out, researchers can refine their questionnaires by administering them to a small group of people similar in characteristics to the intended respondents. Those who have done so have been amazed at the types of error, not just typographical, that can be detected. The first and most efficient way to find out how good a questionnaire is is to test or 'pilot' it. The responses will give the researcher a fair idea of whether all the respondents understand the questions in the same way, whether the format of the questions is the most suitable for this population, whether they understand the instructions and how relevant the questions are. She can also find out whether the length of the questionnaire and its structure are likely to affect responses. Researchers who take the opportunity to consider respondents' views on the above aspects of the questionnaire, listen to the problems encountered by them, and seek to resolve some of the doubts they (the researchers) have about their questionnaires, are likely to learn a lot about the strengths and weaknesses of their tools. Researchers are professionals whose 'language' and culture can be different from those of the potential participants in their study. It is important for them to realise that their questionnaires reflect their value positions and may create a different impression on respondents from the one they anticipate.

CRITIQUING QUESTIONNAIRES

Many authors of reports or articles do not give a detailed description of the questionnaires for readers to assess their validity and reliability. Only on rare occasions are questionnaires included as an appendix, often only a brief description of the number of items is given. Other information that is frequently missing includes pilot testing, validity and reliability tests and reminders or follow-ups to increase response rates. Moody *et al.* (1988), who carried out an analysis of 720 articles in six prominent nursing research journals published between 1977 and 1986, reported:

> Current or past reliability on one or more instruments was reported in 47% of the studies; 43% addressed some form of validity, usually content or face validity, on one or more instruments.

When assessing the use of a questionnaire in a research study, you must look for evidence of the source of the content. Did the researcher formulate the items only from her own experience and/or the literature? Content validity is likely to be enhanced if efforts were made to consult the literature or other instruments for relevant items to be included. If a questionnaire is borrowed and adapted, does the author comment on how the validity and reliability of the original instrument has been affected? You should also determine whether the questionnaire was piloted, with whom, how and with what results. More than one round of piloting is an indication that serious attempts have been made to refine it. You must also find out other measures taken to enhance validity and reliability. How were face or content validity ensured? Was the question-naire given to one or more 'experts' to comment and make suggestions? Construct validity, especially in studies that use existing, well-established tools, is sometimes reported. For most self-designed questionnaires, it is not fair to expect the author(s) to comment on concurrent, predictive or construct validity, as the data to establish these are not always readily available.

It is sometimes possible to evaluate the wording or formats of questions only when these appear in the article or report. When the questionnaire is available, you can assess its content validity, how appropriate or effective the question formats are, and the possibility of biases in the wording. The structure of the questionnaire must facilitate rather than hinder respondents in providing answers. The questionnaire as a whole must make sense and the questions should not jump from one topic to another and back again. You can find out whether the instruc-tions are clear and whether the length and presentation are likely to encourage respondents to complete it. Your task in assessing a question-naire is to find out how valid and reliable it is in answering the research questions. However, it is important to remember that it is easier to critique a questionnaire than to construct one. Perhaps for this reason alone, researchers rarely attach their questionnaires to their articles.

ETHICAL ASPECTS OF QUESTIONNAIRES

The self-administered questionnaire is one of the few methods of data collection that can potentially keep respondents anonymous. This can be an advantage because it gives them the opportunity of making their views known without being identified, unless of course, each question-naire is numbered or coded for the purpose of sending reminders to those who have not replied. One way to maintain anonymity and increase response rates is to send a reminder to all participants regard-less of who replied, but bias may be introduced if a respondent replies twice and this is overlooked by the researcher.

Confidentiality and privacy, as with other methods of data collection, must also be respected. However, both confidentiality and respect for privacy are easier to promise than to fulfil. Despite the best efforts and intentions of researchers, there are ways in which respondents can be identified by others or identify themselves. Privacy must mean what it says, that is the questionnaire must be administered to the respondent alone and in a private place. Robinson (1996) relates how, as a patient, 'in the local gynaecology ward, lying in one of those small bays', she overheard a 'private' conversation. As she describes:

> A white coated woman approached the patient in the opposite bed and asked if she would mind answering a few questions. The captive patient of course agreed. To my horror I recognized the intimate questions as part of the cancer epidemiology questionnaire I had approved at the Ethics Committee. We had not specified the interviews should be private, because it had never occurred to us that the researcher would do anything else.

Researchers are expected to obtain informed consent from respondents. However, because the questionnaire seems to be less intrusive than the interview or observation and less interventionist than the experiment, there is a tendency to think that it can cause no harm. Often obtaining approval from an ethical committee is not thought to be necessary. Questionnaires, however, can be intrusive by asking people embarrassing and sensitive questions, and can invade privacy. They can open 'old wounds' with no-one at hand to offer support. The following three consecutive questions taken from a real questionnaire on cervical screening exemplify the potential of questionnaires to do harm.

		Yes	No
Q9	Do you have any history of sexually transmitted disease?	☐	☐
Q10	Have you been sexually abused in the past?	☐	☐
Q11	Does your family have a history of cervical cancer?	☐	☐

Apart from being highly personal, these questions can trigger memories of traumatic experiences. The potential harm of these types of question is awesome. A respondent who has been sexually abused in the past can rightly ask why the researcher wants to know this and why she should tell anyone about it. This questionnaire may not be typical of questionnaires in general, but is shows that researchers can ignore, or be unaware of, the sensitive nature of their questions. The questionnaire, by psychologically assaulting respondents, can itself be an instrument of abuse.

Questionnaires can make people feel guilty about their lifestyles, for example by asking them questions about healthy living. They can identify their lack of knowledge on particular topics. Knowledge questions can be threatening to health professionals as the data may fall into the hands of their employers. One can ask also whether it is ethically right for people to participate in studies and not be told what the findings are, as would be the case for most research studies. The latter are published in journals of which lay people are unaware, and which professionals themselves may not read.

Robinson (1996), writing about the ethical implications of questionnaire design and administration, concluded that 'badly designed research is per se unethical and should not be done at all' and that 'at best it wastes patients' time and at worst it can do outright harm'.

SUMMARY AND CONCLUSION

The questionnaire is the most popular method of data collection in health and social research. Like other methods, it has a number of advantages and disadvantages. It is suitable mainly for collecting data on facts, knowledge, attitudes, beliefs and opinions when it is carefully prepared, constructed and administered. It is clear also that questionnaire data must not be taken at face value. Readers must assess the validity and reliability of the instrument where possible, and researchers must provide evidence of validity and reliability checks they have carried out. If used wisely and sensitively, the questionnaire has the potential to provide valuable data on which policy and practice decisions can be made.

REFERENCES

Aitken R C B (1969) Measurement of feelings using Visual Analogue Scales. *Proceedings of the Royal Society of Medicine*, **62**:989–96.

Allen M, Knight C, Falk C and Strang V (1992) Effectiveness of a preoperative teaching programme for cataract patients. *Journal of Advanced Nursing*, **17**:303–9.

Banyard P and Hayes N (1994) *Psychology: Theory and Application*. London: Chapman & Hall.

Bowles C (1986) Measure of attitude toward menopause using the Semantic Differential Model. *Nursing Research*, **35**(2):81–5.

Brown J S, Tanner C A and Padrick K P (1984) Nursing's search for scientific knowledge. *Nursing Research*, **33**(1):26–32.

Campbell D T and Fiske D W (1959) Convergent and discriminant validation by the multitrait-multimethod matrix. *Psychological Bulletin*, **56**(81):105.

Carr K K and Kazanowski M K (1994) Factors affecting job satisfaction of nurses who work in long-term care. *Journal of Advanced Nursing*, **19**:878–83.

Chamberlain C, Wraight A and Steer P (eds) (1993) *Pain and its Relief in Childbirth*. Edinburgh: Churchill Livingstone.

Cline M E, Herman J, Shaw E R and Morton R D (1992) Standardization of the Visual Analogue Scale. *Nursing Research*, **41**(6):378–80.

Crossby F E, Ventura M R and Feldman M J (1989) Examination of a survey methodology: Dillman's total design method. *Nursing Research*, **38**(1):56–8.

Dockrell J and Joffe H (1992) Methodological issues involved in the study of young people and HIV/AIDS: a social psychological view. *Health Education Research*, **7**:509–16.

DOH (Department of Health) (1996) *The Protection and Use of Patient Information: Guidance from the Department of Health*. London: DOH.

Falicki Z and Monieta A (1984) Higher feelings in schizophrenic patients studied by means of the semantic differential technique. *Psychopathology*, **17**:3–8.

Fitz-Gibbon C T and Morris L L (1987) *How to Analyse Data*. California: Sage.

Fowler F J Jr. (1992) How unclear terms affect survey data. *Public Opinion Quarterly*, **56**:218–31.

Frank-Stromborg M (1992) *Instruments for Clinical Nursing Research*. Boston: Jones & Bartlett.

Fretwell J E (1982) *Ward Teaching and Learning*. London: Royal College of Nursing.

Gröer M W, Thomas S P and Shoffner D (1992) Adolescent stress and coping: a longitudinal study. *Research in Nursing and Health*, **15**:209–17.

Hash V, Donlea J and Walljasper D (1985) The telephone survey: a procedure for assessing educational needs of nurses. *Nursing Research*, **34**(2):126–8.

Heim E, Blaser A and Weidelich (1972) Dyspnea: psychophysiologic relationships. *Psychosomatic Medicine*, **34**:405–23.

Henerson M E, Morris L L and Fitz-Gibbon C T (1987) *How to Measure Attitudes*. California: Sage.

Hicks C (1995) A factor analytic study of midwives' attitudes to research. *Midwifery*, **11**:11–17.

Jacobsen B S and Meininger J C (1985) The designs and methods of published nursing research: 1956–1983. *Nursing Research*, **34**:306–11.

Likert (1932) *A Technique for the Measurement of Attitudes*. New York: Columbia University Press.

Litwin M S (1995) *How to Measure Survey Reliability and Validity*. California: Sage.

Liukkonen A (1991) Physical restraint use with the demented patients. *Hoitotiede*, **3**(2):63–8.

Liukkonen A and Laitinen P (1994) Reasons for uses of physical restraint and alternatives to them in geriatric nursing: a questionnaire study among nursing staff. *Journal of Advanced Nursing*, **19**:1082–7.

Lydeard S (1991) The questionnaire as a research tool. *Family Practice*, **8**(1):84–91.

McDowell I and Newell C (1987) *Measuring Health: A Guide to Rating Scales and Questionnaires*. Oxford: Oxford University Press.

Mechanic D (1989) Medical sociology: some tensions among theory, method and substance. *Journal of Health and Social Behaviour*, **30**:147–60.

Moody L E, Wilson M E, Smyth K, Schwartz R, Tittle M and Cott M L V (1988) Analysis of a decade of nursing practice research: 1977–86. *Nursing Research*, **37**(6):374–9.

Mulliner C M, Spiby H and Fraser R B (1995) A study exploring midwives' education in, knowledge of and attitudes to nutrition in pregnancy. *Midwifery*, **11**(1):37–41.

Nay-Brock R M (1984) A comparison of the questionnaire and interviewing techniques in the collection of sociological data. *Australian Journal of Advanced Nursing*, **2**(1):14–23.

Nolan M L (1995) A comparison of attenders at antenatal classes in the voluntary and statutory sectors: education and organisational implications. *Midwifery*, **11**:138–45.

Osgood C E, Suci G J and Tannenbaum P H (1957) *The Measurement of Meaning*. Chicago: University of Illinois Press.

Palmer M H, German P S and Ouslander J G (1991) Risk factors for urinary incontinence one year after nursing home admission. *Research in Nursing and Health*, **14**:405–12.

Parahoo K (1993) Questionnaire: use, value and limitations. *Nurse Researcher*, **1**(2):4–15.

Polit D F and Hungler B P (1995) *Nursing Research: Principles and Methods*, 5th edn. Philadelphia: J B Lippincott.

Quinless F W and Nelson M A M (1988) Development of a measure of learned helplessness. *Nursing Research*, **37**(1):11–15.

Reid M G (1985) *Wards in Chancery?* London: Royal College of Nursing.

Robinson J (1996) It's only a questionnaire... ethics in social science research. *British Journal of Midwifery*, **4**(1):41–4.

Rosenfield S N and Stevenson J S (1988) Perception of daily stress and oral coping behaviors in normal, overweight, and recovering alcoholic women. *Research in Nursing and Health*, **11**:165–74.

Schaeffer N C (1991) Hardly ever or constantly? Group comparisons using vague quantifiers. *Public Opinion Quarterly*, **55**:395–423.

Sharp L M and Frankel J (1983) Respondent burden: a test of some common assumptions. *Public Opinion Quarterly*, **47**:36–53.

Sharp T (1990) Relatives' involvement in caring for the elderly mentally ill following long-term hospitalization. *Journal of Advanced Nursing*, **15**:67–73.

Sikorski J, Clement S, Wilson J, Das S and Smeeton N (1995) A survey of health professionals' views on possible changes in the provision and organisation of antenatal care. *Midwifery*, **11**:61–8.

Smith H W (1991) *Strategies of Social Research*, 3rd edn. St Louis: University of Missouri.

Smith L N (1994) An analysis and reflections on the quality of nursing research in 1992. *Journal of Advanced Nursing*, **19**:385–93.

Sparrow N (1993) Improving polling techniques following the 1992 General Election. *Journal of Market Research Society*, **35**(1):79–89.

Stone D H (1993) Design a questionnaire. *British Medical Journal*, **307**:1264–6.

Tall G (1988) Why use a questionnaire? The questionnaire as an evaluation tool in schools. *Pastoral Care*, December, 33–6.

Tettersell M J (1993) Asthma patients' knowledge in relation to compliance with drug therapy. *Journal of Advanced Nursing*, **18**:103–13.

Waltz C F, Strickland O L and Lenz E R (1991) *Measurement in Nursing Research*, 2nd edn. Philadelphia: F A Davis.

12 INTERVIEWS

It is the province of knowledge to speak and it is the
privilege of wisdom to listen (O W Holmes, 1858)

INTRODUCTION

The beliefs, attitudes, experiences and perception of clients and staff are
important for the organisation, delivery and evaluation of care and
treatment. The interview has an important part to play in collecting
data to inform the decisions and actions of health professionals, as well
as in providing insights into how clients access and use health services
and their experience of them.

This chapter will discuss the use of interviews in clinical practice
and in research, the different forms of research interviews and their
advantages and disadvantages. It will also explore the ethical implications, as well as the validity and reliability, of different forms of
interviewing. Finally, what you should look for when critiquing studies
that use interviews will be suggested.

INTERVIEWS IN CLINICAL PRACTICE

In our everyday life, we engage in interactions that involve asking, and
being asked, questions. We can say that we all are 'interviewers' and
'interviewees'. Verbal communication is the most effective means
available to humans with which to convey our feelings, experiences,
views and intentions. However, we do not normally call these verbal
interactions interviews; most of the time they are merely casual conversations. Some of us have experienced or watched job or TV interviews;
you may yourself have undergone an interview to gain a place on a
particular course. These interviews are different from casual conversations in that they have (or should have) a clearer agenda, often prepared
in advance and a specific purpose, and are limited in duration. Health
professionals, too, carry out interviews for the purpose of obtaining
information from clients that can be used to assess, plan, implement and
evaluate care and treatment. Nurse–client interactions involve both
formal interviewing and casual conversations throughout the time that
the client is in contact with the professional. With clinical interviews,
the aim is not only to obtain valuable information, but also to build trust
between the professional and the client. Thus a therapeutic relationship
is initiated and developed. Hein (1980, cited in Holt, 1995) defines a
nursing interview as the 'deliberate use of verbal behaviours... to

communicate with the patient in a manner directly concerned with the promotion, maintenance and restoration of his health'.

A number of authors (Price, 1987; Thompson, 1990; Newell, 1994) have called for more time to be devoted to developing nurses' interviewing skills. According to Newell (1994), interviews in nursing are 'by and large poorly' carried out. He explained the implications of poor interviewing for decision-making:

> If the negative consequences of poor interviewing for the clinician are few, the consequences for the client, by contrast, are potentially grave. At its simplest level, the clinician is likely to receive inadequate or inappropriate information due to poor interviewing, with the result that any decisions made regarding the presenting problem are likely to be equally inadequate or inappropriate.

In Chapter 1, we explained that some knowledge of, and skills in, research methods can help to sharpen nurses' ability to ask questions, listen and observe.

RESEARCH INTERVIEWS

A research interview, on the other hand, is a verbal interaction between one or more researchers and one or more respondents for the purpose of collecting valid and reliable data to answer particular research questions. In the clinical interview, the client is the *raison d'être* of the interview, while in a research interview, the interest in the respondent is as far as the interview goes. In some types of interview, the degree of interaction is greater than in others, but the researcher's aim is not to develop therapeutic relationships. The purpose of clinical interviews is to collect data to enhance the health of the client; the data collected in research interviews serve to satisfy the researcher's curiosity and, if the findings are valid and reliable, they may be ultimately used to enhance client care.

Interviews can be face to face, by telephone and 'as seen on TV' via satellites. They are used in both qualitative and quantitative research. They collect data inductively and deductively. Although interviews are more suited to survey designs, they are used in case studies and experiments as well. There are different forms of interviews, the main ones explained here being structured, qualitative, semistructured and focus group interviews.

STRUCTURED INTERVIEWS

In the previous chapter, it was pointed out that questionnaires can be administered by researchers in person. This is called a *structured* interview. It involves the researcher asking all the questions as they are formulated in the questionnaire. Neither the wording nor the sequence of the questions can be altered. The questionnaire, in this case, is normally referred to as an 'interview schedule'. Davis (1980) refers to this type of interview as the 'scheduled standardized interview'. In other forms of interviews, this schedule or list may be more flexible.

The presence of the researcher can be beneficial in many ways. If the researcher wants to prevent respondents from consulting other sources in answering the questionnaire, as is the case with knowledge questions, she can administer it in person. The main reason for the interviewer's presence, however, is to offer clarification and support, if needed. Sometimes respondents provide incomplete or inadequate responses or 'skip' questions altogether. Their non-verbal behaviour may also communicate their confusion or lack of understanding of certain questions. In such cases, the task of the researcher is to clarify terms without changing the meaning of the questions. To obtain complete and accurate responses, the interviewer can ask 'such non-directive probes as: "In what way?", "How do you mean?", "Could you say a bit more?"' (Cartwright, 1986). As can be seen from these probes, the interviewer does not seek in-depth information but encourages the respondent to think more seriously about the questions and provide more detail in the responses. Her task is to make sure that the respondent understands the question and that she, in turn, understands the answer. Another reason for structured interviews is for the interviewer to help those who have difficulty in reading questions or formulating written responses. By asking the questions and recording the answers, the interviewer also facilitates the research process since the meaning of what is said can be clarified on the spot and she does not have to decipher handwriting other than her own. In some cases, the interviewer codes the responses as they are offered.

The fewer the number of interventions by the interviewer, the more structured the interview. Consistency in asking the questions as they appear on the schedule and in making the same information available to all respondents are the hallmarks of structured interviews. The aim is to achieve standardisation.

As the purpose of the structured interview is to collect data from a predetermined and structured questionnaire, and the interviewer's role is to administer the questionnaire in the same way to all respondents without any alterations, the structured interview is a quantitative method of data collection.

Structured interviews, like structured questionnaires, are employed in the collection of data on knowledge, attitudes, beliefs, opinions and behaviours. Nay-Brock (1984) also explain that 'standardized interviews are designed to allow classification, identification and comparisons and for such purposes the same information must be gained from each respondent'. According to Waltz *et al.* (1991), 'the structured interview is used most appropriately when identical information is needed from all respondents, when comparisons are to be made across respondents who are relatively homogeneous in background and experience, and when large or geographically dispersed samples are used'.

Davis (1980) explains that the rationale for structured interviews 'rests on the belief that for any study, the respondents have a sufficiently common vocabulary so that it is possible to formulate questions that have the same meaning for each of them'. However, self-administered questionnaires may be more appropriate for data of an embarrassing or private nature, since the structured interview negates one of the main strengths of questionnaires – the potential for respondents to remain anonymous.

Validity and reliability of structured interviews

Since the questionnaire is the tool of data collection in structured interviews, it is subject to the same validity and reliability threats as the questionnaire (see Chapter 11). Equally, the same tests of validity and reliability can be carried out. The main advantage of the structured interview over the self-administered questionnaire is the opportunity provided to respondents to seek clarification. By helping them, where necessary, to understand the question, they are more able to give appropriate and relevant answers, thereby enhancing the validity of the instrument. In structured interviews, it is also possible for the researcher to observe non-verbal signs that alert her to occasions when respondents experience difficulties with the questionnaire.

Since all the questions are ideally asked in the same way, structured interviews have a high degree of reliability, but interviewers may have difficulty in ensuring that the amount and type of clarification they give to respondents is more or less uniform. When more than one interviewer is used in the same study, it is possible that some are more able than others to extract information from respondents. Since structured interviews seek to achieve a high degree of standardisation, these issues are pertinent to the reliability of the tool and can, to some extent, be resolved through interviewer training.

The presence of the interviewer can, on the other hand, introduce a number of biases. Respondents may be more inclined to give socially desirable answers or at least mould their responses to fit the occasion.

Personal characteristics of interviewers, such as gender, age, race, clothing, language and accent, can all affect the responses; there are numerous examples in the sociological literature of how personal characteristics can interfere with the collection of valid and reliable data (see for example Hyman, 1954; Sudman and Bradburn, 1974; Cartwright, 1986). According to Davis (1980), even the manner in which respondents are greeted can cause 'unintended variations in responses'. As she explains, 'a difference in some set with the chummy "Hi" as opposed to the slightly more formal "Hello" to the even more formal "How do you do?" creates a different interactional climate'.

RE 35 describes the use of structured interviews in one study.

RESEARCH EXAMPLE 35 Neadley *et al.* (1995)
Health and memory in people over 50: a survey of a single-GP practice in England

An example of a structured interview

Two of the authors and an epidemiologist designed a questionnaire:

> to elicit information concerning general background details, knowledge of local services for elderly people and if they use them, their current health status, i.e. whether they considered themselves to be suffering from an acute or chronic illness, if they were being treated for blood pressure problems, whether they suffered from anxiety/depression and the time span since they last consulted their GP or practice nurse. Their mobility was assessed by a question on the ability to shop unaided, with help or not able at all.

The questionnaire (or interview schedule) is included as an appendix to the article.

Comments

1. All the questions were predetermined (i.e. decided prior to the interview) and standardised (i.e. all respondents were asked the same questions without any addition). Not all the questions were highly structured, in the sense that they were all closed-ended. There were also some open-ended questions, which may have prompted Neadley *et al.* (1995) to describe their interviews as semistructured. However, they were not designed to collect any in-depth information. Instead, respondents were restricted merely to naming or identifying services they 'know about' or 'use', or to answer yes or no, as in the following examples:

   > Can you name any services available locally? These may be provided by the local authority or the health authority.

   > Did you contact your doctor about this on each occasion?

2. The purpose of a structured interview is to offer clarification of terms that respondents may not understand. In this study, the interviewer was allowed to substitute the word 'nerves' for 'anxiety/depression' in the question 'have you ever suffered from anxiety/depression?' in case they did not understand these terms.

3. The data were reported quantitatively as in the following example:

   > Eleven per cent of the participants were availing themselves of some of the services for elderly people.... However, there were also mean differences in age between the users and non-users.

QUALITATIVE INTERVIEWS

A number of terms have been used to describe qualitative interviews. Among the most common are unstructured, in-depth, depth, informal, non-directive, focused and open. Sometimes a combination of these has been offered, such as 'in-depth focused' (Walker *et al.*, 1995), 'unstructured formal' (Hogston, 1995) and even 'in-depth semi-structured' (Nolan *et al.*, 1995). Others, such as Hanson (1994), describe their method simply as 'qualitative interviews'. The array of terms reflects both the various ways in which qualitative interviews are carried out and the liberal use of terminologies in describing these methods.

The term 'unstructured' has become synonymous with 'qualitative'. Yet, as Jones (1985) points out, 'there is no such thing as a totally unstructured interview' and 'the term is over-used and often carelessly used'. Hammersley and Atkinson (1983) believe that some structure is inevitable in research interviews. To avoid confusion, it would be more helpful if researchers simply described their methods as qualitative (if this is the case) and explained in detail their assumptions, purposes and process.

'*Qualitative interview*' is a broad term used to denote a family of interviews that share the common purpose of studying phenomena from the perspective of the respondent. In its most unstructured form, the qualitative interview resembles 'everyday conversations for the purpose of collecting and validating data' (Chenitz, 1986). However, not all qualitative interviews are completely unstructured, as everyday conversations are supposed to be. The degree of structure and control, as well as the process of interviewing, vary from interview to interview.

Structure and control

With structured interviews, the researcher must ask everyone the same questions in the same manner. A researcher wishing to explore, by means of a qualitative interview, a phenomenon such as students' experience of preparing for examinations may not have a list of questions or topics but may decide to let them talk about their experiences. This type of interview is known as 'non-directive' as the interviewer does not 'direct' interviewees to topics but allows them free expression. The task of the interviewer, in this case, is to facilitate the flow of information with as little interruption as possible. As topics are brought up by the students, the interviewer may focus on some rather than others. Often new topics or new perspectives on the same topics are introduced as the interviews progress. Interviewers choose to have little control over the agenda in completely non-directive interviews.

Bennett (1991) carried out 'unstructured non-directive' interviews with 'adolescent girls about their experience of witnessing marital violence'. As she explains:

> Although spontaneous descriptions were encouraged, when a participant had difficulty getting started, a prompt... was used: for example, 'Describe a typical day in your home'. For the most part, however, questions were used only to clarify or to encourage further description.

Completely unstructured interviews are difficult to manage. Some researchers introduce a degree of structure by selecting a number of areas within a topic to 'focus' the interview on. Waltz *et al.* (1991) describe the 'focused interview' as beginning:

> with a rather loose agenda, for example, a list of topics to be covered. However, the interviewer may move freely from one topic area to another and allow the respondent's cues to help determine the flow of the interview. Although the interviewer may work from a list of topics to be covered, the way in which questions are phrased and the order in which they are asked are left to the discretion of the interviewer and may be changed to fit the characteristics of each respondent.

This degree of control that interviewers have in focused interviews should not turn the interaction into a rigid question and answer session (as is the case in structured interviews) but should be as near as possible to normal conversation. The list of topics provide a guide to researchers on what they want respondents to talk about. It is not intended in any way to achieve uniformity or to prevent respondents in taking the initiative to let their perspectives be known. For example, Brown and Williams (1995) explain, in their study of 'women's experiences of rheumatoid arthritis', that:

> a topic guide was developed from the existing literature in order to provide a basis from which interviews could proceed. Utilising nursing skills of listening and encouraging, the researcher allowed the women to introduce anything they felt to be important. The women's role as experts in knowing about rheumatoid arthritis was explicitly emphasized throughout the interviews.

Focused interviews also vary according to how 'loose' the lists of topics are. They can be broad or fairly specific, as an extract from the list of questions in a study by Gilloran (1995) on 'gender difference in care delivery and supervisory relationship' in psychogeriatric nursing shows:

Interview schedule:

A. Care delivery: the patients
1. Main objectives of the care provided ?
2. Differences between male and females patients (needs or demands)?
3. Prefer caring for men or women?
4. Favourites – what is it that attracts?
5. Advantages and disadvantages of mixed wards (for patients and for staff)?

Sometimes the extent of focus varies between interviews in the same study. Walker *et al.* (1995) carried out 'in-depth focused interviews to explore women's experiences regarding all aspects of their care during labour and delivery'. As they explain:

> Initial interviews were broadly focused to encourage respondents to recount experiences of personal relevance in relation to their maternity care. Audiotapes of the interviews were listened to, notes made and used to focus later interviews in order to elaborate fully upon all aspects of experience...

The qualitative interview process

The process of qualitative interviews can also vary. As explained above, some researchers 'allow' respondents to talk without too many interruptions and facilitate the process by listening and probing as appropriate. In this type of interview, the researcher does not reveal her own values and experience. Other interviewers share their experiences with respondents and find that their 'disclosures' help to build a trust between themselves and the respondents in the same way that happens in everyday interactions. Not only do some people feel they have to divulge a little bit of themselves in order for others to be more forthcoming with their own disclosures, but also this type of 'give and take' brings people closer when they know that both of them have some experience of the same phenomenon. Wilde (1992) comments that 'sharing part of ones' personal life would seem to have an effect on the subject's view of the researcher, who becomes, in the subject's eyes, less of a professional and more of a human being'.

In her study of 'women living with fibromyalgia', Schaefer (1995) explains that, during in-depth interviews, 'every effort was made to keep the relationship non-hierarchical and to encourage discussion' and that 'experiences were frequently shared and validated by the interviewer and the participant'.

Even when the researcher tries not to influence respondents by revealing her thoughts, it is not always possible to avoid it. Wilde (1992) found herself sharing views with participants although she had not intended to do so. As she explains, 'on occasions the author found herself being drawn into sharing and disclosing her view of the situation, despite succeeding the majority of times in refraining from doing so'. Fontana and Frey (1994) warn that while 'close rapport with respondents opens doors to more informed research' it may also create problems as the researcher may lose her objectivity.

The degree to which interviewers adopt passive roles in qualitative interviews can also vary. Gray (1994) describes how she had to adopt passive and active roles during her interviews on 'the effects of supernumerary status and mentorship on student nurses':

> I had to be flexible and able to alternate between an active and passive role depending on the nature of the interview and the amount of probing required to encourage the respondent to share information. Not to have this flexibility would result in either adopting a rigidly passive role (which would allow the respondents to focus on irrelevant material) or a role which allows the pace of the interview to gallop away uninhibitedly.

These real-life experiences of interviewers show that the interviewer–interviewee interaction in qualitative interviews differs from situation to situation, so researchers have to be flexible in their approaches. With structured interviews, although not all respondents take the same amount of time to answer all the questions, the duration of the interview is guided by the number of questions and would not normally vary greatly between interviews in the same study. This is not the case with qualitative interviews. The latter are time-consuming because of the in-depth nature of the information required and the diminished control of the researcher over the interview agenda. They vary in length in the same study, because each interaction between the interviewer and interviewee is unique. They could last between 30 minutes and 2 hours. It is unlikely that any phenomenon could be explored in depth in less than half an hour. On the other hand, a 2-hour interview would tire researchers and respondents and cast doubt on their ability to concentrate on the task at hand. Buckeldee (1994) describes her experience of interviewing carers in the community:

> it became apparent that carers were not only too willing to make time to talk with me, often about very personal matters and frequently for much longer periods than I had anticipated. I often spent between one and two hours with them.

In her study of 'women living with fibromyalgia', Schaefer (1995) reported that in-depth interviews lasted from 1 to 2.5 hours. These examples show that qualitative interviews in the same study can vary greatly in length. The freedom and opportunity for respondents to talk and the difficulty that researchers face in keeping them 'on track' often make qualitative interviews last longer than they should. The following excerpts from Buckeldee (1994) illustrate this point:

> Many participants did not often have the time and/or the opportunity to sit and talk and it may have been that they took advantage of this situation. Others rarely saw other people and so may have used this opportunity to simply socialize.

> The readiness of many carers to talk also brought with it the practical problem of encouraging talk and yet ensuring that it was broadly immersed in long and detailed stories of their lives which apparently bore no relevance to my study. As a relatively novice interviewer I found it very difficult to guide participants back onto the broad aims of the interview.

In quantitative research, once a structured interview has been carried out, the researcher cannot go back to the respondents to ask for clarifications or to verify whether what was said was correctly understood by the interviewer. In qualitative research, the opportunity to go back to respondents exists and is often grasped. The reason for this is to continue the previous conversation, to find out whether people feel or think differently about the phenomenon on a different day, and mainly to validate their responses.

Therefore, each unstructured interview is different in process from the next. The researcher's role can vary from a passive one to one in which the sharing of experiences between interviewer and respondent is a key strategy in obtaining data. The duration of interviews within the same study can vary, and researchers have the freedom to interview the same respondents more than once if they so wish.

The content of qualitative interviews

Even with a list of topics, it is unlikely that every interview in the same study will cover strictly the same content. The aim of qualitative interviews is to know all possible ways in which respondents view or experience phenomena. As new perspectives are uncovered and new insights gained, the interviewer finds that earlier interviews are different in content from later ones. Qualitative interviews build on one another. The researcher accumulates perspective and experiences until a broad understanding of the phenomenon is obtained. And when saturation of data is reached (that is no new data emerge), the researcher may stop interviewing even if she had intended to do more interviews.

Researchers comment that their own skills improve as they do more interviews in the same study. Buckeldee (1994) relates her own experience:

> Transcribing and preliminary coding of early interviews helped in several ways. First it gave me feedback about my interviewing skills (or lack of them at times!) which proved invaluable. It also helped to identify areas requiring further exploration which in turn helped to direct later interviews. Furthermore as the interviews progressed my own confidence and skill in conducting interviews increased and was verified in later transcripts of interviews.

To sum up this section, we find that while the structure, process and content of structured interviews are characterised by *consistency* and *standardisation*, the key features of qualitative interviews are, in contrast, *flexibility* and *versatility*. These are reflected in the diversity of ways in which qualitative interviews are conducted.

Reliability and validity of qualitative interviews

The concepts of reliability and validity belong to quantitative research and as such have been criticised as having little relevance to qualitative studies. This does not mean that qualitative researchers are less rigorous in the way they collect, analyse and interpret data. As already described, the term 'reliability' refers to the degree of consistency with which the instrument produces the same results if administered in the same circumstances. In qualitative interviews, no structured, predetermined or standardised tools are used. In their most structured form, qualitative interviews consist of a list topics about which respondents are asked to talk. The qualitative interviewer is also a 'tool' of data collection. She sifts and analyses data in her mind during the interview, as well as transcribes and makes sense of the data thereafter. Each interview in the same study is a unique interaction and is not replicable. The same researcher would conduct the interview differently were it to happen again, and another researcher would also have conducted the interview differently. In contrast, structured interviews can be replicated and the data can be examined for consistency. In the quantitative sense, it can be said that the reliability of qualitative data is difficult to establish. However, to qualitative researchers, reliability is secondary to getting to the core of the phenomena they investigate. As Deutscher (1966) explains:

We concentrate on consistency without much concern with what it is we are being consistent about or whether we are consistently right or wrong. As a consequence we have been learning a great deal about how to pursue an incorrect cause with a maximum of precision.

Some qualitative researchers reject the concepts of reliability and validity and offer instead such terms as 'accuracy', 'truth' and 'credibility'. To ensure rigour, they adopt a number of strategies, including reflexivity and validation of data by the interviewees themselves.

Reflexivity is the continuous process of reflection by the researcher on her own values, preconceptions, behaviour or presence and those of the respondents, which can affect responses. For example, a researcher may reflect on how the data she collects can be influenced by how she is perceived by the respondent. Wilde (1992), in her qualitative study of 'nurses' descriptions of difficult, challenging and satisfying experience at work', explains how she kept various types of memo:

> where she wrote down any observations or reflections on the methodology being used. She included comments on her interviewing style, observations about the transcribing and analysis processes, and other working notes. They served as memos on her behaviour in the research process, and provided invaluable stimuli for the formulation of her ideas on the interaction between researcher and participant in the formal interview. In the diary, the author reflected on her style of interaction and effect on the participants' disclosures.

Reflexivity by the researcher is, however, not enough nor easy to carry out. It is not always possible to stand back and examine the effect of one's preconceptions, especially if one is not always aware of what they are. This is why some researchers return to interviewees to find out whether or not they agree with the data. This data validation process by respondents is useful in providing the opportunity for clarification and for the researcher to recognise her own prejudices, if this is the case. In his study of 'nurses' perceptions of quality nursing care', Hogston (1995), after coding and categorising the data, returned to five of the informants to confirm that 'the interpretation was in keeping with what the informants meant'.

Another way to validate the data is to ask other researchers to examine all or part of the transcripts. The common practice of tape-recording interviews and transcribing the data verbatim (word for word) allows others to have an insight into what transpired between the researcher and the respondents and to compare their perception of it with that of the researcher. In her study of 'adolescent girls' experience of witnessing marital violence', Bennett (1991) describes how she sought help to verify her theories:

An individual with research and clinical experience in family violence read all transcriptions, individual-level descriptions, condensed and transformed meaning-unit statements and the general-level description for the purpose of consensual validation.

Qualitative researchers recognise the subjective component in the interviewing process and seek to utilise it in order to obtain meaningful data. Some believe that building trust between researcher and respondent is crucial in getting access to the latter's perception of the phenomenon. To do so, the interviewer has to bend and mould the interview method to suit the phenomenon. For example, some interviewers, as explained earlier, may share their experiences in order to encourage respondents to 'open up'. This inevitably makes the interview a very subjective and unique experience. To achieve a degree of objectivity, it is therefore necessary to resort to some of the strategies mentioned above. While the same interviews cannot be repeated, other researchers can in time study the same phenomenon in a different setting with the same or different methods and the data can be compared.

Finally, in some cases, the hypotheses and theories developed out of qualitative interviews can be further tested by quantitative approaches.

See RE 36 for an example of qualitative interviews in one study.

SEMISTRUCTURED INTERVIEWS

In semistructured (also referred to as semistandardised) interviews, respondents are all asked the same questions, but there is 'flexibility in the phrasing and order of the questions' (Hutchinson and Wilson, 1992). According to Barriball and While (1994), the semistructured interview provides 'the opportunities to change the words but not the meaning of questions' because it 'acknowledges that not every word has the same meaning to every respondent and not every respondent uses the same vocabulary'. Validity is enhanced because respondents can be helped to understand the questions and interviewers can ask for clarifications and probe for further responses, if necessary.

The tool of data collection in semistructured interviews is called an interview schedule. It differs from an interview guide in focused interviews in that the latter has broad areas or questions but allows the researcher the freedom to ask additional questions. The interview schedule in a semistructured interview is in fact a questionnaire consisting of a list of preformulated questions, which can be neither omitted nor added to.

Semistructured interviews have elements of quantitative and qualitative research. They are similar to structured interviews in that the number and types of question are the same for all respondents, although

RESEARCH EXAMPLE 36   Bluff and Holloway (1994)
They know best: women's perceptions of midwifery care during labour and childbirth

A qualitative interview

The purpose of this study was to examine the experiences of women of their labour and the birth of their baby. A purposive sample of 11 women from a maternity unit of a general hospital was interviewed. Bluff and Holloway describe their 'in-depth interview' thus:

> Collection of data was by means of unstructured interviews to obtain information in the participants' own words, to gain a description of the situation and to elicit detail (Lofland and Lofland, 1984). On average, the interviews lasted for about one hour. They took place in the unit within 48 hours of delivery and avoided the early period of elation and the 'maternity blues' which may occur postpartum. While the women were interviewed, staff cared for their babies in the nursery.

> Each interview took place in an empty room nearby with a 'do not disturb' notice on the door and began with a very informal conversation about the baby. As soon as it appeared that the woman being interviewed felt at ease with the interviewer and the tape recorder, the interview began with an open question about their experience of labour. The interviewer did not take control in the discussion but initially built her questions on the answers which the woman provided. As ideas emerged, the interviewer asked more focused questions. An occasional probe such as 'can you tell me a little more about this' helped to elicit more information about the participants who were also assured that there were no right or wrong answers to the questions. At the end of each interview, after a short discussion about the research, the participants were again asked whether they still wished to be part of the study.

Comments

1. Qualitative interviews vary, among others, according to their purpose and process. This is only an example of one type of qualitative interview. Reading accounts of other interviews will help you to get an idea of the variety of this method of data collection.
2. In this study, the interviewer began with an open-ended question and only used an 'occasional probe'; there is no mention of a list of questions. This indicates that the interviewer is interested in the issues raised by the respondents themselves. Indeed, earlier on in the article they refer to Parse et al. (1985), who 'argue that a qualitative approach to research identifies the perspectives of the research participants and uncovers their characteristics and experiences'.
3. At the beginning, 'the interviewer did not take control in the discussion', but as the interview progressed she asked more focused questions based on the ideas that emerged. Within the same interview, the degree of 'interviewer control' increased as the researcher became more interested in some ideas than in others. This demonstrates one aspect of the flexibility of qualitative interviews.

the actual wordings may be varied for the purpose of making sure that respondents understand the question. As with structured interviews, it emphasises the notion of standardisation, that is respondents must be subjected to the same questions with minimal variations. In a semistructured interview, the researcher is allowed some flexibility to 'probe'. The *Oxford Dictionary* describes probe as 'penetrating investigation'. The use of probes in semistructured interviews is limited to seeking clarification and obtaining more complete answers rather than to uncovering new perspectives. It is a cautious use of probes to ensure that the respondent is not 'led' nor influenced in any way by the interviewer. In contrast, as we have seen earlier, in qualitative interviews the researcher often uses subjectivity to obtain rich and meaningful data.

In semistructured interviews, the researcher is very much in control of the interview process, and the predetermined questions provide the structure to the interview. In qualitative interviews, the degree of control and structure on the part of the interviewer is minimal to allow topics and perspectives to emerge. The researcher does not know in advance all the questions to ask and is very much guided by what respondents say. The researcher has to decide during the interview what questions to ask and how to formulate them.

Some semistructured interviews have a mixture of closed and open-ended questions, while others may have only open-ended ones. This use of closed questions ensures a high degree of standardisation since all the responses fall within the categories offered by the researcher. Open-ended questions can be specific or broad. Specific open-ended questions, such as 'can you list the items of food which you have stopped consuming since you have started to take medication X?' or 'please give as many reasons as possible as to why you do not take medication Y?', limit the range of responses. On the other hand, broad open-ended questions such as 'can you describe feelings when you were first told that you have diabetes?' can prompt respondents to 'open up' and make it difficult for the researcher not only to probe cautiously and objectively, but also to offer the same amount and depth of probing to all respondents. Therefore, one can see how some semistructured interviews are closer to quantitative and others to qualitative interviews. By trying to keep standardisation and yet be flexible, the researcher uses a mixture of quantitative and qualitative methods, which purists may frown upon.

Researchers conducting semistructured interviews must recognise the tension between trying to have both standardisation and flexibility. Although this method produces 'qualitative-type' data, it is not a qualitative method in the same way that a Likert-type scale (a few statements put together, the origin of which is not known) is not a Likert scale (which is constructed by the rigorous and systematic generation and selection of statements). Many qualitative researchers label their interviews as semistructured when in fact they are focused interviews (which have a list of broad questions to guide the interaction rather than constrain it).

In practice, it is questionable whether in semistructured interviews researchers ask exactly the same number of questions of all respondents and try to maintain the same degree of objectivity with all of them. If this does happen, the semistructured interview can be said to fit more into the quantitative approach. If the researcher departs from the list of questions she comes with and starts probing deeply, the interview can be said to be focused and thus qualitative. The degree of standardisation or flexibility can provide clues to how quantitative or qualitative a semistructured interview is.

Semistructured interviews are popular precisely because they can provide quantitative- and qualitative-type responses that allow comparisons between respondents in the same study and can be applicable to other similar settings. They are useful in the study of sensitive topics and in increasing response rates. As with other methods, researchers must have a good rationale for using semistructured interviews.

In their study of 'the perceptions and needs of continuing professional education among nurses', Barriball and While (1994) explain why they chose semistructured interviews:

> Semi-structured interviews were selected as the means of data collection because of two primary considerations. First, they are well suited for the exploration of the perceptions and opinions of respondents regarding complex and sometimes sensitive issues and enable probing for more information and clarification of answers. Second, the varied professional, educational and personal histories of the sample group precluded the use of a standardised schedule.

The validity of responses in semistructured interviews is enhanced by the presence of the researcher, who can clarify the questions and seek clarification from the respondents. Because semistructured interviews share elements of quantitative and qualitative interviews, they are subject to some of the same validity and reliability threats described earlier in this chapter. For an example of a semistructured interview, see RE 37.

FOCUS GROUP INTERVIEWS

A *focus group interview* can be described as an interaction between one or more researchers and more than one respondent for the purpose of collecting research data. It is likely that only one researcher is present in most focus group interviews, but the number of respondents can vary. The focus group interview is a popular method in market research, although it is frequently also used in health research. Some of the

RESEARCH EXAMPLE 37

Kuremyr et al. (1994)
Emotional experiences, empathy and burnout among staff caring for demented patients at a collective living unit and a nursing home

A semistructured interview

The aim of this study was to describe the staff's emotional experiences when caring for elderly demented patients and to estimate their experiences of burnout and empathy in a collective living unit and a nursing home.

The data collection methods were, 'the empathy construct rating scale, the burnout measure', and a semistructured interview. An interview 'form' containing 60 questions was used.

Questions focused on four areas:
1. The staff. For example: Do you feel emotionally exhausted? Do you feel worthless?
2. The patient. For example: How would you describe the demented patient you have the best contact with? What are the patient's main problems?
3. The staff–patient relationship. On a scale of 1 to 5, for example: How strong is your emotional bond to the patient you have the best contact with? What are your feelings in situations when you have close contact with the patient?
4. The staff's occupational situation. For example: Do you get feedback from your work? If you feel emotionally exhausted and/or have feelings of burnout, what kind of support do you want? (Kuremyr et al., 1994)

Comments
1. The prepared form or list of 60 questions was administered to all respondents, thereby imposing a high degree of 'researcher control' and standardisation in the interviewing process. However, the questions were open ended and allowed respondents to answer in their own words. By not providing a list of answers for respondents to choose from (as is the case with structured interviews) and by seeking to listen to the respondents' own views, one can say that the researchers were collecting qualitative data. This is, however, different from a qualitative interview, in which respondents are allowed to speak freely and introduce new ideas which the researcher explores further (as in RE 36). The researcher is in control of the content and the process of the interview.
2. In this study, the researchers know enough about the phenomena (emotional experiences, empathy and burn-out) to know what questions to ask. For example one of questions they ask is 'do you feel worthless?' This assumes that they know that this is one of the feelings which staff can experience while 'caring for demented patients'. On the other hand, we can assume that the researchers do not know the answers and set out to find them. In a quantitative study using the structured interview as a method of data collection, the assumption is that the interviewer knows what questions to ask and also knows the answers (as indicated by the provision of closed and multiple choice categories). All they want is for respondents to choose which answers apply to them. In qualitative interviews, researchers do not know enough about the phenomenon to know what questions to ask. They therefore have to wait for ideas to emerge in the interview (see RE 36) in order to formulate the questions.

phenomena that have been studied using this method include 'the design of a smoking prevention program' (Heimann-Ratain *et al.*, 1985), 'recreation needs assessment questionnaires' (Mitra, 1994) and 'the phenomenon of death: a study of Diploma in Higher Education Nursing students' reality' (Johnson, 1994).

The purpose of focus group interviews differs from that of individual interviews. When researchers want different perspectives on a phenomenon, they can gather people who can offer such insight in one or two sessions. Purposive sampling may be used to group people known to have different views on the topic. However, researchers sometimes have to rely on volunteers, which may bias the findings.

Focus group interviews can follow or lead into individual interviews. Issues raised during these interviews can be pursued in more detail in the privacy of individual interviews. Alternatively, focus group interviews can be conducted in order to validate data previously collected in individual interviews. In the latter, respondents are asked their views or perceptions, free from group pressure. The interviewer can concentrate on one individual at a time and pursue the topic in greater depth. In focus group interviews, it is only possible to deal with general, and not personal, issues. For example, in a group interview the researcher studying burn-out may be able to find out what the respondents think generally of 'burn-out' and may be interested in finding out whether people agree or disagree with its meaning. It is not possible to assess each individual's level of 'burn-out'. The researcher can also answer general questions or attend to the concerns that participants may have in taking part in the study, thus allaying their anxieties.

Focus group interviews provide opportunities to brainstorm, perhaps for the purpose of generating items for a questionnaire. They can also be used to check question wording and formats, and provide opportunities to 'pilot-test' an instrument fairly quickly and cheaply. When focus group interviews are to be followed by individual interviews, the former can help to familiarise the interviewer with prospective or potential interviewees.

The major advantage of focus group interviews is that valuable data can be obtained quickly and cheaply. Some people are also more comfortable in voicing their opinions in the company of friends and colleagues than on their own, with an interviewer. Focus group interviews provide the opportunity for participants to reflect on, and react to, the opinions of others, with which they may disagree or of which they are unaware. Apart from the range of opinions that can potentially be obtained, underlying conflicts are often revealed that would otherwise have remained unknown to the researcher. Even when there is no heated discussion or disagreement, the sharing of experiences can provide valuable insight into phenomena.

One of the major disadvantages of focus grou[p]
dominant personalities or factions can monopolis[e]
express their views at the expense of others. Some
be shy, unassertive or unable to articulate their
interview requires group management as well
The larger the group, the more difficult the task to m[a]
interviewer is skilled, it is possible that the contribution of thos[e]
frightened to voice their opinions will not be fully maximised. Focus
group interviews are also not suitable for the study of sensitive and
personal issues and behaviours that do not conform to the norm.

Recording data can also present difficulties. Taking notes when
many people are talking at the same time is not feasible. Tape-recorders
may only record those who are near to them, although video-recordings
can be more effective as they are not only able to capture what is said,
but can also reveal the group dynamics. Analysis of data from focus
group interviews can also be daunting.

The process of focus group interviews varies, among other things,
according to the number of participants, the skill of the researcher and
the purpose of the interviews. If the purpose is to brainstorm, the
process may be more flexible, with opportunities for spontaneous contribution. If the purpose is to seek respondents' views on a number of
specific issues or if the researcher wants to validate findings from
individual interviews, the agenda will dictate a more directive approach.

Focus group interviews are not replicable. The reliability and
validity of the findings are difficult to ascertain on their own but can be
compared with the findings of individual interviews or other methods, if
used in the same study. Researchers have to reflect on the motives or
reasons for what was said and by whom. They must also realise the
potential effect of group pressure on the type of data they collect.
Kitzinger (1994, cited in Milburn *et al.*, 1995) reported that researchers
found heterosexual men to display more macho and sexually harassing
behaviour in groups than in individual interviews. She emphasised the
importance of examining and understanding 'how social contexts
affect respondents' behaviours and expressed attitudes in research
settings as well as in real life' (Milburn *et al.*, 1995). The interest in the
behaviour of people when in groups, is not new. Hume, in his *Treatise of
Human Nature* in 1739, wrote:

> Everyone has observed how much more dogs are animated when they
> hunt in a pack, than when the pursue their game apart. We might,
> perhaps, be at a loss to explain this phenomenon, if we had not experience
> of a similar in ourselves.

RE 38, Cowley *et al.* (1996) describe how they carried out a focus
up interview with community nurses.

RESEARCH **38** Cowley *et al.* (1996)
EXAMPLE **Establishing a framework for research: the**
example of needs assessment

A focus group interview

Focus group interviews were carried out as part of large study aimed at investigating
'the changing educational needs of community nurses' (district nurses and health visitors), 'with regard to needs assessment and quality of care'. The data from the interviews were to be used to develop the observation and interview instruments, and the
analytical framework for the main body of the research project.

The researchers describe below how participants were recruited:

> 'Typical' consumers from each these services were invited to participate in two
> separate focus group discussions. No attempt was made to arrange a representa-
> tive sample in just two meetings, but efforts were made to arrange a cross-section
> covering a variety of different backgrounds, ages, socio-economic and ethnic
> groups. There were a total of 22 participants; some were identified through con-
> sumer organisations, and others from personal, community nursing contacts.

Cowley *et al.* also describe the process of this group interview:

> In each group, a facilitator introduced the topics, making a conscious effort to ensure
> an accepting, non-threatening atmosphere, asking open questions and inviting par-
> ticipants to consider the points. Further explanation of some of the points was
> sought by some participants. Group members were invited to comment on the ver-
> bal interpretations and information pack, so a variety of opinions were expressed.

Comments
1. Focus group interviews were carried out in the preliminary part of the study to
   generate ideas for the development of structured observation schedules, items for
   personal semistructured interviews as well as a theoretical framework.
2. Some focus group interviews are more focused than others. Here, the researchers
   had a clear agenda and therefore 'guided' the interviews. In a study by Donovan
   (1995) 'of men during their partners' pregnancies', the researcher minimised 'leader
   dominance' by making every effort 'to allow the men themselves to determine the
   direction of the conversations within the given framework for the session'.
3. In this study, a second researcher was present, 'making minimal contributions to the
   discussions, but taking fieldnotes'. The difficulty of leading a group discussion and
   taking notes has been emphasised in the text. In this study, the discussions were
   also tape-recorded.
4. The researchers reflected on the group dynamics. For example, in their analysis of
   data, they paid attention not only to 'the more clearly articulated' themes and ideas,
   but also to those which 'remained undeveloped' during the group interview.

ETHICAL IMPLICATIONS OF INTERVIEWING

Interviewing shares with experiments and postal questionnaires some of the ethical concerns discussed in previous chapters. Unlike the self-administered questionnaire, however, the researcher knows who she is talking to and the respondent cannot therefore remain anonymous. The researcher has a moral obligation to keep the respondent anonymous from others, and the data collected must remain confidential. Anonymity and confidentiality are only two of the many ethical issues that researchers and others must consider if the rights of individuals are not to be compromised. The behaviour of the interviewer before, during and after the interview has the potential of harming respondents.

Before the interview

The issue of consent, especially in relation to patients as a captive population, has been discussed in earlier chapters. Even when people are interviewed in their own homes, they can still feel obliged to help health professionals, either because they are grateful for the services they have received or because they may require them later on. Interviewing as a method of data collection puts particular pressure on respondents to take part. The physical presence of researchers or the sound of their voice over the telephone has more 'weight' than a questionnaire through the letter box. Interviews are sometimes preferred precisely because they yield higher response rates than questionnaires.

To obtain consent, researchers must give as much information as possible to respondents to enable them to make up their minds. Among these may be people who are bereaved, depressed, recovering from a suicide attempt, an abortion or miscarriage, or have just been diagnosed as having a terminal illness. They constitute a vulnerable population who may not be in a position to fully comprehend and digest all the information given to them and may not be able to give proper informed consent. Even when they are not experiencing, or recovering from, an illness or a tragic event, the respondents' living conditions may make them vulnerable and open to exploitation. Many people who live alone crave to have someone to talk to. Many researchers have been surprised to find that they cannot take their leave because respondents want to carry on talking.

During the interview

The interview process itself is potentially harmful. Individuals have a right to privacy, which can be easily invaded once they have given consent. According to Waltz *et al.* (1991), 'a generally accepted ethical position is that subjects should be free to participate or withdraw from participation without recrimination or prejudice'. It is unlikely that this right is frequently exercised. On the other hand, a 'skilful' interviewer can make the respondent reveal intimate details before the latter notices what is happening. Waltz *et al.* (1991) explain that 'the right to privacy asserts essentially that an individual should be able to decide how much of himself or herself (including thoughts, emotions, attitudes, physical presence, and personal facts) to share with others'.

Smith (1992) suggests:

> researchers, who interview people and perhaps particularly women, need an awareness and a sensitivity to the fact that, although a subject may have agreed to take part in a study, it cannot be known for certain what that interview will uncover or give rise to. It could be argued that to be allowed a private view of another person's past or opinions or pain is a privilege.

Qualitative interviews depend on in-depth probing and, as such, have the potential to violate the right to privacy. Fontana and Frey (1994) state:

> A growing number of scholars... feel that most of traditional in-depth interviewing is unethical, whether wittingly or unwittingly, and we agree wholeheartedly. The techniques and tactics of interviewing are really ways of manipulating respondents while treating them as objects or numbers rather than individual human beings.

Qualitative interviews, although individual-centred, operate on the basis that respondents will reveal their inner thoughts if the researcher is skilful enough and if a trust is built up with the respondent. However, in some cultures it is offensive to probe into people's lives. Qualitative interviewers must pay particular attention to cultural norms in order to avoid violating the moral and ethical conduct of particular groups.

Interviews have the potential to reveal views, beliefs, attitudes and behaviours that can be damaging to respondents. In the course of the study, the researcher's view of the respondent may be confirmed or altered, this may not be very important if the respondent never comes into contact with the researcher again, but it has implications if, for example, the respondent is a student on a course in which the researcher is involved.

It is not unusual for research to be carried out in order to make services more cost-effective, and this may eventually lead to a cut in services. It is a bold researcher who divulges the potential of her research to lead to such actions. Buckeldee (1994), in her study of 'carers in the community', remarked that the information given by respondents 'could potentially have been used to support arguments that they may have disagreed with'.

Interviews, especially qualitative ones, can arouse emotions and lead to catharsis. The subject matter of such interviews can be highly sensitive and emotionally charged. In Smith's (1992) study of 'the help-seeking behaviours of alcohol dependent and problem drinking women', 'the content of the discussions ranged over many areas and included references to events which could only be described as highly personal, emotionally charged and, in some cases, unresolved: for example, the giving up of children for adoption; rape; violence to themselves as well as being violent towards others'.

Smith (1992) believes that the researcher has 'an ethical responsibility to handle such material with sensitivity and judgement'; she 'can listen and acknowledge the event but she must not probe in such a way as to produce and encourage emotional pain'. The author also contends that 'to interview and then leave someone in emotional distress without adequate support or safeguards is morally wrong' (Smith, 1992).

In one-to-one interviews, the researcher is in a position to observe overt or subtle changes in the verbal and non-verbal behaviours of the respondent and may therefore respond to them. In focus group interviews, it is difficult for her to observe and respond to the distress of some individuals. Smith (1995) believes that 'when discussing sensitive topics, it is important to have a coleader with clinical experience to adequately monitor the group's comfort level'. In structured interviews, researchers may use questionnaires or other tools that can also arouse emotions and cause distress. Waltz et al. (1991) explain the potential psychological risks 'associated with many of the measurement instruments commonly employed in nursing':

> A measurement instrument or activity may inadvertently expose the subject to stress resulting from loss of self-esteem, generations of self-doubt, embarrassment, guilt, disturbing self-insights, fright, or concern about things of which the subject was previously unaware.

Waltz et al. (1991) illustrate their point with the following examples:

> an instrument measuring parent–adolescent relations may include items that cause the parent to worry about aspects of the relationship or the adequacy of specific parenting behaviors; a measure that requests factual information or recall of specific events may embarrass a subject who is not able to respond; or psychological inventories may provide the subject with insight into aspects of personality or interpersonal relationships that alter previous perceptions and cause distress.

The interview can have the effect of raising expectations and changing respondents' perceptions. In asking them about the services they do or do not use, the interviewer may create expectations that they should avail themselves of these. Similarly, interviews may make respondents aware of their plight and leave them to consider their sad state of affairs. Buckeldee (1994) found this in her study of 'carers in the community'. She writes:

> not only did most carers willingly talk with me but many also freely talked about themselves, including personal and intimate matters. At times this process also resulted in participants exploring new feelings and ideas they had not previously considered or acknowledged. This commonly occurred when we explored their feelings and perceptions of their caring role.

As part of a course, a student carried out a case study during which he interviewed a technician and her boss. The student soon became aware that issues (such as the appraisal of the technician's work) had not been considered by the boss prior to the interview and, because she raised them, it was likely thereafter to have implications for the technician. In doing the student a favour by granting her the interview, she created the conditions that could potentially alter her working practice.

The interview process gives rise to a number of dilemmas that researchers have to face and which may cause themselves stress as well. Buckeldee (1994) gives an idea of her own feelings when exploring the feelings of her respondents. She describes the 'depth of sorrow and sadness', which she felt at times was 'overwhelming'. Respondents may tell researchers in confidence things which can become difficult to ignore and overlook. For example, a respondent may tell the interviewer of her intention of committing suicide or may describe the abuse of patients that she has recently witnessed. The researcher faces the dilemma of doing nothing about it or breaking the confidentiality. Nurse researchers often have to deal with the conflict between their roles as nurses and as researchers. There are numerous examples in the nursing literature (see Smith, 1992; Wilde, 1992; Buckeldee, 1994) of the implications of this conflicting role and of how researchers have dealt with it. Wilde (1992) reports that 'most authors advocate that the researcher resists the temptation to make interventions during the interview, and that they postpone answering questions or making comments until the end of the interview'.

After the interview

What happens after the interview also has ethical implications. Should researchers care about their respondents when the interview is over? What responsibilities do researchers have towards respondents after the interview? Buckeldee (1994), referring to her study, expresses this dilemma:

> Having 'got my data' I did not know whether I should leave the carers in the hope that they would solve or deal with their problems in their own way or whether, having caused them to realise feelings not previously acknowledged, I had a responsibility to help them in some way. If the latter was the case I needed to know what the nature of that responsibility was.

What happens to the data after they are collected is also important. There is the possibility that the views of respondents may be misrepresented. According to Smith (1992), 'it is clear that the interpretation of interview data is never wholly objective and dispassionate despite any effort made to be so' and that 'data interpretation is influenced by life experience and intellectual ability'. This is why some researchers go back to respondents for them to validate their (the researcher's) interpretation of what was said. Since, usually, not all respondents are consulted in this exercise, could it be that interviewers go back to those who are more receptive and hospitable and avoid those who are controversial?

It has also been suggested that debriefing sessions are necessary to deal with some of the stresses that respondents face. Researchers also need such help to relieve some of *their* stresses as well. In focus group interviews, individuals may be distressed and frustrated if they feel that they have not been able, for whatever reason, to express their views. Researchers can help to allay some of these frustrations by talking to them individually afterwards.

The safety of group members must also be of concern to the researcher. Some of the participants may be open to victimisation for the views they have offered. Researchers must be sensitive to these issues. Buckeldee (1994) gives an example from her study of a case where the husband insisted that his wife (his carer) be interviewed in his presence. Buckeldee explains how this 'inhibited her responses', that 'with hindsight she should have anticipated that this could happen' and that she could have arranged the interview when the client was out. While this may have solved a methodological problem, it could, unwittingly, have caused a conflict between the couple had the husband become aware that his wife was asked questions related to his care behind his back.

These are some of the main ethical issues in interviewing. In some cases, the worst possible scenarios have been described and, of course, they do not necessarily apply to all types of interview. They are discussed here for researchers and others to be alert and sensitive to the ethical implications of what could be seen as harmless activities, for which some researchers think (often wrongly) that no approval from an ethical committee is required.

CRITIQUING INTERVIEWS

Critiquing or evaluating interviews is problematic, mainly because very often little information is provided on what takes place between the interviewer and the interviewee. No two interviews are the same. Researchers must therefore describe the interview process in some detail. For example, in structured interviews, although the list of questions is predetermined, structured and standardised, readers need to know whether the input of the interviewer (or interviewers) was the same across all the interviews and, if not, how this affects the data. In qualitative interviews, one can ask whether the researcher was more or less directive, whether she used disclosures to encourage respondents to talk, whether the same questions were asked of all of them or whether the researcher built upon issues raised in the previous interview. Answers to these questions can help to determine how much the topics discussed reflect the interviewer's or the respondents' perspective. For semistructured interviews, one can question the extent to which the prepared list of questions provided a loose or a rigid structure. For example, were respondents simply asked to provide answers to open-ended questions or did the researcher follow up issues raised in these answers? This is to determine whether there was limited or ample scope for respondents to talk freely. In focus group interviews, the rationale for adopting this approach as opposed to personal interviews, as well as information about the size and relevant profile of the group and how the participants were recruited, must be provided. Readers can decide whether the group seemed too large for the interviewer to handle and, depending on the purpose of the group interview, whether the recruitment method was biased or not.

The duration of the interview is often an indication of whether or not it was rushed. While it is not possible to say with certainty that in a 2 hour interview respondents were able to talk freely, it is difficult to comprehend how a qualitative interview can last less than 30 minutes, especially when only one interview is carried out per respondent. It takes that length of time for the interviewer and interviewee to exchange 'civilities' and begin to engage in a conversation let alone talk 'in depth' about anything.

As with other methods of data collection, researchers are better able than readers to reflect on whether their data can be taken at face value. Only they can tell whether their dress, appearance, accent, gender, race and other characteristics, or other events, had any bearings on the data collected.

Researchers must also explain how informed consent was obtained, access to respondents negotiated and respondents' privacy respected. They also have to report on where the interview took place and who else was present.

Measures taken for ensuring the validity and reliability of data must be fully explained. These should give an indication of the length to which the researchers have gone in order to ensure the credibility of their data. Finally, researchers should reflect on the limitations of their studies and indicate whether their findings can apply to other settings or whether they should be treated with caution.

SUMMARY AND CONCLUSION

The interview is one of the main methods of data collection and takes different forms. In structured interviews, the questions are pre-determined, standardised and highly structured, with only limited scope for clarification and elaboration.

Qualitative interviews are characterised by flexibility and versatility, the researcher moulding the interaction in order to obtain in-depth information about phenomena. Semistructured interviews combine elements of both of these types: they give respondents some freedom to express themselves while answering a set number of questions. Finally, focus group interviews make use of group dynamics to obtain a variety of perspectives cheaply and quickly on the same phenomenon.

Each of these interviews has its value and limitations. We have discussed the strategies that researchers adopt to ensure that the data they collect are credible. They should describe the interview process in relevant detail to enable readers to evaluate these data.

Finally, interviews, whatever the type, have ethical implications that researchers must seriously consider. Respondents' human rights must always take precedence over any research consideration.

REFERENCES

Barriball K L and While A (1994) Collecting data using a semi-structured interview: a discussion paper. *Journal of Advanced Nursing,* **19**:328–35.

Bennett L (1991) Adolescent girls' experience of witnessing marital violence: a phenomenological study. *Journal of Advanced Nursing,* **16**:431–8.

Bluff R and Holloway I (1994) 'They know best': women's perceptions of midwifery care during labour and childbirth. *Midwifery*, **10**:157–64.

Brown S and Williams A (1995) Women's experiences of rheumatoid arthritis. *Journal of Advanced Nursing*, **21**:695–701.

Buckeldee J (1994) Interviewing carers in their own homes. In Buckeldee J and McMahon R (eds) *The Research Experience in Nursing*. London: Chapman & Hall.

Cartwright A (1986) *Health Surveys in Practice and Potential*, 2nd edn. London: King Edward's Hospital Fund for London.

Chenitz W C (1986) The informed interview. In Chenitz W C and Swanson J M (eds) *From Practice to Grounded Theory. Qualitative Research in Nursing*. Berkshire: Addison-Wesley.

Cowley S, Bergen A, Young K and Kavanagh A (1996) Establishing a framework for research: the examples of needs assessment. *Journal of Clinical Nursing*, **5**:53–61.

Davis A J (1980) Research as an inactional situation: objectivity in the interview. *International Journal of Nursing Studies*, **17**:215–20.

Deutscher I (1966) Words and deeds: social science and social policy. *Social Problems*, **13**:233–54.

Donovan J (1995) The process of analysis during a grounded theory study of men during their partner's pregnancies. *Journal of Advanced Nursing*, **21**:708–15.

Fontana A and Frey J H (1994) Interviewing: the art of science. In Denzin N K and Lincoln Y S (eds) *Handbook of Qualitative Research*. California: Sage.

Gilloran A (1995) Gender differences in care delivery and supervisory relationship: the case of psychogeriatric nursing. *Journal of Advanced Nursing*, **21**:652–8.

Gray M (1994) Personal experience of conducting unstructured interviews. *Nurse Researcher*, **1**(3): 65–71.

Hammersley M and Atkinson P (1983) *Ethnography: Principles and Practice*. London: Routledge.

Hanson E J (1994) An exploration of the taken-for-granted world of the cancer nurse in relation to stress and the person with cancer. *Journal of Advanced Nursing*, **19**:12–20.

Heimann-Ratain G, Hanson M and Peregoy S M (1985) The role of focus group interviews in designing a smoking prevention program. *Journal of School Health*, **55**(1):13–17.

Hein E C (1980) *Communication in Nursing Practice*, 2nd edn. Boston: Little, Brown.

Hogston R (1995) Quality nursing care: a qualitative enquiry. *Journal of Advanced Nursing*, **21**:116–24.

Holt P (1995) Role of questioning skills in patient assessment. *British Journal of Nursing*, **4**(19):1145–8.

Hutchinson S and Wilson S H (1992) Validity threats in scheduled semi-structured research interviews. *Nursing Research*, **41**(2):117–19.

Hyman H H (1954) *Interviewing in Social Research*. Chicago: University of Chicago Press.

Johnson H R (1994) The phenomenon of death: a study of diploma in higher education nursing students' reality. *Journal of Advanced Nursing*, **19**:1151–61.

Jones S (1985) Depth interviewing. In Walker R (ed.) *Applied Qualitative Research*. Aldershot: Gower.

Kitzinger J (1994) The methodology of focus groups: the importance of interaction between research participants. *Sociology of Health and Illness*, **16**:103–121.

Kuremyr D, Kihlgren M, Norberg A, Astrom S and Karlsson I (1994) Emotional experiences, empathy and burnout among staff caring for demented patients at a collective living unit and a nursing home. *Journal of Advanced Nursing*, **19**:670–9.

Lofland J and Lofland L H (1984) *Analysing Social Settings: A Guide to Qualitative Observation and Analysis*. Belmont, CA: Wadsworth.

Milburn K, Fraser E, Secker J and Pavis S (1995) Combining methods in health promotion research: some considerations about appropriate use. *Health Education Journal*, **54**:347–56.

Mitra A (1994) Use of focus groups in the design of recreation needs assessment questionnaires. *Evaluation and Program Planning*, **17**(2):133–40.

Nay-Brock R M (1984) A comparison of the questionnaire and interviewing techniques in the collection of sociological data. *Australian Journal of Advanced Nursing*, **2**(1):14–22.

Neadley A W, Kendrick D C and Brown R (1995) Health and memory in people over 50: a survey of a single-GP practice in England. *Journal of Advanced Nursing*, **21**:646–51.

Newell R (1994) *Interviewing Skills for Nurses and Other Health Care Professionals: A Structured Approach*. London: Routledge.

Nolan M, Owens R G and Nolan J (1995) Continuing professional education: identifying the characteristics of an effective system. *Journal of Advanced Nursing*, 21:551–60.

Parse R R, Coyne A B and Smith M J (1985) *Nursing Research – Qualitative Methods*. Maryland: Brady Communications.

Price B (1987) First impressions: paradigms for patient assessment. *Journal of Advanced Nursing*, **12**:699–705.

Schaefer K M (1995) Struggling to maintain balance: a study of women living with fibromyalgia. *Journal of Advanced Nursing*, **21**:95–102.

Smith L (1992) Ethical issues in interviewing. *Journal of Advanced Nursing*, **17**:98–103.

Smith M W (1995) Ethics in focus groups: a few concerns. *Qualitative Health Research*, **5**(4):478–86.

Sudman S and Bradburn N (1974) *Response Effects in Surveys*. Chicago: Aldine.

Thompson D (1990) Too busy for assessments? *Nursing*, **4**(21):35.

Walker J M, Hall S and Thomas M (1995) The experience of labour: a perspective from those receiving care in a midwife-led unit. *Midwifery*, **11**:120–9.

Waltz C F, Strickland C L and Lenz E R (1991) *Measurement in Nursing Research*, 2nd edn. Philadelphia: F A Davis.

Wilde V (1992) Controversial hypotheses on the relationship between researcher and informant in qualitative research. *Journal of Advanced Nursing*, **17**:234–42.

13 OBSERVATIONS

> Where observation is concerned, chance favours only the
> prepared mind. (Louis Pasteur, 1854)

INTRODUCTION

In a practice-based profession such as nursing or midwifery, observation is perhaps the most important method of collecting information. As a research tool for the study of human behaviour, it is invaluable on its own or when used in conjunction with other methods. Thus, in this chapter, we will explore briefly the use, value and limitations of observation in nursing practice and nursing research. The main two types of observation, structured and unstructured, will be described and discussed. We will examine the ethical implications of using observation to collect data on people in general, and patients and nurses in particular. Finally, some suggestions will be made to facilitate those who undertake a critical reading of observational studies.

OBSERVATION AND NURSING PRACTICE

Researchers did not invent observation. Adler and Adler (1994) remind us that 'for as long as people have been interested in studying the social and natural world around them, observation has served as the bedrock source of human knowledge'.

Although observation is part of daily life, some professionals, in particular nurses, need to be skilled at it. Without observation, effective nursing care is not possible. The process of nursing care, from assessment to evaluation, greatly depends on precise and accurate observation. The ability to observe, although naturally possessed by some, can be developed with training. While observation is usually associated with sight, the other four senses – hearing, touch, smell and taste – are also involved. These senses vary in the extent to which they are used in nursing practice. Sight and hearing are understandably the most frequently used, although touch and smell provide valuable information as well.

Humans have also devised aids to increase their ability to observe, the most common being telescopes, microscopes and sound amplifiers. In nursing practice, thermometers, sphygmomanometers and stethoscopes are but some of a whole array of devices and equipment designed to make observations of body functions and changes as precise and accurate as possible, and to venture where normal human senses cannot reach.

To assess and monitor clients, practitioners have to observe verbal and non-verbal signs. Many of the clients whom nurses treat, however, are either not able or are unwilling to speak. The ability to assess their conditions and attend to their needs depends greatly on nurses' observational skills. According to Rose-Grippa (1979), 'non-verbal communication, or the transmission of messages without the use of words, is the most basic form of communication' and 'it is estimated that in everyday communication between people, only one third of the message are transmitted verbally, while two thirds are transmitted nonverbally'.

'Doing the obs' is a well-known expression in nursing, which normally means recording the temperature, pulse rate, respiration rate and blood pressure of the patient. Many of the observations carried out by nurses involve the use of more than one sense simultaneously. In 'taking' blood pressure, the nurse may use touch to find a vein, listen for the 'beats' and watch the movement of the 'needle' or 'mercury'. Apart from occasions when nurses are asked to 'observe' or 'special' a patient or to carry out specific observations, they are, according to Peplau (1988), participant observers in most relationships in nursing. As she explains:

> This requires that [the nurse] use herself as an instrument and as an object of observation at the same time that she is participating in the interaction between herself and a patient or a group. The more precise the nurse can become in the use of herself as an instrument for observation, the more she will be able to observe in relation to performances in the nursing process.

OBSERVATION IN NURSING RESEARCH

The purpose of observation in nursing practice differs from that in nursing research. Nurses use observation to collect information to attend to the needs of clients, while researchers conduct observations for the purpose of answering research questions. Many nursing observations, such as the monitoring of temperature, pulse and respiration or blood pressure, require the utmost rigour and precision. However, many other observations are casual, accidental or haphazard. They are made, as Peplau (1988) described above, during everyday interactions between nurses and patients. Therefore observations are made as part of the process of care and are not necessarily the focus of interactions. On the other hand, the researchers' main purpose is not to deliver care but to observe. Therefore interactions are a means to an end, which is to collect research data. Adler and Adler (1994) explain how lay observations differ from research observations:

What differentiates the observations of social scientists from those of every-day life actors is the former's systematic and purposive nature. Social science researchers study their surrounding regularly and repeatedly, with a curiosity spurred by theoretical questions about the nature of human action, interaction, and society.

As the nature of nurses' work requires them to observe all the time, a knowledge of how and why researchers carry out observations can enhance nurses' understanding of the complexity and implications of this method of collecting information. Some of the issues that will be raised in this chapter should, hopefully, help you to reflect on your own knowledge of, and skill, in observation. Like interviews, observations can be carried out during surveys, experiments and case studies. They are used in inductive, deductive, qualitative and quantitative research. They are more suited to some phenomena than others and can be used in conjunction with other methods, such as questionnaires and interviews. The need to choose the most appropriate method, however, cannot be overemphasised. Observations are particularly suited to the study of psychomotor activities and other non-verbal activities, while knowledge, attitudes and beliefs are better studied by questionnaires and interviews. Polit and Hungler (1995) list some of the phenomena amenable to observation. These include 'characteristics and conditions of individuals, verbal and non-verbal communication behaviors, activi-ties, skill attainment and performance and environmental characteris-tics'. Not all observations need to be of people. Gould and Ream (1994), in a study of 'nurses' views of infection control', used a 'ward facilities checklist' to document the availability of resources.

Human behaviour is normally studied by asking questions or by observation, and in many cases by a combination of both. As explained in Chapter 11, there are a number of problems with asking people about their behaviour, including perception bias, memory-gaps, ulterior motives or that respondents may not be aware of how they behave. Despite the fact that some phenomena are more amenable to observa-tion than others, researchers do not always choose the most appropriate method. In a review of studies on nurses' performance, Fitzpatrick *et al.* (1994) found that 'disappointingly, few studies have been located in the literature which adopt an observational approach'. Fitzpatrick *et al.* (1994) make reference to Kerlinger (1977) and Cormack (1984), who argue that 'direct observation is potentially a more comprehensive method to ascertain how a nurse performs in a real situation and to identify differences, if any, in the practice of nurses'.

Some of the phenomena that have been studied by observation include 'the work of the charge nurse in acute admission wards of psychiatric hospitals' (Cormack, 1976), 'communication between nursing staff and patients in intensive therapy/care unit' (Ashworth 1980), 'measurement of nurse–patient touch' (Porter *et al.*, 1986), 'characteristics of effective nursing interventions in the management of challenging behaviour' (Lowe, 1992), 'effectiveness of a handwashing program' (Day *et al.*, 1993) and 'the effects of pain on infant behaviours' (Fuller and Conner, 1995).

In advocating observation as a choice method of studying behaviour, both verbal and non-verbal, it is recognised that behaviour cannot be fully understood without obtaining the views and feelings of the people concerned. Researchers and practitioners interested in the link between knowledge, attitude and practice often find that there are discrepancies between them. Salmon (1993) points out that 'in nursing care as in other aspects of behaviour, attitudes have been found to be a poor guide to behaviour'. Salmon (1993) carried out observations of 27 nurses and administered a questionnaire to them all in his study of the 'interactions of nurses with elderly patients' to find out whether or not there was a link between their attitudes and the way they interacted with patients. Another reason for using multiple methods is because different methods often reveal different realities. For example, Lowe (1992) carried out semistructured interviews and participant observation 'in order to investigate the interventions used by psychiatric nurses when faced with challenging behaviour'. In the interviews, he paid particular attention 'to situations in which the observations of different witnesses to the same event were conflicting' (Lowe, 1992).

Limitations of observations

Observation, like other methods, has its own limitations and ethical implications (discussed in a later section). One of the main problems is the effect of the observer on the 'observed'. The awareness of being observed is likely to lead people to be self-conscious and may influence them to behave in ways they would not normally behave. A classic study by Roethlisberger and Dickson (1939) set out to elucidate the effect of illumination levels on productivity at the Hawthorne plant of Western Electric in Chicago. They experimented with different levels of lighting over a period of 2.5 years and found that no matter what the levels were, productivity continued to increase. Roethlisberger and Dickson (1939) concluded that the workers produced more, mainly because they were being observed rather than as a result of different lighting. This type of observer effect is now known popularly as the 'Hawthorne effect'.

While the effect of the observer's presence cannot be fully eliminated, researchers have found that it is not always possible for people to change their normal behaviour and sustain it for long periods. They have noticed that, after a while, the observer can become 'part of the furniture'. In Cormack's (1976) study, in which he observed the work of the charge nurse in an acute psychiatric setting, he reported clues that led him to believe that his presence as an observer did not entirely affect the behaviour of those he studied. These clues included 'tea drinking staff groups, which left the entire ward without nursing supervision or observation', staff playing cards among themselves, derogatory remarks made about patients, and patients discussing issues in his presence which they insisted were 'highly confidential to be shared with the doctor only'. Some of the strategies to reduce this effect will be discussed later.

Researchers are also best placed to know whether they are aware that their presence has influenced the data they collected and that they must reflect on it. There is no perfect method, and some trade-off is often necessary for the collection of valid and reliable data. To some extent, the video can be used to reduce observer's effect (this is discussed below).

Another problem with observations is that they can be costly and impractical over long periods of time. For example, watching and waiting for aggressive behaviour among psychiatric patients can be time-consuming. The researcher's ability to observe with precision can wane over time as fatigue sets in. The difficulties of observing different aspect of the same phenomenon that occur at the same time, and the ways in which researchers cope with these and other problems, are discussed further in the next section.

STRUCTURED OBSERVATION

A *structured observation* is one in which aspects of the phenomenon to be observed are decided in advanced (that is predetermined). For example, if the verbal content of nurse–patient interactions is to be observed, the researcher can break down 'verbal content' into a number of *units* or *categories*. Ashworth (1980), who carried out observations of staff communication in five intensive therapy/care units, used the following categories for her observation of verbal content:

a. Social superficial – for example 'Hello' or some other social remark which might have been made to anyone and does not specifically relate to the patient as an individual.
b. Social concerned – communication about the patient's family, home or personal interest, or sympathetic remarks such as apologies for causing discomfort.
c. Short-term informative – information about the next activity – for example, 'I'm just going to give you an injection'.

d. Questions – many of these were queries by the nurse to try to confirm what the patient had tried to communicate, or to ascertain what the patient wanted – for example, tea or coffee to drink.

e. Longer-term informative, teaching or orienting – for example, 'The machine is helping you to breathe now but soon you will be able to breathe on your own' or 'You had an accident on your motor-bike on Sunday, and you've been here at X hospital for two days, so it is Tuesday afternoon now'.

f. Command or request – for example 'Hold your arm out please'.

g. Other – anything which did not fall into any other category. Frequently this was used when the nurse called the patient's name to see if there was any response.

Ashworth added a further category (h), which she termed 'reassuring noises' such as 'Don't worry' and 'alright'.

The reason for specifying aspects of the phenomenon in advance is mainly to find out whether they are present and, if so, to what extent. The same type of data is required from each observation, thereby introducing standardisation into the process.

To carry out structured observation, a 'checklist' or 'schedule' is devised. It is similar to a questionnaire and can be highly or loosely structured. For example, in a study of touch in nurse–patient interaction, the observer could be asked to indicate the 'site' of touch without providing her with any categories of site. She then has to decide which term she wants to use to describe where the touch was applied. Alternatively, as Oliver and Redfern (1991) did, 'site of touch' was further divided into 'head, face, shoulder, axilla, arm, hand, chest, abdomen, back, leg, foot, bottom and genitals'; the observer simply had to select the appropriate category. This avoids the problem that arises when different observers use different terms to describe the same site. A highly structured observation schedule leaves little for the observer to record other than 'ticking' the appropriate columns or boxes.

Observation units or categories have been described as 'molar' and 'molecular' (Lobo, 1992). *Molar* units are broad and sometimes abstract, making the task of the observer more difficult since the category is not defined in enough detail for it to be instantly recognised. An example of molar categories comes from a study by Salmon (1993) of 'interactions of nurses with elderly patients', in which 'interactions with patients were subdivided into: positive (informing, questioning, general conversation) negative (ordering, rebuking) and neutral'. Informing itself is a broad term that can be subdivided into further categories. The observer in this case has first to decide what constitutes informing before deciding whether the behaviour is positive. *Molecular* units, on the other hand, are more detailed and precise, and therefore allow for more accurate recording. In a study by Fuller and Conner (1995) of 'the effect of pain on infant behaviors', 'cries' were described as follows:

> Cry duration. A single phonation with more than 3 seconds of silence preceding and following another phonation was defined as a cry. Phonations with less than 3 seconds separating each other were labeled subcries. A cry bout is a series of subcries separated by more than 3 seconds from a cry or second cry bout. The duration in seconds was measured for all cries, subcries, and cry bouts contained on each videotape.

The more molecular categories there are, the more structured the checklist or schedule is. Some phenomena lend themselves more to molecular subdivisions than others. Both approaches have their uses and limitations. As Polit and Hungler (1995) state:

> The choice of approaches depends to a large degree on the nature of the problem and the preferences of the investigator. The molar approach is more susceptible to observer errors and distortions because of the greater ambiguity in the definition of the units. On the other hand, in reducing the observations to more concrete and specific elements, the investigator may lose sight of the activities that are at the heart of the enquiry.

To facilitate recording and analysis, categories are given codes. The following example of the use of codes is taken from Oliver and Redfern (1991).

Non-verbal response	Code
Laughter	L
Touch	T
Smile	S
Cry	C
Mumble	M
Groan	GR
Gesture	GT
Gaze	G
Other	O

While codes are helpful in making it easier and quicker to record a category, especially in observations where behaviours are happening simultaneously, they nevertheless have to be memorised. This can be a difficult and challenging task for observers in studies where large number of codes have to be committed to memory.

In structured observation, the phenomenon to be studied must be operationally defined. The categories or units depend on the particular definition which the researcher chooses. An existing definition can be used, or researchers may formulate their own after reviewing the literature. Felce *et al.* (1980), in their study 'measuring activity of old people in residential care', formulated their definition of 'engagement in purposeful activity' by 'using the literature on behavioral observation, available manuals on measuring engagement in various settings, and the authors' informal observations of residents' behavior in the homes for the elderly'. Whatever the definition, it must adequately represent the phenomenon and be operationally feasible (see Chapter 7). This means that it must describe behaviours that *can* be observed. Lobo (1992) offers the following operational definition of 'lack of cooperation' and 'cooperation' in children during a burn dressing procedure:

> Crying, struggling to 'get away,' arm thrashing, screaming, and back arching may be defined and categorized as behaviors indicating a lack of cooperation. Sitting or lying quietly, talking in a 'usual' tone of voice, (further defined) holding still, walking to the treatment room, and assisting in the procedure may be defined and categorized as behaviors indicating cooperation.

From these definitions, a list of units or categories can be derived that can facilitate the observation and recording of the cooperation and lack of cooperation of children.

Structured observations and structured interviews are similar in that both use predetermined, structured and standardised tools. The observer and interviewer also adopt a non-participative or non-interventionist stance. As with the administration of questionnaires, the observer stands 'outside' what is being observed and tries not to influence events or behaviours in any way. In structured observations, researchers seek to quantify specific aspects of the phenomena being observed. They usually want to find the presence or absence of a particular behaviour or characteristic and the frequency or intensity with which it may happen. For example, in Salmon's study of nurses interactions with elderly patients, he set out to find, among others, the *number* of nurses' interactions that involved patients and the *proportion* of these interactions that 'were concerned with physical care (medication, meals and dressing)' or 'informal reality orientation periods' (Salmon, 1993). Structured observations adopt mostly a deductive approach since the behaviour or activity is observed against units of observation that are specified in advance. The underlying assumption in the use of structured observations is that researchers know what constitutes the behaviour or activity and seek only to discover to what extent they are present in the population under study.

Sampling in structured observation

It is not always feasible or possible to observe every behaviour or activity on a continuous basis; prolonged observation of patients and nurses can cause them unnecessary stress. Therefore researchers resort to time sampling where appropriate. Nurses are familiar with the concept of time sampling. Patients are monitored at set intervals, as in the case of four hourly recording of TPR. In the same way, if patient activities are being observed, the researcher may decide to carry out observations during the first 15 minutes of each hour for the duration of the shift. This can be done if it is believed that these 15 minute periods are able to give an accurate and representative picture of activities during the whole shift. Macdonald *et al.* (1985), analysing data from a study of 'activity and contacts of old people in residential settings', reported that 'a single hour of observation is sufficient to form an accurate representation of what might be achieved by a whole day's study'. They did concede, however, that 'it is possible that this particular hour is only representative... because of the relative lack of activity, and contacts, in the settings studied'. Therefore the selection periods of observation must be justified as it is likely that some behaviours or activities may happen only at certain times.

Intermittent observation, as is the case in time sampling, may not be appropriate in cases where the behaviour or activity happens rarely or unpredictably. For example, if a researcher wants to observe aggressive behaviour among psychiatric patients, continuous observation is advisable. This can be achieved either by observing whole shifts or by dividing the day into, for example, 4 hourly sessions from 8.00 am to midnight. The researcher then carries out the 8.00 am to 10.00 am observation on day 1 and the 10.00 am to 2.00 pm session on day 2. This is continued until all four sessions are covered. In this way, data for the whole period between 8.00 am and midnight are obtained, although not all in one day. Patients and nurses thus do not have to 'suffer' the presence of the researcher for one whole day.

Alternatively, the researcher may want to observe aggressive behaviours during specific 'events' such as meal times or in discussion groups. In this case, these events become the focus of the study. However, not all meal times may be observed. The researcher may select a sample of meal times, for example lunch on Monday and Friday, dinner on Tuesday and Saturday and breakfast on Wednesday and Sunday. Thus a sample of meal times can be chosen to represent meal times in general on that particular ward. This is known as event sampling: the event becomes the sampling unit.

Limitations of structured observation

Behaviours and activities happen simultaneously, and the observer may not be able to notice and record all of them. The position of the observer may be such that the behaviour may be outside her observation range or she may be obstructed, as in the case where a nurse is in the observer's line of vision and the patient cannot be observed. In a study by Porter *et al.* (1986) measuring nurse–patient touch, 'fifteen per cent of the observations had to be discarded, primarily because of obscured vision for one of the observers'. Some movements or changes may be so subtle or rapid that the researcher is unable to capture them. For example, eye contacts can be fleeting or a facial expression can last a fraction of a second. As Lobo (1992) explains:

> If the behavior occurs very infrequently, it may be missed altogether because the length of the observation is not sufficient to capture the behavior. Or if the event is fleeting and the observation is over a long period of time, a fatigued observer may miss the event.

In a busy environment, it is possible for the observer to be distracted, especially if she is concerned about what happens to other people. In continuous observation, fatigue may set in, leading to lack of concentration. According to Porter *et al.* (1986), 'circadian variation may affect the accuracy of the observer at different times of day'.

One of the major problems with structured observation is the difficulty of deciding which category or unit the observed behaviour or activity belongs to, especially when the molar approach is used. Some categories are not adequately operationally defined. In Porter *et al.*'s (1986) study, the observers found difficulty in recording the 'patient response to touch' because, as the authors admitted, response-type 'was not sufficiently well operationally well defined'. Some categories require the observer to make more subjective judgements than do others. For example, in the above study, there was more agreement between observers on such categories as 'duration of touch' and 'type of touch' than on 'response type' or 'intensity of touch'. This was because the observers had to decide subjectively what constituted 'response type' or 'intensity of touch'. On the other hand, 'duration of touch' can be measured by a stop watch and 'type of touch' was sufficiently well defined for the observers not to rely too much on their subjective judgement.

Researchers can overcome some of above problems by providing adequate operational definitions, by piloting their observation schedule, by training observers and by making the use of audio- and video-taping, where possible, appropriate and ethical.

Mason and Redeker (1993) suggest video-taping as an answer to observer fatigue. Video-recording has the advantage of providing continuous data over long periods of time. It has frame-by-frame, close-up (useful for subtle movements) and play-back facilities. It may also reduce the observer's effect, although it is likely that people will be aware of being observed by an 'electronic eye'. According to Lobo (1992), 'a benefit to videotaping the data is that a new coding schema can be applied to the data if a new observation tool is being developed'. However, video-taping in the natural environment is problematic unless subjects are confined to one room (Mason and Redeker, 1993), and 'live observations also have the advantage of the data collector being able to record anecdotal information, which tells more about the ambience of the environment' (Lobo, 1992).

Validity and reliability of structured observation

When structured observations are carried out, 'the reliability and validity of observations depend upon the reliability and validity inherent in the observational aids and in the ability of the observer to identify and record the specified behaviors or events' (Waltz et al., 1991). For structured observations to have validity, the observer must observe what she is supposed to observe. Observation schedules can be assessed for content validity in the same way as questionnaires (see Chapter 11). The operational definition of the phenomenon must be clear and precise, and the categories or units must represent the phenomenon. To ensure content validity, the observation schedule can be given to a panel of experts for review.

The observer's presence can also affect the validity of the data. As mentioned earlier, the observer's effect can be reduced when those observed 'get used' to the presence of the observer. Sometimes the observer spends little time in the setting prior to the observation period and therefore has little or no opportunity for 'settling in'. The personal attributes, such as gender, race, dress or manner, of the observer may influence how people behave when they are observed. Researchers must be sensitive to this possibility and make allowances for this when they analyse and interpret data.

When a number of people witness an accident, it is unlikely that their individual accounts of the event will be entirely consistent, even if it happened only 5 minutes earlier. Police officers are familiar with instances of witnesses giving different descriptions of the same burglary or assault. Research observers, too, are not immune from such inconsistencies. The observation schedule, the instructions to observers and the opportunity to record behaviours as they happen facilitate the observation process. However, observers are human and can be influenced by a number of factors that can distort their perception; or they may simply make mistakes.

Reliability in structured observation refers to the consistency with which the observer matches a behaviour or activity with the same unit or category on the observation schedule and records it in the same way each time it happens. *Intraobserver* reliability is the consistency with which one observer records the same behaviours in the same way on different occasions. Observations in the same study are often carried out by two or more observers. It is important that they observe, interpret and record the same behaviour or activity in the same way. *Interobserver* or *interrater reliability* can be monitored by asking two or more observers to record the same behaviours, their findings then being statistically computed. A '1.00' indicates total agreement and thereby excellent reliability, while a score of below 0.60 (an agreement in 6 instances out of 10) is of doubtful reliability. However, each study may set its own acceptable levels of reliability depending on the type of phenomenon. The more difficult they are to observe, the less likely to achieve a score closer to 1.00. There is normally a consensus in the research literature on what constitutes an acceptable reliability level, depending on the complexity of the observational task. In their study of 'nurse–patient touch', Porter *et al.* (1986), referring to Cicchetti (1984), set the following levels: 0.75–1.00, excellent interobserver reliability; 0.60–0.74, good reliability; 0.40–0.59, fair reliability; and less than 0.40, poor reliability.

A high level of agreement between two or more observers usually means that they consistently recognised and recorded the same behaviour in the same way. However, they could also be consistently wrong. In their study of 'interpersonal communication between nurses and elderly patients', Oliver and Redfern (1991) reported that two observers 'recorded that no non-verbal response' to touch had occurred during their observations. Oliver and Redfern (1991) explained that:

> This is unlikely to be true; it is much more likely that the non-verbal responses that did occur were not observed because the observers were busy recording other components. Non-verbal responses contain such a range of behaviours that they require a more focused and 'close-up' observation technique than was used in this study. Videorecording would be an appropriate technique for this.

When dealing with reliability, it is important to remember that researchers can be consistently right or consistently wrong. Different types of error may affect the reliability of observation data. The most common error is when the same researcher faced with the same behaviour or activity interprets it differently, or when different observers use different categories to classify the same phenomenon. Another error is when, due to lack of concentration or because the behaviour happens too quickly, observers use the wrong codes (especially when there are a large number of them).

The observers' interpretation of behaviour can be influenced by their experience and prejudices. Our professional backgrounds often make us see things differently from others, for example assertiveness can be interpreted as aggressiveness by different people. Lobo (1992) gives this example of how prejudices can influence observation:

> if mother–baby interaction is observed and the data collector knows that all of the mothers have had histories of drug use, the observer may score all of the mothers lower, or if the data collector knows the mothers are all upper middle class and highly educated, the scores may be higher.

The training of observers is crucial if a high level of reliability is to be achieved. Apart from live sessions, observation practice on video-recorded observations can be useful as well. According to Booth and Mitchell (1988, cited in Lobo, 1992), 'it may take as many as 30 practice sessions to obtain interrater reliability'.

When observations do not match, observers must discuss their perception of the particular behaviours or activities in dispute and arrive at an agreed interpretation of them. The validity and reliability of structured observations depend mainly on how the observation schedule is constructed and used.

In RE 39, Day *et al.* (1993) carried out structured observations in their study of handwashing.

UNSTRUCTURED OBSERVATION

Maupassant, a French novelist, in a preface to *Pierre and Jean* in 1887, wrote:

> In everything there is an unexplored element because we are prone by habit to use our eyes only in combination with the memory of what others before us have thought about the thing we are looking at. The most significant thing contains some little unknown element. We must find it.

According to Kirk and Miller (1986):

> In science, as in life, dramatic new discoveries must almost by definition be accidental ('serendipitous'). Indeed, they occur only in consequence of some kind of mistake.

RESEARCH **39** Day et al. (1993)
EXAMPLE **39** **Effectiveness of a handwashing program**

Structured observations

As the authors explain:

> The purpose of this pilot project was to determine the effectiveness of a formalized handwashing program for a group of grade 1 students... The objectives of the study were to (a) develop and evaluate a handwashing program for children with disabilities and (b) compare the incidence of infectious illness, use of antibiotics, and visits to doctors during the study period and for the same period of the previous year.

Day et al. also explain that:

> The researchers designed an observation checklist to evaluate the required handwashing behaviors. The tool was developed by basing the items on the components of handwashing found in the infection control literature and from recommendations from nurses.

> The checklist contained 11 categories as follows: 'washes front of hand', 'washes back of hand', 'washes side of hand', ' washes thumb', 'washes between fingers', 'washes with water', 'washes with soap', 'washes for 30 seconds', 'dries hands with towel', 'washes after toileting' and 'washes before eating'. If the child washed or attempted to 'wash using correct technique', a tick (✔) was made on the record sheet. If no attempts to 'wash using the correct technique' were made, an 'X' was recorded.

Comments

1. The information to be collected was decided in advance. Observers were required to look for the presence or absence of the behaviours (handwashing techniques, that is, how to wash, and the timing of handwashing activities, that is, when to wash) specified in the checklist. In quantitative research, observers collect only the information specified in advance and are not expected to deviate from this task.
2. The content validity of the tool was determined in an independent review by nurse experts and other health-care professionals (Day et al., 1993).
3. Observing behaviours with the use of a checklist can be problematic. In this study, the observers found it difficult to 'accurately assess handwashing behavior at appropriate times'. They suggest the use of video cameras 'placed in a number of sites to capture handwashing behaviors at appropriate times, particularly those times when the children sneezed or coughed'.

They relate how radioactivity was discovered when Henri Becquerel 'tossed the uranium salts into a drawer with his photographic materials and knocked off work'. Alexander Fleming also found that 'some kind of mold got into his staphylococcus culture and ruined the bacteria' and accidentally discovered penicillin (Kirk and Miller, 1986).

Although the ability to understand what happens is based on prior knowledge, these examples also show the need to study phenomena with fresh eyes and an open mind. By adopting a deductive approach, researchers collect data to validate what is already known. The categories to be observed are formulated in advance, based on previous knowledge. Alternatively, researchers can observe phenomena without any pre-determined categories and allow these to emerge from the data collected.

When we observe people's behaviour on buses we do not have categories to 'tick'. Instead, we record and analyse mentally what we watch. We may notice that some people sit by themselves rather than join others, younger people sit at the back, some sit comfortably while others sit at the edge of their seat or some people read while others meditate or talk to others. We would have, in fact, carried out 'unstructured' observations. In the latter, the researcher does not start with any predetermined categories but instead constructs them while she observes or after all the observations have been made. Unstructured observations therefore adopt an inductive approach and are described as qualitative observations. Those who favour this type of observation 'claim that structured, quantitatively-oriented methods are too mechanistic and superficial to render meaningful account of the intricate nature of human behavior' (Polit and Hunger, 1995).

Unstructured observations are appropriate in cases where little is known about the phenomenon. The knowledge gained can be used afterwards to construct categories for structured observations. In the above example, a researcher can thereafter try to see whether people on buses in fact behave as described above. To do so, she has to construct an observation schedule containing the various behaviours mentioned above and record their presence or absence and their frequency.

Unstructured observations are also undertaken when researchers believe that the existing knowledge of phenomena is either lacking or invalid. For example, Samarel (1989), in her study of how hospice nurses meet the needs of terminally ill and acutely ill patients, in which she used unstructured observation, found that the 'observed interactions of the participant nurses differed from that suggested by the literature regarding ways nurses interact with dying patients'. In this case, unstructured observations provided data to challenge existing knowledge.

In structured observations, the boundaries of what is to be observed are set prior to data collection. Observers are only expected to collect information required in the schedule or checklist. Each observation session lasts about the same amount of time and the researcher also carries out the same observation for each and every session. Unstructured observations are less standardised and more flexible. Each observation session is treated as a unique event and no two sessions are considered to be the same. What is learnt in the first session can be built upon in the later sessions, as is the case with qualitative interviews. In everyday life, we learn by accumulating 'facts', which are confirmed or rejected as we come across the same event time and time again. This 'cumulative' process of confirmation and validation is adopted by researchers as they move from one observation to the next. The purpose of an unstructured observation is to arrive at as complete an understanding of the phenomenon as possible. For this to happen, researchers must be flexible enough to make the most of the observation situation and should not feel constrained to observe only the categories decided in advance.

Unlike the case in structured observations, no specific research questions, objectives or hypotheses are set at the beginning of unstructured observations. Researchers decide during the observation what to focus on. Usually, the initial observations are 'unfocussed and general in scope', and later when observers become more familiar in the settings, their attention may be more focused (Adler and Adler, 1994). In Millman's (1976) study of 'life in the backrooms of American medicine', she describes this process:

> At first, my research interests were quite general. I soon found, however, that my attentions were drawn toward two intriguing issues. One was the variety of ways that doctors define, perceive and respond to medical mistakes – both their own mistakes and those made by hospital colleagues... The second major issue I came to focus on is the competing interests and conflicts among various group of doctors within the hospital.

Unstructured observations are also flexible in the duration of the sessions. They do not all necessarily have to be carried out over the same period of time. In a study by Hewison (1995) of 'nurses' power in interactions with patients', the unstructured observation sessions 'ranged from $2^1/_2$ to 4 hours in duration'.

In structured observation, researchers make recordings on the schedule or enter the data directly into a portable computer. These 'tools' are essential; without a checklist no observation can take place, in the same way that one cannot conduct a survey without a questionnaire. In unstructured observation, researchers take notes in a variety of ways. As explained before, in a qualitative study the researcher is herself a tool of data collection and analysis during the process of data collection. This is sometimes supplemented by note-taking in one form or other, ranging from scribbles to extensive descriptions and tape-recordings. Notes are usually taken as inconspicuously as possible so as not to disturb the normal flow of events. Nyström and Segesten (1994), in their study of 'sources of powerlessness in nursing home life', explain that 'observational notes were usually written in an empty corner of the ward on several occasions during the day, but they were occasionally directly recorded in the presence of the patients'. For another study in which observation is carried out (on a labour ward), see Hunt and Symonds (1995).

Analysis of data collected by unstructured observations is similar to that for qualitative interviews. Researchers have used the phenomeno-logical (Hallberg *et al.*, 1995) and grounded theory (Hewison, 1995) methods in their analysis of data from observations. Nyström and Segesten (1994) describe how they analysed their data:

> Analyses searched for events or conditions which were connected to power aspects, and which seemed to result in reactions signifying positive or negative experiences. Components, categories, and patterns were identified. Salient themes were further elaborated. Themes found were presented to and verified by the registered nurses and the nursing home chief, and by teaching staff in the nursing college.

One of the main problems with this type of observation is that the researcher can be selective in what to focus on, and this may reflect her personal interest. For example, in the above study by Millman (1976), there may have been other aspects of hospital life on which she could have focused, but instead she was 'attracted' to the two she mentioned. Another researcher may have taken an interest in aspects other than those chosen by Millman.

Hewison (1995), commenting on the limitations of his study of 'nurses' power in interactions with patients', points out that:

> While every effort was made to overcome the selective inattention (Spradley, 1980) which can result in obvious everyday activity being overlooked, what was actually observed also constitutes a limitation. The selection of interactions to be recorded was mediated by what was felt to be pertinent to the research problem. Observation is always selective (Carter, 1991), and the content of this study is no exception.

Analysis of data can also be a problem. By not deciding in advance which aspects to observe, it is likely that a large mass of data will be collected. This can make data analysis particularly difficult, laborious and time-consuming, as is also the case with qualitative interview data.

The problem of the observer effect is also real in unstructured, as it is in structured, observation. To offset this limitation, researchers have to use strategies to 'blend into' the environment and reflect on the effect of their presence.

Validity and reliability of unstructured observation

By not seeing behaviours and activities through the lens of predetermined categories, it is possible to some extent to observe a phenomenon 'as it is'. The purpose of unstructured observations is to seek as many different ways in which the phenomenon manifests itself. As explained earlier, each observation builds on the previous one by providing data that contribute towards an in-depth understanding of the phenomenon.

The flexibility of unstructured observations allows the researcher to search for the 'truth' whenever she can find it. This means that she can observe for longer or shorter periods in some sessions if the data are considered valuable. Thus the validity of unstructured observation is increased. The selectivity bias present in this type of observation is one of the main limitations. As explained earlier, there is little doubt that different researchers are likely to collect different data while observing the same phenomenon.

It is not possible for others to replicate unstructured observational studies. However, their data can be compared with those collected by different methods and in similar settings. The validity and reliability of unstructured observations will be further discussed in the next section.

RE 40 contains an account of the use of unstructured observation in Woodgate and Kristjanson's (1996) study.

PARTICIPATION IN OBSERVATION

Observers can adopt a detached role or can participate fully in the activities which they observe. In between these two stances, there are a number of positions that observers can occupy. Gold (1958) suggested the following four roles: 'the complete participant, the participant-as-observer, the observer-as-participant and the complete observer'. Adler and Adler (1994) describe the complete observer role as:

> researchers who are fundamentally removed from their settings. Their observations may occur from the outside, with observers being neither seen nor noticed. Contemporary varieties of this role might include the videotaping, audiotaping, or photographing noninteractive observer. This role most closely approximates the traditional ideal of the 'objective' observer.

RESEARCH **40** Woodgate and Kristjanson (1996)
EXAMPLE   **A young child's pain: how parents and nurses take care**

Unstructured observation

This qualitative study was undertaken to describe how parents and nurses respond to hospitalised young children experiencing pain from surgical intervention. The authors describe how data were collected on two surgical units of a university-affiliated children's hospital in Central Canada:

> The primary means of data collection involved participant observation. This method optimizes the researcher's ability to understand motives, beliefs, unconscious behaviours, and customs (Lincoln and Guba, 1985). Children were observed from the immediate post-operative period until their discharge day. Their responses to pain and how caregivers (i.e. parents and nursing staff) reacted to them were noted. To capture the most detailed descriptions of the children's pain experiences, a variety of care events were observed (e.g. bathing, changing a dressing, ambulating a child) at various time periods (i.e. day and evening shifts). Observation periods lasted from 2 to 8 hours daily. The number of observation hours totalled approximately 250 for all 11 children.

> Data were recorded in detailed field notes at the time the observations were made or as close as possible to the time of the observed event.

Comments

1. The qualitative approach in this study was justified by the lack of 'descriptions and explorations of the context in which pain is experienced by children', although 'there has been a lot of research focusing on childhood pain'.
2. No prepared scheduled was used to carry out the observations. Instead, one researcher recorded fieldnotes, from which categories or themes emerged. According to the authors, an outcome of the study was a model describing the young child's pain experience.
3. Consistent with participant observation (see below), the observer also interviewed the participants in order 'to extend the observational data and to clarify meanings the subjects themselves attributed to the situation'.

The complete participant's role is described as one in which the researcher is one of the participants in the activities or events that are observed without, however, revealing that she is in fact also carrying out research observations while being part of the group. This covert role has serious ethical implications, which will be discussed later. The rationale on which this covert, total participative role is based is that observers can never fully avoid the effect of their presence. They believe that, by revealing their role as researchers, they are not observing what would normally have happened were they not present, and thereby do not collect valid data.

The other two roles, participant-as-observer and observer-as-partici-pant, are similar. The former reflects a more participative role, the latter a more research role. Gold's classifications (which are four points on a continuum with 'complete participant' at one end and 'complete observer' at the other) are ideal types; in practice, these four roles may be more problematic than one might think. For example, although researchers may be overt about their role, how much they reveal can affect the data. Some observers ask permission to observe but do not reveal the exact nature of their study. Nurse researchers may also conceal the fact (or do not volunteer the information) that they are trained nurses. Making others aware that one is a researcher is not enough to remove the charge of 'covert' research.

The nature of participation differs from observer to observer even when a participant-as-observer role is adopted. For example, a trained nurse's participation in this role will differ from that of a non-nurse. Her participation in nursing care and access to information would be different from that of, for example, Millman, a sociologist, who could only 'follow' surgeons around in operating theatres and attend ward rounds and various staff meetings (Millman, 1976). Had she been a surgeon, she would have participated in their conversations in a way which a sociologist could not, and although she may not have carried out operations, the 'surgeon researcher' would have taken part in other activities as well. In being allowed or able to do some tasks, the surgeon researcher would have some experiential understanding of what she observed in a way that Millman could not.

When researchers adopt a non-participative role, their very presence is likely to alter the situation. Luker and Kenrick (1992), in their study of 'clinical decisions of community nurses', explain:

> Although the researcher restricted conversation with patients to social pleasantries and took no part in the nurse–patient dialogues, she was clearly a participant by way of her presence in the same room, which may have exerted an influence on the interactions both from the nurses' and patients' points of view.

Finally, in the same study, it is not always possible or desirable to maintain the same degree of participation in the pursuit of valid data. Samarel (1989) describes how her participation varied as her study of 'caring for the living and the dying' progressed:

> The primary mode of data collection was participant observation with the role of the researcher ranging from observer-as-participant to participant-as-observer... During the early phase of data collection the researcher was present in the hallways, lounges, offices, nurses' station and at staff

meetings... After two months of observation in this manner, the investigator's presence began to be accepted by the staff as natural. The investigator then began to take a more active role (observer-as-participant).

Samarel (1989) went on to explain that, thereafter, she had minimal participation 'in informal patient care conferences in which patients' needs were discussed and nursing care planned'. She also 'assisted the participant nurses with such aspects of patient care as moving, bathing or bed making'.

PARTICIPANT OBSERVATION AND ETHNOGRAPHY

The term 'unstructured observation' is often used interchangeably with that of 'participant observation'. They should not be confused, as it is possible to observe a phenomenon inductively (without predetermined categories) yet refrain from taking part in the action.

Participant observation is the choice method in ethnographic studies. Layder (1993) describes the benefits that sociologists derive from such an approach:

> The method of 'participant observation' allows the closest approximation to a state of affairs wherein the sociologist enters into the everyday world of those being studied so that he or she may describe and analyse this world as accurately as possible. Participant observation represents the ideal form of research strategy because this method requires that the sociologist for all intents and purposes 'becomes' a member of the group being studied.

Davies (1995) explains that 'ethnographic research uses observational skills that people use in their everyday lives' and that 'we constantly make sense of speech, body movement and facial expressions in different social settings'.

To get a glimpse of people's feelings and behaviour, ethnographers not only have to be present where the action is but also, as much as possible, be part of their environment and become an insider. The purpose of participating is to try to see things from the subjects' point of view. According to Millman (1976):

> Every social world has its own rules about what is to be attended, and how. To be a participant or insider means that one is guided by this socially shared 'definition of reality'. Thus, doctors come to see things in ways which are consistent with their particular positions and interests in their world.

The ethnographer can never fully participate in the action in the same way as those she studies. The sociologist cannot do what the doctor does but can be close enough to get an understanding of the world of doctors. In her study of 'life in the backrooms of medicine', Millman (1976) describes how this became possible:

> By spending so much time with individuals and by accompanying them through their entire days for weeks or months at a time I was able to get a feeling for the texture and quality of staff life in the hospital. I was able to observe how the various groups of doctors viewed and gave meaning to the situations which arose, and how they chose to pay attention to some things and not to others.

One of the strengths of the ethnographic approach is that observations and interviews go hand in hand (see RE 40). This allows for a more complete understanding of what is being studied. Thus the ethnographer can ask why people behave the way they do and clarify inconsistencies that arise between what people say and do. Ethnographic interviews take the form of normal conversations, as is the case when a student spends a day 'shadowing' or accompanying a community nurse on her visits. However, formal interviews can also be carried out. An important feature of the ethnographic approach is that participants can ask questions of the researcher. According to Frankenberg (1982), 'it often happens to the field worker that the questions he is asked are more important than the questions he asks'.

One of the problems with ethnography is overidentification of the researcher with the participants in the study. As Millman (1976) explains:

> Learning to be an effective participant-observer generally involves an extensive training and learning process. The observer learns how to enter a 'social world' such as a hospital, how to make his or her way through it (without creating too much havoc) and how to get close enough to the regular inhabitants to understand how they see their world. At the same time the observer learns how to avoid identifying too much with the observed and with their perspectives. It is no wonder that sociologists talk frequently about 'entry' and 'departure' from the 'field', for the borders between participation and observation are continuously crossed.

Frankenberg (1982) describes entry into the field as 'going native'. This can compromise the objectivity of the researcher. The latter can also be affected as a consequence. According to him:

what they (sociologists and anthropologists) all have in common is the experience of having submerged themselves for anything from a year to three or four years in a cultural environment different from their own. What few recognise is that they can never look on society in quite the same way again.

ETHICAL IMPLICATIONS OF OBSERVATION

Research observation, whether overt or covert, is an intrusion into other people's privacy. When informed consent is given, the observer has a duty to keep the confidentiality of the information obtained. Johnson (1992) makes clear the distinction between privacy and confidentiality:

> Privacy would allow the individual nurse, for example, to carry out work without the scrutiny of a researcher, just because people ought to be able to avoid the inconvenience of observation if they so choose. Confidentiality would mean that a person having agreed to be observed, those observations would not be disclosed to others in any identifiable way.

With all the best intention and goodwill, it is not always possible to maintain confidentiality. Mander (1995), drawing from her own research experience, concludes that 'in the course of research, confidentiality carries many benefits for all parties, but may present the researcher with some practical difficulties'. She adds:

> Data, including personal experience seeking access, collected during my recent studies indicate that the implementation of confidentiality is difficult, inconsistent and occasionally falls short of the recommended standard. It is necessary to conclude that in research, the practice of confidentiality does not always equate with that which is preached.

Obtaining informed consent to enter the private world of others does not give the right to researchers to treat the data as they like.

Considerable stress can also be put both on patients and their carers if observations take place over long periods or if they cause interference. Researchers can face the dilemma of intervening, or not, in cases where they observe malpractice or unsafe practices. Other actions may include reporting these incidents. This can lead to the investigation and suspension of the very people who granted access in the first place. Mason and Redeker (1993) point out that 'videotaping may also raise ethical and legal issues in health care delivery settings, where the videotaping or observation may record errors in health care practices'.

Another problem relates to the selection of some and not all patients in the same ward or clinical area. While many would not be affected, others may feel that they are being 'neglected' and that those who are observed are getting all the attention. In one study, 10 out of 21 patients in a ward were observed. If no explanation is given to those who are not observed, it may cause some concern to them or their visiting relatives.

The political implications of observations are many. Johnson (1992) points to the potential 'political and managerial gain from use or misuse of information' from observations. The image of particular institutions can be tarnished if observational data show deficiencies in services. It is likely that managers and others may want to take some actions to remedy the situation, and this may affect some of the individuals who took part in the study. Although researchers should not identify by name the setting where observations are carried out, it is not possible to keep anonymity when a study is carried out in full view of others. According to Johnson (1992) 'in an increasingly market-oriented health care system, providers are more nervous than ever of 'bad' publicity about their services'.

Research data can be used to inform decision-making. Data from observations may therefore be used to alter the very situation which the researcher was granted access to observe. By providing the researcher with information, the working conditions and even the livelihood of those observed could be seriously at risk. Davies (1995), referring to her ethnographic study of 'initial encounters in a midwifery school', relates how some of her informants 'responded with amusement and others with initial consternation to the discovery that their friend and student researcher was "the person who had the power to close us down"': Davies was an officer of the Welsh National Board.

Many people are reluctant to have their working practices observed. Some associate this type of research activity with the infamous 'time and motion' studies carried out to find ways of increasing production and reducing the workforce. Understandably, people may be suspicious of the motives of researchers, many of whom do not show any concern for those they observe once the data are collected and would probably not allow others to observe their own practices.

Covert observation brings with it particular ethical implications. Three main, but not mutually exclusive, reasons are given to support this type of observation. Firstly, some researchers believe that the only way to obtain valid data is not to let participants know they are being observed. In this way, it is possible to observe things 'as they are' normally, unaffected by the observer's presence. Secondly, access to research sites may be denied by gatekeepers for various reasons. For example, the owners of a private nursing home may not want a researcher to 'pry' around. Thirdly, there are those who believe that research is a political act and that the results benefit some people at the expense of others, especially the more deprived groups such as the mentally ill, those with a learning difficulty and the elderly in institutions. Those who carry out covert research may believe that although the rights of some participants are infringed, the findings will benefit a larger number of people in a similar situation to theirs. To some extent, according to this argument, the rights of the few can be sacrificed for the benefit of the collective. Johnson (1992), discussing some of the ethical implications of a study by Field (1989), in which a research student worked as a nursing auxiliary to collect data on dying patients, concludes that 'it is impossible to say whether Field's approach is absolutely right or wrong'. Johnson (1992) suggests that researchersshould 'give a clear account of their moral justification for infringing human freedoms' so that 'their approach can be better understood'.

CRITIQUING OBSERVATIONS

To evaluate data from structured observations, readers need to know exactly what phenomenon was observed and how it was defined. Researchers must also provide adequate information on how the observations were carried out. This includes information relating to how the research tool was constructed and comments on its content validity. If an observation checklist is provided, you can attempt to assess its face validity. Researchers must also explain how intra- and interrater reliability were achieved, and what other steps were taken to ensure the validity and reliability of the instrument.

The context in which the observations are conducted and the strategies designed to reduce the observer effect need to be explained; the sampling of periods to be observed must be justified. For example, is 1 hour's observation every 4 hours appropriate for a study of ward teaching? If the observations take place at 9.00 am, 1.00 pm, 5.00 pm and 9.00 pm, it is likely that the last three sessions may not be appropriate as they could be the times that staff are at lunch, on coffee break and handing over to the next shift, respectively.

The observer is also in a position to explain whether or not difficulties were experienced when observing certain behaviour or events. If this was the case, she must discuss how this may have affected the collection of valid and reliable data. In Day et al.'s (1993) study of handwashing (see RE 40), the researchers acknowledged the difficulty of observing certain behaviours and recommended the use of video cameras. They were also concerned that because 'after washing, the children received a stamp on the back of their hands from a common stamp and stamp pad', this may have affected the results as 'organisms from the stamp and pad were transmitted to each child'. As one of the objectives of this study was 'to compare the incidence of infectious illness', the use of a common stamp and pad would have been a serious limitation of the study.

For unstructured observations, researchers must provide information on the type of observation and their degree of involvement with the participants. The thought processes and the actions of the observer during the observation must be conveyed for readers to have an idea of what happened. Information on how the participants were recruited, the reasons for their selection and a description of the setting must also be provided. Finally, the measures taken to ensure rigour and respect for people's rights (this also applies to structured observations) should be described in detail.

SUMMARY AND CONCLUSION

Observations provide useful information for clinical and research purposes. They are particularly suited to the study of non-verbal behaviour. They are used in qualitative and quantitative studies and in both experimental and non-experimental designs. As a quantitative tool, observation can be structured, predetermined and standardised. Researchers know in advance the data required and use a schedule or checklist constructed prior to the collection of data. Qualitative researchers prefer not to be influenced by prior knowledge and instead allow phenomena to unfold before their eyes. From the data collected, they aim to formulate themes, conceptual models, hypotheses and theories. The degree of researcher participation with the people, and in the setting where the observations take place, varies according to the aims of the study. Each type of observation has its value, limitations and ethical implications. As with other research methods, the challenge to researchers is to find ways to collect useful data without infringing people's rights.

REFERENCES

Adler P A and Adler P (1994) Observational techniques. In Denzin N K and Lincoln Y S (eds) *Handbook of Qualitative Research*. California: Sage.

Ashworth P (1980) *Care to Communicate*. London: Royal College of Nursing.

Booth C L and Mitchell S K (1988) Observing human behaviour. In Woods N F and Catanzaro M (eds) *Nursing Research: Theory and Practice*. St Louis: C V Mosby.

Carter D (1991) Descriptive research. In Cormack D (ed.) *The Research Process in Nursing.* Oxford: Blackwell Scientific.

Cicchetti, D V (1984) On a model for assessing the security of infantile attachment: issues of observer reliability and validity. *Behaviour and Brain Science*, **7**:149–50.

Cormack D (1976) *Psychiatric Nursing Observed.* London: Royal College of Nursing.

Cormack D F S (1984) *The Research Process in Nursing.* Oxford: Blackwell Scientific.

Davies R M (1995) Introduction to ethnographic research in midwifery. *British Journal of Midwifery*, **3**(4):223–7.

Day R A, St Arnaud S and Monsma M (1993) Effectiveness of a handwashing program. *Clinical Nursing Research*, **2**(1):24–40.

Felce D, Powell L, Lunt B, Jenkins J and Mansell J (1980) Measuring activity of old people in residential care. *Evaluation Review*, **4**(3):371–87.

Field D (1989) *Nursing the Dying.* Tavistock: Routledge.

Fitzpatrick J M, While A E and Roberts J D (1994) The measurement of nurse performance and its differentiation by course of preparation. *Journal of Advanced Nursing*, **20**:761–8.

Frankenberg R (1982) Participant observers. In Burgess R G (ed.) *Field Research: A Sourcebook and Field Manual.* London: Allen & Unwin.

Fuller B F and Conner D A (1995) The effect of pain on infant behaviors. *Clinical Nursing Research*, **4**(3):253–73.

Gold R L (1958) Roles in sociological field observations. *Social Forces*, **36**:217–23.

Gould D and Ream E (1994) Nurses' views of infection control: an interview study. *Journal of Advanced Nursing*, **19**:1121–31.

Hallberg I R, Holst G, Nordmark A and Edberg A (1995) Cooperation during morning care between nurses and severely demented institutionalized patients. *Clinical Nursing Research*, **4**(1):78–104.

Hewison A (1995) Nurses' power in interactions with patients. *Journal of Advanced Nursing*, **21**:75–82.

Hunt S C and Symonds A (1995) *The Social Meaning of Midwifery.* Basingstoke: Macmillan.

Johnson M (1992) A silent conspiracy?: some ethical issues of participant observation in nursing research. *International Journal of Nursing Studies*, **29**(2):213–23.

Kerlinger F N (1977) *Foundations of Behavioural Research*, 2nd edn. New York: Holt, Rinehart & Winston.

Kirk J and Miller M L (1986) *Reliability and Validity in Qualitative Research.* California: Sage.

Layder D (1993) *New Strategies in Social Research.* Cambridge: Polity Press.

Lincoln Y S and Guba E G (1985) *Naturalistic Inquiry.* Newbury Park, CA: Sage.

Lobo M L (1992) Observation: a valuable data collection strategy for research with children. *Journal of Paediatric Nursing*, **7**(5):320–8.

Lowe T (1992) Characteristics of effective nursing interventions in the management of challenging behaviour. *Journal of Advanced Nursing*, **17**:1226–32.

Luker K A and Kenrick M (1992) An exploratory study of the sources of influence on the clinical decisions of community nurses. *Journal of Advanced Nursing*, **17**:457–66.

Macdonald A J D, Craig T K J and Warner L A R (1985) The development of a short observation method for the study of the activity and contacts of old people in residential settings. *Psychological Medicine*, **15**:167–72.

Mander R (1995) Practising and preaching: confidentiality, anonymity and the researcher. *British Journal of Midwifery*, **3**(5):289–95.

Mason D J and Redeker N (1993) Measurement of activity. *Nursing Research*, **42**(2):87–92.

Millman M (1976) *The Unkindest Cut. Life in the Backrooms of Medicine*. New York: Morrow Quill.

Nyström A E M and Segesten K M (1994) On sources of powerlessness in nursing home life. *Journal of Advanced Nursing*, **19**:124–33.

Oliver S and Redfern S J (1991) Interpersonal communication between nurses and elderly patients: refinement of an observation schedule. *Journal of Advanced Nursing*, **16**:30–8.

Peplau H E (1988) *Interpersonal Relations in Nursing*, 2nd edn. London: Macmillan.

Polit D F and Hungler B P (1995) *Nursing Research: Principles and Methods*, 5th edn. Philadelphia: J B Lippincott.

Porter L, Redfern S, Wilson-Barnett J and Lemay A (1986) The development of an observation schedule for measuring nurse–patient touch, using an ergonomic approach. *International Journal of Nursing Studies*, **23**(1):11–20.

Roethlisberger F J and Dickson W J (1939) *Management and the Worker*. Cambridge: Harvard University Press.

Rose-Grippa K (1979) Nurse communicator. In Bower F L and Bevis E O *Fundamentals of Nursing Practice: Concepts, Roles and Functions*. St Louis: C V Mosby.

Salmon P (1993) Interactions of nurses with elderly patients: relationship to nurses' attitudes and to formal activity periods. *Journal of Advanced Nursing*, **18**:14–19.

Samarel N (1989) Caring for the living and dying: a study of role transition. *International Journal of Nursing Studies*, **26**(4):313–26.

Spradley J (1980) *Participant Observation*. New York: Holt, Rinehart & Winston.

Waltz C F, Strickland O L and Lenz E R (1991) *Measurement in Nursing Research*, 2nd edn. Philadelphia: F A Davis.

Woodgate R and Kristjanson L J (1996) A young child's pain: how parents and nurses 'take care'. *International Journal of Nursing Studies*, **33**(3):271–84.

14 MAKING SENSE OF DATA

The essence of life is statistical improbability on a colossal scale. (Dawkins, 1988.)

INTRODUCTION

Collecting data is a crucial part of the research process, but data in themselves do not answer research questions or support or reject hypotheses. Researchers have to make sense of them before presenting them to readers in ways that they, in turn, can understand. In this chapter, some of the common methods of data analysis and presentation in quantitative and qualitative studies are examined. A brief outline of some of the descriptive and inferential statistics in quantitative analysis is given. Finally, some of the ways in which researchers make sense of, and report, qualitative data are described.

WHAT DOES MAKING SENSE OF DATA MEAN?

In Chapter 2, it was explained that data means all the information collected during the process of research for the purpose of answering questions, testing hypotheses or exploring a phenomenon. In the course of a study, a large mass of data are collected. All the individual bits of information from questionnaires, interviews or observations are known as 'raw' or 'crude' data. Like vegetables or meat, they have to be cleaned and processed before they can be appreciated. In themselves, crude data do not immediately make sense. The answers to research questions do not 'jump out' of the pile of questionnaires; they have to be 'teased out' or analysed, a process called data analysis.

The analysis of data in quantitative studies tends to take place after all the data have been collected. However, it is not an after-thought but an integrated part of the research design. The level of research (descriptive, correlational or experimental), the research questions, objectives or hypotheses and the type of data collected determine which type of analysis is required. Those who have left decisions about data analysis to the end phase of a research project have learnt that this can be a serious mistake.

In qualitative research, data analysis begins during the data collection phase. The researcher processes the information, looks for patterns during the interview or observation and selects themes to pursue. Data analysis continues between interviews and after all the data are collected. In the first part of this chapter, we will focus mainly on data analysis in quantitative studies.

Quantitative Data Analysis

In Chapter 2, it was explained that the purpose of quantitative research is to measure phenomena. Some of these can be measured more accurately and easily than others. For example, we can measure respondents'weight with more precision than we can measure their satisfaction with nursing care. For measurement to take place, there must be numbers. Some measures are already in the form of numbers. For example, weight is expressed in grams, height in centimetres and quality of life in the score obtained on a quality of life scale. Others have to be converted into numbers if they are to be analysed quantitatively. For example, if health visitors are asked to rate the degree of importance of research to their practice according to whether it was 'high', 'moderate' or 'low', these categories would be allocated numbers to reflect their order of importance.

Quantitative analysis can only be carried out with numbers, but numbers in themselves have no intrinsic worth: they have to be given meaning by those using them. For example, number 1 can mean first or it can be the lowest value on a scale of 1 to 10. To make sense of numbers, they are given a value, usually according to a scale. For example, when respondents are asked to rate in order of frequency their sources of health information on a scale of 1 to 10, the researcher must specify whether 1 is the highest or the lowest frequency.

Levels of measurement

To measure one needs a scale. As explained earlier, not all phenomena are readily amenable to measurement, nor can they all be measured with the same degree of precision. The scales devised to measure them also differ in their degree of precision. Mathematicians have classified scales into a hierarchy of four levels. The lowest is nominal, followed by the ordinal, interval and ratio.

Nominal scale

Some of the variables with which quantitative researchers deal cannot in themselves be measured, although some aspects of them can. For example, men cannot be measured against women, although their weight and height can be measured and compared. In the same way, when a researcher asks respondents to state their professional qualifications, she cannot measure and compare adult nursing with mental health nursing; for example, it would be arbitrary and controversial to assign more value to one qualification than to the other. However, these variables (gender or qualifications) are given a number for the purpose of quantitative analysis. When researchers code their questionnaires for manual or computer analysis, they may assign numbers as follows.

Adult nursing	1
Mental health nursing	2
Care of people with a learning difficulty	3
Children's nursing	4

While the scale is 1 to 4, the numbers in this case have no value: 4 does not mean twice as good or as many as 2. It is simply a way of labelling or coding the variable 'qualification'. This type of scale is known as 'nominal'. The *Oxford Dictionary* describes 'nominal' as 'existing in name only, not real or actual'. The numbers on a nominal scale are therefore in name only and do not have any real worth or value: they serve only to distinguish one variable from another.

Ordinal scale

Sometimes respondents are asked to state whether or not they are satisfied with the care or treatment they receive, using a scale similar to the one below.

Very satisfied
Satisfied
Neither satisfied nor dissatisfied
Dissatisfied
Very dissatisfied

The ranking of these categories from 'very satisfied' to 'very dissatisfied' implies a hierarchy or ordering of satisfaction. In coding responses from this type of question, the researcher may allocate numbers as follows.

Very satisfied	5
Satisfied	4
Neither satisfied nor dissatisfied	3
Dissatisfied	2
Very dissatisfied	1

While those allocated number 5 have a higher satisfaction than those with a 4, there is no equal distance implied between the numbers. Those who are satisfied (4) are not twice as satisfied as those who are dissatisfied (2), only more satisfied. The ordinal scale is different from a nominal scale in that the numbers signify the order or hierarchy of these variables. The higher numbers indicate that the respondents have more of the property (in this case, satisfaction) than do the lower numbers, but the scale cannot specify by how much.

Interval scale

An interval scale is a more precise ordinal scale. In it, the distances between the numbers on the scale are known. A thermometer is an example of an interval scale; the degrees are numbered in such a way that the distance between 5 degrees and 10 degrees is the same as between 75 degrees and 80 degrees.

Ratio scale

A ratio scale is an interval scale with an absolute zero. In the above example, the centigrade or farenheit thermometers have no absolute zero, since there are degrees below zero. Zero degrees centigrade does not mean 'nil' temperature. Twenty degrees is warmer than 10 degrees, but it does not mean that it is twice as warm: it means that it is 10 degrees warmer. Rulers and weighing scales, on the other hand, have an absolute zero. A zero on a ruler means no length and 20 centimetres is twice as long as 10 centimetres. Therefore, the numbers on a ratio scale tell us not only the amount which they differ (i.e. by 10 degrees) but also by how many times (twice as long or four times as heavy).

The distinction between these four levels is usually made because there is a view that 'the level of measurement specifies the type of statistical operations that can be properly used' (Waltz *et al.*, 1991). Others believe that the choice of statistical techniques should not depend on levels of measurement but 'on the nature of the research question addressed' (Waltz *et al.*, 1991). We will pursue this theme later in this chapter.

To sum up, the purpose of quantitative research is to measure, and measurements are carried out by scales consisting of numbers. There are different levels of measurement and different levels of scale. The meaning of the numbers differs from scale to scale: numbers can be used as labels, as indicating order or rank, or can have values.

STATISTICAL LEVELS

How data are analysed and presented depends on the type of question which researchers ask. In Chapter 8, three levels of quantitative research were identified – descriptive, correlational and experimental. The types of question that can be asked depend on these levels.

There are two types of descriptive question that are usually asked. The first refers to the sample, especially its demographic characteristics (for example, how many respondents are there in the sample?, what is their age and gender distribution?). The second type refers to their responses (for example, how many respondents indicated a preference for primary nursing rather than team nursing?, what were the scores of respondents on the 'assessment of pain scale'?).

At the correlational level, researchers are mainly interested in finding answers to two types of question: whether there is a relationship between variables (for example between educational background and compliance with treatment) and whether there are differences between groups (for example, is there a difference between male and female nurses' attitudes to nursing research?).

At the experimental level, the main question asked is whether changes in one or more independent variables actually cause changes in one or more dependent variables (for example, does an educational programme cause an increase in patients' knowledge of diabetes?).

Descriptive statistical analysis is carried out to answer descriptive questions, while correlational and causal relationships are explored by the use of *inferential* statistics.

DESCRIPTIVE STATISTICS

Statistics has a language and logic of its own. If you were asked to describe a car to someone who has not seen it, you can convey a picture of it by referring to its colour, size, make, engine capacity, age and number of doors. These main features are essential to adequately describe the car. Similarly, when researchers describe data, they normally report the main features, which can give an idea of what the data consist of without the need to see the crude data.

To describe quantitative data, researchers use terminologies for which there are agreed meanings. Some layman's terms, such as 'average' or 'majority', are vague and may not have the same meaning for everyone. Statisticians have not only devised terms that describe the essential features of data, but also explained precisely what they mean. The three main features that researchers use to describe and summarise data are:

- frequency
- central tendency
- dispersion.

Frequency

The most basic analysis of quantitative data involves counting the number of times a variable appears in the data. Samples are described in terms of frequency as, for example, in a study of 'midwives' attitudes to fetal monitoring' by Dover and Gauge (1995), in which they reported:

> The greater proportion of midwives (73%, n = 85) had past delivery suite experience and 51 (43%) were presently allocated to this area. Less than half (36%, n = 42) the midwives either had, or were studying for, some sort of relevant continuing education qualification.

Dover and Gauge reported frequency both in terms of absolute numbers (denoted by the letter 'n') and in percentages. It is sometimes difficult to compare absolute numbers. If 20 out of 60 male students and 12 out of 48 female students prefer lectures to seminars, the difference between these numbers is not immediately obvious since the sizes of the groups are not similar. When converted to proportions or percentages, they can make more sense. Fink, A (1995) defines a proportion as 'the number of observations or responses with a given characteristic divided by the total number of observations'. In the above example, the proportion of male students who prefer lectures is:

$$\frac{20}{60} \quad \frac{\text{(responses given)}}{\text{(total number of observations)}} \quad = \frac{1}{3}$$

and for female students

$$\frac{12}{48} = \frac{1}{4}$$

Thus by converting these numbers into proportions, it is possible to see that proportionately more male than female students prefer lectures.

Percentages also facilitate comparisons. A percentage is a proportion multiplied by 100 (Fink, A, 1995). In the above example, the percentage of male students is:

$$\frac{1}{3} \times 100 = 33.3\%$$

Frequencies are commonly reported in the form of tables, bar charts and pie charts. An example of data reported in tabular form (Table 14.1) comes from a study by Sutton *et al.* (1994), entitled 'Incidence and documentation of patient accidents in hospital'.

Table 14.1 Comparison of patients' and nurses' descriptions of reported accident causes. (Reproduced by kind permission of *Nursing Times*.)

Accident causes	Patient responses		Nurse responses	
	No.	%	No.	%
1 Loss of balance, unsteady	21	10.1	36	17.2
2 No assistance	0	0.0	25	12.0
3 Confusion	2	1.0	3	1.4
4 Slip, trip	15	7.2	13	6.3
5 Faint, fit, dizziness	21	10.1	21	10.1
6 Contrary activity	1	0.5	8	3.8
7 Condition of footwear	5	2.4	5	2.4
8 Treatment, medication	2	1.0	2	1.0
9 Other patient factors	40	19.1	23	11.1
10 Condition of floor	13	6.3	4	1.9
11 Faulty equipment	5	2.4	7	3.4
12 Staff factors	6	2.9	4	1.9
13 Other environmental factors	14	6.7	7	3.4
14 Miscellaneous	0	0.0	2	1.0
15 Multiple	11	5.3	9	4.3
16 Unknown	52	25.0	39	18.8
	208	100.0	208	100.0

In this table, the authors give a frequency distribution of responses from patients and staff in absolute numbers and in percentages.

Tables facilitate the presentation of large amounts of data in a concise way. To report the data from the above table in the text would require more than a number of sentences, which would have to be read a number of times to be fully comprehensible and digestible. A quick glance at the table not only gives the frequency of the different responses, but also enables instant comparisons between the two groups.

Diagrammatic presentation of data is designed to attract readers' attention and give a sense of proportion; this is important if the purpose is to compare data. A bar chart is one type of diagram used for this purpose. An example of a bar chart (Figure 14.1) comes from the same study. The bar chart shows the occurrence of accidents for each hour over a 24-hour period. At a glance it is possible to identify the times when the number of accidents is high or low.

The sense of proportion is conveyed graphically by the relative height of the bars. Some bar charts can have multiple bars and can be presented sideways as well.

Pie charts, although less popular and less versatile than bar charts, are also used to convey the sense of proportion in data. Unlike bar charts, the numbers must be converted into proportions or percentages before the pie chart is constructed, although absolute numbers can additionally be included. Oldham (1993) describes the pie chart as a 'circle (360 degrees) which represents 100 percent of the sample' and 'the various parts of the sample are converted into fractions of the 360 degrees'. An example of a pie chart (Figure 14.2) is taken from a study by Willmott (1994) on career opportunities in the nursing service for prisoners. The segments show how qualifications are distributed among the staff.

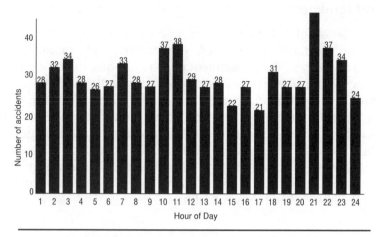

Figure 14.1 Reported patient accidents by hour of day. (Reproduced by kind permission of *Nursing Times*.)

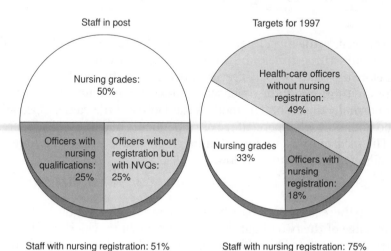

Figure 14.2 Staff in post in the nursing service for prisoners as at March 1994 and targets for staffing, target year 1997. (Reproduced by kind permission of *Nursing Times*.)

Bar charts and pie charts have an advantage over textual reporting in that they can present large amounts of data in a concise and visual form. They must, however be clearly labelled and, where appropriate, properly shaded, as shading often fades in the process of photocopying. Tables, bar charts and pie charts must not be overloaded with data and should require little effort on the part of readers to understand them.

Central tendency

To make sense of information, we use such concepts as 'average', 'typical' or 'common'. We may ask 'how many people, on average, are admitted to the casualty department of the local hospital on a Saturday night', or 'what is the "typical" injury or illness with which they attend the casualty department'. In effect, in statistical terms, we are looking for the *central tendency* rather than for extreme cases. The statistical measures of central tendency are the mode, median and mean. To explain these terms, we will use Example A. Suppose 10 patients on a medical ward were administered a 'satisfaction with nursing care scale' and the scores (from 0 to a possible 100) for each patient (represented here by the letters A to J) were as follows.

Example A

A	B	C	D	E	F	G	H	I	J
50	40	60	50	70	40	20	50	90	60

The *mode* is the most frequent value. In the above example, the value '50' occurs three times and no other value occurs as many times. Therefore the mode is 50. However, knowing that the mode is 50 does not tell us anything about the other scores (if we did not have access to them, as is normally the case). The mode is therefore of little value, especially if we do not know what percentage of respondents had this typical score.

The *median* is the midpoint value when the scores are arranged in ascending order, as shown below.

20   40   40   50   50   50   60   60   70   90

Since there are 10 scores, there is no one single midpoint. Therefore the average of the two middle values is the median, which in this case is 50 (this is calculated by adding the two middle values and dividing the total by 2).

Fifty per cent of the values fall below and 50 per cent above the midpoint. By knowing that the median is 50, we also know that half of the respondents scored below and half above 50.

The *mean* is the arithmetic average of a set of values. It is calculated by adding all the scores and dividing by the number of responses. The total score in the above example is 530 and the number of responses is 10. Therefore the mean is:

$$\frac{530}{10} = 53$$

Unlike the mode and the median, the mean is actually determined by a calculation that takes into account all the other scores. If one score is greatly increased or reduced, it may not affect the mode or median but it will change the mean. For example, if the score of patient 'J' were 90 instead of 60, the mode and the median would remain 50 while the mean would increase to 56.

The limitations of the mode, median and mean can be demonstrated by Example B, showing the satisfaction scores of the same 10 patients.

Example B

A	B	C	D	E	F	G	H	I	J
20	30	20	30	40	70	90	90	90	90

The mode is 90
The median is (40 + 70) / 2 = 55
The mean is 570 / 10 = 57

The mode in this case gives the impression that patients scored very high, yet only 40 per cent did. The median indicates that five patients scored less than 55, but it fails to show that some patients scored very low and others very high. The mean of 57 is deceptive as it suggests that the level of satisfaction of these 10 patients is medium (57), yet as the crude scores show, none of them had medium level satisfaction. What these measures of central tendency do *not* tell us is how the scores vary. In Example A, the scores bunched around 50 (with only two extreme scores – 20 and 90) and the mean was 53. In Example B, there were four very low and four very high scores, and the mean was 57. We may conclude that the patients in Example B were more satisfied with the care they received (mean 57) than the patients in Example A (mean 53), yet only one patient scored below 40 in Example A, while four patients in Example B did.

Dispersion

Central tendency measures are, therefore, not enough to make sense of the data. We need to know the variance of the scores (i.e. how they vary). The three measures which can describe variance are:

- range
- interquartile range
- standard deviation.

The range is the easiest to report as it comprises the lowest and the highest values. In Example B, the range is between 20 (the lowest) and 90 (the highest). It is also sometimes expressed as the difference between these two scores. The range is also least helpful in explaining the distribution of spread of the scores, as the lowest and the highest scores may be extreme.

The interquartile range gives a better description of variance in the data. If you recall that the median is the value or score below which 50 per cent of the values fall, this can be called the *semiquartile* range. Two other ranges, the lower quartile and the upper quartile, can also be calculated in the same way as the median. To understand what the lower and upper quartiles are, we have to know the median. The *lower quartile* is the midpoint between the lowest value and the median, and the *upper quartile* is the midpoint between the highest value and the median. We can refer to Example A to show the lower and upper quartiles. The scores (arranged in ascending order) of the 10 patients were as follows.

G	B	F	A	D		H	C	J	E	I
20	40	40	50	50	▼	50	60	60	70	90

The median is 50. This was obtained by arranging the scores in ascending order and selecting the midpoint score. As the number of values is even (10), there are two midpoint scores: 50 and 50. The median lies between them, as shown above.

The lower quartile is calculated by finding the midpoint of the scores *below* the median. There are five scores and the midpoint is 40. Similarly, the upper quartile is the midpoint of the five scores *above* the median, in this case 60.

Having obtained the range, median, lower quartile and upper quartile, we can have a better sense of the data. We know, in the above example:

- the lowest score is 20;
- the highest score is 90;
- 50 per cent of the scores lie below 50;

- 25 per cent of the scores lie below 40;
- 25 per cent of the scores lie above 60.

The lower, semi- and upper quartiles are also known as the first, second and third quartiles respectively.

The mode, median, mean, range and interquartile range describe, to a limited extent, the distribution of scores in the data. Researchers resort to the *standard deviation* (SD) when they want to convey the distribution of the scores, more specifically how they vary (or deviate) from the mean. The SD is a 'kind of average deviation of the observations from their mean' (Moore, 1985).

If the scores are homogenous, there is little or no deviation from the mean and therefore the SD is zero or close to zero. The larger the SD, the more the scores deviate from the mean. This deviation from the mean can be positive or negative. If the mean of 10 scores is 65 and the SD is ± 1.75, this means that the average deviation from 65 is 1.75. The scores are closely bunched around 65. If, on the other hand, the mean is 65 and the SD 30.5, many of the individual scores are far from the mean. Below is an example of how SD is reported, from a study by Williams (1989) on empathy and burn-out in male and female helping professionals:

> The subjects ranged in age from 23 to 80 (M = 37.4, SD = 10.6) and had practiced from 1 to 44 years (M = 12, SD = 9).

This means that years of practice varied more from their mean (M = 12, SD = 9) than age of respondents did from its mean (M = 37.4, SD = 10.6). The SD is, therefore, always reported in conjunction with the mean.

Frequency, central tendency and dispersion are main measures of descriptive statistics. Together, they can convey the main features of data, although the most commonly reported ones are frequency, mean and standard deviation.

Finally, the term 'normal distribution', needs to be explained. In normal distribution, most of the scores cluster around the mean, and the extreme scores are few and are more or less equally distributed above and below the mean. This is illustrated in Figure 14.3 and is referred to as a 'bell-shape' distribution:

A normal distribution has the following characteristics: 34 per cent of all scores fall between the mean and 1 SD on either side of the mean; similarly, 28 per cent of all scores fall between 1 SD and 2 SD from the mean, as in Figure 14.3.

As explained later on, some statistical tests can only be performed if the distribution is normal.

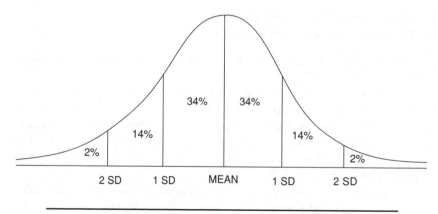

Figure 14.3 A normal distribution curve.

INFERENTIAL STATISTICS

Researchers using quantitative approaches such as surveys and experiments seek to find relationships between variables and, where possible, to establish the exact nature of these relationships, with the aim of making predictions. They also seek to generalise the findings from their samples to equivalent populations. To do so, they resort to inferential statistics.

To find out whether there are relationships between variables, researchers formulate null hypotheses. The null hypothesis is a statement that there is no actual relationship between variables and that any such observed relationship is only a function of chance or sampling fluctuations (Polit and Hungler, 1983). Data are collected to accept or reject the null hypothesis.

Errors are sometimes made in the testing of null hypotheses. A *type I error* happens when a statistically significant relationship is found, in the study sample, between two variables (for example educational attainment and the practice of breast self-examination) when, in fact, no such relationship exists in the population. A *type II error* occurs when no such relationship is found in the sample when, in fact, it exists in the population.

To establish statistical significance, researchers can select from a number of tests, some of which will be described later. The results from these tests will signify whether or not there are relationships between variables. However, there is always a probability that the results were obtained by chance. You have perhaps seen the following:

$p > 0.05$

The letter 'p' is used to denote the probability of a chance occurrence. The figures and decimal points (e.g. 0.05) are the levels set by researchers above which they will accept that the results were obtained by chance. The symbol > denotes greater than and < less than. p > 0.05 means that the researcher will accept the results if they are statistically significant 95 times out of 100.

SELECTING A TEST

The choice of statistical tests depends, among others, on sample size and sampling method (i.e. random or not), on the level of measurement (nominal, ordinal, etc.) and on whether the variables to be measured in the sample are normally distributed in the population. For parametric tests, the variable has to be normally distributed, while for non-parametric tests no such assumption is made. Munro *et al.* (1986) explain:

> The main difference between these two classes of techniques is the assumptions about the population data that must be made before the parametric tests can be applied. For t-tests and analysis of variance (ANOVA), for example, it is assumed that the variable under study is normally distributed in the population and that the variance is the same at different levels of the variable. The nonparametric techniques have relatively few assumptions that must be met before they can be used.

In this section, we will take a brief look at some of the commonly used tests in nursing research, namely Pearson product moment correlation coefficient, t-test and chi-square test.

The *Pearson product moment correlation coefficient* is the 'most usual method by which the relationship between two variables is quantified' (Munro *et al.*, 1986) and it relates to parametric data. Correlation coefficients (represented by the letter r) can be positive or negative. They vary between +1 (a perfect positive relationship) and −1 (a perfect negative or inverse relationship). There is no consensus, however, on how large a correlation should be for a relationship to be established. This depends mainly on the size of the samples.

Fink, A (1995) suggests the following interpretation:

> 0 to +.25 (or −.25) = little or no relationship
> +.26 to +.50 (or −.26 to −.50) = fair degree of relationship
> +.51 to +.75 (or −.51 to −.75) = moderate to good relationship
> over +.75 (or −.75) = very good to excellent relationship

In a study on 'the influence of family resources and family demands on the strains and well-being of care giving families', Fink, S V (1995) used the Pearson product moment correlation 'to examine the relationships between the study variables and the length of time the family had provided assistance and family socio-economic status' and reported that:

> Length of time was significantly and negatively related to family well-being, $r = -.23$, $p < 0.05$, but was not related to any of the independent variables. Socioeconomic status was significantly related to internal family system resources, $r = .25$, $p < .05$, and family well-being, $r = .40$, $p < .01$.

The *t-test* is a parametric test to compare the means of two samples, for example the mean knowledge scores of one group of patients who were given verbal information about their illness and of another group who were given written information. According to DePoy and Gitlin (1994), the 't-test must be calculated with interval level data and should be selected only if the researcher believes that the assumptions for the use of parametric statistics have not been violated'. As they explain:

> The t-test yields a t value that is reported as $t = x$, $p = 0.05$ where x is the calculated t value and p is the level of significance set by the researcher. There are several variations of the t-test.

An example of the use of a t-test is from an experimental study by Koh and Thomas (1994), in which they compared the degree of satisfaction with nursing care among patients receiving postoperative pain relief via patient-controlled analgesia (PCA) with that of those receiving traditional intramuscular injection (IMI) regimes. They reported:

> The mean quality index was 76.12% for the experimental ward and 68.92% for the control ward which indicated a higher perceived quality care for the experimental ward using PCA. t-Test revealed that this was statistically significantly different ($t = 2.06$, df $= 77$, $P < 0.05$).

To find whether the t value (2.06) is statistically significant, we have to use a table known as distribution of t-probabilities. The table consists of p values (probability value) and the df (degrees of freedom) values. It is beyond the scope of this book to explain what degrees of freedom are. What is important to know is how they are calculated and how to use them in reading the t-value. The df in a t-test are calculated by subtracting 1 from the number of subjects in each group. In the above study by Koh and Thomas (1994), there were 49 patients in the experimental ward and 30 in the control ward. As there are 2 groups, the df is 77 (49+30−2). The p value was set by the researchers at 0.05 level. With a df of 77 at $p > 0.05$, the corresponding value in the table is approximately 2.660. As this is larger than the t-value (2.06), it led Koh and Thomas (1994) to state that the results were statistically significant.

The *chi-square test* (χ^2) can be used when comparing proportions and is normally used with non-parametric data. For example, 100 smokers attend antismoking sessions and only 60 stopped smoking after a month, while in another group of 80 smokers, who received no sessions, 20 stopped smoking. The chi-square test can be used to find whether the differences between these proportions (60 out of 100 and 20 out of 80) are statistically significant. To understand how to read a chi-square result, the figures from the above example must first be placed in a table, as below.

	Stopped smoking	Did not stop	Total
Number attending a smoking session	60	40	100
Number of those not attending session	20	60	80
Total	80	100	180

The df are calculated by subtracting 1 from the number of rows and multiplying this by the number of columns minus 1. This can be expressed as

$$(R - 1) \times (C - 1)$$

where R = rows and C = columns.

In the above examples, there are two columns and two rows. Therefore df is $(2 - 1) \times (2 - 1) = 1$. Once the df value and the p value (a level set by the researcher) are known, it is possible to read the distribution of χ^2 Probability Table). The corresponding value in the table must exceed the 2 value if the results are to be statistically significant.

It is beyond the scope of this book to explain how these tests are carried out or to discuss other tests. If you are in doubt about statistical data, you should consult a statistics text or a statistician. Two useful references are Hicks (1990), *Research and Statistics – A Practical Introduction to Nurses,* and Reid (1993), *Health Care Research by Degrees.*

QUALITATIVE DATA ANALYSIS

Quantitative research is described as objective partly because it is believed that the research process, including data analysis, can be replicated. If the crude data are made available to other researchers, it is possible for them to carry out the same statistical tests and obtain the same results. It is also possible to carry out other tests or challenge the original tests. Qualitative data analysis is to some extent subjective, although researchers have developed strategies to allow others to follow and validate their actions.

In quantitative research, data analysis starts once all the data are collected. In qualitative research, data analysis takes place during data collection and thereafter. The researcher processes the data as they are received and makes judgements relating to aspects of the phenomenon to pursue. For example, as she carries out more and more interviews, she has to remember some of what was said in previous interviews. She analyses and synthesises the information while talking to respondents.

The analysis of data 'as they come in' during interviews is a subjective process. No two researchers can assimilate and react to the incoming information in the same way. To reduce the subjective effect, an audit trail is sometimes left for others to follow the thinking processes and the actions of the researcher (Lincoln and Guba, 1985). Morse and Field (1996) explain that the audit trail is useful for understanding the researcher's 'decisions, choices and insights', especially when 'the focus of interview questions changes as themes or concepts begin to emerge from the data'. According to them, 'it is important to be able to report at what time and for what reason the changes occurred'.

Apart from processing information during interviews and observations, written notes are kept and/or interviews audio-taped. The fieldnotes and the verbatim transcriptions of tapes represent the crude data in qualitative studies. They need to be made sense of, although in most cases qualitative researchers have a feel for what eventually emerges even before the transcripts are read.

Data analysis of fieldnotes

Morse and Field (1996) identify four processes in the analysis of qualitative data. These are comprehending, synthesising (decontextualising), theorising and reconceptualising. As they explain:

> These processes occur more or less sequentially, for the researcher must reach a reasonable level of comprehension before being able to synthesize (i.e. to make generalized statements about the participants), and until the researcher is able to synthesize, theorizing is not possible. Recontextualisation cannot occur until the concepts or models in the investigation are fully developed.

Before engaging in these processes, data have to be transcribed word for word and read many times. Computer packages are now available to help in identifying words or phrases that occur frequently, and in coding them (see Tesch, 1990). Themes, patterns and concepts can become apparent.

The researcher's task is to make sense of them, to find out how they are related and, if possible, to formulate propositions, models or theories.

In grounded theory, there are two analytic procedures to the coding process (Strauss and Corbin, 1990). As they explain:

> The first pertains to the *making of comparisons*, the other to the *asking of questions*. In fact, grounded theory is often referred to in the literature as 'the constant comparative method of analysis' (Glaser and Strauss, 1967, pp. 101–16). These two procedures help to give the concepts in grounded theory their precision and specificity.

Phenomenological methods of data analysis have also been developed by, among others, VanKaam (1966), Colaizzi (1978) and Giorgi (1985). Each of these authors describes in detail the steps that can be taken to read, analyse and validate data. For example Colaizzi's procedural steps are as follows (Ryan, 1996):

1. All interviews are transcribed *verbatim* and read in order to get a feel for them.
2. Significant statements and phrases that pertain to the experience under investigation are extracted.
3. Meanings are formulated from these significant statements.
4. Significant statements are organised into clusters of themes.
5. The themes are used to provide a full description of the experience.
6. Researcher returns the description to its original source for confirmation of validity.

Whether the researcher follows closely the grounded theory or a phenomenological method, the task of analysing qualitative data is arduous and intellectually demanding. It is a process of discovery as the researcher is most likely to tread on ground not before attempted by others.

Hallgren *et al.* (1995) describe below how they began to make sense of the data they collected during their study of women's perceptions of childbirth:

> After verbatim transcription, each interview was read by the first author in order to acquire a sense of the whole text and to obtain ideas for further analysis. The impressions and ideas were written down. Nine of the interviews were read by the first three authors and impressions and ideas were discussed until consensus was reached. The first author then continued the analysis. Meaning units connected to birth, to childbirth education and to other ways of preparation were identified in each interview, and themes were formulated. With the insight from each theme in each interview, the

women's perceptions of childbirth and childbirth education were interpreted. From the interpretations of the first interview with each woman, four perceptions of childbirth were formulated and the women's interviews were sorted into these four groups. Then the development of the perceptions of childbirth and childbirth education were described for the women in each group. The second author independently analysed six of the 33 interviews, randomly selected. After discussion, agreement was reached about these interviews and the sorting of all interviews into the four groups as well as of the development of the perceptions.

The laborious process of analysing qualitative data is captured in this description by Hogston (1995), in his study on the quality of nursing care:

1. After each interview, the transcript was manually transcribed by the researcher onto a personal computer, providing an opportunity for identifying themes as the tape was transcribed.
2. Following transcription, a print-out was obtained and the tape replayed making notes onto the transcript. Notes included comments about tone of voice, recurrent themes and the researcher's own initial thoughts and feelings about the nature and significance of the data.
3. The transcripts were re-read and codes assigned to recurrent themes. This is known as 'open coding', whereby the data are examined word by word and line by line (Stern, 1980), and codes were freely generated, often reflecting the words of the respondents themselves. For example, the code 'skill mix' was given to the response:

    (quality is all about) staffing levels, skill mix of staff that are on. (R2)

4. The global codes were then reviewed and sorted into broader codes. This is what Miles and Huberman (1984) refer to as data reduction, whereby the data are condensed, focused and simplified. For example, the code 'patient information' was initially given to the response:

    The patient is happy with the knowledge that they have been given about their condition that has brought them into hospital. (R1)

    This was collapsed into the substantive code of 'patient satisfaction' as it was congruent with similar comments about being happy and satisfied with the care given:

    I think that if the nurse feels happy with the care and the patient does then I think that's good care, it's not always possible I don't think to achieve the highest, but if you are happy and the patient is happy then that is the best good patient care that there is. (R14)

5. Once the data were coded, they were re-examined to look for similarities which would allow the global codes to be collapsed into substantive codes and grouped together into categories. Categories are groups of data which cluster together (Stern, 1980). The coded data were then cut up and pasted onto cards which reflected the substantive codes and categories.

6. Finally, the informant's pathway through the transcript was traced by colour coding the categories within the transcript. In grounded theory this relates to the 'fit' of categories, whereby all instances of the phenomena under question relate to the developing category (Glaser and Strauss, 1967) and the 'fractured' data come together as coherent whole (Glaser, 1978). By working with the data and revisiting the original transcripts, the meaning and accuracy of the categories became clearer.

Researchers are sometimes so immersed in their studies that they may not be totally objective in their analysis. To ensure rigour, they often enlist the help of others to read their transcripts and fieldnotes. Woodgate and Kristjanson (1996) explain how, in their study of children's pain, they left an audit trail and sought the help of others:

The use of analytic memos representing the written form of the researcher's abstract thoughts about the data, codes, and categories was ongoing. When no new information emerged data collection and analysis were considered complete. All categories were independently reviewed by three researchers with expertise in qualitative analysis to confirm the organization and relationships of the derived properties and categories. For a categorization to be validated all reviewers were required to agree. Analysis of themes that did not meet this criterion were re-examined and re-classified until consensus was achieved.

Qualitative data are sometimes reported in quantitative forms, however, the purpose of qualitative research is to gain insight into phenomena rather than to collect data on frequency or prevalence. While the findings of quantitative studies are reported in, among others, descriptive and inferential statistical forms, qualitative findings are reported textually, supported by relevant quotes from respondents. This is in keeping with the belief in qualitative research in the importance of describing the experience of people from their own points of view.

SUMMARY AND CONCLUSION

In this chapter, the purpose and process of quantitative and qualitative data analysis were described. In quantitative studies, descriptive and inferential statistics help researchers and readers to make sense of the data. The main measures in descriptive statistics are frequency, central tendency and dispersion. Inferential statistics help researchers to determine whether relationships exist between variables and whether there are differences between groups.

In qualitative research, the process of data analysis is laborious and ongoing. It starts during data collection and continues after the field notes and/or tapes have been transcribed. Grounded theory and phenomenology provide frameworks that researchers can use to analyse qualitative data. Researchers have also developed ways of allowing others to understand their thinking processes and actions. The purpose of qualitative analysis is ultimately to gain insights into phenomena. The themes, patterns and categories generated can lead to the development of hypotheses and theories.

REFERENCES

Colaizzi P (1978) Psychological research as the phenomenologist views it. In Valle R and Kings M (eds) *Existential Phenomenological Alternative for Psychology*. New York: Oxford University Press.

Dawkins R (1988) *The Blind Watchmaker*. London: Penguin.

DePoy E and Gitlin L N (1994) *Introduction to Research*. St Louis: C V Mosby.

Dover S L and Gauge S M (1995) Fetal monitoring – midwifery attitudes. *Midwifery*, **11**:18–27.

Fink A (1995) *How to Analyse Survey Data*. California: Sage.

Fink S V (1995) The influence of family resources and family demands on the strains and well-being of care giving families. *Nursing Research*, **44**(3):139–46.

Giorgi A (1985) *Phenomenology and Psychological Research*. Pittsburg: Duquesne University Press.

Glaser B G (1978) *Theoretical Sensitivity: Advances in the Methodology of Grounded Theory*. Mill Valley, CA: Sociology Press.

Glaser B G and Strauss A L (1967) *The Discovery of Grounded Theory. Strategies for Qualitative Research*. Chicago: Aldine.

Hallgren A, Kihlgren M, Norberg A and Forslin L (1995) Women's perceptions of childbirth and childbirth education before and after education and birth. *Midwifery*, **11**:130–7.

Hicks C M (1990) *Research and Statistics: A Practical Introduction for Nurses*. London: Prentice Hall.

Hogston R (1995) Quality nursing care: a qualitative enquiry. *Journal of Advanced Nursing*, **21**:116–24.

Koh P and Thomas V J (1994) Patient-controlled analgesia (PCA): does times saved by PCA improve patient satisfaction with nursing care? *Journal of Advanced Nursing*, **20**:61–70.

Lincoln Y S and Guba E G (1985) *Naturalistic Inquiry*. California: Sage.

Miles M B and Huberman A M (1984) *Qualitative Data Analysis: A Sourcebook of New Methods*. London: Sage.

Moore D S (1985) *Statistics: Concepts and Controversies*, 2nd edn. New York: W H Freedman.

Morse J M and Field P A (1996) *Nursing Research: The Application of Qualitative Approaches*, 2nd edn. London: Chapman & Hall.

Munro B H, Visintainer M A and Page E B (1986) *Statistical Methods for Health Care Research*. Philadelphia: J B Lippincott.

Oldham J (1993) Statistical tests. Part 1: Descriptive statistics. *Nursing Standard*, **7**(43):30–5.

Polit D F and Hungler B P (1983) *Nursing Research: Principles and Practice*, 2nd edn. Philadelphia: J B Lippincott.

Reid N (1993) *Health Care Research by Degrees*. London: Blackwell Scientific.

Ryan S (1996) Living with rheumatoid arthritis: a phenomenological exploration. *Nursing Standard*, **10**(41):45–8.

Stern P N (1980) Grounded theory methodology: its uses and processes. *Image*, **12**(1):20–33.

Strauss A and Corbin J (1990) *Basics of Qualitative Research: Grounded Theory Procedures and Techniques*. California: Sage.

Sutton J, Standen P and Wallace A (1994) Incidence and documentation of patient accidents in hospital. *Nursing Times* **90**(33):29–35.

Tesch R (1990) *Qualitative Research: Analysis Types and Software Tools*. New York: Falmer Press.

VanKaam A (1966) *Existential Foundations of Psychology*. Pittsburg: Duquesne University Press.

Williams C A (1989) Empathy and burnout in male and female helping professions. *Research in Nursing and Health*, **12**:169–78.

Willmott Y (1994) Career opportunities in the nursing service for prisoners. *Nursing Times*, **90**(24):29–30.

Woodgate R and Kristjanson L J (1996) A young child's pain: how parents and nurses 'take care'. *International Journal of Nursing Studies*, **33**(3):271–84.

Waltz C F, Strickland O L and Lenz E R (1991) *Measurement in Nursing Research*, 2nd edn. Philadelphia: F A Davis.

15 EVALUATING RESEARCH STUDIES

INTRODUCTION

The previous chapters have described, explained and discussed the basic concepts and the research process in qualitative and quantitative research. Issues relating to the validity and reliability of methods and findings have been extensively covered. Where appropriate, suggestions have been made on how to critique particular aspects of research studies.

This chapter provides a structure for the evaluation of research studies and a summary of the relevant questions to ask. Sources of bias and some of the common practices in the reporting of research are identified. In addition, the role of researchers in facilitating evaluation will be raised.

CRITIQUING SKILLS

The terms 'critique' and 'evaluate' will be used interchangeably here to mean making a value judgement on what is reported. By now, readers should have the necessary knowledge and comprehension to begin to read research studies critically. In particular, they should be able to describe the aim of the research, its methodology and findings. However, description is only the first step towards evaluation. The latter requires a judgement on the part or the reader of the actions and interpretations of the researcher. This can be done mainly by weighing what was done against accepted practice by researchers, although new and unconventional approaches should be considered on their own merit. For example, there is consensus among researchers that if a sample is not randomly selected, the findings cannot be generalised to the target population. Therefore, if a researcher states that her findings can be generalised when the sample is one of convenience, the reader can question the validity of this claim. Although individual readers may critique a study differently, the criteria they use during their evaluation must be objective. One cannot state that a literature review is inappropriate or inadequate without giving reasons to explain why. The task of critiquing is a challenging one and can only be acquired through much practice. Church and Lyne (1994) explain that:

> The process of critically appraising research reports takes a long time. It cannot be hurried. It requires intensive, detailed reading and careful

checking of the conclusions against the evidence provided. Full-time researchers often find this to be the most taxing and time-consuming part of their working lives.

Although nurses are expected to implement research findings in their practice, it is unsafe to base their decision on one single study, however good it is. Reviewing studies with a view to using them in practice must also be done by experienced practitioners and researchers. The Cochrane Collaboration and the York Review and Dissemination Centre (see Chapter 1) carry out reviews to facilitate health practitioners in using research findings. The Royal College of Nursing also develops clinical practice guidelines, mainly by reviewing and evaluating existing studies.

To keep an interest in, and be up to date with, research developments in their areas of care, nurses must be able to evaluate research studies. The benefits of research awareness and research-mindedness have been fully discussed in Chapter 1. According to Stevens *et al.* (1993):

> Whatever the reasons for evaluating research, the exercise requires skills and knowledge as well as a questioning and positive attitude to research. One does not become an efficient evaluator overnight. The beginner may find this task quite daunting. Often an evaluation carried by a group of practitioners may provide valuable learning opportunities.

A STRUCTURE FOR EVALUATION

Individuals may approach the evaluation of a study in different ways. Beginners sometimes prefer to be guided through the process. A step-by-step guide is provided here for this purpose. Other frameworks or guidelines that can be used to evaluate research studies include those of Stevens *et al.* (1993) and Hek (1996).

Only a summary of the main questions to ask is included, as relevant chapters already have a section on critiquing; readers are strongly advised to consult these for more details. The following headings (based on the format in which both quantitative and qualitative research are most often reported) provide a structure for the evaluation of research articles:

- Title of article
- Abstract
- Literature review
- Methodology
- Results
- Discussion and interpretation
- Recommendations.

Title of article

The title should draw readers' attention to the precise area of study and make reference to the population from whom data are collected. For example, the title 'An exploratory study of research utilization by nurses in general and surgical wards' (Rodgers, 1994) makes clear the phenomenon being investigated (research utilisation) and the population under study (nurses in general and surgical wards). Too much information in the title can make it long and inelegant. For example, 'Nurses' creativity, tedium and burnout during one year of clinical supervision and implementation of individually planned nursing care: comparisons between a ward for severely demented patients and a similar control ward' (Berg *et al.*, 1994) is very informative, but some of the details could perhaps be confined to the abstract. There is no right or wrong title, only a misleading or confusing one.

Abstract

An abstract is a short summary of a study (the number of words is normally stipulated by the journal). The purpose of an abstract is to give readers enough information for them to decide whether or not the article is of interest to them. The abstract should state briefly the aim of the study, the design, including the method(s), sample(s) and sampling, and the main findings. This information is essential as it describes what the study is about, how it was carried out and what was found. Readers should not ask too much from an abstract as details are provided in the rest of the article.

Literature review

Readers may want to know why the current study is important, what research, if any, has been carried out previously and what the research will contribute. The four functions of a literature review described in Chapter 5 can be used as a framework for evaluation. In particular, the following questions may be asked:

- Is a rationale provided? If so, what is it? How convincing are the reasons? Does the author support it with evidence such as research findings, statistical data and, to a lesser extent, expert opinion?
- Does the author provide a critical overview of similar research carried out?
- Are the relevant concepts and issues dealt with adequately?
- Is there a conceptual framework? How does the author propose to use it?

- Is there reliance on primary or secondary sources? Are the references dated? Is it likely there may be more recent material? Has the author been selective in her review of the literature?

Remember that the author is restricted by word limits, but if the lack of information affects your understanding of the study, this is a good indication that the information should have been provided.

In qualitative studies, researchers may not want to be influenced by previous research. They should, however, give a rationale and make reference to the relevant literature.

The title, abstract and literature review have little bearing on the reliability and validity of the findings. Readers are advised not to spend too much time critiquing them. The methodology of the study determines the quality of the research and, as such, deserves the most attention.

Methodology

The framework suggested in Chapter 3 (philosophical assumptions, methods of data collection and techniques of data analysis) can be used to find out whether the study is qualitative, quantitative or a mixture of the two.

Questions to ask of the methodology include:

- Are the research questions, objectives or hypotheses clearly stated?
- Are the operational definitions adequate? The criteria of clarity, precision, validity, reliability and consensus (see Chapter 7), can be used for this purpose.
- Is the design the most appropriate for the phenomenon under study? If, for example, the researcher uses a cross-sectional design to study the difficulties that mothers face breast-feeding in the first 6 months, is a longitudinal design more appropriate? What are the limitations of a cross-sectional design for this study (see Chapter 8)?
- What are the methods of data collection? Are there any instruments (questionnaires, interviews or observation schedules) used in this study? Are they constructed for the purpose of the current study? Do they have face, content or other forms of validity? How was this achieved? Where do the items in the instruments come from?
- Is the instrument reliable? Was a test–retest or a split-half test, if appropriate, carried out (see Chapter 11)?
- Was the instrument borrowed? What is its established validity and reliability? How extensively has it been used in other similar studies?
- If the borrowed instrument is modified for the purpose of the current study, what are the changes made? How does it affect the validity and reliability of the original instrument? What are the

measures taken to ensure the validity and reliability of the modified instrument?

In qualitative studies, the researcher must explain clearly what she proposes to do. The process of data collection must be described in sufficient detail for readers to assess the degree of control exerted by the interviewer and the extent and nature of the interaction between researchers and respondents. The steps taken to ensure rigour during the data collection phase must be described. Readers may also ask whether an audit trail was left (see Chapter 14).

One important aspect of methodology on which researchers sometimes omit to provide information is the sampling method. The questions to ask are:

- Who was selected? From what population were they selected? What was the precise method of selection? What implications does the sampling method have for the validity, reliability and generalisability of the findings?
- What was the response rate? What implications do the non-responses have for the findings?

Although in qualitative studies, non-probability samples are most frequently used, researchers must also explain their sampling method and give reasons why those in the sample were chosen, as this may have implications for the findings (see Chapter 10).

In addition to the above aspects of methodology, researchers must describe the steps taken to ensure that the rights of individuals are respected. They must also explain how access to the study population was obtained as this may have implications for the data.

Results

The method of data analysis, whether in quantitative or qualitative studies, must be described and justified. Researchers are often selective in their presentation of results. Readers should refer back to the questions or hypotheses set at the start of the study to find out whether they are addressed in the results section. Tables and figures must also make sense.

The way in which some results are presented can be misleading. Stevens et al. (1993) give the following example:

> when an author writes that sixty per cent of respondents state that they drink alcohol because of stress, it must be explained that they were asked to choose from a list of reasons provided by the researcher. By not stating the

format of the question, i.e. whether it was an open or a multiple-choice one it is difficult for the reader to put the responses in context.

Beginners may find it difficult to understand statistical tests and jargon. A good journal referee should query mistakes or inconsistencies in the analysis. If you are in doubt about some of the calculations, you should, if possible, consult someone who knows about statistics. What is more important is for the author to explain what the results mean.

In qualitative research, the measures taken to ensure the objectivity in data analysis and interpretation, such as asking other researchers to read the transcripts or going back to respondents, must be explained.

Discussion and interpretation

Results can be presented on their own or with discussion and interpretation. Whatever the choice of presentation, it is important that results are explained, discussed and interpreted. One of the first tasks of a critical reader is to find out if the research questions, objectives or hypotheses set at the start of the study have been addressed, and if not reasons should be provided. Sometimes researchers only discuss results in which they are interested and/or support their particular views. As much as possible all results, positive or negative, should be discussed. To contribute to the pool of knowledge, results should be compared with findings from other studies and when these are different, possible explanations should be offered.

It is not enough to report that the results are statistically significant; researchers must also explain the clinical significance of the results or identify why the results are not (perhaps on their own) clinically significant. It may be that the results of the study show that, with the new treatment, people are cured of their illness more quickly. However, their degree of discomfort with the new treatment may be greater than with the usual one.

The discussion and interpretation of data often reflect the subjective opinion of researchers. To evaluate this aspect of a study, Stevens et al. (1993) suggest the following questions:

- Can you follow the steps leading to the conclusions?
- Are there any gaps in the development of the arguments?
- How consistent are the arguments?
- Is the author contradicting himself?
- Do the arguments make sense according to your experience?
- Does your experience lead you to see different meanings in the data?
- Basically, do you agree with the data and/or the interpretation of the author?

Recommendations

Readers must first ask whether the recommendations are based on the research findings of the present study. Researchers are often in favour of certain policies or practices and they peddle them in the form of recommendations even when the findings of their studies are not conclusive. The recommendations made must also be practical, feasible and well thought out. In fact, researchers should be expected to discuss the limitations of their recommendations rather than simply state them.

SOURCES OF BIAS

Biases represent the greatest threat to the reliability and validity of data. To ensure rigour, researchers must avoid bias or, if this not possible, account for them. The main sources of bias are:

- respondents
- researchers
- methods of data collection
- the environment
- the phenomenon.

Respondents' motivation, perception, social class affiliation, personal and collective agendas or even communication skills (or their lack), among others, can bias the results. Similarly, researchers' own prejudices, values, beliefs or lack of research skills, and other factors, can affect the collection, analysis and presentation of data. Questionnaires may contain leading or ambiguous questions, and interview and observation schedules may not be valid or reliable. The environment can also influence the findings. Captive populations may yield different data than if they were studied in their own homes. In experimental studies, data contamination can occur when subjects in the control group share information with those in the experimental group, especially when both are on the same ward. Finally, the phenomenon may not reveal itself in its usual form on days when it is studied. For example, if the researcher sets out to observe aggression among patients, it may not necessarily occur in the way it normally does while the researcher is present.

These and other sources of bias are extensively discussed in this book. The few examples given are only a reminder to readers.

OMISSION AND EXAGGERATION

There are two types of omission – deliberate and unintentional. Deliberate omission is an attempt to deceive. Most omissions, however, are not intentional. Some of the common omissions identified in the earlier chapters include sampling methods, the description of interventions in control groups and the precise method of randomisation in RCTs. In qualitative studies, researchers often omit descriptions of the process of data collection as well as the rationale for their method of sampling.

Sometimes researchers are so familiar with their studies that they assume that readers also are. Jargon and specialist terminologies, when not frequently used in the literature, must be avoided or explained. The lack of information about a study may lead readers to make their own assumptions. Stevens *et al.* (1993) point out:

> It is a common mistake on the part of readers to assume what the author means when the meaning is obscure. It is better to keep an open mind than to assume what the meaning is. The assistance of colleagues, fellow students and lecturers may be helpful in clarifying ambiguities.

Researchers are also prone to exaggeration in their reporting. Apart from overplaying the significance of their findings, especially from small-scale studies, they often use terms indicating their position on particular issues. For example, it is not unusual for one researcher to report '45 per cent of the population' as 'almost half the population' and another as 'less than half the population'.

THE ROLE OF RESEARCHERS IN FACILITATING EVALUATION

It is the researchers' responsibility to present data clearly and in sufficient detail for others to understand how the research was carried out. Equally important is the researcher's own reflection on and evaluation of the study and its findings. Unfortunately, some researchers treat their findings as sacred and fail to be critical of them. If researchers were expected to include a section in their papers in which they attempted to falsify their own findings, readers would be better informed. In any case, researchers, as mentioned before, should be required to offer other plausible explanations for their findings. After all, it is they who know the circumstances in which the data were collected and are, therefore, in a position to identify possible sources of bias and error. They are also in possession of the raw data.

While the research enterprise is about asking questions, we must realise we cannot always find answers to them. However, in the process of inquiry, we come to learn more about ourselves and others and about the means by which we study people. We are, therefore, the richer for it. Very often, researchers and readers learn more from the process of research than from the findings.

Journal editors and referees, too, have an important part to play in making sure that articles are written and presented in a form that informs rather than confuses readers. There is perhaps a case for some referees to be given training in evaluating research; some of them are clinical experts but have little research experience.

Finally, there is a lot to learn when reading research studies. The task of evaluation should be approached with an open and inquiring mind. As Parahoo and Reid (1988) conclude:

> Critical reading of research helps to develop a research imagination. With practice, the individual's sense of enquiry will be heightened as his or her disposition to passive acceptance of the written and spoken word diminishes. Healthy scepticism rather than negative, cynical attitudes will transform a fault finding activity into a learning experience which can only lead to the development of research-mindedness.

SUMMARY AND CONCLUSION

In this chapter, a structure for the evaluation of research studies was offered. The main questions to ask when reading research articles were summarised and sources of bias, as have some of the common practices in the reporting of research, were identified. The role of researchers in facilitating evaluation was also emphasised.

This book, as a whole, provides the necessary knowledge and insight to enable nurses and others to read, understand and critique research studies. It is hoped that by putting research in perspective, readers will realise the value, potential and limitations of research in contributing to the advancement of knowledge.

REFERENCES

Berg A, Hansson U W and Hallberg I R (1994) Nurses' creativity, tedium and burnout during 1 year of clinical supervision and implementation of individu-ally planned nursing care: comparisons between a ward for severely demented patients and a similar control ward. *Journal of Advanced Nursing*, **20**(4):742–9.

Church S and Lyne P (1994) Research-based practice: some problems illustrated by the discussion of evidence concerning the use of pressure relieving device in nursing and midwifery. *Journal of Advanced Nursing*, **19**:513–18.

Hek G (1996) Guidelines on conducting a critical research evaluation. *Nursing Standard*, **11**(6):40–3.

Parahoo K and Reid N (1988) Critical reading of research. *Nursing Times*, **84**(43):69–72.

Rodgers S (1994) An exploratory study of research utilization by nurses in general medical and surgical wards. *Journal of Advanced Nursing*, **20**(5):904–11.

Stevens P M J, Schade A L, Chalk B and Slevin O D'A (1993) *Understanding Research*. Edinburgh: Campion Press.

16 THE UTILISATION OF RESEARCH IN CLINICAL PRACTICE

INTRODUCTION

The integration of research and practice requires the combined effort and commitment of nurses, managers, educators and researchers. Despite the proliferation of research and the increase in research training and education of nurses and midwives, research findings are being used only sporadically in practice. This chapter reports on barriers to the implementation of research, strategies that have been used to facilitate its use and related issues.

USING RESEARCH IN PRACTICE

Nursing is a practice-based discipline, and the knowledge generated by research should inform this practice. Of the many ways in which this knowledge can be used, we can distinguish between conceptual or cognitive use and instrumental use (Weiss, 1979). Stetler and DiMaggio explain conceptual or cognitive use thus:

> [it] refers to use of information to change one's understanding of something, or the way one thinks about a situation. With such 'enlightenment', an individual may 'conceptualize problems differently or extend the range of alternatives considered rather than as direct input into specific decisions (Stetler and DiMaggio, 1991, quoting Cook *et al.*, 1980).

and instrumental use as:

> utilization that is concrete, such as adoption of an explicit nursing intervention or other information that will help facilitate decision making.

It is hard to believe research has had little or no impact on the way in which nurses think. Improved quality of articles, both research and non-research, written by students and staff nurses point to a better awareness of research and its potential. Nursing textbooks make more reference to research now than they did 10 years ago. Research is a mandatory part of the curriculum in initial training in the UK and in many other countries. As discussed in Chapter 1, research provides a logical thinking frame that must influence some of those who undertake or read research. Closs and Cheater (1994) explain that 'the nature of many research projects is such that direct changes to practice are inappropriate – rather they may extend the way that nurses think about what they do, how they relate to the people they care for, and generally stimulate more reflecting and questioning attitudes'.

Empirical evidence on conceptual use is, however, hard to come by. Stetler and DiMaggio (1991), in a study of 24 clinical nurse specialists, found that '75 per cent of the sample reported their most frequent level of use as conceptual' and that 'subjects used it to improve their understanding or influence their way of thinking about issues'. More studies need to be carried out to shed some light on the conceptual use of research in practice.

The instrumental use of research, on the other hand, has been the focus of much research (Myco, 1981; Gould, 1986; Funk *et al.*, 1991; Harris, 1992). The literature abounds with evidence and statements that the implementation of findings, across countries and clinical specialties, is not happening on a mass scale. Gould (1986), writing about the UK, concluded:

> For more than 20 years pressure sore prevention and the treatment of established pressure sores have continued to generate research by nurses and those in allied disciplines. Pressure sore aetiology is established and much is known about the healing of chronic wounds, but little impact has been made on clinical nursing practice.

In their book *Nursing Rituals: Research and Rational Actions?* Walsh and Ford (1990) asked, ' despite all the research that has shown that the best wound healing environment is a moist one... why does a staff nurse spend 20 precious minutes twice a day hosing down and drying out a pressure sore with piped oxygen?'. Three years later, O'Connor (1993) found 'great confusion and inaccuracies' in her sample of staff nurses' knowledge relating to wound healing.

Webb and Mackenzie (1993), after completing a study of 94 nurses in one health authority in England, commented:

> It is... hard to avoid the conclusion that nursing, at least in the area studied, is still far from being a research-based profession and that research minded-ness is not an approach that has been adopted. The extent to which this situation is general in UK nursing cannot be stated on the basis of this study, but it seems likely that similar findings would be found in many district general hospitals.

In a survey of 100 midwifery and medical staff of a large general hospital in the UK, Harris (1992) found that:

> many treatments offered for the relief of postpartum perineal pain are not research-based. Where important research-based findings are available they are not being implemented, while the research which has affected current clinical practice has been inappropriately applied.

Similarly, in the USA, Funk *et al.* (1991) observed that, 'despite the dramatic growth of the quality and quantity of clinically oriented research in recent years, the use of research findings in practice has remained sporadic at best'. In Canada, Hodnett *et al.* (1996) found that despite excellent summaries of the best research evidence concerning helpful and harmful intrapartum practices that are available to practitioners, three studies in Southern Ontario hospitals revealed that intrapartum care was often not based on research findings.

At the same time, there is some evidence that nurses and midwives have more positive attitudes than they did a decade ago (Ehrenfeld and Eckerling, 1991; Hicks, 1993; Lacey, 1994). In a national survey of midwives, Hicks (1993) found that '75 per cent of the sample studied were positively disposed towards research as a routine aspect of their professional activities'.

The research–practice gap or 'the gap between producers and users of knowledge' (Caplan, 1982) is not restricted to nursing. Hunt (1987) pointed out that 'no awareness is shown by nurses writing on this subject that these are problems identified by other occupational groups with more appropriate educational and research dissemination processes than have been developed in nursing systems'. The *Sunday Times* (5 February, 1995), under the sensational headline 'Hundreds killed by doctors relying on outdated manuals', reported:

> Doctors have admitted that they have killed hundreds of patients by relying on 'lethal' outdated textbooks and by giving outmoded treatments after they have been found ineffective or even dangerous... Their candid disclosures highlight the pressing need for measures to ensure that doctors involved in treatment, training and research are kept up to date with the latest medical findings.

In the field of social policy, Caplan (1982) observed:

> As a result of recent empirically-based studies, it has become evident that even with the increased production of policy-relevant knowledge and improved technological procedures for transfer and dissemination, the frequency of use and the impact of knowledge has not increased substantively.

Some much-quoted historical examples of the research–practice gap include the delayed uptake of lemon juice to prevent scurvy. According to Haines and Jones (1994), 'in 1601 James Lancaster showed that lemon juice was effective, but it was not until 1795 that the British Navy adopted the practice (and not until 1865 in the case of the Merchant Navy)'.

We can conclude that the problem of non-utilisation of research findings is not confined to the present time, to any discipline or to any particular country. One can, therefore, ask why it is perceived as a contemporary problem. The main reason seems to be that the volume of research has increased and that, through vastly improved means of communication, we are more aware of it. There is an expectation, therefore, that research utilisation should have increased significantly as a consequence (see Chapter 1 for other reasons for this).

Another conclusion is that there a gap between the time that knowledge is produced and the time when it is used. According to Drucker (1985), 'the lead time for knowledge to become applicable technology and begin to be accepted on the market is between 25 and 30 years' and 'this has not changed much throughout recorded history'.

Drucker (1985) puts the 'lead time' down to 'the nature of knowledge'. Caplan (1982), on the other hand, points to other factors that influence the non-use of research findings:

> Simply because information is timely, relevant, objective and given to the right people in usable form, its use has not been guaranteed. Thus, the 'intelligence' value of the information conveyed does not directly relate to its utilization... . Bureaucratic, ethical, attitudinal, and social considerations take precedence over the value of information in its own right.

BARRIERS TO THE IMPLEMENTATION OF RESEARCH FINDINGS

Dr Margaret Clark, addressing a conference in Scotland in 1994, warned 'that there was little use in setting priorities and funding research if the findings were not implemented'. She added, 'no one has yet cracked the nut on what blocks implementation of research' and 'that subject is worthy of some independent research itself' (*Nursing Standard*, 1994).

In this section, we examine some of the major factors that act as barriers to the implementation of research findings in nursing and midwifery practice. These barriers can be grouped according to one of the following three overlapping headings:

- personal factors
- contextual factors
- factors relating to research and its presentation.

Personal factors

Among the personal factors influencing the use of research are attitudes and knowledge, which are intertwined. A nurse who has positive attitudes to research may want to know more about research, while, on the other hand, reading research articles can foster a positive attitude towards it. A review of the literature by Champion and Leach (1989) revealed that attitude is an important variable in research utilisation. In their study of 59 nurses from a community hospital in the USA, they reported that 'attitude was found to have the greatest correlation with research utilization'. In a pilot study by Lacey (1994) in the UK, attitude alone was found to be 'a powerful predictor of utilization'. These findings were supported in Hick's (1995) study of 550 midwives of all grades in England, Scotland and Wales.

While positive attitudes are important, it is difficult without knowledge for nurses to make use of findings. Knowledge refers in this instance to knowledge of and knowledge about research. Knowledge *of* research refers to the understanding and evaluating of research studies, while knowledge *about* research refers to the awareness of research relating to clinical practice. These two types of knowledge are not mutually exclusive. Evaluating research, although a prerequisite for the implementation of findings, is a skill that cannot easily be acquired. It can, however, be developed over a period of time through evaluating a large number of articles, often with the help of more experienced colleagues. It is doubtful whether an 'introduction to research' module can equip nurses with the skills necessary to be fully able to read research critically. As Lelean (1982) explains, 'assessing the strengths and weaknesses of a research design calls for considerable knowledge about research methods, so that each stage of the research process can be questioned and evaluated'. It is clear that what nurses learn in their first research module has to be built upon.

Awareness of research findings is another prerequisite for their use. Learning how to critique does not mean that nurses will read relevant research regularly. Webb and MacKenzie (1993) concluded from their study that, 'only a minority of nurses read journals regularly and that they do not read research journals'. This issue will be discussed below.

Even when research findings are available in 'digestible' form, as in the case of pressure sores and wound healing, there is evidence that many nurses continue their usual practices (Gould, 1986; O'Connor, 1993; Koh, 1993). Sleep (1992), referring to the non-implementation of findings in midwifery practice, warns that 'no matter how much clinicians learn about research in the educational setting, there is a problem about transferring this knowledge into the real world of practice'.

Hunt (1987), who experienced many obstacles when undertaking a project aimed at evaluating and implementing research findings, points out the limitations of focusing solely on research education. As she explains, 'the hope that if individual nurses could be educated to read research they could change their practice accordingly seems, on the basis of this study, to be too simplistic'.

Education is, therefore, a necessary but not sufficient condition for integrating research and practice. The context in which the implementation takes place is of utmost importance. As DeMey (1982) succinctly puts it:

> A solution which seems theoretically very sound and elegant might change into an awkward and inefficient scheme because in the 'context of application' new and unforeseen factors drastically alter the picture.

Contextual factors

Funk *et al.* (1991) surveyed a random sample of 5000 nurses of various educational backgrounds in the USA and found that all eight items in their scale relating to the characteristics of the setting 'were rated among the top ten barriers' to using research findings in practice. Below is a list of the top ten statements rated by the sample of nurses (Funk *et al.*, 1991):

1. The nurse does not feel she/he has enough authority to change patient care procedures.
2. There is insufficient time on the job to implement new ideas.
3. The nurse is unaware of the research.
4. Physicians will not cooperate with implementation.
5. Administration will not allow implementation.
6. Other staff are not supportive of implementation.
7. The nurse feels results are not generalizable to own setting.
8. The facilities are inadequate for implementation.
9. Statistical analyses are not understandable.
10. The nurse does not have time to read research.

Other studies (Champion and Leach, 1989; Pettengill *et al.*, 1994; Rizzuto *et al.*, 1994) have reported similar findings. Of the contextual factors, the most cited are administrators'/managers' support, time, availability of research findings, autonomy and resistance to change. Champion and Leach's (1989) review of the literature suggests that institutional support was the most important variable determining the use of findings. This is no surprise as institutional support can influence the other contextual factors mentioned above.

Mercer (1984), cited in Champion and Leach (1989), reported a direct relationship between research use and reinforcement by nursing administration, while Champion and Leach (1989) found in their own study that, 'nurses who felt they had support from their nursing leaders utilized research'.

The respondents in Funk *et al.*'s (1991) study identified 'administrative support and encouragement' as the best way to facilitate the use of research-based innovations and suggested 'incorporating research in staff responsibilities and allowing time to review the literature, explore ideas, pilot test innovations, and develop protocols and policies to fully implement changes in practice'.

Champion and Leach (1989) make similar and other suggestions:

> Administration could begin by allowing nurses time while on duty to read related research. In-service programmes and continuing education could also be developed by nursing administration to help nurses utilize research in specific areas. The availability of a clinical nurse researcher could also aid nurses in understanding and utilizing research results. Support for using nursing research might be incorporated into yearly evaluations, with credit being given for those nurses who attempted to use research in clinical practice.

One of the contextual factors that has been reported by nurses as being a major barrier to implementation is the lack of time available to read, process and use research in their practice. Funk *et al.*'s (1991) findings that 75.1 per cent of the sample felt that there was 'insufficient time on the job to implement new ideas' were echoed in Pettengill *et al.*'s (1994) study, in which 50 per cent of educators and 51 per cent of service nurses ranked 'lack of time' as the 'most discouraging factor' in their use of research findings in their practice. Rizzuto *et al.* (1994) also found that nurses wanted on-duty time for research activities.

Recent changes in the health service in the UK have put more pressure on nurses' time. Expecting nurses to use their off-duty time to read and evaluate research makes research an optional and separate activity from practice, thereby enlarging rather than closing the theory–practice gap. To introduce and manage innovations in practice requires more time than that usually spent on current practice. However, time may be saved in the long term if practice becomes more efficient and effective.

Lack of autonomy is identified by many nurses as another barrier. As can be seen in the list above from Funk *et al.*'s (1991) findings, the statement 'The nurse does not feel she/he has enough authority to change patient care procedures' came top of the nurses' responses. One of Lacey's (1994) conclusions was 'the biggest deterrent to the implementation of research findings is lack of autonomy, particularly nurses who feel unable to go against doctors' wishes'. She cited cases in which anaesthetists and theatre staff were opposed to reducing preoperative fasting periods to 3 or 4 hours, although there was research evidence to support the change.

Opposition can also come from ward and unit managers who feel comfortable with the *status quo* and wish to maintain it. The relationship between manager and staff nurse, often characterised by its rigid, demeaning, authoritarian and hierarchical structure, can militate against the democratisation potential of research. Bircumshaw (1990) points out that 'the successful implementation of change not only requires individual nurses at ward level to be receptive and willing to implement research, it also requires the support and encouragement of ward sisters and nurse managers'. Policy directives frequently constrain our practices, and authority may play an important part in what nurses are 'allowed' to do (Bray and Rees, 1995).

All changes involve a degree of disruption and discomfort. There is little surprise that there is often resistance to alter one's practice. Resistance to change is cited by several authors as a major influence inhibiting the introduction of research into clinical care (Sleep, 1992). Resistance can come from other health professionals as well as nursing managers and one's own colleagues. The pressure to conform to existing ward practices has been well documented in the nursing literature (Luker, 1984; Melia, 1984; Kane and Parahoo, 1994).

Other context-related factors mentioned in the research literature include the lack of reward, the poor opinion of other professionals of nursing and midwifery research, and heavy workloads.

Factors related to research and its presentation

The research itself and the way in which it is presented and communicated can determine whether or not it is eventually used. No matter how skilful nurses are at evaluating research, how positive their attitudes are or how much support they get from their managers, if the research itself (the product) is not known to nurses, is of poor quality or is hardly comprehensible, it will not be used.

The failure to find studies relating to clinical practice was reported to be a common impeding factor (Pettengill *et al.*, 1994). In the same study, respondents reported that 'methods to keep them informed about study findings encouraged research utilization'. These methods included 'a monthly research newsletter' (ranked as most helpful), 'research meetings, continuing education programmes, computer networks, interactive software, and research study guides' (Pettengill *et al.*,1994). The nurses in Funk *et al.*'s (1991) study also said that accessibility of the research and the way it was presented were a problem. They suggested that research be reported in journals frequently read by clinicians and written so as to give more specific explanations of the clinical implications in a 'how to' format.

The best studies are of little value if they are incomprehensible to those who could benefit most from them – practitioners. The language and style of research reports often present difficulties for practitioners and even for those who are knowledgeable about research. Funk *et al.* (1991) made the following observations:

> Research reports are commonly full of research jargon intended for other researchers, not clinicians; they emphasise the reliability and validity of measurements rather than what was actually measured; they focus on the statistical tests performed rather than on the meaning of the findings; they rarely indicate what information may be applicable to practice, even when supporting research has been published.

Not all research findings are relevant, valid or reliable. They may also not be generalisable to all settings. It is the responsibility of researchers to make findings relevant to clinical practice. Edwards-Beckett (1990) suggested that 'for results to be of interest to clinicians, researchers need to spell out the meaning of their results in their manuscripts, identify previous studies that contributed to the current findings and clearly state the limits of generalizability'.

Hunt (1996) points out that less attention is given to the responsibility for non-utilisation held by researchers, mainly that they:

- do not produce their findings in usable form;
- do not study the problems of practitioners;
- do not manage to persuade and convince others of their value;
- do not develop the necessary programmes for the acceptance and introduction of innovation;
- do not have the necessary authority/access.

In conclusion, from many of the studies cited above, a number of factors influencing the use of research have been identified. Although factors related to the context in which research is to be implemented are more frequently reported than are personal factors, it does not mean the same barriers will exist in every setting. It is also understandable that administrators'/managers' support is one of the common impeding factors since it can influence, in turn, the time allocated to nurses, the distribution of workloads, access to research, opportunities for further training and education, financial rewards, autonomy, resistance to change and a host of other factors. However important the contextual factors are, without a positive attitude and basic research training to evaluate research, the use of findings will be severely impeded. The starting point seems to be to create a culture in which learning about research is valued and opportunities to acquire knowledge and skills are present. This can be followed by devising strategies to implement research findings, where appropriate.

Strategies to Facilitate the Use of Research

A number of strategies have been adopted at national, institutional and individual levels to remove some of the barriers to the use of research in nursing and midwifery practice. As mentioned earlier, the introduction of research as a compulsory component in initial training in the UK is aimed at helping students to acquire a basic knowledge of research. Research is also well established in degree and other postbasic programmes. At an individual level, the credit for the positive attitude of nurses and midwives to research must go to those who at great costs (financial, domestic and social) enrol on these courses in order to continue their professional development.

At the institutional level, research support groups, journal clubs and other similar groups engage in activities to promote the understanding and use of research. Sometimes imaginative ways are devised to attract participation. For example, a 'sacred cows' contest was organised by the research committee at Kelowna General Hospital, in British Columbia, Canada. As Brown (1993) explains:

> At one of our monthly meetings we had the idea of a contest to identify the sacred cows of nursing. The idea originated from a review of articles published in a journal for operating room managers. In nursing, sacred cows are those routine practices we do not even think about any more. Blessed by time, these practices normally escape scrutiny. Yet, research might show that these practices are no longer justified, if they ever were. Identifying some of nursing's sacred cows could help us to develop researchable questions of a very practical nature.

The membership of support groups varies with institutions. The core members are the practitioners themselves, with managers, teaching staff and sometimes other health professionals. Some groups are run on more formal lines than others. Research support groups also vary in their functions. These have included, among others, the identification of research problems, the presentation of completed projects by members, discussions of methodological and ethical issues and papers by guest speakers. Journal clubs are more focused on the communication of research information. Burrows and Mcleish (1995) explain that the purpose of these clubs:

> is to give interested practitioners an opportunity to keep up to date with the latest developments and research in nursing... . Club members take it in

turns to be responsible for reading a journal for a month, selecting one article to summarize, share, and discuss with other participants.... . Equally, anyone may attend purely to listen to the summaries and join in the discussion.

Access to research information in the UK has continued to improve. Closs and Cheater (1994) give us some examples:

Quicker and more efficient methods of literature retrieval, for example, computerized on-line search facilities, are now increasingly available in college of nursing and university libraries. Research databases such as the Index of Nursing Research and the Midwifery Research Database are also valuable information resources.

Evaluating research studies for the purpose of implementing findings in practice is a 'tall order' for individual nurses. It may be dangerous to implement findings on the basis of one study. Collective efforts to review the research literature on selected aspects of clinical practice are likely to instil more confidence in practitioners who carry out the implementation. In 1992, the St Georges Group in London published a research-based document prepared by a team comprising 'a number of nurses, a surgeon, a geriatrician, a pharmacist, a physiotherapist and a dietician' on 'pressure sore prevention and wound management policies' (Smith, 1993). Not only does this represent a multidisciplinary approach, but it is also a concerted effort of a group of people to review the literature, thereby facilitating the task of individual practitioners.

The renewed interest in clinical guidelines is expected to result in an improved quality of care. The relationship between guidelines and research is clearly described by Duff et al. (1996):

A key defining attribute of clinical guidelines is that they are based on research evidence. It may be that for some aspects of care insufficient research evidence is available and reliance has to be on expert opinion, pending adequate research studies. Those elements of a clinical guideline that are included on the basis of research and have important implications for patient/client outcome can be specified as recommended.

Sleep (1992), explaining that midwives often 'lack the skills to critically evaluate published research as the basis of changing practice', points out that they are, however, fortunate to be supported:

by the availability of an invaluable resource which offers a comprehensive review of all current research evidence in which alternate forms of care have been formally evaluated: *Effective Care in Pregnancy and Childbirth* (ECPC) (Chalmers et al., 1989).

At a national level, too, there are agencies that evaluate and disseminate research findings to enable practitioners to make use of them. Titler *et al.* (1994) describe one such initiative, the Agency for Health Care Policy and Research (AHCPR) which:

> reviews available research on selected topics and makes recommendations for clinical practice in areas such as pain, urinary incontinence, skin care and depression. The unique form in which AHCPR guidelines are published and distributed has great potential for stimulating their use by bedside caregivers because research findings are synthesised for health care providers.

As explained in Chapter 1, the UK Centre for Reviews and Dissemination (CRD) was established in 1994 'to provide the NHS with important information on the effectiveness of treatments and the delivery and organisation of health care' (CRD, 1994). The CRD explains how it expects to achieve this objective:

> Through our dissemination work we aim to provide important information in an easily accessible form. We will use a range of methods to promote implementation, such as bulletins, NHS networks, workshops, and continuing medical education. We will also disseminate information to members of the public through patient leaflets and other media.

Hunt (1981) gave five reasons why nurses do not use research findings in clinical practice. These are:

1. They do not know about them.
2. They do not understand them.
3. They do not believe them.
4. They do not know how to apply them.
5. They are not allowed to use them.

The strategies and initiatives described above seem to address the first three reasons. The other two depend largely on contextual factors, more specifically the support that practitioners need when trying to implement findings. One cannot generalise about the strategies used by managers because different settings differ in the amount and type of support, if any, that is available. Some of the strategies used include the creation of a 'research and development' (or similar) post in clinical areas in the UK, the provision of on-duty time to set up and attend research support groups, administrative support for typing and photocopying, funding to attend workshops, seconding nurses to undertake part-time or full-time studies, and releasing nurses for short periods from clinical duties to carry out research projects. Anecdotal evidence suggests that some hospitals do little or none of the above, while others offer a lot of support. The research and development nurses' role also varies across the country. By and large, they act as consultants to managers and practitioners on research and clinical issues, some carrying out projects on their own or with others, most being involved in promoting research-based practice.

There have been few initiatives that have addressed the use of research from the critical review of findings to their implementation and final evaluation. One such project was undertaken by the Western Interstate Commission for Higher Education (WICHE) in the USA in the 1970s. Bircumshaw (1990) describes how the WICHE:

> took nurses from various settings and taught them methods relating to the change process and research utilization in 3-day workshops. Research related to a problem was reviewed and a plan for instituting research-based change and evaluation of the change was arrived at.

A better known project, the Conduct and Utilization of Research in Nursing (CURN) (Horsley *et al.*, 1983) was developed over a period of five years, 1975–80, to:

> increase utilization of research findings in the following ways: (1) disseminating findings; (2) facilitating organisational modifications necessary for implementation; and (3) encouraging collaborative research that was directly transferable to clinical practice. (Burns and Grove, 1987)

In the UK, Hunt (1987) led a project involving nurse teachers and librarians from the schools of nursing on the management of mouth care and preoperative fasting. After evaluating and synthesising the literature on these topics, policies were drawn up following consultation with the relevant personnel, including central sterile supply department (CSSD) staff, anaesthetists, pharmacists, dental consultants and nursing staff. When staff found it difficult to translate the policy into practice, problem-solving and quality circles groups were set up. Hunt (1987) discussed a number of difficulties experienced during the project. These included the fact it took nearly 2 years for seven nurse teachers and a librarian to identify, evaluate and synthesise relevant information and produce a 'reference' package. Hunt (1987) explained that 'even at the end of two years' work the information collected on mouth care could not be regarded as up to date' and 'by the time the package was put together it was in need of updating'. She also found resistance to change among ward sisters. As she explained:

> not all ward sisters were found to conform to the guidelines disseminated to them from the nurse teachers and the Nursing Procedures Committee,

although ward sisters were involved in workshops to discuss the proposed changes. This indicated the extent of the autonomy exercised by ward sisters in ignoring policy decisions and the lack of an effective management system to ensure that agreed practice changes were implemented and maintained.

On the other hand, she found 'when medical, catering and housekeeping staff were approached they responded positively and co-operatively to the surprise of the nurses indicating that nurses appeared to view themselves as victims rather than initiators of change' (Hunt, 1987).

As pointed out earlier, one of the barriers to implementation was resistance from other health professionals. This shows that each setting has its own barriers and that generalisations should be avoided.

Collaborative partnerships in nursing research

In Chapter 8, action research was shown to be a research design and a strategy to bridge the research–practice gap. There are other initiatives that do not describe themselves as action research but which involve collaboration between outside researchers and practitioners. One such study by Tierney and Taylor (1991) demonstrates the benefits of this type of collaboration. As they explained, 'what we came to appreciate as we worked together was that our respective contributions to the research process seemed to be so naturally complementary rather than in conflict'.

They found the practitioners' 'practical ability and knowledge of the setting, its day-to-day workings and the patient population' valuable, and that they facilitated 'the recruitment of patients to the study', attended to the 'practical business of data collection' and 'provided support and encouragement for the researcher in what otherwise would have been a long, rather lonely and emotionally draining period of fieldwork'. On the other hand, the researcher provided 'easy access to the literature', was able 'to plan the study', analysed data and drafted the initial report (Tierney and Taylor, 1991). Finally, at the interpretation and discussion stages, the contribution of the practitioner was appreciated. As Tierney and Taylor (1991) reported:

> In the interpretation and discussion of the findings... and especially in the drafting of recommendations, there was great value in having the more objective and stuffy approach of the academic researcher tempered by clinically-oriented and down-to-earth observations and criticism.

Practitioner research

An approach that is becoming popular with nurses is practitioner research. Reed and Procter (1995) identify the following three research positions.

Researcher positions

'Outsider'	'Hybryd'	'Insider'
A researcher undertaking research into practice with no professional experience	A practitioner undertaking research into the practice of other practitioners	A practitioner undertaking research into their own and their colleagues' practice

Reed and Procter (1995) point out that the practitioner researcher, by virtue of being an insider, has the knowledge, insight and opportunities to select relevant problems to research, be sensitive to the issues related to the process of collecting data, have a better understanding of the data and be more committed to the dissemination of the findings.

Some of the examples of practitioner research studies given by Reed and Procter (1995) include 'a study of family networks and relationships in community midwifery' (Davies, 1995), 'patients' feelings about patients' (Skeil, 1995) and 'reflections on evaluating a course of family therapy' (Stevenson, 1995).

Research and development units

One important development in the last decade is the formation of nursing, midwifery and health visiting development units throughout the UK, in which research has played an important part in developing practice. Drawing from the experiences of practitioners and researchers, working models of the interface between research and practice have been developed. As Vaughan and Edwards (1995) explain, these models 'offer a range of ways in which research and practice can be brought together' and that they all have advantages and disadvantages. The authors concluded:

> the opportunities to develop unified roles, to have access to research skills within the team, or to develop partnerships between academic and clinical sites seem to be the most exciting, since they bring together the expertise from both settings and can meet both the developmental and research needs most fully.

Collaborative ventures between researchers and practitioners seem to be on the increase, judging by the nursing research literature. This trend is likely to continue well into the 21st century. However, such worthwhile projects may have limited impact on the overall use of research findings in practice, as the majority of clinical areas remain untouched by them. A number of issues need to be addressed seriously if research is to become an integral part of practice.

USING RESEARCH: WHOSE RESPONSIBILITY IS IT ANYWAY?

The contribution of nurse education in imparting research knowledge and fostering a positive attitude to research among nurses must be recognised. However, educational programmes in the UK have so far focused on 'understanding and awareness of research' and on acquiring skills to carry out research (Clark and Sleep, 1991). The situation in the USA is no different, as Stetler and DiMaggio (1991) point out:

> The conduct of research and the utilization of research are different processes. In the past, the former has received primary attention in educational programmes. It is perhaps time that equal attention be given to both.

Funk *et al.* (1991) explain that 'no matter how practitioners learn about research in the educational environment there is a problem about transferring this knowledge into the real world of practice'.

To teach nurses how to implement change means entering the world of the micropolitics of the ward, hospital or other clinical area. It entails challenging power and authority – the type of activity nurses are rarely trained to engage in and, as a result, shy away from. If, as Caplan has stated, the implementation of research findings is a 'political process' (Caplan, 1982), nothing short of a political education for nurses will suffice. The challenge is for educators and others to devise courses to meet the political education needs of nurses. According to Walsh and Ford (1990), 'what is needed is assertiveness, and this is sadly lacking, not only because of the subservient tradition of nursing, but also because as most nurses are women, they have been socially conditioned out of any assertive tendencies they may have'.

Assertiveness is one, albeit an important, component of the political education of nurses. The latter also involves learning about the tension and conflict present in the implementation of change, understanding power, gender and class relationships and how they operate in occupational settings such as wards, hospitals and clinics, and obtaining the insight and skills to use appropriate strategies to effect change. It can be argued that these topics are already adequately covered in current nursing curricula. Anecdotal evidence, however, suggests they are rarely dealt with in sufficient depth to make a difference. Some courses address macropolitical issues such as democracy, elections and pressure group politics. Social policy, in one form or another, figures in a number of curricula. While these are important topics in their own right, they tend not to address the political issues that impact daily on the lives of practitioners working with other professionals in settings where bureaucratic, authoritarian and hierarchical structures tend to stifle creativity and innovation.

Cang in 1979 wrote, 'to a significant number of members of the nursing profession "research" has become something of a dirty word'. While attitudes to research are much more positive in the 1990s, 'politics' still remains a dirty word for nurses. It is an emotional issue conjuring images of strikes, but there is more to politics than strikes. A political education must aim at empowering practitioners who will be able to interact with others as fully mature professionals who feel valued and confident of their ability, not as subordinates to others. Sleep (1992) warns, 'it is unrealistic for educational programmes to place upon practitioners the burden of introducing research into the workplace, unless the climate prevailing in both service and management spheres is receptive to change'.

For the full potential of a political education to be realised, the environment in which practitioners work must be facilitative and supportive, as explained earlier. Lack of managerial support has been reported as a key barrier to the implementation of research findings. Where successes have been recorded, the role of managers have been crucial. Managers must also support nurses in their struggle to be autonomous practitioners of equal status to others, in particular doctors, to many of whom nursing research remains a peripheral activity of little importance. The onus is on nurses to make the case for innovation strong enough to convince others of its value. Lacey (1994) reported from her study that:

> the implementation of research findings was seen to be possible where a sound rationale could be put forward to those in authority. Those nurses who felt they had a certain degree of autonomy in clinical practice were more confident of their ability to do this than those... who felt they could not alter practice without agreement of others, notably doctors.

Nurse managers have an important role in coordinating efforts aimed at making other health professionals aware, and appreciative, of nursing research. The potential for the advocacy role of nurse managers must not be underestimated. Sleep (1992), writing about midwifery practice, describes the challenge facing supervisors of midwives. She writes:

> Clinicians should be actively encouraged to develop and use their creative skills in planning innovative strategies for the integration of research into

practice. Supporting and facilitating this process is one of the greatest challenges facing supervisors of midwives who are in a unique and privileged position to act as midwife advocates.

The creation of an environment in which nurses can question and make suggestions is another challenge facing managers. As Funk *et al.* (1991) conclude, 'only when staff believe the environment is conducive to questioning current practice and searching for more effective practice will they believe they have the authority to change practice using research methods'.

The essence of research is to question; it cannot survive in an environment that constrains it. Research has a liberating potential to free practitioners from the shackles of unsafe and ineffective conventional and traditional practices, also empowering those who participate in it.

The creation and maintenance of a culture in which research is valued, rather than paid lip service to, is of utmost importance for the integration of research and practice. Closs and Cheater (1994) point out that, even in the NHS, 'government-driven changes in the health service have rarely been based on research and many changes in nursing practice have been made without a sound research base'.

Casey (1995) pointed out, in an editorial in the *Nursing Standard*, that 'while the health department has invested in research and development and is pushing evidence based practice, it does appear that research is not research in the government's eyes if the findings are contrary to its policies'. She was referring to the government's rejection of the report *Mental Health and Stress in the Workplace*, which claimed that working more than 40 hours a week doubles the risk of heart disease. According to Casey (1995), the report damages 'the government's case against the European directive on working hours which lays down a maximum 48 hour working week'.

Many nurse educators can hardly claim that they base their teaching on the findings of educational research. One can also ask how many curricula are planned and delivered according to pecuniary imperatives rather than being based on research findings. Managers and teachers must lead by example. Researchers, too, have the responsibility of doing quality, relevant research and presenting it in ways that can be understood by practitioners. They must endeavour to turn the mystique of research into an everyday activity in which practitioners can participate and value.

Therefore, the empowerment of nurses through education, the creation of a supportive environment in practice and the promotion of a culture in which research is valued, can together be the solution to the wholesale rather than sporadic and selective use of research in nursing and midwifery practice.

Smith (1995) in an editorial in the *Journal of Advanced Nursing* in which he reviewed the WHO publication *Nursing and Midwifery Beyond the Year 2000: Rhetoric, Research and Reality* (WHO, 1994) concluded:

> I believe that nurses and midwives will never become a powerhouse for change until the shelves full of nursing and midwifery reports are converted into action. I believe that that requires well educated, articulate and assertive practitioners, who are both research-minded and intuitive, who practice ethically, who possess professional maturity, who espouse social justice and equity, and who demonstrate personal commitment and political astuteness. In other words, we need nurses and midwives who use their hands, hearts and heads.

Summary and Conclusion

In this chapter, we have shown how, despite evidence of an increase in knowledge of and positive attitudes to research, nurses and midwives are not using research in their practice. The barriers to implementation relate to personal and contextual factors and to the quality of research and its presentation. Nurse education has so far focused on 'understanding research' and 'how to do it'. What is required now are educational programmes that can teach nurses how to use research in their own settings. This education should aim at empowering nurses so that they can themselves effect change. Educators, managers, researchers and practitioners all have an important contribution to make towards the integration of research and practice.

References

Bircumshaw D (1990) The utilization of research findings in clinical nursing practice. *Journal of Advanced Nursing*, **15**:1272–80.

Bray J and Rees C (1995) The relevance of research. *Practice Nursing*, **6**(7):33–4.

Brown G (1993) The sacred cow contest. *Canadian Nurse*, **89**(1):31–3.

Burns N and Grove S K (1987) *The Practice of Nursing Research: Conduct, Critique and Utilization*. Philadelphia: Saunders/CWB.

Burrows D E and McLeish K (1995) A model for research-based practice. *Journal of Clinical Nursing*, **4**:243–7.

Cang (1979) Nursing research: problems of aim, method and content. *Journal of Advanced Nursing*, **4**(4):453–8.

Caplan N (1982) Social research and public policy at the national level. In Kallen D B P, Kosse G B, Wagenaar H C, Kloprogge J J J and Vorbeck M (eds) *Social Science Research and Public Policy-Making: A Reappraisal*. Netherlands: NFER.

Casey N (1995) Editorial. *Nursing Standard*, **10**(3):3.

CDR (Centre for the Dissemination of Research) (1994) *NHS Centre for Reviews and Dissemination* (leaflets). York: University of York.

Chalmers I, Enkin M and Kierse M J N C (eds) (1989) *Effective Care in Pregnancy and Childbirth.* Oxford: Oxford University Press.

Champion V L and Leach A (1989) Variables related to research utilization in nursing: an empirical investigation. *Journal of Advanced Nursing,* **14**:705–10.

Clark E H and Sleep J (1991) The what and how of teaching research. *Nurse Education Today,* **11**:172–8.

Closs S J and Cheater F M (1994) Utilization of nursing research: culture, interest and support. *Journal of Advanced Nursing,* **19**:762–73.

Cook T, Levinson-Rose J and Pollard W (1980) The misutilization of evaluation research. *Knowledge: Creation Diffusion and Utilization,* **1**:477–98.

Davies J (1995) A study of family networks and relationships in community midwifery. In Reed J and Procter S (eds) *Practitioner Research in Health Care.* London: Chapman & Hall.

DeMey M T (1982) Action and knowledge from a cognitive point of view. In Kallen D B P, Kosse G B, Wagenaar H C, Kloprogge J J J and Vorbeck M (eds) *Social Science Research and Public Policy-Making: A Reappraisal.* Netherlands: NFER.

Drucker P F (1985) *Innovations and Entrepreneurship: Practice and Principles.* London: Heinemann.

Duff L A, Kitson A L, Seers K and Humphris D (1996) Cinical guidelines: an introduction to their development and implementation. *Journal of Advanced Nursing,* **23**:887–95.

Edwards-Beckett J (1990) Nursing research utilization techniques. *Journal of Nursing Administration,* **20**(11):25–30.

Ehrenfeld M and Eckerling S (1991) Perceptions and attitudes of registered nurses to research: a comparison with a previous study. *Journal of Advanced Nursing,* **16**:224–32.

Funk S G, Champagne M T, Wiese R A and Tornquist E M (1991) Barriers to using research findings in practice: the clinician's perspective. *Applied Nursing Research,* **4**(2):90–5.

Gould D (1986) Pressure sore prevention and treatment: an example of nurses' failure to implement research findings. *Journal of Advanced Nursing,* **11**:389–94.

Haines A and Jones R (1994) Implementing findings of research. *British Medical Journal,* **308**:1488–92.

Harris M (1992) The impact of research findings on current practice in relieving postpartum perineal pain in a large district general hospital. *Midwifery,* **8**:125–31.

Hicks C (1993) A survey of midwives' attitudes to, and involvement in, research: the first stage in identifying needs for a staff development programme. *Midwifery,* **9**:51–62.

Hicks C (1995) A factor analytic study of midwives' attitudes in research. *Midwifery,* **11**:11–17.

Hodnett E D, Kaufman K, O'Brien-Pallas L, Chipman M, Watson-MacDonell J and Hunsburger W (1996) A strategy to promote research-based nursing care: effects on childbirth outcomes. *Research in Nursing and Health,* **19**:13–20.

Horsley J A, Crane J, Crabtree M K and Wood D J (1983) *Using Research to Improve Nursing Practice: A Guide.* New York: Grune & Stratton.

Hunt J (1981) Indicators for nursing practice: the use of research findings. *Journal of Advanced Nursing*, **6**:189–94.

Hunt J (1996) Barriers to research utilization. *Journal of Advanced Nursing*, **23**:423–5.

Hunt M (1987) The process of translating research findings into nursing practice. *Journal of Advanced Nursing*, **12**:101–10.

Kane M and Parahoo K (1994) Lifting: why nurses follow bad practice. *Nursing Standard*, **8**(25):34–8.

Koh S (1993) Dressing practices. *Nursing Times*, **89**(42):82–6.

Lacey E A (1994) Research utilisation in nursing practice – a pilot study. *Journal of Advanced Nursing*, **19**:987–95.

Lelean S R (1982) The implementation of research findings into nursing practice. *International Journal of Nursing Studies*, **19**(4):223–30.

Luker K A (1984) Reading nursing: the burden of being different. *International Journal of Nursing Studies*, **21**(1):1–7.

Melia K M (1984) Student nurses' construction of occupational socialisation. *Sociology of Health and Illness*, **6**(2):132–51.

Mercer R (1984) Nursing research: the bridge to excellence in practice. *Image: Journal of Nursing Scholarship*, **14**:47–51.

Myco F (1981) The implementation of nursing research related to the nursing profession in Northern Ireland. *Journal of Advanced Nursing*, **6**:51–8.

Nursing Standard (1994) New section, **8**(40):14.

O'Connor H (1993) Bridging the gap? *Nursing Times*, **89**(32):63–6.

Pettengill M M, Gillies D A and Clark C C (1994) Factors encouraging and discouraging the use of nursing research findings. *Image: Journal of Nursing Scholarship*, **26**(2):143–8.

Reed J and Procter S (1995) (eds) *Practitioner Research in Health Care*. London: Chapman & Hall.

Rizzuto C, Bostrom J, Suter W N and Chenitz W C (1994) Predictors of nurses' involvement in research activities. *Western Journal of Nursing Research*, **16**(2):193–204.

Skeil D (1995) Patients' feelings about patients. In Reed J and Procter S (eds) *Practitioner Research in Health Care*. London: Chapman & Hall.

Sleep J (1992) Research and the practice of midwifery. *Journal of Advanced Nursing*, **1**:1465–71.

Smith J P (1993) Pressure sore prevention and wound management policies. *Journal of Advanced Nursing*, **18**:687.

Smith J P (1995) Nursing and midwifery beyond the year 2000: rhetoric, research and reality. *Journal of Advanced Nursing*, **21**:815–16.

Stetler C B and DiMaggio G (1991) Research utilization among clinical nurse specialists. *Clinical Nurse Specialist*, **5**(3):151–5.

Stevenson C (1995) Reflections on evaluating a course of family therapy. In Reed J and Procter S (eds) *Practitioner Research in Health Care*. London: Chapman & Hall.

Sunday Times, 5 February 1995, pp. 1, 2.

Tierney A J and Taylor J (1991) Research in practice: an 'experiment' in research–practitioner collaboration. *Journal of Advanced Nursing*, **16**:506–510.

Titler M G, Kleiber C, Steelman V *et al.* (1994) Infusing research into practice to promote quality care. *Nursing Research*, **43**(5):307–13.

Vaughan B and Edwards M (1995) *Interface between Research and Practice: Some Working Models.* London: King's Fund Centre.

Walsh M and Ford P (1990) *Nursing Rituals: Research and Rational Actions.* Oxford: Heinemann Nursing.

Webb C (1990) Partners in research. *Nursing Times*, **86**(32):40–4.

Webb C and Mackenzie J (1993) Where are we now? Research-mindedness in the 1990s. *Journal of Clinical Nursing*, **2**:129–33.

Weiss C (1979) The many meanings of research utilization. *Public Administration Review*, **39**:426–31.

Weiss C H (1991) Reflections on 19th-century experience with knowledge diffusion. *Knowledge: Creation, Diffusion, Utilization*, **13**(1):5–16.

WHO (World Health Organisation) (1994) *Nursing Beyond the Year 2000: Report of a WHO Study.* Technical Report Series no. 842.

GLOSSARY

abstract A brief summary usually found at the beginning of an article. It states briefly the aim of the study, the design (including the method/s, sample/s and sampling) and the main relevant findings.

accidental sample It is a sample of convenience in which only those units which are available have a chance of being selected.

action research Action research involves using research in order to plan, implement and evaluate change in practice.

alternative-form test Alternative-form reliability test (also known as equivalence) is carried out by asking questions in different forms and comparing the data.

bias Factors, other than those investigated, which may influence the findings of a study.

bracketing It is the suspension of the researcher's preconceptions, prejudices and beliefs so that they do not interfere with or influence her description and interpretation of the respondent's experience.

case study Case studies focus on specific populations (usually small) and events which are bounded by time and well defined. In-depth information can be collected by using a variety of methods.

central tendency This term refers to 'average' or 'typical' scores, not extreme ones. The statistical measures of central tendency are the mode, median and mean.

clinical effectiveness The most efficient and cost-effective way to assess, organise, deliver and evaluate care and treatment in order to achieve optimum benefit for clients.

cluster random sample A cluster or multistage random sample involves sampling the clusters before drawing samples from the selected clusters.

comparative studies The purpose of a comparative study is to compare policies, practices, events and people.

conceptual/theoretical framework The use of concepts and/or theories to underpin a study.

construct validity This refers to the extent to which the questionnaire or scale reflects the construct which is being assessed or measured.

content validity The degree to which the questions or items in a questionnaire or observation schedule can adequately study or measure the phenomenon being researched.

control To account for the effect of unwanted variables, researchers introduce control in their experiments by making sure that another group (control group), similar in all respects (except for the intervention) to the experimental group, takes part in the experiment. Control is also exercised by the objective allocation of subjects to groups.

covert observation This is a form of participant observation in which researchers do not divulge that they are making observations for research purposes and when 'participants' are not aware they are being observed as part of a research study. Covert observation has serious ethical implications.

criterion-related, concurrent and predictive validity
A questionnaire's criterion-related validity can be assessed by comparing the data collected with data from other sources. When other such data are currently available, the concurrent validity of the questionnaire can thus be assessed. Predictive validity refers to data which may be available in the future and which may confirm the validity of the data from the present questionnaire.

deduction   Deduction is the process of knowledge acquisition by the formulation of a theory or hypothesis and the collection of data thereafter in order to support or reject it.

Delphi technique   This is a form of survey which consists of gathering the views of experts, normally individually, on a particular issue. It involves a number of rounds during which feedback is provided to respondents to allow them to reconsider their initial opinion, if necessary, for the purpose of reaching a consensus.

dependent and independent variables   Anything which varies can be called a variable. Variables can be dependent or independent. In the statement 'lack of exercise causes constipation', the independent variable is 'lack of exercise' and the dependent one is 'constipation'. It is the relationship between variables which determines whether they are dependent or independent, not the variables themselves. In the statement 'the degree of constipation determines one's level of well-being', constipation is the independent variable.

descriptive and correlational studies   In descriptive studies researchers describe phenomena about which little is normally known. From the data collected, patterns or trends may emerge and possible links between variables can be observed but the emphasis is on the description of phenomena.
In correlational studies the primary aim is to examine or explore relationships between variables.

descriptive statistics   This type of statistics answers descriptive questions and does so by such measures as frequency, central tendency and dispersion.

determinism   It is the belief that phenomena have causes and effects and that experiments can find the answer to them.

dispersion   To describe how scores vary, measures of dispersion such as standard deviation, variance, range and quartiles are used.

ethnography   This is a research approach developed by anthropologists who go and live among the people they study. Ethnographers study human behaviour as it is influenced or mediated by the culture in which it takes place.

evaluative studies   An evaluative study is normally carried out when a researcher wants to find out if, how and to what extent, the objectives of particular activities, policies or practices have been or are being met.

evidence-based practice   Practice based on the most valid and reliable research findings, the judgement and experience of practitioners and the views of clients.

extraneous and confounding variables   Extraneous variables are those which researchers are aware of at the start of the study but do not seek to study. They need to be controlled in order that they do not interfere with the experiment. Confounding variables are extraneous variables which researchers fail to or cannot control but which may work in the same or opposite direction with the independent variable. Sometimes the two terms are used interchangeably.

face validity Face validity is one form of content validity. It involves giving the questionnaire to anyone, not necessarily an expert on the subject, who can 'on the face of it' assess whether the questions or items reflect the phenomenon being studied.

focused group interview This can be described as interactions between one or more researchers and more than one respondent for the purpose of collecting data on a specific topic.

frequency This involves describing scores in absolute numbers, percentages and proportion.

grounded theory This term was coined by Glaser and Strauss (1967) to mean an inductive approach to research whereby hypotheses and theories emerge out of, or are 'grounded' in, data.

hypothesis A statement which normally specifies the relationship between variables.

hypothetico-deductive
An approach whereby hypotheses and theories are put to the test by the deductive (see above) process during the course of research, especially experiments.

induction This means that after a large number of observations have been made, it is possible to draw conclusions or theorise about particular phenomena.

inferential statistics Inferential statistics describe correlational or casual links between variables.

internal and external validity of experiments Internal validity is the extent to which changes, if any, in the dependent variable can be said to have been caused by the independent variable alone. External validity is the extent to which the findings of an experiment can be applied or generalised to other similar populations or settings.

interpretivism It is the belief that people continuously make sense of the world around them and different people may have different interpretations of the same phenomena.

Interpretivism is a blanket term for a collection of approaches broadly called 'qualitative' that share an opposition to the logical positivists' notion (see *positivism* below) of studying humans as objects or particles.

interval scale The numbers allocated to variables signify the order or hierarchy of these variables and they indicate the precise distance between them.

intervention/manipulation The term intervention is used in an experiment to describe the independent variable whose effect the researcher is trying to assess or measure. Examples of interventions include medications, information programmes and therapies. By giving different medications (or the same medication in varying amounts) to different groups, the researcher is in fact manipulating the intervention, hence the term manipulation.

intra- and inter-observer reliability
Intra-observer reliability is the consistency with which the same observer records the same behaviours in the same way on different occasions. Inter-observer reliability is the consistency with which two or more observers record the same behaviours in the same way on different occasions.

intuition A form of knowing and behaving not apparently based on rational reasoning.

longitudinal and cross-sectional studies A longitudinal study is one in which data are collected at intervals in order to capture any change which may take place over time. The same sample (cohort) is usually 'followed-up' over a period of time.

In cross-sectional studies, data are collected from different groups of people who are at different stages in their experience of the same phenomenon.

matched-pairs Matched-pairs allocation takes place when researchers try to pair a subject in the experiment with another in the control group, in terms of characteristics such as age, gender, illness condition, and so on. Usually researchers enter a subject in one of the two groups and allocate someone else with similar characteristics to the other group.

mean The mean is the arithmetical average of a set of values.

median The median is the mid-point value when the scores are arranged in ascending order.

meta-analysis This is a form of research on research. In its pure form it involves the statistical analysis of research findings in order to arrive at one final finding.

mode The mode is the most frequent value.

molar and molecular These are observation units or categories. Molar units are broad and sometimes abstract. Molecular units are more detailed and precise.

nominal scale In a nominal scale the numbers allocated to variables have no value and are only used to label them.

normal distribution In a normal distribution of scores most of the scores cluster around the mean and the extreme scores are few, and are (more or less) equally distributed above or below the mean.

nursing research All research which pertains to the organisation, delivery, uses and outcomes of nursing care. It, therefore, includes research on clients, nurses, resources and nursing practice.

observer's effect Observer's effect, reactivity and the Hawthorne effect are terms used to describe changes in the participants 'usual' or 'normal behaviour' as a reaction to being observed for research purposes.

operational definition The process of communicating precisely the meaning of concepts and the ways in which they can be observed and recorded.

ordinal scale In an ordinal scale, the numbers allocated to variables signify the order or hierarchy of these variables, but cannot specify the exact difference between them.

paradigm A research paradigm can be described as the beliefs and values which particular research communities share about the type of phenomena which can or cannot be researched and the methodologies to be adopted.

phenomenology This is a philosophical theory about the way humans experience consciousness. The phenomenological approach focuses on individuals' interpretations of their lived experiences and the ways in which they express them.

placebo A placebo is a substance of no pharmacological or therapeutic property which resembles, in all physical characteristics, the intervention used in the experimental group. Placebos are used in experiments to overcome the possible suggestive effect of new interventions.

positivism A movement in the social sciences which evolved in the 18th century as a critique of the supernatural and metaphysical interpretations of phenomena. It is based on the belief that the methods of the natural sciences can be used to study human behaviour as well. It is the belief that only what can be observed by the human senses can be called facts. Logical positivism is one branch of positivism which makes use of mathematics in the interpretation of research findings.

primary and secondary sources
Original publications are primary sources while publications which report, quote from or comment on original works are known as secondary sources.

probability and non-probability samples With probability samples, every unit in the sample frame has a more than zero chance (known in advance) of being selected. Non-probability samples are made up of units whose chances of selection are not known.

prospective, retrospective and historical studies A prospective study is one in which the researcher investigates a current phenomenon by seeking data which are to be collected in the future. A retrospective study relies on information from the past in order to understand a current problem. Both prospective and retrospective studies have a 'foot' in the present. A historical study does not need to have a link with the present. It seeks to understand phenomena embedded in the past.

purposive or judgmental sample
This involves making a judgement or relying on the judgement of others in selecting a sample. Researchers use their knowledge of potential participants to recruit them. The purpose of this type of sampling is to obtain as many perspectives of the phenomenon as possible.

qualitative interview This is a broad term to denote a family of interviews with varying degrees of flexibility for the purpose of studying phenomena from the perspective of respondents.

quasi-experiment Such an experiment does not meet all three components of a true experiment, but it must have an intervention. A quasi-experiment may or may not have a control group – and if it does, it does not have randomisation.

quota sample When different groups of people take part in a study, the researcher allocates the number in each group beforehand and then uses non-probability sampling methods to select the units.

randomisation The process of allocating subjects to experimental and control groups by an objective method.

randomised controlled trial (RCT)
These are true experiments which are normally carried out in clinical practice.

range This is the lowest and highest value. Sometimes it is expressed as the difference between these two values.

ratio scale A ratio scale is an interval scale with an absolute zero. The numbers on a ratio scale tell us not only the amount by which they differ but also by how many times.

reductionism It means reducing complex phenomena to simple units that can be observed or recorded.

reflexivity It is the continuous process of reflection by researchers of how their own values, perceptions, behaviour or presence and those of the respondents can affect the data they collect.

replication This refers to the process of repeating the same study in the same or similar settings using the same method(s) with the same or equivalent sample(s).

research It is the study of phenomena by rigorous and systematic collection and analysis of data. It is a private enterprise made public for the purpose of exposing it to the scrutiny of others, to allow for replication, verification or falsification, where possible.

research awareness   The term has three main components: the adoption of a questioning stance to one's practice, knowledge of existing research and the ability to use it.

research-based practice   It is a term to denote the use of research to inform and justify one's practice.

research design   This is a plan of how, when and where data are to be collected and analysed.

research questions   Research involves asking questions. The term research question is used mainly to describe the broad question which is set at the start of a study. Some researchers may prefer to state aims, objectives or hypotheses instead.

sample and population
A proportion or subset of the population is known as a sample. A population can be defined as the total number of units (such as individuals, organisations, events or artefacts) from which data can potentially be collected.

sample frame   A list of all the units of the target population from which random samples are normally drawn.

semi-quartile, lower-quartile and upper-quartile   The semi-quartile ranges are scores which fall below and above the median. The lower-quartile is the mid-point between the lowest value and the median. The upper-quartile is the mid-point between the highest value and the median.

semi-structured interview   In this type of interview respondents are all asked the questions from a pre-determined list but there is flexibility in the phrasing and sequence of the questions.

simple random sample   Each unit in the sample frame has an equal chance of selection.

single-blind and double-blind trials
A single-blind trial is when either the subjects or the researcher is unaware which group is control or experimental. A design in which both subjects and researchers are unaware of which intervention each group is receiving is called a double-blind trial.

snowball sample   In this type of sampling, the first respondent refers someone they know to the study, who in turn refers someone they know until the researcher has an adequate sample.

split-half test   This test (of reliability) involves dividing or splitting the instrument (normally a scale) into two equal halves and finding out if their scores are similar.

standard deviation   The standard deviation is an average deviation of the scores from the mean.

stratified random sample
A stratified random sample is drawn by separating the units in the sample frame into strata (layers), according to the variables the researcher believes are important for inclusion in the sample, before drawing simple random samples from each strata.

structured interview   In this type of interview, researchers ask all the questions as they are formulated on an interview schedule. They have some flexibility to rephrase the question but cannot alter the content or sequence of the question.

structured observation
A structured observation is one in which aspects of the phenomenon to be observed are decided in advance (predetermined) and a schedule or checklist is constructed (structured) and the same information is required of all observations (standardised).

survey A survey is a research design which aims to obtain descriptive and correlational data usually from large populations, usually by questionnaires, interviews and to a lesser extent, by observations.

systematic random sample
A systematic random sample is drawn by choosing units on a list at intervals decided by the researcher in advance. Every unit on the list has an equal chance of selection.

systematic review This is one form of literature review in which all available research studies on a particular topic are identified, analysed and synthesised.

target population The target or study population is the population which meets the criteria for inclusion stipulated by the researcher.

test–retest Test–retest involves administering the questionnaire to the same respondents on two or more occasions and comparing their responses for the purpose of assessing the reliability of the questionnaire.

theory In its basic form a theory is an explanation of how and why a phenomenon occurs. Scientific theories are more precise in that they specify relationships between variables.

theory-generating research The aim of this type of theory is to generate hypotheses and/or theories. From the data collected researchers identify themes, patterns or relationships.

theory-testing research The aim of this type of research is to test particular hypotheses and/or theories. Researchers set hypotheses (often derived from theories) and collect data to confirm, modify or reject them.

time and event sampling These types of sampling are used mostly in studies which use observation. In time sampling, the sampling unit is time instead of people. Researchers may decide to sample the first 15 minutes of every hour of the day instead of observing the whole day. When 'events' are the focus of a study, the events become the units from which a sample is drawn.

true experiment In research terms a true experiment is characterised by three components: intervention (manipulation of), control and randomisation.

validity and reliability Validity refers to the degree or extent to which a questionnaire, interview or observation schedule and other methods of data collection studies or measures the phenomenon under investigation. Reliability refers to the consistency of a particular method in measuring or observing the same phenomena.

volunteer sample It is a sample of convenience over which the researcher has little control but instead is dependent on the sample volunteering to take part.

within-subject and between-subject designs When the same group of subjects receive the usual intervention and the experimental intervention alternatively, the design is described as within-subject or cross-over. A between-subject design is one in which different subjects constitute the control and the experimental groups.

INDEX

A

Abstract 362
Accidental sampling 230–1
Action research 170–3
Alternate-form test 273
Analysis
  qualitative data 326, 353–7
  quantitative data 339–53
Anonymity 79, 263, 276
Attitude scales 257–9, 266
Audit trail 354, 357
Average 347

B

Bar charts 345
Belief systems 32–5
Between-subject design 184–5
Bias 38, 63, 95, 181, 189, 196–7,
  225, 366–7
Blind techniques 188, 206
Body of knowledge 17–18, 81, 117
Books 78
Bracketing 44, 137, 154

C

Captive population 233, 266
Case studies 148–9, 192
Categories 54, 314, 357
Cause and effect 40–1, 103, 147,
  180
Central tendency measures 342, 346
  mean 347
  median 346
  mode 346–7
Centre for Reviews and Dissemination
  15, 380

Checklist 353
Chi-square 353
Closed questions 252–4
Cluster sampling 228–31
Cochrane Collaboration 15, 361
Cohort 158
Comparative studies 166–8
Concepts 7, 51, 128, 138
Conceptual definition 129–30
Conceptual framework 109–12
  in qualitative research 116–17
  in quantitative research 112–16
Conceptual literature 82–3
Conceptual model 109–10
Concurrent validity 271
Confidentiality 79, 276–7, 332
Confounding variables 196–7
Consent 79, 172, 188, 205–6
Consistency 38, 64, 265
Constant comparative method 57,
  355
Constructs 101, 249
Construct validity 272–3, 276
Content validity 270–1, 275
  of observation schedules 320, 334
  of questionnaires 270–1
Control groups 183–7
Convenience sampling 230–1
Correlation 36, 126, 143–5, 350
Correlational study 146
Covert observation 328, 333
Credibility of qualitative research
  292, 307
Criterion-related validity 271–2
Critiquing
  experiments 212–14
  interviews 306–7
  literature review 96–8

observations 334–5
operational definitions 139
questionnaires 275–6
questions 139
research process 77
sampling 240–4
skills 360–1
studies 360–8
theory 118–19
Crossover design 186–7
Cross-sectional design 159–60
Culture 8, 42–3, 105, 150–2

D

Data
analysis 53–4, 151–2
qualitative 353–7
quantitative 329–53
saturation 290–1
Data collection
qualitative 52–3
quantitative 52–3
Deduction 36–7, 107–9, 248, 317, 324
Degrees of freedom 352
Delphi technique 168–70
Dependent variable 126, 128, 182
Descriptive
designs 143–5
level 143
statistics 342–9
theories 102
Design
between-subject 184–5
in qualitative research 150–6
levels 143–8
selection of 143
Solomon four 185
types 148–50
within-subject 186
Determinism 40
Deviation of scores 349
Disclosure 79, 206, 288–9
Dispersion 348–9
Disseminating findings 15, 371, 380
Double-barrelled questions 268
Double-blind techniques 188

E

Effectiveness, clinical 13–16
Empiricism 40
Empowerment 60–1
Ethical issues
for questionnaires 276–8
in experiments 203–7
in interviewing 301–6
in observations 332–4
Ethical principles 78–9
Ethnograph 42–3, 152
Ethnography 137, 150–2, 330–2
Evaluating
abstract 362
conceptual frameworks 118–19
experiments 212–14
interviews 306–7
literature review 96–8, 362–3
methodology 363–4
observations 334–5
operational definitions 139
questionnaires 275–6
research process 77
research questions 139
sampling 240–4
Evaluative studies 164–6
Event sampling 318
Evidence-based practice 13–16, 94
Experience as a source of knowledge 9–10
Experiments
characteristics of 181–90
control in 183–9
ethics of 203–7
example of 147
external validity 200–3
internal validity 196–200
meaning of 179
problems with 207–8
quasi- 190–6
single-subject 190–3
value of 58
Ex post facto research 149
External validity 236
Extraneous variables 183

F

Face to face interviews 282
Face validity 271
Feminist research 61
Fidelity 78
Focus group interviews 296–300, 306
Formulating
  aims and objectives 123–5
  hypotheses 125–7
  purpose 123–4
  questions 122–4
Frequency distribution 349–50
Funding 6, 24–7, 212

G

Generalisability 38, 236, 239–40
Grounded theory 45–6, 154–7

H

Hawthorne effect 313
Historical studies 161
History effects 198
Homogeneous population 219
Hypotheses 125–7, 181–3
  inverse 127
  null 127, 350
  positive 127

I

Identification of research question 73, 122
Independent variables 126, 128, 182
Induction 36, 107, 109, 116, 247, 324
Inferential statistics 350–3
Informed consent 79, 207, 301
Instrumentation effects 198–9
Internal validity 196–200
Interpretation 365
Interrater reliability 321–2
Intervention 181–3
Interview bias 284–5
Interview effects 263–76

Interviews
  content of 290–1
  ethical implications of 301–6
  focus group 296–300
  qualitative 286–91
  reliability and validity 284–5, 291–3
  research 282
  semistructured 293–6
  structured 282–6
Intraobserver reliability 321
Intuition 9

J

Journals 85–6
Judgemental sampling 232–3
Justice 78

K

Knowledge
  metaphysical 33–4
  need for 31
  scientific 33–5
  supernatural 32–3
Known-groups technique 272

L

Levels of research 143–8
Likert scale 258–9
Limitations
  experiments 207–8
  interviews 284–5
  observations 313–14
  questionnaires 262–4
Literature 82–8
Literature review
  critiquing 96–8
  functions of 89–94
Logical positivism 40–1
Longitudinal studies 156, 158–60

M

Manipulation 192
Matched-pairs 184
Mean 347
Measurement levels 339
    interval 341
    nominal 339–40
    ordinal 340–1
    ratio 341
Median 346–7
Memory distortion 266
Memory gaps 266
Meta-analysis 95, 173–4
Metaphysical beliefs 33–5
Methodology 142–3, 363–4
Mixing approaches 64–8
Mode 346
Molar categories 313–14
Molecular categories 313–14
Mortality 159, 200
Mortality effects 200
Multiple choice questions 253
Multistage sampling 230
Multitrait–multimethod approach
    272
Mythical beliefs 32–5

N

Nominal scale 339–40
Non-maleficence 78
Non-parametric tests 352
Non-participant observation 327
Non-probability sampling 222–3
    accidental 230–3
    convenience 230
    purposive 232–3
    quota 235–6
    snowball 234–5
    volunteer 233–4
Normal curve 350
Null hypothesis 127, 350
Nursing research
    development of 4–7
    funding 6, 24–7, 212
    meaning of 7
    role of nurses in 18–24
    utilisation of 22–3, 369–72
Nursing theory 117–18

O

Objectives 125
Objectivity 63–4
Observation
    categories 314–15
    checklist 315–16
    critiquing 334–5
    ethical implications of 332–4
    in nursing practice 310–11
    limitations of 313–14
    participation in 327–32
    structured 314–22
    unstructured 322–7
    validity and reliability of 320–2,
    327
Observer's effect 313, 320
Open-ended questions 254–7
Operational definition 136, 317, 319
    in nursing practice 128–9
    in quantitative research 136
    in qualitative research 136–8
Ordinal scale 340–1

P

Pain measurement 262
Paradigms 39, 46–7
Parametric tests 352
Participant observation 327–32
Participatory action research 60–2
Pearson product moment correlation
    coefficient 351–2
Phenomenological approach 43–5
    description of 152, 153
    example of 155
Phenomenon 11
Philosophical assumptions 51–2
Piloting questionnaire 263, 275
Placebo 188
Population 218–19
    captive 301
    target 219–20
    theoretical 219
    units of 218–19
Positivism
    description 39–41
    logical 40–1
Post-test 181, 185, 195
Practitioner research 383

Predictive validity 271
Pre-test 181, 185, 195
Primary sources 84–5
Privacy 276–7, 301–2, 332,
Probability sampling 224
    cluster random 228–9
    simple random 224–5
    stratified random 226–7
    systematic random 227–8
Probing in interviews 288–9
Professionalisation 16–18
Prospective studies 160, 163–4
Publications 85–8
    primary 84–5
    secondary 84–5
Purposive sampling 232–3, 298

Q

Qualitative analysis 53–4, 151–2,
    353–8
Qualitative research
    limitations 62–3
    process 288–90
    value of 59–62
Quantitative research 54–5
    limitations 58–9
    value of 54, 57–8
Quasi-experiment 192–6
Questionnaires 246–78
    administration 262
    advantages 262–4
    critiquing 275–6
    disadvantages 263–4
    ethical aspects of 276–8
    fatigue 264
    use of 246–7
    validity and reliability of 264–75
Question formats 250, 252–62
    checklist 252
    closed 252–4
    double-barrelled 269
    double negative 269
    hypothetical 269
    leading 269
    multiple choice 253
    open-ended 254–7
    rank order 253
Quota sampling 235–6

R

Randomisation 189–90
Randomised controlled trials 190–1,
    208–11
Random sampling 224
    cluster 228–30
    simple 224–6
    stratified 227
    systematic 227–8
Range 348
Rating scales 259
Ratio scale 341
Reflexivity 292
Reliability
    alternate-form 273
    definition of 38
    external 200–3
    interrater 321–2
    intraobserver 321
    split-half 274
    test–retest 273
Reactivity 313, 320
Refereed journals 86
Replication 38
Research 10–13, 37–9
    clinical effectiveness and 13–16
    definition of 38
    limitations of 11–13
    professional development 16–18
    questions 122–3
    role of nurses in 18–23
    utilisation 22–3, 269–87
Research and development units
    383–4
Research-mindedness 19–20
Research process 71–2
    critiquing the 77
    in qualitative research 75
    in quantitative research 75
    meaning of 71–2
    nursing process 72
    stages of 73–5
Response rate 243, 264, 267
Results 364–5
Retrospective designs 160–2
Rigour 38, 257
Royal College of Nursing 14, 16, 20

S

Sample 218
  frame 220–1
  non-probability 222–3
  probability 222–3
  selected and achieved 221–2
Sample setting 243
Sample size 241–2
Science 35
  and knowledge 33–4, 47–8
  and research 36–7
Scientific beliefs 33–5
Scientific method 39
Secondary sources 84
Selection effects 199–200
Semantic differential scale 259–60
Semiquartile range 348
Simple random sample 224–6
Single-subject experiment 190–2
Snowball sample 234
Social desirability 266
Solomon four group design 185
Split-half test 274
Standard deviation 349
Statistical analysis 341–2
  descriptive 342–9
  inferential 350–3
Stratified random sample 226–8
Subjectivity 63–4
Surveys 148–9, 248
Systematic random sample 227–9
Systematic reviews 94–5

T

Target population 219
Test–retest 273
Themes in qualitative research 54,
  56–7, 116, 151, 326, 354
Theoretical framework 109–18
Theory
  definition 100–1
  generating 108–9
  levels of 103–5
  practice and 105–7
  research 105–18
  testing 108
  types of 102–3
Time sampling 318
Time series design 195
Tradition as source of knowledge 8–9
Trial and error 10, 180
Triangulation 64–8
t-test 352
Type I and type II error 350

U

Units of observation 314–17
Unstructured interviews 286
Unstructured observations 322–7
Utilisation of research 22–3, 269–87

V

Validity 38
  concurrent 271
  construct 272–3, 276
  content 270–1, 275
  criterion 271–2
  external 236
  face 271
  internal 196–200
  predictive 271
Variables 126, 128, 182–3, 196–7
Variance 348
Veracity 78
Verbatim 354–5
Video-taping in observation 319–20
Visual analogue scales 260–1
Volunteer sampling 233–4

W

Within-subject design 186–7